KT-171-415

PENGUIN BOOKS
LUCREZIA BORGIA

'Bradford does much to put the record straight and has fulfilled her aim of letting Lucrezia Borgia speak for herself and allowing the world in which she lived to come alive for the reader' *Sunday Telegraph*

'Richly detailed ... Bradford writes authoritatively on the politics of the time' *Sunday Times*

'Sarah Bradford writes with cool authority and her research in Italian archives is exemplary. No other biography is likely to bring us closer to Lucrezia' *Spectator*

'Bradford brings her subject fully into focus and provides a very full, readable and soundly based account' *The Times Literary Supplement*

'If you want a brilliant and erudite study of the continually changing balances of power in the Italian princely and ducal states, and the power of the Vatican, this book could not be bettered' *History Today*

'Bradford's juicy work [is] a mouthwatering prospect' *Tatler*

Lucrezia Borgia

Life, Love and Death in Renaissance Italy

SARAH BRADFORD

PENGUIN

PENGUIN BOOKS

Published by the Penguin Group
Penguin Books Ltd, 80 Strand, London WC2R ORL, England
Penguin Group (USA), Inc., 375 Hudson Street, New York, New York 10014, USA
Penguin Group (Canada), 90 Eglinton Avenue East, Suite 700, Toronto, Ontario, Canada M4P 2Y3
(a division of Pearson Penguin Canada Inc.)
Penguin Ireland, 25 St Stephen's Green, Dublin 2, Ireland
(a division of Penguin Books Ltd)
Penguin Group (Australia), 250 Camberwell Road,
Camberwell, Victoria 3124, Australia (a division of Pearson Australia Group Pty Ltd)
Penguin Books India Pvt Ltd, 11 Community Centre,
Panchsheel Park, New Delhi – 110 017, India
Penguin Group (NZ), cnr Airborne and Rosedale Roads, Albany,
Auckland 1310, New Zealand (a division of Pearson New Zealand Ltd)
Penguin Books (South Africa) (Pty) Ltd, 24 Sturdee Avenue,
Rosebank 2196, Johannesburg, South Africa

Penguin Books Ltd, Registered Offices: 80 Strand, London WC2R ORL, England

www.penguin.com

Published by Viking 2004
Published in Penguin Books 2005

4

Copyright © Sarah Bradford, 2004

Printed in England by Clays Ltd, St Ives plc

Contents

Author's Note

Money Values

Economic historians now regard equating the value of fifteenth- and sixteenth-century coinage with today's money as unrealistic owing to the number of factors involved in the calculation. However, a rough rule of thumb would be to multiply each currency (gold coins such as ducats, francs, florins and scudi were all much the same) by one hundred to arrive at a modern sterling equivalent.

Time Calculations

In fifteenth- and sixteenth-century Italy there were twenty-four hours in the day (like ours) but, instead of starting the day at midnight as we do, the Italians began the day half an hour after sunset: thus the twenty-fourth hour was the last hour of daytime.

List of Illustrations

Every effort has been made to trace the copyright holders and we apologize in advance for any unintentional omission. We would be pleased to insert the appropriate acknowledgement in any subsequent editions.

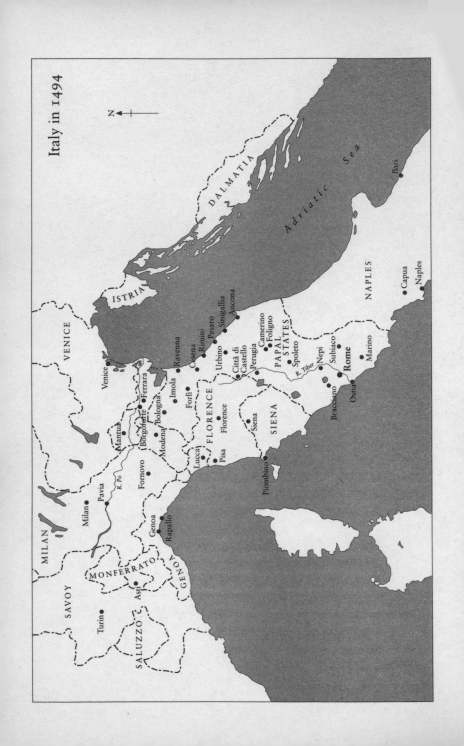

Italy in 1494

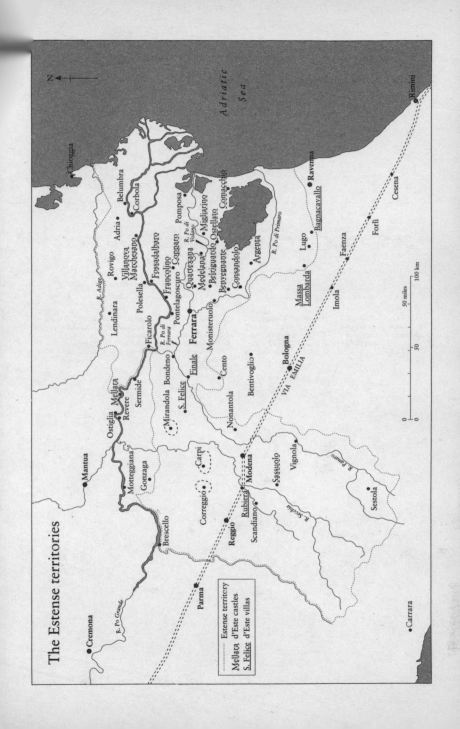

The Estense territories

N

Adriatic Sea

Chioggia

Belumbra
Corbola
Adria
Rovigo
Villanova
Marchesano
R. Adige
Lendinara
Polesella
Ficarolo
R. Po di Ferrara
Fossadalbaro
Francolino
Pontelagoscuro · Coppare
Quartesana
Medelana
Belriguardo · Ostellato
Benvignante
Consandolo
Argenta
Pomposa
Migliarino
R. Po di Volano
Comacchio

Mantua
R. Po Grande
Cremona
Ostiglia
Mellara
Revere
Sermide
Motteggiana
Gonzaga
Brescello
Mirandola
Bondeno
S. Felice
Finale
Ferrara
Monisteruolo
Cento
Bentivoglio
Nonantola
Carpi
Correggio
Rubiera
Modena
Scandiano
Sassuolo
Vignola
R. Secchia
R. Panaro
Sestola
Parma
Reggio
VIA EMILIA
Bologna
Massa Lombarda
Imola
Faenza
Forlì
Cesena
Lugo
Bagnacavallo
Ravenna
R. Po di Primaro
Argenta
Rimini

Carrara

---- Estense territory
[Mellara] d'Este castles
<u>S. Felice</u> d'Este villas

0   50   100 km
0   50 miles

The Descendants of Alexander VI

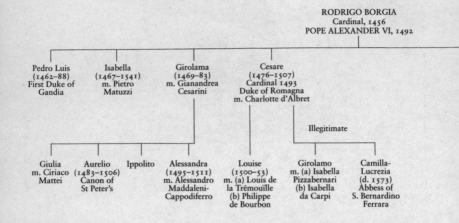

RODRIGO BORGIA
Cardinal, 1456
POPE ALEXANDER VI, 1492

Pedro Luis
(1462–88)
First Duke of
Gandia

Isabella
(1467–1541)
m. Pietro
Matuzzi

Girolama
(1469–83)
m. Gianandrea
Cesarini

Cesare
(1476–1507)
Duke of Romagna
Cardinal 1493
m. Charlotte d'Albret

Illegitimate

Giulia
m. Ciriaco
Mattei

Aurelio
(1483–1506)
Canon of
St Peter's

Ippolito

Alessandra
(1495–1511)
m. Alessandro
Maddaleni-
Cappodiferro

Louise
(1500–53)
m. (a) Louis de
la Trémouïlle
(b) Philippe
de Bourbon

Girolamo
m. (a) Isabella
Pizzabernari
(b) Isabella
da Carpi

Camilla-
Lucrezia
(d. 1573)
Abbess of
S. Bernardino
Ferrara

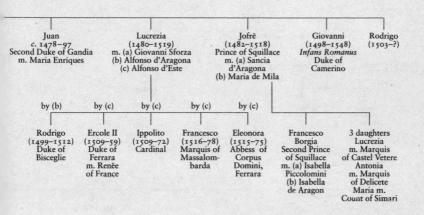

Juan
c. 1478–97
Second Duke of Gandia
m. Maria Enriques

Lucrezia
(1480–1519)
m. (a) Giovanni Sforza
   (b) Alfonso d'Aragona
   (c) Alfonso d'Este

Jofrè
(1482–1518)
Prince of Squillace
m. (a) Sancia
       d'Aragona
   (b) Maria de Mila

Giovanni
(1498–1548)
Infans Romanus
Duke of
Camerino

Rodrigo
(1503–?)

by (b)

Rodrigo
(1499–1512)
Duke of
Bisceglie

by (c)

Ercole II
(1509–59)
Duke of
Ferrara
m. Renée
of France

by (c)

Ippolito
(1509–72)
Cardinal

by (c)

Francesco
(1516–78)
Marquis of
Massalom-
barda

by (c)

Eleonora
(1515–75)
Abbess of
Corpus
Domini,
Ferrara

Francesco
Borgia
Second Prince
of Squillace
m. (a) Isabella
       Piccolomini
   (b) Isabella
       de Aragon

3 daughters
Lucrezia
m. Marquis
of Castel Vetere
Antonia
m. Marquis
of Delicete
Maria m.
Count of Simari

The House of Este

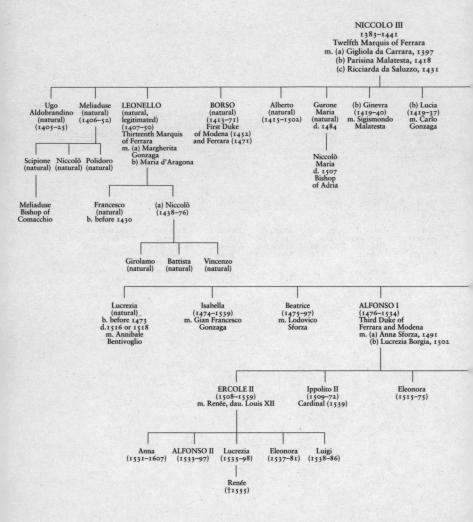

NICCOLO III
1383–1441
Twelfth Marquis of Ferrara
m. (a) Gigliola da Carrara, 1397
   (b) Parisina Malatesta, 1418
   (c) Ricciarda da Saluzzo, 1431

Ugo
Aldobrandino
(natural)
(1405–25)

Meliaduse
(natural)
(1406–52)

LEONELLO
(natural,
legitimated)
(1407–50)
Thirteenth Marquis
of Ferrara
m. (a) Margherita
Gonzaga
b) Maria d'Aragona

BORSO
(natural)
(1413–71)
First Duke
of Modena (1452)
and Ferrara (1471)

Alberto
(natural)
(1415–1502)

Gurone
Maria
(natural)
d. 1484

(b) Ginevra
(1419–40)
m. Sigismondo
Malatesta

(b) Lucia
(1419–37)
m. Carlo
Gonzaga

Scipione
(natural)

Niccolò
(natural)

Polidoro
(natural)

Niccolò
Maria
d. 1507
Bishop
of Adria

Meliaduse
Bishop of
Comacchio

Francesco
(natural)
b. before 1430

(a) Niccolò
(1438–76)

Girolamo
(natural)

Battista
(natural)

Vincenzo
(natural)

Lucrezia
(natural)
b. before 1473
d.1516 or 1518
m. Annibale
Bentivoglio

Isabella
(1474–1539)
m. Gian Francesco
Gonzaga

Beatrice
(1475–97)
m. Lodovico
Sforza

ALFONSO I
(1476–1534)
Third Duke of
Ferrara and Modena
m. (a) Anna Sforza, 1491
   (b) Lucrezia Borgia, 1502

ERCOLE II
(1508–1559)
m. Renée, dau. Louis XII

Ippolito II
(1509–72)
Cardinal (1539)

Eleonora
(1515–75)

Anna
(1531–1607)

ALFONSO II
(1533–97)

Lucrezia
(1535–98)

Eleonora
(1537–81)

Luigi
(1538–86)

Renée
(†1555)

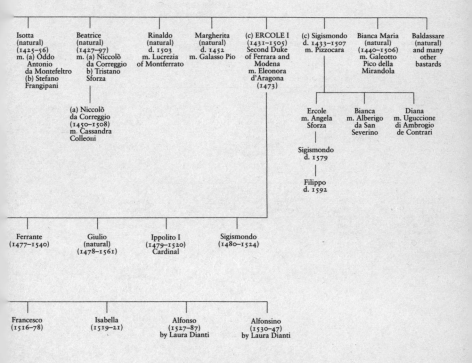

Isotta
(natural)
(1425–56)
m. (a) Oddo
Antonio
da Montefeltro
(b) Stefano
Frangipani

Beatrice
(natural)
(1427–97)
m. (a) Niccolò
da Correggio
b) Tristano
Sforza

Rinaldo
(natural)
d. 1503
m. Lucrezia
of Montferrato

Margherita
(natural)
d. 1452
m. Galasso Pio

(c) ERCOLE I
(1431–1505)
Second Duke
of Ferrara and
Modena
m. Eleonora
d'Aragona
(1473)

(c) Sigismondo
d. 1433–1507
m. Pizzocara

Bianca Maria
(natural)
(1440–1506)
m. Galeotto
Pico della
Mirandola

Baldassare
(natural)
and many
other
bastards

(a) Niccolò
da Correggio
(1450–1508)
m. Cassandra
Colleoni

Ercole
m. Angela
Sforza

Bianca
m. Alberigo
da San
Severino

Diana
m. Uguccione
di Ambrogio
de Contrari

Sigismondo
d. 1579

Filippo
d. 1592

Ferrante
(1477–1540)

Giulio
(natural)
(1478–1561)

Ippolito I
(1479–1520)
Cardinal

Sigismondo
(1480–1524)

Francesco
(1516–78)

Isabella
(1519–21)

Alfonso
(1527–87)
by Laura Dianti

Alfonsino
(1530–47)
by Laura Dianti

The Neapolitan House of Aragon (d'Aragona)

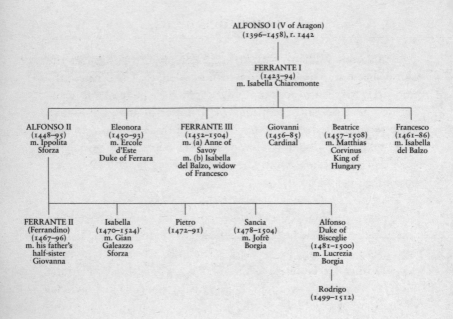

ALFONSO I (V of Aragon)
(1396–1458), r. 1442

FERRANTE I
(1423–94)
m. Isabella Chiaromonte

ALFONSO II
(1448–95)
m. Ippolita
Sforza

Eleonora
(1450–93)
m. Ercole
d'Este
Duke of Ferrara

FERRANTE III
(1452–1504)
m. (a) Anne of
Savoy
m. (b) Isabella
del Balzo, widow
of Francesco

Giovanni
(1456–85)
Cardinal

Beatrice
(1457–1508)
m. Matthias
Corvinus
King of
Hungary

Francesco
(1461–86)
m. Isabella
del Balzo

FERRANTE II
(Ferrandino)
(1467–96)
m. his father's
half-sister
Giovanna

Isabella
(1470–1524)
m. Gian
Galeazzo
Sforza

Pietro
(1472–91)

Sancia
(1478–1504)
m. Jofrè
Borgia

Alfonso
Duke of
Bisceglie
(1481–1500)
m. Lucrezia
Borgia

Rodrigo
(1499–1512)

Acknowledgements

My husband, William Bangor, has been my co-author in the sense that only someone with his knowledge of late fifteenth- and early sixteenth-century Italy could have helped me transcribe the thousands of pages of manuscript material which have formed the basis for this book. Without his help, it would have taken far longer to complete. The admiration which he developed for Lucrezia in the course of his work has been a sustaining inspiration.

So many people with great knowledge of this subject have been generous with their help. I would like to distinguish for particular gratitude Raffaele Tamalio, *the* expert on the archives at Mantua and the Gonzaga family, and his wife Lynn. In Ferrara, Dott. Giuseppe Muscardini, Bibliotecario presso i Musei Civici di Arte Antica di Ferrara, went out of his way to guide us round the city and archives and to provide me with every possible information and help.

I am also grateful to the following: Philip Attwood, Dr Silke Ackermann; the Reverend Father Miquel Batllori, S.J., Dott. Maria Barbara Bertini, Director of the Archivio di Stato di Milano, Dott. Mario Bertoni, Archivist of the Archivio di Stato di Modena, Harriet Bridgeman, Dr R. J. Bridgeman, Jose Maria Burrieza, departmental head of References at the Archivio General de Simancas; Dr Ann G. Carmichael, Edward Chaney, Dr Cecil H. Clough, Dr Barrie Cook, Margaret Critchley; Dott. Alessandra Farinelli, Responsabile Fondi Antichi, Biblioteca Comunale Ariostea di Ferrara; Dott. Daniela Ferrari, Director of the Archivio di Stato di Mantova, Simonetta Fraquelli, Antonia Fraser; Nicole Garnier, conservateur, the Musée Condé at Chantilly; Alberto Govi, Professor Guido Guerzoni; Mary Hollingsworth, Dr Charles Hope; Professor Douglas Johnson; Professor Robert J. Knecht; Dr Jilly Kray, Librarian of the Warburg Institute; Dott. Laura Laureati; Sarah Lawson; Carmelo Lison; Alvaro Maccioni; Dr Michael Mallett; Philip Mansel; Professor Joan Francesc Mira; Kenneth Montgomery; Dr Ornella Moscucci; Professor Reinhold Mueller; Dott. Andrea Nascimbeni of the Fondazione Cassa di Risparmio di Ferrara; Jette Nielsen and Vivian Nutton of the Wellcome Library; the Reverendissimo Padre Prefetto Sergio Pagano of the Archivio Segreto Vaticano; Lucia Panini; Dr Stephen Parkin, Curator Italian Printed Books 1501–1850 at the British Library; Milo Parmoor; Dott. Paola Pelliccia of the Biblioteca Comunale in Subiaco; Guy Penman of the London Library, Antonio Pettini; Luciana Pignatelli; Dr Dennis Rhodes; Padre Nazzareno Romagnollo; the late Professor Nicolai Rubinstein; Maude Sallansonet, archivist, the Musée Condé at Chantilly; Diana Scarisbrick; Jane and Tony Scheuregger of the Minstrels Gallery; Eva Soos, photoservices, the Pierpont Morgan Library; Dott. Angelo Spaggiari, Director of the Archivio di Stato di Modena; Dr David Starkey; Julien Stock; Simon Stock; Baron Berti von Stohrer; Professor Roy Strong; Hugh Thomas; Priscilla Thomas; Peter Thornton; Dr Dora Thornton; Albert Torra, Vic-Director, Archivio de la Corona de Aragon; Dott. Francesca Trebbi of the Biblioteca dei Musei Civici in Pesaro; Dr Thomas Tuohy; Anna Uguccioni of the Prefettura in the Palazzo Ducale in Pesaro; Dott. Gianna Vancini; Professor Laurent Vissiere; Maureen Waller; John Wells, Assistant Under Librarian, Department of Manuscripts and University Archives, University Library, Cambridge; Roger S. Wieck, Curator, Medieval and Renaissance Manuscripts, the Pierpont Morgan Library.

On the publishing side grateful thanks are due to the following for their contribution: Andrea Cane of Mondadori; Helen Fraser, Juliet Annan and Carly Cook of Viking, London; Lynda Marshall, picture research; Antonia Till for her kindness in reading the type-script; Richard Collins for his skilful editing; Douglas Matthews for his compiling of the index; Camilla Eadie, for all her help and technical expertise; Wendy Wolf and Clifford J. Corcoran, Viking, New York; Gillon Aitken, Sally Riley and Ayesha Karim Khan of Gillon Aitken Associates. Finally, I would like to thank Keith Taylor, Elisabeth Merriman and Sarah Day for their invaluable help in the production of this book.

Foreword

Lucrezia Borgia's name has been a byword for evil for five hundred years, her life distorted by generations of historians and seen through the prism of the crimes of her family, themselves magnified by hostile chroniclers of the time. Lucrezia herself has been charged with murder by poisoning and incest with her father, Pope Alexander VI, and her brother, Cesare Borgia. As an archetypal villainess she has featured in works by Victor Hugo and Alexandre Dumas, an opera by Donizetti and a film by Abel Gance – to name but a few. Byron was so fascinated by her reputation that, after viewing her love letters in Milan, he stole a strand from the lock of her blonde hair which accompanied them.

A cautious rehabilitation of her reputation began in the nineteenth century, but the general conclusion was that, if she were not a murderer and a whore, she was no more than an empty-headed blonde, helpless victim of the males in her family. The truth is that in a world where the dice were heavily loaded in favour of men, Lucrezia operated within the circumstances of her time to forge her own destiny. Born the illegitimate daughter of one of the most notorious of Renaissance popes, Alexander VI, she was married at the age of thirteen to a man she had never met, then divorced from him at the behest of her father and brother and remarried to a second husband who was murdered on the orders of her brother when she was just twenty. It was then that she took her fate into her own hands and was actively involved in the promotion of her third marriage, to Alfonso d'Este, the future Duke of Ferrara, whom she knew to be violently opposed to the idea of her as his wife. As Duchess of Ferrara, Lucrezia came into her own, showing a powerful intelligence and skill in managing her life. Winning over her hostile in-laws – with the notable exception of the formidable Isabella whose husband she took as a lover – she ruled over a magnificent court with herself as the focus of a circle of poets and intellectuals. In times of war and plague, she administered justice and oversaw the defence of Ferrara. As she had survived the violence of the papal court of the Borgias she survived the inbred violence of the Este family; only childbirth, the curse of the age for women, ultimately defeated her.

More recent historians have imposed their own patterns on Lucrezia: in going back to the original sources, the thousands of papers in the archives of Modena, Mantua, Milan and the Vatican, I have let Lucrezia speak for herself. This is her story.

London, November 2003

The Scene

At the time of Lucrezia Borgia's birth in 1480, Italy was famously a geographical expression rather than a country, a peninsula divided into independent states bound by the weakest sense of common nationality. Neapolitans, Milanese and Venetians were Neapolitans, Milanese and Venetians first and foremost: the concept of Italy as a political whole did not exist beyond a vague xenophobia in which non-Italians were perceived as barbarians. Italians saw themselves as richer, more cultivated and sophisticated than the rest of Europe. At a time when Europe was unified by the Catholic religion with the Pope, wielding both spiritual and temporal powers, at its head, Rome, as the seat of the papacy, was the centre of the Western world, or Christendom as contemporaries would have known it.

The principal Italian states in the late fifteenth century were (from north to south) Milan, ruled by the Sforza family; Venice, a merchant empire ruled by an oligarchy of patrician families headed by a doge; Florence, then ruled by the Medici as a hereditary despotism in the person of Piero, son of Lorenzo the Magnificent; the Papal States, the temporal dominion of the Pope whose authority in practice was devolved to 'papal vicars', principally the Este of Ferrara, but including smaller city states such as Bologna, Rimini, Pisa, Siena, Camerino, Forlì, Faenza and Pesaro, where families such as the Bentivoglio, the Malatesta, the Petrucci, the Varani, the Riarii and the Manfredi held sway. Mantua was held as a fief of the Holy Roman Empire by the Gonzaga family. In this fragmented state the smaller entities bound themselves to the larger ones for protection, sometimes, as in the case of the Este and the Gonzaga, also to outside powers, notably France or, in the case of Naples, to Spain. Round Rome the

great baronial families the Orsini and Colonna, Savelli and
Caetani officially owed allegiance to the Pope but in practice
often fought against him, their loyalties given to the highest
payer among the major states. To the south the Kingdom of
Naples, at this time ruled by a junior branch of the royal house
of Aragon in Spain, included not only Naples itself and the
Neapolitan Campania but also Puglia and Calabria. The possession of Naples lay at the heart of the foreign invasions in
Lucrezia's lifetime, the throne being disputed by both its present
Aragonese kings and the descendants of the previous rulers, the
French house of Anjou. The Pope, as temporal lord, had the
right of investiture of the crown of Naples, and it was this power
which placed him at the heart of the Italian wars, as the two
outside powers, France and Spain, claimed hereditary rights to
the Kingdom.

In his *History of Italy* the Florentine historian Francesco
Guicciardini saw 1492, the year of Lucrezia's father's election as
Pope Alexander VI, as marking the end of a golden age and the
beginning of Italy's troubles:

Italy had never enjoyed such prosperity, or known so favourable a situation as that in which it found itself so securely at rest in the year of
our Christian salvation 1490, and the years immediately before and
after. The greatest peace and tranquillity reigned everywhere; the land
under cultivation no less in the most mountainous and arid regions
than in the most fertile plains and areas. Dominated by no power other
than her own, not only did Italy abound in inhabitants, merchandise
and riches, but she was also highly renowned for the magnificence of
her many princes, for the splendour of so many noble and beautiful
cities, as the seat and majesty of religion, and flourishing with men
most skilful in the administration of public affairs and most nobly
talented in all disciplines and distinguished and industrious in all the
arts. Nor was Italy lacking in military glory according to the standards
of that time, and adorned with so many gifts that she deservedly held
a celebrated name and reputation among all the nations.[1]

That peace in the country regarded as the richest and most civilized on earth had been kept over the last forty years by the Italian League, the alliance between Naples and Milan, held together by Lorenzo de'Medici ('the Magnificent') and cemented by a common fear of the power of Venice. Lorenzo de'Medici died prematurely in April 1492, aged only forty-three; on his death the strains which had developed within the League burst apart, rupturing the hermetic seal which had protected Italy from the newly centralized European powers without. The ambitions of Ludovico Sforza, brother of Cardinal Ascanio, to dethrone the legitimate ruler of Milan, his nephew, Gian Galeazzo Sforza, married to Isabella d'Aragona, niece of the King of Naples, had led to an intense family quarrel between Milan and Naples. This spilled over the Italian borders when Ludovico (always known as 'il Moro', a play on his dark complexion and his emblem, the mulberry) invited the young King of France, Charles VIII, to invade and claim his right to the throne of Naples on the grounds of his descent from the former Angevin rulers of the Kingdom. Hungry for glory, in 1494 Charles descended on Italy with a large, well-equipped army in pursuit of his claim, ushering in a period of war and foreign invasion which would be the background to Lucrezia Borgia's entire life.

Cast of Principal Characters

Borgia (in Spanish de Borja)

LUCREZIA BORGIA: illegitimate daughter of Rodrigo Borgia, later Pope Alexander VI, and his mistress Vannozza Cattanei. Married (1) 1493, Giovanni Sforza, lord of Pesaro, (2) 1498, Alfonso d'Aragona, Duke of Bisceglie, (3) 1501, Alfonso d'Este, later Duke of Ferrara

ALONSO DE BORJA, of Jativa in Valencia: Rodrigo's uncle and Lucrezia's great uncle, founded the family fortunes when elected Pope Callixtus III in 1455

RODRIGO BORGIA, also of Jativa in Valencia: Lucrezia's father. Elected Pope Alexander VI in 1492

CESARE BORGIA: Lucrezia's eldest brother, illegitimate son of Rodrigo Borgia and Vannozza Cattanei. Cardinal of Valencia and then Duke of Valentinois, known as 'il Valentino'. Married Charlotte d'Albret, sister of the King of Navarre

JUAN BORGIA: Lucrezia's second brother, illegitimate son of Rodrigo Borgia and Vannozza Cattanei. Better known as second Duke of Gandia. Married Maria Enriques and was the unworthy grandfather of St Francis Borja

JOFRE BORGIA: supposed son of Rodrigo Borgia by Vannozza Cattanei but suspected by Rodrigo to be Vannozza's son by her third husband, Giorgio della Croce. Created Prince of Squillace, married Sancia d'Aragona (see below)

VANNOZZA CATTANEI: Rodrigo Borgia's long-time mistress and mother of his favourite children

ADRIANA DE MILA: Rodrigo Borgia's first cousin, married to Lodovico Orsini-Migliorati. Lucrezia's guardian until she married, mother-in-law of Rodrigo's mistress, Giulia Farnese

ANGELA BORGIA: illegitimate cousin of Lucrezia, known for her beauty which caused havoc among the Este brothers at Ferrara. Married Alessandro Pio da Sassuolo

GIOVANNI BORGIA: known as the '*Infans Romanus*', illegitimate son of Alexander VI and a Roman woman and therefore Lucrezia's half-brother. Often reputed to be the product of an incestuous relationship between Lucrezia and her father, a rumour which was almost certainly unfounded

RODRIGO BORGIA (the younger): illegitimate son of Alexander VI, born in the last year of his papacy and therefore another half-brother of Lucrezia.

Aragona

KING FERRANTE I OF NAPLES: grandfather of Lucrezia's second husband, Alfonso Bisceglie

KING ALFONSO II OF NAPLES: known as Duke of Calabria before his accession, father of Alfonso Bisceglie (illegitimate)

KING FERRANTE II OF NAPLES: son of Alfonso II, known as Ferrantino

KING FEDERICO III OF NAPLES: brother of Alfonso II

ALFONSO D'ARAGONA, Duke of Bisceglie: Lucrezia's second husband, illegitimate son of Alfonso II

SANCIA D'ARAGONA, Princess of Squillace: illegitimate daughter of Alfonso II and sister of Alfonso Bisceglie, married Jofre Borgia

RODRIGO D'ARAGONA, second Duke of Bisceglie: Lucrezia's only son by Alfonso Bisceglie

Sforza

LUDOVICO MARIA SFORZA: known as 'il Moro', Duke of Bari and then of Milan, married Beatrice d'Este (see below)

ASCANIO SFORZA: cardinal, brother of the above

GIOVANNI SFORZA, lord of Pesaro: illegitimate son of Costanzo Sforza. Lucrezia's first husband

Este

ERCOLE I, Duke of Ferrara: Lucrezia's father-in-law

ALFONSO I, Duke of Ferrara: eldest son of Ercole, Lucrezia's third husband

FERRANTE D'ESTE: Ercole's second son

ISABELLA D'ESTE. See GONZAGA. Alfonso's sister, married to Francesco Gonzaga, Marquis of Mantua (see below)

IPPOLITO D'ESTE: cardinal, Ercole's third son

GIULIO D'ESTE: Ercole's illegitimate son

SIGISMONDO D'ESTE: Ercole's youngest legitimate son

ERCOLE II: Alfonso and Lucrezia's eldest son and heir

IPPOLITO D'ESTE: Alfonso and Lucrezia's second son, later also Cardinal d'Este and builder of the Villa d'Este

FRANCESCO D'ESTE: Alfonso and Lucrezia's third son

ELEONORA D'ESTE: Alfonso and Lucrezia's only surviving daughter

Gonzaga

FRANCESCO GONZAGA, Marquis of Mantua: husband of Isabella d'Este and lover of Lucrezia

ELISABETTA GONZAGA: sister of the above, married to Guidobaldo da Montefeltro, Duke of Urbino

LEONORA GONZAGA: daughter of Francesco and Isabella, married Francesco Maria della Rovere, Duke of Urbino, after the death of Guidobaldo da Montefeltro in 1508

FEDERICO GONZAGA: son and heir of Francesco and Isabella, succeeded his father as Marquis in 1519 and later became first Duke of Mantua

Della Rovere

GIULIANO DELLA ROVERE: Cardinal of San Pietro in Vincula, Rodrigo Borgia's great rival for the papacy in 1492, later succeeding as Julius II (see below)

FRANCESCO MARIA DELLA ROVERE: nephew of the above, married Leonora Gonzaga (see above) and succeeded to the dukedom of Urbino

Popes (with the dates of their papacy)

INNOCENT VIII (Giovanni Battista Cibo of Genoa) 1484–92
ALEXANDER VI (Rodrigo Borgia, see above) 1492–1503
PIUS III (Francesco Piccolomini of Siena) 1503
JULIUS II (Giuliano della Rovere of Albisola, near Genoa, see above) 1503–13
LEO X (Giovanni de'Medici of Florence, son of Lorenzo the Magnificent) 1513–22

Spanish sovereigns (with the dates of their reigns)

(For Aragonese Kings of Naples see Aragona above)
FERDINAND OF ARAGON (1479–1516) married ISABELLA OF CASTILE (1474–1504) in 1469 when they became known as 'the Catholic Kings'. Rodrigo Borgia's patron and occasional foe

French sovereigns (with the dates of their reigns)

CHARLES VIII (1483–98)
LOUIS XII (1498–1515)
FRANCIS I (1515–47)

PART ONE

The Pope's Daughter
1480–1501

1. The Pope's Daughter

'She [Lucrezia] is of middle height and graceful in form. Her face
is rather long, the nose well cut, hair golden, eyes of no special
colour. Her mouth is rather large, the teeth brilliantly white, her
neck is slender and fair, the bust admirably proportioned. She is
always gay and smiling'

– A contemporary description of Lucrezia
by an eyewitness, Niccolò Cagnolo of Parma

Rome, 26 August 1492. Rodrigo Borgia, recently elected as Pope
Alexander VI, rode in scorching heat through the lavishly decorated streets of Rome from St Peter's to take formal possession
of the papacy in the basilica of San Giovanni in Lateran. In the
opinion of experienced courtiers this was the most sumptuous
pontifical ceremony ever seen. Thirteen squadrons of men in
armour on colourfully caparisoned horses led the way out of the
piazza of St Peter's. Behind them marched the households of
the cardinals in a blaze of crimson, purple and rose-coloured satin,
green velvet, cloth of gold and silver, lion-coloured velvet, the
cardinals themselves in mitres and robes, their horses draped in
white damask. Count Lodovico Pico della Mirandola bore the
Pope's personal standard: a shield with a grazing red bull on a
gold ground halved with three black bands surmounted by the
mitre and keys of St Peter. The roar of cannon from the Castel
Sant'Angelo rumbled in the background, the Romans shouted
'Borgia, Borgia' with a wild enthusiasm which they were not later
to feel. The streets were lined with blue cloth, strewn with flowers and herbs, the walls of palaces hung with magnificent tapestries and at intervals triumphal arches proclaimed the most

idolatrous slogans: 'Caesar was great, now Rome is greater:
Alexander reigns – the first was a man, this is a god.' In front of
the Palazzo San Marco a fountain in the form of a bull spurted
water from horns, mouth, eyes, nose and ears, and 'most delicate
wine' from its forehead. The heat exhausted everyone, particularly the heavily built Pope: at the Lateran basilica he had one of
his recurrent fainting fits and had to be revived with a dash of
water in his face, an evil omen in the opinion of observers.

At sixty, Rodrigo Borgia, a Catalan from the Kingdom of
Valencia in southern Spain, now occupied one of the most powerful positions in the known world. As Pope, he was regarded as
God's supreme vicar on earth in both temporal and religious
spheres, having inherited the spiritual authority of St Peter and
the earthly powers of the Emperor Constantine. With the return
of the popes to the city sixty-two years before, after the Great
Schism, Rome was again the undisputed centre of the Christian
world. The scruffy medieval town clinging to the shattered monu-
ments of the classical city was being transformed; a succession of
popes demonstrated their position as heirs to the imperial glories,
building bridges, levelling roads and beautifying St Peter's and the
Vatican, the centre of their operations. The cardinals, princes of
the Church nominated by the popes for their loyalty and political connections rather than their spiritual qualities, vied with
each other in building splendid palaces to display their wealth
and importance. Rome now saw its identity in classical terms:
since the fall of Constantinople to the Turks in 1453, classical
texts and Greek and Latin scholars had flooded into Italy. Men
saw their lives in terms of the heroes of ancient Greece and
Rome, not of the saints and patriarchs. In the city itself, excava-
tions revealed the glories of imperial Rome, such as the Golden
House of Nero, confirming the citizens in their feelings of identity as inheritors of Republic and Empire. The popes were arbiters
of Europe and beyond; in 1492 Columbus had landed on
Hispaniola and, as Alexander VI, Rodrigo Borgia was to supervise the carving up of the New World between the Spanish and
Portuguese sovereigns. In Europe he retained the symbolic power

to crown the Emperor and to confirm or refuse the investiture of the Kingdom of Naples. He had the power to initiate alliances and call crusades against the ever more powerful Ottoman Turks, while he directly controlled a large portion of central Italy, the Papal States or 'the Patrimony of St Peter', where local lords or 'papal vicars' held their lands from him.

Born in 1431, Rodrigo Borgia had been at the centre of this web of power from a very early age when, probably still in his teens, he emigrated from his native town of Jativa in Valencia to Rome to join the Catalan train of his uncle, Cardinal Alonso de Borja, brother of his mother Isabella. He had been well educated as the pupil of the humanist Gaspare da Verona who conducted a smart 'preparatory school' for the relatives of eminent churchmen, and then in canon law at the University of Bologna. Alonso's election in 1455 as Pope Calixtus III changed Rodrigo's life. Within a year, at the age of twenty-five, he had been appointed a cardinal, then given the Vice-Chancellorship of the Church, the second most important office after the Pope. He survived the purge of Catalans by the furious Romans after the death of Calixtus in 1458, keeping his office and accumulating rich benefices through the reigns of subsequent popes. He gained immensely in knowledge of the workings of the papal court and of international affairs and contacts, building up his position by the acquisition of key papal fortresses surrounding Rome. In the city itself he lived in the style of a Renaissance prince, with a household of 113, and had built himself one of the finest palaces in Rome which today still forms the nucleus of the Palazzo Sforza-Cesarini on the Corso Vittorio Emmanuele. Pope Pius II likened the splendours of the magnificent building with its tower and three-storey loggiaed courtyards to those of the Golden House of Nero. Rodrigo's ally, Cardinal Ascanio Sforza, who as a member of Milan's ruling family and one of the richest cardinals in Rome, was in a position to judge, was equally impressed:

The palace is splendidly decorated: the walls of the great entrance hall are hung with tapestries depicting various historical scenes. A small

drawing room leads off this, which was also decorated with fine tapestries; the carpets on the floor harmonized with the furnishings which
included a sumptuous day bed upholstered in red satin with a canopy
over it, and a chest on which was laid out a vast and beautiful collection of gold and silver plate. Beyond this there were two more rooms,
one hung with fine satin, carpeted, and with another canopied bed
covered with Alexandrine velvet; the other even more ornate with a
couch covered in cloth of gold. In this room the central table was
covered with a cloth of Alexandrine velvet [a complicated dyeing process
which resulted in a violet blue] and surrounded by finely carved chairs.

Rodrigo Borgia was a man of immense shrewdness and ability, devious and ruthless, avid for money and possessions but at
the same time possessed of overwhelming charm, a quick sense
of humour and a great lust for life and beautiful women. Priest
or not, his sexual power was intense: 'He is handsome; of a most
glad countenance and joyous aspect, gifted with honeyed and
choice eloquence', his former tutor had described him as a cardinal; 'The beautiful women on whom his eyes are cast he lures
to love him, and moves them in a wondrous way, more power-
fully than the magnet influences iron.'[1] A Sienese garden party
held when he was twenty-nine was described by his master, Pope
Pius II, as an orgy, with dancing, lewd women and lascivious
conduct by all present. The Sienese joked that if all the children
fathered on that day were born with the robes of their fathers
they would turn out priests and cardinals.[2] Thirty-three years
later he was still an attractive man, described by Hieronymus
Portius in 1493 as 'tall, in complexion neither fair nor dark; his
eyes are black, his mouth somewhat full. His health is splendid,
and he has a marvellous power of enduring all sorts of fatigue.
He is singularly eloquent in speech, and is gifted with an innate
good breeding which never forsakes him.'[3] Rodrigo was an
impressive figure with his powerful, hooked nose, imposing
manner and heavy but athletic body (he had a passion for hunting). He was possessed of great willpower and would let nothing, not even his children, stand in the way of his ambitions.

He fathered eight, possibly nine, children: the first three, by unknown mothers, were Pedro Luis, born in about 1468; Jeronima, who married the Roman noble Gian Andrea Cesarini in 1482; and Elisabetta, who married a papal official, Pietro Matuzzi, that same year. Two more boys by anonymous mothers were born after he succeeded to the papacy, but his principal mistress and mother of the three children he loved the most, Lucrezia and her two elder brothers Cesare and Juan, was Vannozza Cattanei. Vannozza, the daughter of one Jacopo Pinctoris, (the Painter), was probably born and brought up in Rome, but is believed to have been of Mantuan origin. She must have had a strong personality to have held a man like Rodrigo Borgia for so long; she was certainly attractive enough to marry two husbands while carrying on her affair with the cardinal. Her relationship with Rodrigo ended shortly after Lucrezia's birth, although she claimed that her last child, Jofre, born in 1481/2, was fathered by Rodrigo and would proudly record the fact on her tombstone. Rodrigo himself remained dubious as to Jofre's parenthood and apparently suspected he was the son of Vannozza by her second husband, the Milanese Giorgio della Croce, to whom she was married at the time of Jofre's birth. Vannozza profited greatly from her connection with the powerful Cardinal Borgia, becoming a woman of property, with inns in the smart quarters of Rome and houses which she rented to artisans and prostitutes. From the few letters of hers which survive, she comes across as distinctly unattractive in character – grasping, social-climbing, avid for money and position. She kept in touch with Alexander after their affair ended by which time she was married to a third husband, Carlo Canale, but seems to have played little part in her children's lives as they grew up. While she remained close to her eldest son, Cesare, her relationship with Lucrezia, her only daughter, was a distant one.

Lucrezia was twelve when her father became Pope, having been born on 18 April 1480 in the fortress of Subiaco, one of her father's strategic strongholds round Rome. Her birth outside the city was probably due to Rodrigo's early policy of discretion as to the existence of his illegitimate family, as a result of which we know very little of her early life. She probably spent her first years in her mother's house on the Piazza Pizzo di Merlo in the Ponte quarter of Rome, and it seems probable that she was also educated in the Dominican convent of San Sisto on the Appian Way, a place in which she later took refuge in times of difficulty and stress. She spent her formative years not with her mother but in the vast Orsini Palazzo Montegiordano in the care of Adriana de Mila, her father's first cousin and the widow of a member of the powerful Roman clan. The dominant figure in her life was undoubtedly her father, who loved his three children by Vannozza with an extravagant passion – 'he is the most carnal of men', an observer remarked – so much so that there were later accusations of incest between Rodrigo and Lucrezia.

After his election to the papacy, Alexander moved Adriana and Lucrezia to the Palazzo Santa Maria in Portico near the Vatican. The move brought Lucrezia to the attention of the largely hostile Borgia chroniclers, the gossip columnists of the day, and of the envoys to the papal court of the Italian states, an important part of whose duties was to purvey intimate detail to their employers. The limelight penetrated her hitherto private world where she lived in an ambience which was virtually a papal harem. Lucrezia was brought up in an atmosphere of male sexual power and dominance, in which the women were entirely subject to Rodrigo's will and desires. The head of the household, Adriana de Mila, subjugated herself entirely to his interests, acting as Lucrezia's guardian and chaperone, while at the same time encouraging his relationship with her own son's wife, the beautiful, nineteen-year-old Giulia Farnese Orsini, known as 'Giulia la Bella'. Giulia's cuckold husband Orsino Orsini, nicknamed 'Monoculus' ('One-eyed'), was kept well out of the way at their country estate of Bassanello.

Lucrezia herself, as the only daughter of Rodrigo's relationship with Vannozza, was cherished by her father who loved her, according to the chroniclers, 'superlatively'. Unlike her siblings

she was fair, perhaps an indication of her northern Italian maternal origin. 'She is of middle height and graceful in form', Niccolò
Cagnolo of Parma wrote of her in her early twenties. 'Her face
is rather long, the nose well cut, hair golden, eyes of no special
colour [probably grey blue]. Her mouth is rather large, the teeth
brilliantly white, her neck is slender and fair, the bust admirably
proportioned. She is always gay and smiling.'[4] Other narrators
specifically praised her long golden hair and her bearing: 'she
carries herself with such grace that it seems as if she does not
move'. It is significant of Rodrigo's fashionable identification with
the humanist, classical world that he should take as his papal name
that of the Greek hero and conqueror Alexander, while naming
one of his favourite sons Cesare (i.e. Caesar) and his daughter
Lucretia after the Roman matron who committed suicide rather
than live with the dishonour of being raped. The name Lucretia,
symbolizing as it did womanly chastity, would make her the subject
of unseemly mirth among many of her contemporaries. She was
a woman of her time, well educated in humanist literature, speaking Italian, Catalan, French and Latin and capable of writing
poetry in those languages; she also had an understanding of Greek.
She had been taught eloquence and could express herself elegantly
in public speech. She loved music and poetry both Spanish and
Italian, owning volumes of Spanish *canzones* and of Dante and
Petrarch. Like upper-class women – and men – of her time she
learned to dance with skill and grace, an important part of courtly
pastimes.

Lucrezia was brought up in a world in which male dominance
was taken for granted; while her brother Cesare might believe
Alberti's dictum 'a man can do anything he wills', a woman's
dilemma was that of Lorenzo the Magnificent's sister, Nannina
Rucellai, who wrote to her mother in 1470, 'Whoso wants to do
as they wish, should not be born a woman.'[5] She was also a
Borgia, with her father's charm, graceful manners and administrative ability, his resilience and understanding of the workings of
power. Like him, she well knew how to turn events to her advantage; she accepted situations as they were and went her own way,

bending to circumstances but never defeated by them. She shared the curious mixture of piety, sensuality and complete indifference to sexual morality that was a feature of her family but, when she was in a position to express herself, she would prove to be a good, kind and compassionate woman.

Of her immediate siblings she was closest to her brother Cesare, born in 1476,[6] the most brilliant and ruthless of all the Borgias, including his father. Cesare was to be the evil genius of Lucrezia's life: their love and loyalty to each other were such that he, like his father, would be accused of incest with her; even that his obsessive love for her led him to murder. Accusations of incest at the time have to be viewed with a degree of scepticism: sexual innuendo was a favourite ingredient of Italian gossip. It was, however, not always unjustified. Cesare's contemporary Gian Paolo Baglioni, lord of Perugia, openly received ambassadors while lying in bed with his sister.

Cesare grew up to be the handsomest man of his day: at twenty-five the Venetian envoy Polo Capello, who by then had reason both to hate and to fear him, wrote '[he] is physically most beautiful, . . . tall and well-made'. The Mantuan envoy Boccaccio, who visited him in his palace in the Borgo, the newly built quarter next to the Vatican, in March 1493 described him aged seventeen to the Duke of Ferrara: 'He possesses marked genius and a charming personality. He has the manners of a son of a great prince: above all he is lively and merry and fond of society . . .' By then Cesare, destined by his father for the Church, had been accumulating rich ecclesiastical benefices since the age of seven. At fifteen, to the outrage of his future flock, he was appointed Bishop of Pamplona, the ancient capital of the Kingdom of Navarre, although he had not yet even taken holy orders. After his elevation to the papacy, Alexander had bestowed on Cesare his own former archbishopric of Valencia, with a huge income of 16,000 ducats a year. When Boccaccio visited him the only sign of his clerical status was 'a little tonsure like a simple priest': otherwise he was dressed for the hunt in a 'worldly garment of silk with a sword at his side'. 'The Archbishop of Valencia,' the envoy remarked, 'has never had any inclination for the priest-hood.'

Indeed, Cesare had inherited none of that streak of piety which ran through his family. Alexander was a devotee of the Virgin Mary while Lucrezia developed a deep sense of religion over the years. Cesare's great-nephew, grandson of his worthless younger brother Juan, even became a saint. But there is little to suggest that Cesare cared anything for God or religion. As a man of the Renaissance, he believed in an egocentric world, taking as his role model his namesake, Caesar. Following the Renaissance concept of the ancient world he believed that the ultimate aim of a man's life was not heaven but fame and power on this earth, a goal to be achieved by his own individual exercise of skill and valour – '*virtù*' – to conquer the unpredictable force of fortune – '*fortuna*' – which ruled the world. Indeed, everything about Cesare pointed to a career other than the one chosen for him. He was a brilliant student – even the hostile historian Paolo Giovio admitted that at the University of Pisa, which he had attended after the University of Perugia, 'he had gained such profit [from his studies] that, with ardent mind, he discussed learnedly the questions put to him in both canon and civil law'. And in a world which valued courage in war and physical prowess in the exercise of arms, he excelled in strength and competitiveness. He shared his father's passion for hunting, for horses and hunting dogs and he learned bullfighting from the Spaniards of his own and his father's households. He had everything with which to succeed, backed, all-importantly, by his father's powerful position; it all depended upon his father's life and that, in the nature of things, could not give him unlimited time. Convinced, as he once said, that he would die young, he became driven, devious, dissembling, ruthlessly crushing everyone who stood in his way. As his career progressed, the legend of the Borgia monster was born.

Yet at seventeen he could still appear to the envoy Boccaccio as 'very modest' and his bearing 'much better than that of the Duke of Gandia, his brother . . .' Lucrezia's other older brother, Juan Borgia, born c. 1478, was a vain, arrogant, mindless, dissolute

youth who shared Cesare's fine features and good looks but none
of his qualities. Notwithstanding this, he was his father's favourite
son, as his stepfather, Vannozza's third husband, Carlo Canale,
informed Francesco Gonzaga, Marquis of Mantua, who was
exploring every avenue of influence with the Pope in order to
have his brother, Sigismondo Gonzaga, made a cardinal. Canale,
formerly a secretary to the previous Cardinal Gonzaga, uncle of
the current Marquis, advised Gonzaga to do everything he could
to conciliate Juan Gandia, such as presenting him with one of
the Gonzaga horses which were coveted throughout Europe.
'Because,' he wrote, '. . . in dealings with His Holiness he could
have no better intercessor than His Lordship because he is the
eye of His Holiness Our Lord.'[7] By this time Canale was so
carried away by his wife's exalted connections that he went so
far as to sign the letter 'Carolus de Cattaneis'. The youngest
member of the quartet, Jofre Borgia, at least a year younger than
Lucrezia and destined to play a minor part in her life, was far
less favoured by Alexander than Vannozza's three other children,
although he deployed him as he did the others as a pawn in his
political plans. Indeed, Jofre's existence was barely noticed by
commentators at that time. Alexander's early discretion as to the
existence of his children had succeeded to the extent that the
Mantuan envoy Fioramonte Brognolo, writing to Francesco
Gonzaga's wife, Isabella d'Este, cautiously referred to both Cesare
and Juan as 'nephews of a brother of His Holiness' as late as
February 1493.

Although born in Roman territory and half Italian on their
mother's side, Lucrezia and her brothers were strongly influenced
by their Catalan ancestry. 'Catalan', as distinct from Spanish, had
a particular connotation in the eyes of Italians and indeed the
Catalans themselves. The Kingdom of Aragon, represented in
Alexander's day by the wily King Ferdinand, included the Catalan-
speaking peoples spread round the western coasts of the
Mediterranean from the territory of Barcelona, the capital, to the
former Moorish kingdom of Valencia in the south and the island
of Mallorca. The reputation of the Catalans as tight-fisted

merchants and ruthless fighters was widespread; as far as the Italians were concerned elements of race and religion also entered into it, particularly in the case of Valencia, a recently conquered Arab kingdom where Moors (Arabs) and Jews had lived side by side with Aragonese. The Moorish kingdom of Granada had only fallen to the Spaniards under Ferdinand of Aragon and his wife Isabella, independently Queen of Castile, in 1492, the year of Rodrigo's election. Valencian Catalans in particular were referred to opprobriously by Italians as *marrani*, meaning secret Jews. The Borgias, or de Borjas, in Rome under Calixtus and subsequently Alexander, represented an alien cell, with their own loyalties and their own language (a mixture of Latin and Provençal). Both Borgia popes, Calixtus and Alexander, gathered a praetorian guard of their Valencian relations and fellow Catalans around them, to the exclusion of native-born Italians. Catalan was the language of the papal court of the Borgias and the family language which they used among themselves. Borgias and their connections swarmed round Alexander in the Vatican to an even greater degree than they had round his uncle Calixtus. Juan de Borja y Navarro, Archbishop of Monreale, was the only cardinal of Alexander's first creation on 31 August 1493. The other Borja connections are too numerous to mention, occupying as they do no less than a dozen pages of the index of the authoritative work on the subject.[8] That Italians were contemptuous of them as *marrani* is evidenced by the chancellor of Giovanni de'Medici (the future Pope Leo X, then a fellow student of Cesare at the University of Pisa in 1491), commenting on Cesare's household: 'It seems to us that these men of his who surround him are little men who have small consideration for behaviour and have all the appearance of *marrani*'.[9]

The awareness of being a race apart, regarded as foreigners in a foreign land, enhanced the Borgias' sense of togetherness – 'us against the world'. They employed their relations and compatriots as the only people they could trust in a potentially hostile environment. In Rome itself and its immediate environs, the independence and security of the papacy were threatened by the great

baronial families with palaces in the city and strongholds in the
Roman Campagna, the Colonna and the Orsini, and their lesser
allies; only the fact that the two families invariably worked against
each other made the situation inside and immediately outside the
city tenable for the holder of the papal throne. And beyond the
Orsini and Colonna, the great families of Italy were linked by a
web of dynastic marriages and ancient alliances going back over
hundreds of years. A chain of intermarriage joined Orsini to
Medici, Este to Sforza, Gonzaga to Montefeltro, branching down
to the smallest lordships. 'So thick was the undergrowth of alliances
among the signorial families', an historian wrote, 'that to strike
one branch was to break another.' This was the family network
which the alien Borgias would attack in their ambitious plans to
establish a dominant Borgia dynasty in Italy.

Alexander's children were the instruments and beneficiaries of
his policies. No stigma was attached to bastardy at the time;
bastards being sometimes preferred over legitimate children.
Nepotism among Renaissance popes was nothing new. It was
taken as normal by Italians of the time that each pope, as soon
as he was elected, would in the usually comparatively short time
available to him take steps to advance his relations to positions
of power and wealth and, if possible, to establish a dynasty on a
permanent basis. Calixtus himself, who led a blameless private
life, had been guilty of excessive nepotism. Alexander, however,
was unique in the lengths to which he would go, and in the
ambition, talent and looks of the children he promoted. Sexual
laxity in the princes of the Church, and indeed in lay society,
was taken as a matter of course and it was not until the kings
and princes felt their interests threatened by Alexander's political
proceedings that the torrent of abuse against him began. At the
time, however, Rodrigo Borgia's election was generally welcomed.
No one beyond the pious Queen Isabella of Castile objected to
his immoral way of life as unsuited to the occupant of the Chair
of St Peter. Indeed, when the Queen later remonstrated with the
papal nuncio Desprats (another Catalan) about Alexander's flaunt-
ing of his children, Desprats retorted that the Queen had clearly

not studied the lives of Alexander's predecessors such as Innocent VIII and Sixtus IV, and that if she had she would not have complained about his present Holiness. 'And I revealed to her some things about Pope Sixtus and Pope Innocent, demonstrating how much more worthily Your Holiness behaved than the aforesaid [pontiffs]', he wrote disingenuously to his patron, Alexander.[10]

Lucrezia's immediate future was inextricably linked with her father's dynastic plan for his family and influenced by the shifts in his political alliances. Before his election to the papacy, Alexander had concentrated on building a power base in his native Valencia with rich benefices for himself and his children, not to mention the dukedom of Gandia and other secular privileges as the fruits of his complex relationship with the Catholic Kings of Spain, Ferdinand of Aragon and Isabella of Castile. The Borgias originated in Aragon but for several hundred years had lived in the territory of the former Moorish kingdom of Valencia. The social ascent of the family from the obscure ranks of the small landowning class of citizens had begun in the fourteenth century, accelerating in the time of Calixtus when his niece, Rodrigo's sister Joana, married a member of the ancient nobility. Their spectacular rise to prominence during the fifteenth century owed itself to the efforts of first Calixtus (who had four sisters and numerous relations living there) and then to Alexander as cardinal and as Pope. Their ascent to the ranks of the high nobility was confirmed when Rodrigo obtained the dukedom of Gandia for his eldest son, Pedro Luis, in 1485. This honour, and the lands which went with it, for which the then Cardinal Borgia paid handsomely and subsequently enlarged, was the foundation stone of the Borja dynasty in Spain. In keeping with their customary position of bargaining between King Ferdinand of Aragon and Rodrigo as one Catalan to another, it seems likely that the dukedom was the reward Rodrigo extracted for his services in influencing the then Pope, Sixtus IV, to grant a Bull of dispensation in 1471 enabling Ferdinand to marry Isabella, thus uniting the Kingdoms of Aragon and Castile. Pedro Luis, whom Rodrigo had named guardian to Juan, died unmarried and without heirs in Rodrigo's palace in Rome in 1488, leaving his titles and Spanish estates to Juan, who also inherited his fiancée, Maria Enriques, cousin to King Ferdinand.

Lucrezia, eight years old at the time, was left 10,000 ducats by the half-brother whom she had barely known. As her father continued to exploit his Spanish connections, she was promised in marriage, aged ten, to Querubi de Centelles, son of the Count of Oliva, on 26 February 1491, when she was described in the agreement between Borgia and Oliva as 'carnal daughter of the said most reverend cardinal and sister of the most illustrious lord Don Juan de Borja, Duke of Gandia'. Within just over two months her father, after her proposed bridegroom married someone else, betrothed her, now aged just eleven, on 30 April 1491, to Don Gaspar de Procida, son of the Count of Almenara and Aversa. This marriage contract too was annulled on 8 November 1492, after Rodrigo's election, when the new Pope no longer saw his daughter's future in Spain. As Alexander trod the difficult path endeavouring to preserve the independence of the papacy between conflicting interests, Lucrezia would be the victim of his shifting pattern of alliances.

2. Countess of Pesaro

'The Pope being a carnal man and very loving of his flesh and
blood, this [relationship] will so establish the love of His Beatitude
towards our house that no one will have the opportunity to divert
him from us and draw him towards themselves'

– Cardinal Ascanio Sforza, to his brother Ludovico, Duke of Milan,
on the marriage of Lucrezia to Giovanni Sforza, 3 February 1493

Alexander's election had been unanimous; neither of his two most
powerful rivals, cardinals Giuliano della Rovere (the future Pope
Julius II), representing the interest of the Kingdom of Naples, nor
Ascanio Sforza, representing the Duchy of Milan, could gain a
majority. Ascanio Sforza, seeing which way the wind was blowing, had swung his partisans behind Rodrigo and in return had
received Borgia's former office, the Vice-Chancellorship, his palace
and various strongholds and benefices in his gift. The usual accusations of simony – the selling of holy offices for money – were
raised: the diarist Stefano Infessura wrote that a train-load of mules
laden with silver had been seen passing from Borgia's palace to
Sforza's, but nothing could be proven beyond the usual wheel-
ing and dealing which attended papal elections. Analysing the
voting records of the conclave which resulted in Alexander's election, the Borgias' most authoritative historian, Michael Mallett,
considered that Alexander won on merit.

Alexander VI was seen as an able 'chief executive' who could
lead the Church through increasingly dangerous times. Even the
Florentine historian Francesco Guicciardini, no friend of the
Borgias, admitted his capabilities: 'Alexander VI possessed singular cunning and sagacity, excellent judgement, a marvellous efficacy

in persuading, and an incredible dexterity and attentiveness in dealing with weighty matters', he wrote. (These qualities, however, he added, were 'far outweighed by his vices: the most obscene behaviour, insincerity, shamelessness, lying, faithlessness, impiety, insatiable avarice, immoderate ambition, a cruelty more barbaric and a most ardent cupidity to exalt his numerous children: and among these were several (in order that depraved instruments might not be lacking to carry out his depraved designs) no less detestable than the father . . .)[1]

Lucrezia's third betrothal and later marriage to Giovanni Sforza, lord of Pesaro, signed on 2 February 1493 and executed by proxy while Sforza was in Pesaro, demonstrated the complete ruthlessness with which Alexander deployed his daughter, still a child even by the standards of the day. It was simply a cynical and temporary response to a temporary situation: by marrying his daughter to a connection of Ascanio Sforza he was not only demonstrating publicly his debt of gratitude for his election but punishing the Sforzas' enemy, Ferrante, the Aragonese King of Naples, for a hostile move against himself the previous September. In the complex minuet – even tit for tat – of Italian high politics, King Ferrante of Naples, angered by Alexander's alliance with Ascanio, had financially backed a move by the Orsini family in September 1492 to buy the castles of Cerveteri and Anguillara near Rome in an attempt to put a stranglehold on the Pope in the first weeks of his papacy. In the month before Lucrezia's betrothal Alexander had negotiated a new line-up of Italian powers with the League of St Mark linking the papacy to Venice and Milan. The child bride Lucrezia was to be a pledge to the Sforzas and a signal to the powers beyond Rome of Alexander's independence. A letter from Ascanio Sforza to his brother Ludovico, announcing the signing of the contract and proxy ceremony the previous night, made clear the importance the Sforzas attached to the marriage: 'The Pope being a carnal man and very loving of his flesh and blood, this [relationship] will so establish the love of His Beatitude towards our house that no one will have the opportunity to divert him from us and draw him towards themselves.'[2] The envoys of the King of Naples, he told Ludovico, had gone to infinite pains in recent days to prevent the Sforza marriage, offering instead as a husband for Lucrezia the son of the Duke of Calabria, Ferrante's grandson (who later became Lucrezia's second husband) with great material inducements. To circumvent the Neapolitan efforts, the proxy ceremony was carried out in the greatest secrecy at the Pope's request – only the Cardinal of Monreale, Cesare, Juan, Ascanio, the Milanese ambassador, Stefano Taberna, four of the Pope's chamberlains and the notary who drew up the contract were party to the affair. Giovanni Sforza was to be given a *condotta* (a military contract to raise and pay a specified number of troops to the profit of the provider, or *condottiere*) by the Pope subsidized by the Duke of Milan.[3] Lucrezia brought with her a dowry of 31,000 ducats.

In dynastic terms of prestige and wealth it was not a great marriage. Giovanni Sforza was a minor prince, the illegitimate son of Costanzo Sforza, Count of Cotignola, the original but far less powerful line of the family to which Ludovico il Moro and Ascanio belonged. Pesaro, a beautiful town on the Adriatic coast of Italy, strategically situated on the Via Emilia, had only been taken over by Giovanni's grandfather, Alessandro, in 1445. Alessandro – a ruthless husband who had twice tried to poison, and then to strangle his second wife, before forcing her into a convent – was otherwise a civilized man who employed the best architects and artists to beautify the town. The court at Pesaro was famous for its festivities: Alessandro expanded his connections with all the great families of Italy and founded a superb library. His son Costanzo, Giovanni's father, a cousin of Ascanio Sforza, made his court a centre for poets and scholars, and married into the Aragonese royal family; his bride was Camilla d'Aragona, niece of King Ferrante. But the marriage produced no legitimate heirs, so Giovanni, the eldest of two illegitimate sons, succeeded as lord in 1483. He enjoyed an annual revenue of 12,000 ducats but, like many lords with a court to maintain, was perennially short of money and earned his living as a *condottiere*. Giovanni

Sforza was handsome and well-connected, not only through his Sforza relations in Milan, but his first wife, Maddalena Gonzaga, had been the sister of Francesco Gonzaga, Marquis of Mantua, and of Elisabetta, wife of Guidobaldo da Montefeltro, Duke of Urbino. He was, however, utterly dependent on his powerful Sforza relations, Ascanio and Ludovico, and had as little choice in the marriage as Lucrezia; he did what the elder Sforzas told him and was destined to play only a fleeting part in Lucrezia's life.

The Sforza marriage took place under the veils of secrecy and dissimulation customary in Alexander's manoeuvres. As early as 4 November 1492, the Mantuan envoy Jacopo d'Atri reported that Giovanni Sforza was staying secretly in the house of the Cardinal of San Clemente, and that the negotiations for his marriage to Lucrezia were far advanced. Secrecy was necessary because Lucrezia's previous fiancé, Procida, had come to Rome to claim his bride, declaring that his marriage had been negotiated by means of the King of Spain. 'There is much gossip about Pesaro's marriage,' the Ferrarese envoy wrote to his master, Duke Ercole d'Este. 'The first bridegroom is still here, raising a great hue and cry, as a Catalan . . .'[4] By a curious twist of fate the man who was to become Lucrezia's third husband, Alfonso d'Este, son of Duke Ercole, was a guest in the Vatican at the time and visited Lucrezia.[5] Procida eventually accepted defeat, compensated by a considerable sum of money in the form of a *condotta* from the Pope, subsidized by the Duke of Milan, in order to buy his silence and give way to Giovanni Sforza.[6] At any rate he was registered as among the leading members of Juan Gandia's household in Valencia the following year.[7]

Lucrezia's marriage to Giovanni Sforza was celebrated with due pomp and festivity in the Vatican on 12 June 1493. Sforza had made a solemn entry into Rome two days earlier, having returned to Pesaro in the interim. The timing of his arrival and indeed of his marriage had been delayed, dictated by Ascanio Sforza's need to seek the advice of his astrologers as to the most favourable date, which irritated the Pope. As it turned out, the astrologers' choice of date made no difference to what was to be an ill-starred marriage. Lucrezia saw her husband-to-be for the first time when he arrived outside the Palazzo Santa Maria in Portico to pay his respects to her from a distance. He must have seemed old to her – he was twenty-six and a widower – although he was handsome enough with a long, straight nose, a fashionable beard and flowing hair. Lucrezia was only just thirteen but no innocent, given the close proximity in which she lived with her father's teenage mistress, Giulia Farnese.

The Pope spared no expense to show off his daughter, endowing her with a sumptuous trousseau which was rumoured to include a dress reputedly worth 15,000 ducats.[8] Giovanni himself had borrowed jewellery from the Gonzaga to put on a good show, and was dressed for his wedding in a long Turkish-style robe of curled cloth of gold, with the Gonzaga gold chain round his neck. At the Pope's orders he was accompanied to the Vatican by the Roman barons and a flock of bishops to a great hall crowded with the noblewomen of Rome. Cesare and Juan Gandia slipped in through a secret door, the younger Borgia dressed with his usual ostentation, in a 'Turcha', like the bridegroom's, of curled cloth of gold down to the floor, his sleeves embroidered with large pearls, a chain of balas rubies and pearls of great price at his neck and wearing a beret studded with a jewel estimated to be worth 150,000 ducats.

The bride herself was described by one observer as 'very beautiful' ('*assai bella*'), in a splendid dress and jewels. She was flanked by the daughter of Niccolò Orsini, Count of Pitigliano, married to Giulia Farnese's brother, Angelo, and by Giulia herself, who quite outshone her and was described by an onlooker as 'truly beautiful to behold and said to be the Pope's favourite'. The bride and groom knelt at the Pope's feet while the Count of Pitigliano held a naked sword above them and an archbishop pronounced the marriage ceremony. Afterwards the Pope led them into an outer room where a 'very polished' pastoral eclogue by Serafino was performed, followed by Plautus's comedy *The Menaechmi*, in Latin, which bored Alexander who ordered it to be cut short.

There was a lavish presentation of wedding presents in the form of magnificent silver from, among others, Cesare, Ascanio and the Duke of Ferrara.[9] After a light collation the couple were accompanied to the Palazzo Santa Maria in Portico by all the barons, prelates and ladies, and that night the Pope gave a 'most sumptuous' private dinner for the gentlemen at which Ascanio Sforza and his Milanese ally, Cardinal Sanseverino, were prominent guests.[10] There was to be no bedding of the bride as was customary since the Pope had ordered that the marriage was not to be consummated before November, either out of consideration for his daughter's age or, equally likely, to enable him to have it dissolved on the grounds of non-consummation in case it no longer suited his plans.

Within a week of Lucrezia's marriage to Sforza, the wily Alexander was hedging his diplomatic bets. Don Diego Lopez de Haro, envoy extraordinary from the King and Queen of Spain, came to offer the Pope homage on their behalf. It was the first prong of a pincer movement designed to draw Alexander back towards the Aragonese cause in Naples. Lopez de Haro advised Alexander that King Ferdinand 'regarded the affairs of Naples as his own' while proffering an irresistible bait: the revival of the marriage project between the Borgias and the royal family of Aragon which had been planned before the death of Pedro Luis. Juan Gandia had taken his late half-brother's place as the fiancé of Dona Maria Enriques, the King's cousin. Alexander leapt hungrily at the lure, hoping, as he told his son Juan, not only for the royal connection but, through Isabella, the prospect of obtaining former Moorish estates in the recently conquered Kingdom of Granada. The Catalan bargaining between king and pope extended to the all-important resolution of the quarrel between Spain and Portugal over the right to explore and colonize the New World, opened up by Columbus's landing on Hispaniola which had become known in Rome in March of that year.

Hard on the Spanish envoy's heels came Federigo d'Aragona, the second son of King Ferrante of Naples (whose death had occurred in January), desperate to prevent Alexander promising the investiture of the Kingdom of Naples to Charles VIII of France. He offered a secret engagement between Jofre Borgia and Sancia, an illegitimate daughter of Ferrante's successor, Alfonso Duke of Calabria, and to negotiate peace between Alexander and Virginio Orsini, who held a *condotta* from the King of Naples, and who was to pay the Pope a large sum in return for the investiture of the castles of Cerveteri and Anguillara. A reconciliation was arranged between Alexander and Giuliano della Rovere. Within weeks all was settled, Juan Gandia left early in August for his wedding in Barcelona, shortly after the publication of the so-called Alexandrine Bulls which resolved the question of the New World on terms favourable to Spain, while on 17 August Jofre was married by proxy to Sancia. Alexander's diplomacy had won hands down, with rich marriages for his children, money and independence for himself. Although he intended to keep on good terms with all parties, his new pro-Aragonese stance did not in the end bode well for the Sforzas.

'This Duke [Gandia] leaves very rich and loaded with jewels, money and other valuable portable goods and silver. It is said he will return within a year but leave all his goods in Spain and come back to reap another harvest,' the Mantuan envoy reported.[11] A document from the archives of Valencia cathedral headed 'Inventory of the property which His Holiness Our Lord ordered to be put in caskets for the Lord Duke' provides a truly staggering view of the ostentatious wealth and resources of the Borgias. Boxes and boxes of rich velvet, damask, brocade, cloth of silver, satin and furs were loaded aboard his ship, curtains, cushions, bedcovers studded with gold, bed hangings in white damask brocade with gold fringes and crimson satin lining, tapestries woven with the history of Alexander the Great, and of Moses, huge quantities of table silver engraved with the ducal arms. One box contained jewels for Gandia and his duchess: a pendant to be worn in his cap consisted of a great emerald with a huge diamond above it, and a large pendant pearl, and a golden cross studded with pearls and diamonds to be given to the Duchess in which the Pope with his own hands had placed a piece of the True Cross.[12]

Even before he left, Alexander had issued Juan with firm instructions to make sure that he was assiduous in his attentions to the Spanish royal family, and particularly to the Queen, in order to obtain the fine estate which Lopez de Haro had indicated would be given to him.[13] Alexander's instructions to Gandia's treasurer and secretary, Genis Fira and Jaume de Pertusa, were equally commanding: he hoped for great things for Juan of the Spanish sovereigns – the marquisate of Denia in Valencia and, beyond that, a lordship in the Kingdom of Granada, adding pertinently that he expected both – 'one favour does not prevent another'.[14]

But in his greedy haste and joy Alexander had neglected his usual caution. Gandia received a splendid reception when he reached Barcelona on 24 August, and Alexander prepared the last and most important of the Bulls opening the way for Castile to conquer any lands in the west not yet occupied by other Christian powers. The Bull was promulgated on 25 September but, preoccupied with other matters, neither Ferdinand nor Isabella attended Gandia's wedding at the end of the month, nor were any favours yet forthcoming. While Isabella the Catholic thought it unseemly to be granting favours to the Pope's bastard, Ferdinand saw Gandia as a useful hostage to ensure Alexander's loyalty over Naples should he have to intervene, and his interest lay in prolonging the affair. Alexander was mortified: he was still more so as reports began to come in of Juan's bad behaviour and neglect of his wife, including an (unfounded) accusation of non-consummation of the marriage, which roused him to fury. Even Cesare, newly promoted as Cardinal of Valencia by his father, wrote a reproving elder brotherly letter to Juan, in Valencian Catalan, the family language, at his father's instigation:

However great my joy and happiness at being promoted cardinal, and they were certainly considerable, my annoyance was greater still when I heard of the bad reports His Holiness had received of you and your behaviour. Letters . . . have informed His Holiness that you had been going round Barcelona at night, killing cats and dogs, making frequent visits to the brothel, gambling for large sums, speaking disrespectfully and imprudently to important people, showing disobedience to Don Enrich and Dona Maria [Juan's father and mother-in-law] and finally acting throughout in a way inconsistent with a gentleman of your position.[15]

Juan's bad behaviour and, most of all, the report of his non-consummation of the marriage, frightened and disturbed Alexander who was not comforted by the report he received from his nuncio, Desprats, of a conversation he had had with Queen Isabella, who, he said, 'had received great annoyance and displeasure from certain things concerning Your Beatitude, principally those which were such that they caused scandal . . ., specifically the festivities at the wedding of Dona Lucrecia, and the creation of the cardinals, that is of Valencia [Cesare Borgia] and the Cardinal Farnese [Giulia's brother, Alessandro] . . .' Desprats' advice to the Pope was not to pursue the cause of Gandia and his siblings with such fervour.

Among other family duties expected of Gandia were the execution of certain commissions given him by his father, specifically 'small tiles' (*rajoletes*) for the decoration of the Borgia Apartments in the Vatican, and by 'his dearest sister' Lucrezia. An accounts book of 27 January to 29 June 1494 lists money for various presents for Lucrezia, including gold jewellery and shoes: 'sandals of gold and silk: 168 escudos for the sandals and shoes of the Lady Lucrecia . . . three hand lengths of blue satin to make two pairs of sandals for the Illustrious Lady Lucrecia'.[16]

In Rome, with the spotlight on the male members of her family, Lucrezia slipped from the attention of observers, who, however, recorded that Giovanni Sforza, as a result of a case of plague in his household, had gone out of Rome to Civita Castellana on 4 August.[17] There was no mention of Lucrezia going with him and at the end of that month Alexander was reported to be considering leaving Rome to get fresh air, because he was in danger of the plague and felt constricted in the Vatican as did 'our children' ('*nostri nepoti*').[18] Cesare was out of Rome

at Caprarola in August and with Alexander in Viterbo in October.
The Pope had left Rome after the stormy consistory in which
he had finally succeeded in imposing his will on the rebellious
cardinals and pushing through the blatantly nepotistic nominations of Cesare and Farnese, and also of the fifteen-year-old
Ippolito d'Este. Otherwise, Alexander had been politically even-
handed in his nominations for the cardinalate; only Ferrante of
Naples, to his fury, was unrewarded.

Lucrezia was certainly in Rome at the beginning of November
when Cattaneo reported that Giovanni Sforza was expected there
'to do reverence to His Holiness Our Lord and to keep company
in all respects [*'accompagnarsi in tuto'*] with his wife'. The clear
inference was that Sforza had been given permission to consummate his marriage, although this is the only contemporary
evidence we have that he did so. Lucrezia, still only thirteen, was
clearly of adult intelligence, since Cattaneo spoke of her as 'a
most worthy lady and very favourable to the cause of our
Monsignore' (Sigismondo Gonzaga, Francesco's brother, for
whom the Gonzaga were urgently pressing elevation to the cardinalate). Gonzaga's friends, he said, strongly recommended that the
Marquis treat Lucrezia as a 'sister and sister-in-law' (*sorella e cugnata*)
and pay more attention to her than he had in the past, 'especially
her being the daughter of [the Pope]' and 'full of goodwill' towards
Gonzaga.[19]

The direct route to papal favour led through the Palazzo Santa
Maria in Portico, as the astute princes of Italy and their envoys
were well aware. Adriana de Mila marshalled the suitors, while
Lucrezia and Giulia, the women Alexander loved most, obtained
the results. As Girolama Farnese, Giulia's sister, wrote to her
husband, the Florentine Puccio Pucci, on 21 October 1493, 'You
will have received letters . . . and have learned . . . all that Giulia
has secured . . . and you will be greatly pleased.'[20] Pucci's brother,
Lorenzo, who was in Rome that winter, left a vivid description
of the domestic scene at Santa Maria in Portico on Christmas
Eve, when he visited Giulia and found her drying her hair by
the fire with Lucrezia and Adriana. After Lorenzo had thanked

her for her favours to his family, Giulia replied, 'that such a trifle deserved no thanks. She hopes to be of still greater help to me, and says I shall find her so at the right time. Madonna Adriana joined in saying I might be certain that . . . it was owing to the favour of Madonna Giulia herself that I had obtained the benefices . . . Madonna Giulia asked with much interest after Messer Puccio and said, "We will see to it that some day he will come here as ambassador: and although, when he was here, we, in spite of our endeavours, were unable to effect it, we could now accomplish it without any difficulty."' Also present was Giulia's daughter, Laura, born the previous year and generally reputed, although almost certainly without foundation, to be the Pope's child. Alexander, devoted as he was to his children, never showed the slightest interest in her, and the evidence of a jealous letter he was to write to Giulia suggests that he was convinced Laura was Orsino's child. Pucci described Giulia as 'a most beautiful creature. She let her hair down before me and had it dressed; it reached down to her feet; never have I seen anything like it; she has the most beautiful hair. She wore a headdress of fine linen, and over it a sort of net, light as air, with gold threads woven in it. In truth it shone like the sun!' Lucrezia, perhaps irritated by Pucci's obvious admiration for Giulia's beauty, left the room to change from a 'robe lined in the Neapolitan fashion' similar to the one Giulia was wearing, and returned soon afterwards wearing 'a gown almost entirely of violet velvet'.

Giovanni Sforza himself boasted to the Mantuan envoy Brognolo that 'all these ladies who have access to the pontiff' were worth cultivating, but 'principally his wife'. 'I hear from all quarters,' Brognolo informed Francesco Gonzaga, 'that she [Lucrezia] has great access and could not be better, and certainly I understand that for her age she has great intelligence . . . I wished to inform Your Lordship of this in order that you should understand that the majority of those who want favours [of the Pope] pass through this door and it has already been signalled to me that it would be good to show some gratitude . . .'[21] The Gonzaga sent presents of prized fish (*carpioni*) from Lake Garda and cheese to the Pope, food appropriate for the Lenten season. Alexander turned to one of his Spanish intimates and told him to see that these were distributed to Cesare 'and to the ladies'.[22] But hard currency, a commodity always in short supply at Mantua, was necessary, Brognolo bluntly told Isabella d'Este, wife of Francesco, a few days later. Money was offered but, for reasons of his own, Alexander told the envoy not to send it at present but to defer it for a week. Jewels, however, were acceptable – for Lucrezia, as the envoy sent to present them informed Francesco Gonzaga, but Giovanni Sforza advised him that he had better keep the jewels intended for Giulia 'since the Pope would take it badly'.[23]

Giovanni Sforza was clinging to his marriage and to Lucrezia, his all-important link with the Pope in what was, from his point of view, an increasingly dangerous political situation. King Ferrante of Naples had died in January and on 22 March 1494 Alexander announced that the investiture of the Crown of Naples should go, not to Charles VIII of France, as the French King had demanded, but to the late King Ferrante's son, Alfonso, Duke of Calabria, who would be crowned by Cardinal Juan Borgia. The French invasion of Italy with the conquest of Naples as its object was now a virtual certainty. Sforza's position that spring of 1494 was an uncomfortable one: a plaintive letter to his patron Ludovico retailed an awkward conversation with the Pope:

Yesterday His Holiness said to me in the presence of Monsignor [Ascanio] 'Well, Giovanni Sforza! What have you to say to me?' I answered, 'Holy Father, every one in Rome believes that Your Holiness has entered into an agreement with the King of Naples, who is an enemy of the State of Milan. If this is so, I am in an awkward position, as I am in the pay of Your Holiness and also in that of the State I have named [Milan]. If things continue as they are, I do not know how I can serve one party without falling out with the other . . . I ask that Your Holiness may be pleased to define my position so that I may not act contrary to the obligations into which I have entered by virtue of my agreement with Your Holiness and the illustrious State of Milan . . .

Alexander replied coldly that he should choose in whose pay he should remain according to his contract.[24] Both the Pope and the Duke of Milan wanted to dominate the unfortunate lord of Pesaro 'and make use of his state', as Ascanio had written to his brother in cipher earlier that month,[25] but the Pope was determined that Milan should pay the cost of his *condotta*. Ascanio advised his brother that in the Sforza interest it would be better if Giovanni were in Pesaro, out of the Pope's clutches.

Giovanni, wishing to keep in with both sides, put a brave face on the situation, for in a letter of 18 April 1494, addressed to Juan Gandia, with whom he appeared to be on the most friendly terms, he thanked him for a letter in which Gandia had expressed his joy at the kindness with which the Pope had received Sforza on his return and informed him that he would be leaving shortly for Pesaro to put his affairs in order, to reform his troops and pay them, and that Lucrezia would be accompanying him.[26] As a postscript and additional sweetener he offered to obtain the Sicilian horses Juan wanted from the King of Naples. But Alexander's switch in allegiances was underscored the following month by a Borgia marriage in Naples and lavish grants of money and titles to Alexander's children. On the day of his coronation, 8 May, the new King Alfonso granted Juan Borgia the principate of Tricario, the counties of Carinola, Claramonte and Luria and other lands, each worth 12,000 ducats a year. Jofre was made prince of Squillace, count of Cariaci and protonotary of the Realm with an income of 12,000 golden ducats. Three days later the marriage was celebrated of Jofre to Alfonso's illegitimate daughter, the princess Sancia, who was at least three years older than him. 'He consummated his marriage to the illustrious Dona Sancha, his wife, and performed very well, notwithstanding he is not more than thirteen years old,' Alexander wrote to Gandia.[27]

Although Juan was now known to have consummated his marriage and his wife was pregnant, his extravagance continued to disgust Alexander who had showered him with money and obtained new titles and rich revenues for him.[28] Alexander's unholy love of money and property is revealed in this letter: '. . . your procurators have taken peaceful and expeditious possession in your name of the principate of Tricario, the County of Carinola, Claramonte and Luria and of all your other lands, which, according to their descriptions are lands of greater income even than the King offered, easily more than 12,000 ducats, fine, large and full', he told Gandia gleefully before he burst out into the rage of a self-made man well aware of the value of money, over his son's wasteful dissipation of his funds.

Gandia was by now homesick for his family and longing to return to Rome, as a letter to Lucrezia in the Valencia archives (written but apparently never sent) shows:

I feel a great desire to have news of you for it has been a great while since I received a letter from you and you can imagine, my lady sister, what a great joy your letters are to me for the love I bear you. So do me the favour of writing for my consolation, because already the Duchess my wife complains a great deal of you, that you have never written despite all the letters sent to you from here. She commands us to ask you to write, she is pregnant and in the seventh month. It seems two years since I left. I have written to His Beatitude to order my departure and from day to day I hope for this order . . . I commend myself to the lord of Pesaro, my dear brother, and similarly to Madama Adriana and Madama Julia . . .[29]

Probably around the same time (September 1494) he sent a similar letter to Cesare, imploring him to intercede with the Pope to send galleys to take him to Italy: 'Each day seems like a year to me in the delay of those ships which His Holiness has written in recent days he will send soon . . .'

Despite the political situation, Giovanni Sforza was still in favour with the Borgias: in May, Alexander gave permission for Lucrezia, Adriana and Giulia to visit Pesaro for the first time. A collection of his private papers which remained hidden in the archives of the Castel Sant' Angelo for over a hundred years reveals the Pope's extraordinary dependence on 'his women', his love for Lucrezia and obsession with his beautiful young mistress. The party arrived in Pesaro on 8 June in heavy rain to a tumultuous welcome, as Lucrezia reported to her father, finding themselves provided with a 'beautiful and comfortable house with all the furnishings and gaieties which could be required'.[30] Adriana wrote the same day, praising Pesaro and the care with which its tactful lord attended to her every desire. Both women were, however, alarmed by the report brought by Messer Francesco (Francesc, in his native language) Gacet, a Catalan confidant of the dangerous position in which Alexander found himself in Rome, not merely from the plague but from the pro-French enemies (the Colonna, in particular) who were encircling him. 'Messer Francesco will have informed you,' Lucrezia wrote, 'how we have all understood that at the present time [things] are going very badly [at] Rome, and that we are upset and sorrowful that Your Sanctity should be there. I implore Your Beatitude as much as I can to leave and if you do not wish to, take great care and diligence to guard yourself. And Your Beatitude must not take this as presumption but due to the great and cordial love I bear you and be certain that I will never be content until I hear frequent news of Your Beatitude.' Adriana backed her up with expressions of concern that Alexander remained in Rome in the face of such danger, assuring him that he had nothing to worry about in Pesaro because 'these ladies' (Lucrezia and Giulia) were following his orders and were continually together. Orsino, who must have accompanied his errant wife to Pesaro, also recommended himself, she said, to His Lordship. One Giulia d'Aragona, a member of the numerous royal house of Naples, who accompanied the party, enlarged on the welcome and festivities at Pesaro where she, Giovanni, Lucrezia and Giulia Farnese, in robes of 'pontifical splendour', had danced among the crowds who were astounded by their magnificence. But she assured him that rumours of their total enjoyment were wrong, that both she and Lucrezia were counting the days until they could be with him again. She mentioned her brother, Cardinal Luigi d'Aragona, who was so pleased with the negotiations between the Pope and the new King of Naples that he felt 'as if the Pope had once again made him Cardinal'.[31] No woman, it seems, could ever write to Alexander without attempting to wheedle some favour out of him: four days later, she appealed to him to grant the benefice of the recently murdered Bishop of Rimini to her brother. In a postscript she hinted at some watching brief entrusted to her by the Pope, no doubt concerning the movements of Giulia Farnese, whom the besotted Pope was anxious should return to him as soon as possible. He addressed a long letter to Adriana asking her when the party intended to return and whether Giovanni Sforza would accompany them or remain in Pesaro. He was expecting them at the end of June or beginning of July and would himself return to Rome to meet them. He would expect Giovanni Sforza to remain in Pesaro to raise troops and defend his state, but did not think it advisable that the women should stay there in view of the number of troops wandering the country ahead of the French invasion.

In fact, the high-spirited Lucrezia was enjoying herself too much at Pesaro to write regularly to her embattled father. She excused herself on the grounds that she had been waiting for the letters she and Julia had just received, and because on Sunday the celebrated beauty Caterina Gonzaga had arrived and was still there. Caterina's charms were already known to the Borgias: earlier that year one Jacopo Dragoni had written a humorous Latin poem to Cesare, the 'Divine Caesar, Cardinal Valentia', advising him to 'lay siege to the town of San Lorenzo', where Caterina lived with her husband (i.e. to seduce Caterina), and referring to her husband Ottaviano in contemptuous terms.[32] It is not known whether Cesare took this advice. Lucrezia's account of Caterina was dismissive:

Firstly, she is taller than Madonna Giulia, she has beautiful skin and hands and her figure is also beautiful but her mouth is ugly and her teeth very ugly indeed, her eyes large and pale [?grey], her nose is more ugly than beautiful, a long face and the colour of her hair is ugly and she has a distinctly mannish appearance. I wanted to see her dance and it was not a very satisfactory performance. In fact in all things she does not measure up to her reputation and in my opinion [compare] with the Lady whom I hold as my mother [Adriana] and Madonna Julia whom I hold as my sister . . .[33]

Lucrezia and Caterina did in fact become close friends, a connection which Caterina was eager to exploit in a letter written around this time to the Pope – ostensibly by Lucrezia but actually in Caterina's hand and signed by both women early in July 1494 – in which they earnestly recommended Caterina's husband, Count Ottaviano da Montevegio, to Alexander's protection against his enemies.[34] Caterina followed up this letter with another written on her return home to San Lorenzo praising Lucrezia to the skies for her spirit, intelligence and 'attitudes of a true Lady' and for her friendship. Her own sanity had been restored by the return of her husband from Rome when she had been led to believe he was dead. Now she asked Alexander for support against her brother-in-law, Roberto da Montevegio, and enemies who had taken her rents and were threatening to kill her.

Giulia Farnese had contributed her own description of Caterina's charms in a letter to her ageing lover which produced a doting response:

Julia, darling daughter, a letter we received from you, the longer it was the more it was pleasing to us, so that it took more time to read, although to extend yourself in the description of the beauties of that person who could not be worthy to fit your shoes, we know how she behaves in all other things and does not do so with great modesty. And we know this to be a fact which you well know because everyone who writes to you says that next to you she appeared as a mere lantern near a sun, making out that she is quite beautiful, we thus understand your perfection, of which truly we have never been in doubt. And we wish that like us you recognize this clearly . . .

and that no other woman is loved. And when you make this deliberation, we will acknowledge you as no less wise than you are perfect . . .[35]

As he knew that the three women (Adriana, Lucrezia and Giulia) read each other's letters from him, he said, there was no need for further news.

Alexander was obsessed with his sexual passion for Giulia but he adored his daughter and was thrown into transports of panic at rumours going round Rome at the end of June that Lucrezia was dead, or her life despaired of. 'Dona Lucretia, most beloved daughter,' he wrote. 'Truly you have given us four or five days of grief and grave worry over the bitter news that has spread throughout Rome that you were dead or truly fallen into such infirmity that there could be no hope for your life. You can imagine how such a rumour affected my spirits for the warm and immense love that I have for you. And until I saw the letter which you wrote in your hand, although it was so badly written that it showed you were unwell, I have enjoyed no peace of mind. Let us thank God and Our Glorious Lady that you have escaped all danger. And thus we will never be [truly] content until we have seen you in person.' Giovanni Sforza 'our most dear son', had written to him complaining that the Sforza had given him neither the *condotta* nor money, nothing but words. Alexander, having recently abandoned Milan, the French and the Sforza and come down firmly on the side of the Aragonese of Naples, suggested that Giovanni should follow his example and take service instead with the new King of Naples, Alfonso, whom he, Alexander, was shortly to meet. Cardinal Ascanio, he told her, 'from suspicion and fear' of King Alfonso, had left Rome.[36]

In the circumstances he was furious to learn that in mid July Giulia, accompanied by Adriana, had left Pesaro without his permission, to attend the sickbed of her brother, Angelo, at the family estate of Capodimonte. In fact, on reaching Capodimonte they found Angelo already dead, which, according to Alexander, caused Giulia and her brother the cardinal such distress that they fell sick of the fever. The Pope sent them one of his doctors but vented his rage and frustration on Lucrezia: 'Truly Lord Giovanni and yourself have displayed very little thought for me in this depar- ture of Madonna Adriana and Giulia, since you allowed them to leave without our permission: for you should have remembered – it was your duty – that such a sudden departure without our knowledge would cause us the greatest displeasure . . .'[37] Lucrezia responded immediately to her father's furious missive:

'Concerning the departure of the aforementioned Lady [Giulia], truly Your Holiness should not complain of either my lord or myself: because when the news of the grave illness of Signor Angelo arrived, Madonna Hadriana and Donna Julia decided at all costs to leave immediately. We tried with every efficacy to dissuade them that it was better to await the opinion of Your Beatitude, whose licence would permit them to leave. But so great was their pain and their desire to see him alive that no persuasion was sufficient to keep them here. Indeed with supreme difficulty I persuaded them to wait a little, hoping that so their anxi- ety and determination [to leave] might abate a little. When the messen- ger arrived with the news that he was worse, no persuasion, reasoning or prayers could prevail since they resolved immediately to take horse and go there against every wish of my lord and myself. And the cause of it all was only the tenderness they felt at such a loss. And truly if it had not been forbidden to me I should have kept them company. Your Lordship can be certain that I felt cordial displeasure and extreme bitter- ness: both for the loss of such a lord whom I held as a good brother, and also because I was displeased precisely because it happened with- out the knowledge and will of Your Beatitude, and because I missed their amiable and sweet company. All the same, I have no power over the deliberations of others. They themselves can be witnesses that I did not fail in any way to try to keep them here. I beseech you not to take from this a bad impression of my lord or myself, nor to condemn us for something which was not my fault.[38]

Turning to politics, she commented with a sagacity unusual in a woman of her age, congratulating Alexander on the results to be hoped for from his meeting with King Alfonso at Vicovaro near Tivoli on 14 July and the prospects of an agreement with the Colonna.

Despite the optimistic note in Lucrezia's letter, Alexander's position in Rome was becoming more dangerous by the minute. His principal enemy and rival at the papal court, Giuliano della Rovere, had fled to France demanding the convocation of a General Council to depose Alexander on the grounds of simony. 'If Cardinal Giuliano can be got to ally himself with France,' the Milanese envoy Stefano Taberna had written on 2 May, 'a tremendous weapon will have been forged against the Pope.' On 17 March, Charles VIII had announced his intention of invading Italy, and the news that Giuliano had allied himself with him and his call for a General Council seriously alarmed Alexander. At the end of June, Ascanio Sforza had fled Rome to join the Colonna and succeeded in suborning them from their allegiance to Naples. Ascanio too now demanded a General Council to depose the Pope. Alexander, therefore, was threatened on all sides. At his meeting with King Alfonso of Naples at Vicovaro on 14 July, it was agreed that Virginio Orsini, head of the clan, should remain in the Roman Campagna to keep the Colonna in check, while the mass of the Neapolitan troops under Alfonso's eldest son, Ferrantino, supported by their allies, the Florentines, should make their way north. None of this deterred the King of France: assured of the neutrality of Venice and Milan, he crossed the border between France and Savoy, marching southward.

Yet in the midst of all his troubles, Alexander's yearning to see his mistress was at the forefront of his mind. Giulia Farnese was also in an awkward position. Her husband, Orsino Orsini, far from being complacent at her public and scandalous association with the Pope, had remained at Città di Castello on the pretext of illness so that he would not have to join the Neapolitan forces, and was determined that Giulia should return to him at Bassanello. Alexander, however, prevailed on Virginio Orsini to order Orsino to join the Neapolitan camp of the Duke of Calabria. Virginio, in Rome to confer with the Pope about the betrayal of Ostia to his hereditary enemies, the Colonna and their Savelli allies, took Alexander's side against his own unfortunate kinsman. On 21 September 1494 he wrote to Orsino, clearly (since a draft in the Pope's hand exists in the Vatican Secret Archives) at Alexander's dictation. The letter has hitherto been attributed to Alexander but the terms in which it is written and the fact that it was to be sent from Monterotondo, the Orsini fortress outside Rome, makes it clear that the text was agreed between them during their conference in Rome, and that Orsini dispatched it from Monterotondo, Alexander keeping a draft for his archives.

In this letter Virginio informed Orsino that he had received news that the Duke of Calabria was angry because he had been told that Orsino was now recovered. 'I therefore urge you for your honour and to purge your contumaciousness that you go immediately to the Duke of Calabria who I am sure will receive you kindly,' he wrote, adding that he had hoped to find Adriana and Giulia 'your mother and your wife' in Rome so that he could encourage them not to abandon the Pope in this undertaking for the good of the King of Naples and his state and the benefit of the house of Orsini. He understood that the King had written to the same effect to Adriana: 'And therefore it is necessary and thus we pray and command you that you should write immediately to Madama [Adriana] asking her and expressly ordering your wife that they should immediately come to Rome together and with all their skill and art to urge the Pope to remain firm in this enterprise . . .' In view of the urgency of the matter he was sending his courier with the letter to await a reply confirming the orders Orsino would have given.[39]

The letter was almost certainly prompted by a report from Alexander's confidant Francesco Gacet, which had roused the Pope to fury. He informed Alexander that Adriana had arrived at the Farnese estate of Capodimonte and had told Cardinal Farnese of Alexander's recent resolution that Giulia should go to Rome and the archdeacon be sent to Orsino to persuade him to do the Pope's will. Farnese (the future Pope Paul III), a proud and intelligent man who was well aware that he was known as 'the petticoat cardinal' because of his sister's part in his promotion, stood firm against causing further scandal. He cared nothing for offending Orsino in order to do His Beatitude a service but he could not do this for his own honour and the infamy it would bring on his house. Gacet had suggested that Virginio Orsini should be prevailed upon to intervene and persuade Orsino to go to join the Neapolitan camp and after his departure the women could go to Rome. The cardinal, he stressed, would not for his honour resist Orsino's demands that his wife should go to Bassanello. Fra Theseo, a monk in Giulia's service, wrote from Bassanello warning her that he had never seen Orsino so enraged and that if she was wise she would under no circumstances go to Rome.[40]

Alexander was a man of unusual force of character, always determined to get his own way in all circumstances. He minuted three furious letters to Giulia, Adriana and Cardinal Farnese:

Ungrateful and perfidious Julia, we have received a letter of yours via Navarrico by which you declare that your intention is not to come here without the permission [against the will] of Ursino. And although at this moment we understand your wicked state of mind and that of those who counsel you, however, considering your feigned, dissimulating words can we totally persuade ourselves that you should use such ingratitude and perfidy towards us, having so many times sworn and pledged your faith to be at our command and not to concile yourself with Ursino. That now you want to do the contrary and go to Basanello [sic] with express peril to your life, I would not believe that you would do for any other reason if not to plunge again into that water of Bassanello . . . [a euphemism for resuming marital relations with Orsino which on a previous occasion resulted in the birth of their daughter, Laura].

He hoped that she and the '*ingratissima*' Adriana would come to their senses and repent. Nonetheless, under pain of excommunication and sentence to eternal punishment he ordered her not to leave Capodimonte and still less to go to Bassanello.[41]

He wrote to Adriana along much the same lines, accusing her of revealing her wicked mind and malignity in declaring in her letter brought by Navarrico that she did not wish Giulia to go to Rome against the will of Orsino, and forbidding her to leave Capodimonte without his express permission.[42] To Alessandro Farnese he wrote less venomously, reminding him of how much he, the Pope, had done for him and, with a note of trust betrayed, that he could have so soon preferred Orsino to him. Now, so that Farnese could excuse himself with Orsino and so that Giulia should not have to go to Bassanello, he, Alexander, would send him another papal brief in the hand of the Bishop of Nepi, exhorting and commanding him 'to conform freely to our will'.[43]

But that was far from being the end of the matter: Alexander never gave up, as he informed Gacet. He had seen Fra Theseo's letter to Giulia advising her to go to Bassanello and not to Rome ('I know that friar,' he added menacingly). He had responded by sending a brief to Orsino commanding him under threat of the gravest penalties either to go to the camp of the Duke of Calabria or to come to him in Rome within three days. Intimidated by all this pressure, Orsino capitulated, his brief stand for his honour evaporated: on 28 November he extracted his price, asking the Pope for money to pay his troops. On the 29th, Giulia, with her sister Girolama and Adriana, left Capodimonte for Rome. But they had left it too late and once again Alexander was – temporarily – thwarted in his desires. The party was captured near Viterbo by French troops under the gallant captain Yves d'Alègre and a demand for a ransom of 3,000 ducats was sent to the Pope. Alexander was frantic: he appealed to his former allies, Ascanio Sforza and Cardinal Sanseverino, to intercede for him with the King of France. His request was granted, and on 1 December the ladies arrived at the Vatican to be greeted by Juan Marrades, the Pope's Catalan chamberlain. It was rumoured that Giulia spent the night there.

The ageing Pope's passion and vanity were ridiculed by his many enemies, among them Ludovico Sforza. Giacomo Trotti,

Ferrarese envoy at the court of Milan, reported Sforza's reaction to Duke Ercole:

He gravely reproved Monsignor Ascanio and Cardinal Sanseverino for surrendering Madonna Giulia, Madonna Adriana, and Hieronyma [Girolama Farnese] to his Holiness: for, since these ladies were the 'heart and eyes' of the Pope, they would have been the best whip for compelling him to do everything which was wanted of him, for he could not live without them. The French, who captured them, received only three thousand ducats as ransom, although the Pope would gladly have paid fifty thousand or more simply to have them back again. The . . . Duke [Sforza] received news from Rome . . . that when the ladies entered, His Holiness went to meet them arrayed in a black doublet bordered with gold brocade, with a beautiful belt in the Spanish fashion, and with a sword and dagger. He wore Spanish boots and a velvet biretta, all very gallant. The Duke asked me, laughing, what I thought of it, and I told him that, were I the Duke of Milan, like him, I would endeavour, with the aid of the King of France and in every other way – and on the pretext of establishing peace – to entrap His Holiness, and with fair words, such as he himself was in the habit of using, to take him and the cardinals prisoners, which would be very easy. He who has the servant, as we say at home, has also the wagon and the oxen . . .[44]

Lucrezia, meanwhile, remained safely in Pesaro where life was pleasant enough in the princely palace in the main square and at the beautiful Villa Imperiale on the hill of San Bartolo above the city. Pesarese society, although less cosmopolitan than that of Rome, was far from being dull and provincial. It was, above all, secure: the French army, pouring southward without meeting any resistance, was intent on reaching Rome and taking Naples. In Rome, her father was isolated, supported only by Cesare. Juan was still in Spain, Jofre and Sancia in Naples. Alexander had been betrayed by the Orsini who handed their castle of Bracciano over to the French King, while the Neapolitan army had had to retreat south to defend the Kingdom. On 31 December, as Charles VIII entered Rome through the Porta del Popolo at the head of his troops, Alexander retreated through the covered way from the Vatican to the Castel Sant'Angelo, taking with him his private papers (including the letters quoted above) which were to reveal so much of his family relationships. The Borgias were at bay.

3. The Borgias Renascent

'And when His Excellency asked him [Giovanni Sforza] if this [his
alleged impotence and inability to consummate his marriage to
Lucrezia] were true, he answered no. Rather, he had known her an
infinite number of times. But the Pope had taken her away from
him only in order to have her to himself . . .'

– Antonio Costabili, Ferrarese envoy in Rome to Duke Ercole I of
Ferrara on the subject of Lucrezia's divorce from Giovanni Sforza

By the late spring of 1495 the situation had changed dramatically for the Borgias. With no weapons other than his diplomatic
skills and the power of his personality, Alexander had succeeded
in outwitting the French King with a formidable force at his
back. Charles had received fair words from the Pope and nothing more; having taken the road for Naples with Cesare in his
train as hostage for his father's good behaviour, he was incan-
descent with fury when Cesare, in a pre-arranged plan, escaped
at Velletri disguised as a groom. When it was discovered that he
had disappeared overnight and that all the trunks of his baggage
train were loaded with stones, Charles's mood darkened further.
Furious, he declared, 'All Italians are dirty dogs, and the Holy
Father is the worst of them.' Within a few months of Charles's
departure from Rome, he was to discover what a formidable and
cunning enemy he faced in Alexander who succeeded in uniting a daunting array of powers against him. On 31 March 1495
a Holy League against the French was announced between Milan,
Venice, Spain, the papacy and the Emperor.

Meanwhile, in Naples Charles's position was becoming unten-
able; where he had at first been welcome he was now hated.

Although hideous in appearance – 'more like a monster than a man', as one commentator described him, he was a relentless womanizer. '[He] was one of the most lascivious men in France, and was very fond of copulation, and of changing his dishes, so that once he had had a woman, he cared no more about her, taking his pleasure with new ones . . .' wrote an observer. His soldiery were no better: 'The French were clownish, dirty, and dissolute people . . . They were always to be found in sin and venereal acts.' When the main body of the French army finally left the Kingdom in May, making for home, they took with them not just plunder but syphilis, a terrifying new disease, which spread like wildfire through Europe.

As they approached Rome on their way north, Alexander and Cesare, with nineteen cardinals and a large force of papal, Milanese and Venetian troops, beat a strategic retreat, first to Orvieto and then to Perugia. Realizing there was nothing further to be gained by remaining in Italy, where he could be cut off and trapped by the League, Charles made off northwards. At Fornovo on the River Taro he met the forces of the League under the command of Francesco Gonzaga. The Italians claimed a famous victory and Gonzaga commissioned his favourite painter, Andrea Mantegna, to execute the *Madonna della Vittoria* (ironically, now in the Louvre) to commemorate it, but the inescapable fact was that Charles got away, leaving behind on the field of battle his Neapolitan plunder, including a book containing the portraits of the ladies whose favours he had enjoyed in 'Naples'. At the end of June, the Borgias returned to Rome.

The triumph of the Borgia Pope and his family was celebrated in the heart of the Vatican where Bernardino Pinturicchio had completed the decoration of the Borgia Apartments (which still exist) as a flamboyant demonstration of their Spanish origins and family pride. Here, covering walls and ceiling in almost megalomaniac repetition, are the two Borgia devices, the double crown of Aragon, symbol of the royal house from which, quite fictitiously, they claimed descent, and to which they have added sun rays or flames pointing downwards, and the grazing ox of their original emblem transformed into a rampant, virile, pagan bull.

These rooms have an alien, defiantly Spanish feeling: the tiled floors blaze with the Aragonese double crown, the frames surrounding Pinturicchio's frescoes are coloured, geometric stucco work, recalling the Moorish craftsmanship of Granada and Seville. One fresco depicts the unmistakable, powerful figure of Alexander, clothed in a cope studded with jewels and pearls, his profile expressing not spirituality but a sensual vitality. Frescoes in the adjoining Sala dei Santi incorporated supposed portraits of his children − Cesare, Lucrezia and Juan Gandia.[1]

Lucrezia was still in Pesaro in the spring of 1495 when Giovanni Sforza, in the wake of an exchange of visits between Pesaro and Urbino, wrote to the Gonzaga boasting that 'without fail' he would send his wife to Rome after Easter 'from where she will not leave until she has obtained all we desire [for Sigismondo to be made cardinal] because no one else can achieve this better, I am sending her and she goes willingly to serve Your Excellency to whom she is devoted . . .'[2] But for all his boasting, Sforza did not trust the Borgias, as whining letters he wrote from Pesaro to Ludovico il Moro in March and April demonstrated.[3] On 18 March he wrote to Ludovico telling him that at dawn that morning a messenger from the Pope had arrived, forbidding him to leave home (presumably to go to Rome) and then ordering him to join the service of the Pope, Milan and Venice. Sforza said he planned instead to go to Milan, throw himself into his arms and place himself and his state under Ludovico's protection. One wonders what he was afraid of.

For all Giovanni Sforza's boasting, Lucrezia had not so far succeeded in obtaining the cardinal's hat for Sigismondo Gonzaga, as his brother Francesco complained bitterly to Ludovico Sforza.[4] In his role as Captain General of Venice commanding the forces of the League, Francesco visited both Lucrezia and Cesare when he passed through Rome en route for Naples in March 1496 where the remaining French were besieged in Atella. Alexander presented him with the Golden Rose for his services to the League and the Church but he had preferred to strengthen his

own position by the appointment as cardinals of intimates whose
loyalty was assured: his cousin, Juan de Borja-Llançol, the
Valencians, Juan Llopis and Bartolomeu Marti, and the Catalan
Juan de Castre-Pinos. As the victor of Fornovo and the foremost
soldier in Italy, Francesco Gonzaga, with his dark, sensual looks,
no doubt made an impression on Lucrezia and he was destined
to play a major role in her life. What Gonzaga, married to the
formidable Isabella d'Este and with a mistress by whom he had
three children, thought of the fifteen-year-old Countess of Pesaro
is not recorded. His opinion of her father no doubt coincided
with that of his scatological correspondent, Floriano Dolfo, who
in a long letter wrote of 'this our Pope who brought to this rose
[the Golden Rose] such a stink of trickery, simony, quarrels and
cankers that not even the perfume of so noble a flower can overcome it . . .'[5]

Giovanni Sforza was not in Rome (although he had apparently been in January); rather, he was in Pesaro, putting his troops
in order prior to joining Gonzaga in the Kingdom and going
through the usual protracted negotiations with the Pope and the
Duke of Milan over money for his *condotta*.[6] He arrived in Rome
on 16 April and remained there for ten days extracting money
from the Pope and resisting all attempts to make him leave earlier.[7]
Something was wrong in his relationship with Lucrezia. The
Mantuan envoy Gian Carlo Scalona made dark hints as to the
reason for Sforza's departure on 28 April – 'perhaps he has something at home, something which others would not suspect' –
adding that he had left in a most desperate state of mind and
would not return, 'leaving his wife under the apostolic mantle',
a phrase which has been interpreted as a suggestion of incest. No
hint of this, however, appears in the correspondence of Ascanio
Sforza and the Milanese envoy Stefano Taberna, who, being close
to Giovanni, would have been in a position to know.

With Giovanni Sforza out of the way, the summer of 1496 was
notable for a series of Borgia family reunions, celebrated with
their customary pomp. In May, Jofre and Sancia returned to Rome,
their entry into the city organized by Alexander and Cesare with

all the showmanship of which they were past masters. Entering
by the Lateran Gate, the couple were greeted by the households
of all the cardinals, the commander of the Vatican Guard at the
head of two hundred soldiers, the ambassadors of Spain, Milan,
Naples, Venice and the Empire, with the senators, nobles and leading citizens of Rome. Lucrezia, anxious not to be outshone by
her sister-in-law, of whose attractions she had already heard much,
was gorgeously dressed to meet her. Jofre and Sancia rode to the
Vatican where Alexander peeped down at their approach through
a half-closed shutter before going down with Cesare to greet
them. The atmosphere of sexuality surrounding Sancia, and indeed
the Borgia court, emerges clearly in this description by Scalona:

In truth she did not appear as beautiful as she had been made out to
be. Indeed the lady of Pesaro [Lucrezia] surpassed her. However that
may be, by her gestures and aspect the sheep will put herself easily at
the disposal of the wolf. She has also some ladies of hers who are in
no way inferior to their mistress, thus they say publicly it will be a fine
flock . . . She is more than twenty-two years old, naturally dark, with
glancing eyes, an aquiline nose and very well made up, and will in my
opinion not give the lie to my predictions . . .[8]

He dismissed Jofre as 'dark in complexion and otherwise lasciv-
ious-looking with long hair with a reddish tinge . . . and he is
fourteen or fifteen years of age'.

Sancia's behaviour and reputation were such that, as early as
June 1494, the Catalan master of the Squillace household had felt
it necessary to issue a sworn declaration with the testimony of a
dozen witnesses denying improprieties: 'I, Anthoni Gurrea, give
testimony that in the Household of the Prince of Squillace the
government of the Ladies is so honest and of such good order
as is possible to have. And in the chamber of the Princess no
man whatever is entertained . . .'[9] Jofre was too young and too
insignificant to satisfy Sancia; within months she found a man
more to her taste in Cesare. She and Lucrezia became close
friends: at a service in St Peter's later that month the two girls

shocked the papal master of ceremonies when, during a long and tedious sermon, they climbed to the choir reserved for the canons and sat there laughing and chatting with their ladies.

The Borgia family circle was complete with the arrival from Spain of Juan Gandia on 10 August. The twenty-year-old duke was dressed to the nines in a scarlet cap hung with pearls, a doublet of brown velvet blazing with jewels, black stockings embroidered with the golden crown and rays of Gandia and a long Turkish mantle of gold brocade. His bay horse was adorned with gold fringes and silver bells which tinkled as he rode, and he was accompanied by six squires, including a Moor dressed in gold brocade and crimson velvet, twelve splendid horses ridden by pages and a crowd of dwarfs and jesters. The role for which he was destined by his doting father was to crush the Orsini whose treachery in the last days of 1494 had not been forgotten and whose dominance of the Roman Campagna represented a serious threat to the independence of the papacy. Now, with the head of the clan, Virginio, and his eldest legitimate son, Giangiordano, in prison in Naples after the final surrender of the remaining French, Alexander saw his chance. It was the right strategy at the right moment, but in choosing Juan, a youth with no military experience, to lead the campaign, nominally headed by the cultured but feeble Guidobaldo, Duke of Montefeltro, as Captain General of the League, Alexander was making a serious mistake.

On 26 October, to the sound of trumpets, Gandia was invested in St Peter's with the titles of Captain General of the Church and Gonfalonier (Standard Bearer). Alexander was beside himself with joy and pride while Scalona wrote scornfully: 'The Pope is so swollen up and inflated with this election of his son, that he does not know what to do with himself, and this morning desired to set a feather in his cap with his own hands and sew on a jewel of great value . . .'[10] Unsurprisingly the campaign was a failure: at the great fortress of Bracciano, a woman, Bartolommea d'Alviano, wife of the most able of the Orsini captains, held out. The Orsini rampaged up to the walls of Rome, mocking Gandia by sending into the papal camp a large donkey with a placard 'I am the ambassador of the Duke of Gandia' round its neck and a rude letter addressed to him under its tail. At Soriano in January the papal army was defeated and Guidobaldo captured. The Orsini were now masters of the Roman Campagna and Alexander was left with little alternative but to make peace in February 1497. The Orsini retained all their castles except for Cerveteri and Anguillara which the Pope held as security against the payment of 50,000 ducats. He refused to ransom Guidobaldo and gave the major part of the Orsini indemnity to the undeserving Gandia[11] in compensation for having failed to secure the Orsini lands. In March, Gandia, with the help of the great Spanish general Gonsalvo de Cordoba, took Ostia from the only French garrison remaining on Italian soil.

The exercise of Spanish military might on Alexander's side boded ill for the Sforza; that very week, at the end of March, Giovanni Sforza, who had been at the Palazzo Santa Maria in Portico with Lucrezia since mid January, fled precipitately from Rome to Pesaro, without informing either Ascanio or Ludovico Sforza. It had been clear since the beginning of the year that things had been going wrong in the Sforza marriage, as a letter of 7 January written from Pesaro by Giovanni to Ludovico revealed. The Pope, he said, had been putting pressure on him to return to Rome but he had excused himself on the grounds of indisposition. Recently, however, a brief had arrived from Alexander giving him eight days in which to comply.[12] A report from Scalona to Mantua that Sforza was in high favour with the Pope and that Lucrezia was now content and much in love with him seems to have been wide of the mark.[13] The hastiness and secrecy of his departure – he feigned to be going to a pardon ceremony outside the gates of Rome where in reality he had horses waiting for him – suggests that Giovanni had heard something to make him afraid of the Borgias. It may be that hints had been dropped, probably by Cesare, that as a husband for Lucrezia he was surplus to requirements. Scalona reported that there were rumours the Borgias would have him poisoned but that he himself believed these to be without foundation. Il Moro was seriously concerned at the possibility of a rupture with the Pope: much as he despised and distrusted Alexander, he needed his political support. The unwelcome prospect of a divorce seems to have been in the back of his mind when he drafted a request to be taken to Giovanni: 'We wish that His Lordship will make clear to us the reasons he left so precipitately from Rome. And whether this has arisen because he has not yet consummated his marriage with his wife. Make him understand so that we may find some convenient remedy. And concerning this tell him that we pray he will declare his mind as he should . . .'[14] The wretched Sforza replied that the Pope was furious with him and demanded his return, threatening that if he did not do so of his own accord he would be forced to. He added that the Pope was using his flight as an excuse to deprive him of his wife absolutely without any reason in spite of his just demand (for Lucrezia to go to Pesaro).

By 4 May, Ludovico had learned – presumably from his ambassador Taberna – the cause of Sforza's flight, namely Borgia threats. He was all the more surprised, therefore, to receive a request from the Pope to intervene to obtain Giovanni's return to Rome. Puzzled, he pressed his nephew to tell him the exact reasons both for his abrupt departure from Rome and his refusal to return there; he must do so either by letter or orally if it seemed to him something which should not be committed to paper. He promised Giovanni that he would not force him to return to Rome.[15] Giovanni, clearly still in a state of panic and confusion, assured Ludovico of his loyal gratitude but said that he was sending a trusted messenger to Rome to ask Alexander to permit Lucrezia to come to Pesaro, as was only reasonable, and that if the Pope later wanted them both to return to Rome he would be content to do so. The messenger was instructed to go then to Ludovico with the Pope's answer and to explain to him why Giovanni was unwilling to return to Rome so that Ludovico would understand that he had good reason for his actions.[16] By 1 June, Ludovico had received letters from Ascanio in Rome informing him of the Pope's fixed desire for a dissolution of the marriage. Giovanni rode to Urbino to consult Guidobaldo, who had been released after paying his own ransom, and returned to Pesaro 'ill-content'. The arrival five days later of Fra Mariano, Alexander's envoy, in Pesaro provoked Giovanni into a panic flight to consult with Ludovico in Milan. The Mantuan representative in Urbino, Silvestro Calandra, reported to Francesco Gonzaga on 6 June that he left 'incognito, desperate and in a hurry'. Guidobaldo was sending a trusted servant to inform the Marquis 'of the bad behaviour of the Pope to the damage and shame of Signor Giovanni . . .'[17] In another move of sinister purport to the Sforza interest, there were reports that the Pope had come to an agreement with Ascanio's enemy and rival, Giuliano della Rovere, with whom he had been negotiating for some time, that della Rovere should come back to Rome from France with all his offences pardoned and his benefices restored.

Meanwhile Lucrezia, the victim at the eye of the storm, left the Vatican on 4 June accompanied by her household and took refuge with the nuns of the Dominican convent of San Sisto, a pattern of behaviour she repeated throughout her troubled life at times of particular pressure. No one seems to have penetrated the depths of her feelings at this time but they appear to have been rebellious. One observer[18] said that she had left her father 'as an unwelcome guest', in other words, she had quarrelled with the Pope, presumably over the divorce proceedings, another that she had parted from her husband some months ago 'on unamicable terms'. From the distance of Urbino, Calandra reported that her father had sent the *bargello* (sheriff or constable of police) to fetch her out of the convent, but she did not leave.[19] Most probably she had gone there of her own accord, to escape from the tensions created by her father and brothers, both of whom had declared she should never return to Sforza. Reports of the divorce, and the reasons which were to be put forward for it, were already public, as the always well-informed Venetian diarist Marin Sanudo wrote. The Pope had sent Lucrezia to a convent – 'it was said for two reasons: the first that, before he married her to the said lord of Pesaro, he had promised her to another lord in Spain [Procida];

secondly, it is said that since she was married the said lord has never consummated the marriage because he was impotent. And that he [the Pope] will undertake a process and then, if it was so, will dissolve the marriage . . .'[20] Another report alleged that Juan Gandia would take her with him to Spain because of the divorce, and that the Pope was so set upon the dissolution of the marriage that he had even offered to allow Giovanni Sforza to keep Lucrezia's dowry. Ascanio Sforza wrote to Ludovico on 14 June that the breach between Lucrezia and Giovanni was final, that the Pope, supported by Cesare and Juan, had declared that Lucrezia could not remain in the hands of such a man, that the marriage had never been consummated and could and should be annulled.[21] From Milan the Ferrarese Antonio Costabili wrote to his master, Duke Ercole, reporting that Giovanni Sforza had been there to implore Duke Ludovico to persuade the Pope to allow Lucrezia to return to him; this the Pope had refused to do on the grounds that he had never been able to consummate the marriage despite all the years they had spent together. 'And when His Excellency asked him if this were true, he answered no. Rather, he had known her an infinite number of times. But the Pope had taken her away from him only in order to have her to himself and he expressed himself at length on the subject of His Holiness.' Ludovico unkindly suggested to Giovanni that the Pope should send Lucrezia to the castle of Nepi, then in the hands of his brother Ascanio, where Giovanni could also go and consummate his marriage so that the Pope would restore her to him. Sforza declined the offer and still more the suggestion that he should prove himself 'with Women' in the presence of the papal legate. And given that he (Giovanni) refused both alternatives, il Moro asked him how they could say that he was impotent considering that he had made the sister of the Marquis of Mantua pregnant (Sforza's late wife, Maddalena Gonzaga, had died in childbirth in 1490). To which he replied – 'Your Excellency can see for yourself, they still say that I had her made pregnant by another.' This, Costabili added, made Ludovico think that if the lord of Pesaro were to be given 'two twists of the rope (*due tracti di corda*) he would confess to never having done anything either with the sister of the Marquis of Mantua or with this one [Lucrezia] because if he really was potent he would have wanted to give some proof of himself. This gave His Highness to believe that if Sforza was not constrained to give up the dowry, he would not put up much objection to the divorce.'[22]

Whatever the real truth – and only the Borgia inner circle knew it – Lucrezia was still in San Sisto when a tragedy took place which shook Rome – and the Borgias – to the core. While Lucrezia was apparently out of favour, Alexander had conferred singular favours on her brothers: in a secret consistory (a council of cardinals) on 8 June, Cesare was nominated legate for King Federigo's coronation in Naples, a blatantly nepotistic appointment in view of his youth and lack of seniority. But it was the investiture of Juan, in another secret consistory held the previous day, with the Duchy of Benevento and the cities of Terracina and Pontecorvo, which caused the greatest resentment. The alienation of these important papal cities as hereditary fiefs to Gandia was regarded as an intolerable scandal. Juan, whose arrogance had already earned him powerful enemies, became the primary target of anti-Borgia hostility.

On Wednesday 14 June, exactly one week after his investiture, Juan Gandia disappeared. On the afternoon of that day he had ridden out with Cesare and Cardinal Juan Borgia of Monreale to have supper with Vannozza at her vineyard, or country villa, near Monte San Martino dei Monti. Returning as night was falling, they reached the bridge of Sant'Angelo leading to the Vatican, where Juan told the others that he must leave them as he had to go somewhere alone. Both the cardinals and Gandia's servants, according to Scalona's report, did everything possible so that he should not go unaccompanied; the streets of Rome were not safe at night for a rich young man alone, especially with the enemies Gandia had. But Juan was adamant; the most he would do for his own safety was to send one of his grooms back to his rooms in the Vatican to fetch his light 'night armour', and then tell him to wait for him in the Piazza Judea. He took leave of Cesare and Cardinal Borgia and turned his mule in the direction of the Ghetto. As he did so, a masked man in a black cloak was seen to mount the mule behind him and the two rode off together.

Cesare and Cardinal Borgia, not unnaturally uneasy over these mysterious proceedings, waited some time by the bridge for him to return. When he did not, they rode back to the Vatican 'with considerable anxiety and doubt in their minds'. Juan's groom was attacked on his way to fetch the armour, receiving slight stab wounds but, 'as he was a strong man', says Scalona, he returned to the Piazza Judea to wait for his master. When Gandia did not return, he went back to the Vatican, thinking that Juan was spending the night with some Roman woman, as was frequently his custom. Neither the groom nor Cesare, for the same reason, reported Juan's escapade to the Pope that night.

The following morning Gandia's household informed Alexander that he had not returned. The Pope was still not greatly concerned, being accustomed to Juan's amorous adventures, but his alarm mounted as the day passed with no sign of him and in the evening Alexander sent for Cesare and Cardinal Borgia and begged them to tell him what had happened. They told him what they had learned from Juan's groom, whereupon Alexander, according to Scalona, said 'that if he was dead, he knew the origin and the cause'. Then, 'seized with mortal terror', in the words of the diarist Johannes Burchard, the German papal master of ceremonies, he ordered a search to be made. As Alexander's agents scoured the streets, the city was in uproar: fearful of a vendetta, many Romans closed their shops and barricaded their doors. The Colonna, Savelli, Orsini and Caetani fortified their palaces while parties of excited and angry Spaniards roamed the streets with drawn swords. Finally, on Friday 16 June, feverish inquiries brought to light the report of a timber dealer, Giorgio Schiavi, who was accustomed to keep watch over the wood which he unloaded on the river bank near

the Ospedale of San Girolamo degli Schiavoni. On Wednesday
night, he said:

about the hour of two, while I was guarding my wood, lying in my
boat, two men on foot came out of the alley on the left of the Ospedale
degli Schiavoni, onto the open way by the river. They looked cautiously
about them to see that no one was passing, and not having found
anyone, returned the way they had come into the same alley. Shortly
afterwards two other men came out of that same alley, also looking
furtively round them; not seeing anybody, they made a signal to their
companions. Then there appeared a rider on a white horse, carrying a
body slung across its crupper behind him, the head and arms hanging
to one side, the legs to the other, supported on the right by the two
first men so that it should not fall off. Having reached the point from
which refuse is thrown into the river, the horseman turned his horse
so that its tail faced the river, then the two men who were standing
on either side, taking the body, one by the hands and arms, the other
by the feet and legs, flung it with all their strength into the river. To
the horseman's demand whether the body had sunk, they replied, 'Yes,
sir', then the horseman looked again at the river and saw the dead
man's cloak floating on the water, and asked what it was. They answered,
'Sir, the cloak'. Then he threw some stones at it and made it sink. This
done, all five, including the other two who had come out of the alley
to keep watch, went away by an alley which leads to the Hospital of
San Giacomo.

Asked why he had not reported the incident to the authorities,
Schiavi answered simply: 'In the course of my life, on various
nights, I have seen more than a hundred bodies thrown into the
river right at this spot, and never heard of anyone troubling himself
about them.'

Following this report, all the fishermen and boatmen of Rome
were called in to search the river with promise of a reward. First
the body of an unknown man was discovered; then around midday,
near the church of Santa Maria del Popolo, a fisherman named
Battistino da Taglia brought up in his net the body of a young

man, fully clothed, with his gloves and a purse containing 30 ducats still hanging from his belt. Nine stab wounds were counted on his body, in the neck, head, body and legs. It was Juan Gandia.

Juan's body was taken to the Castel Sant'Angelo where it was washed and dressed in brocade with the insignia of Captain General of the Church. At six o'clock that evening it was borne by the noblemen of Gandia's household in procession from Sant' Angelo to the church of Santa Maria del Popolo to be buried in the family chapel, in a procession led by twelve torch bearers, the palace clerics, the papal chamberlains and squires, 'all marching along weeping and wailing and in considerable disorder', as Burchard commented. 'The body was borne on a magnificent bier so that all could see it, and it seemed that the Duke were not dead but sleeping', he recorded, while another observer remarked that Juan looked 'almost more handsome than when he was alive'. An elegant funeral oration was performed for the dead Duke by the humanist Tommaso Inghirami, known as Fedra.

Alexander's grief for his beloved son was indescribable; even the stolid and normally unsympathetic Burchard was moved:

The Pope, when he heard that the Duke had been killed and flung into the river like dung, was thrown into a paroxysm of grief, and for the pain and bitterness of his heart shut himself in his room and wept most bitterly. The Cardinal Segorbe (Bartolomeu Martì, a cousin of Rodrigo) and some of his servants went to the door, persuading him to open it, which he did only after many hours. The Pope neither ate nor drank anything from the Wednesday evening until the following Saturday, nor from the morning of Thursday to the following Sunday did he know a moment's peace.

By Monday 19 June, Alexander had recovered himself sufficiently to hold a public consistory in which he referred to his son's death in emotional terms: 'The Duke of Gandia is dead. His death has given us the greatest sorrow, and no greater pain than this could we suffer, because we loved him above all things, and esteemed not more the papacy nor anything else. Rather, had we seven papacies we would give them all to have the Duke alive again. God has done this perhaps for some sin of ours, and not because he deserved such a cruel death; nor do we know who killed him and threw him into the Tiber.'

Rumours flew around the city as to the author, or authors, of the crime: the names of Giovanni Sforza, Guidobaldo da Montefeltro and Ascanio Sforza were mentioned. Within a week, however, after Alexander had exonerated those named, all inquiries were suspended. It seemed that the Borgias now had a good idea of who was responsible and intended to bide their time to pursue their vendetta. The most likely candidates were the Orsini, whose vendetta with the Borgias went back to the first year of Alexander's papacy when they had conspired to encircle him by acquiring the castles of Cerveteri and Anguillara; Alexander could not forgive them their desertion to the French at the end of 1494. He had retaliated with his attempt to seize their lands for Gandia in 1496 but the real spark which lit the fuse of Orsini anger was the death of the clan leader, Virginio Orsini, still in prison in Naples for his treachery in 1494, on 13 January 1497, which they held to have been instigated by the Borgias. By the laws of the vendetta, Virginio's death called for revenge, and how better could his family avenge themselves on Alexander than by engineering the death of his favourite son? As a Venetian source reported at the end of the year: 'This Pope plotted to ruin the Orsini because the Orsini for sure caused the death of his son the Duke of Gandia.' The Borgias' pursuit of the vendetta would be carried out with great subtlety and cruelty by Cesare in the years to come.

Grief and anger, however, did not prevent the Borgias from pursuing their political and dynastic aims. At the same consistory in which he had mourned Juan Gandia's death, Alexander had returned to the subject of Lucrezia's divorce from Giovanni Sforza. He and Cesare had already laid their plans for a new marriage for Lucrezia even before the murder. The plan, hatched at the time of the announcement of Cesare as legate for the corona- tion of King Federigo in Naples, was for Cesare to squeeze every advantage he could from the grateful King. This included a Neapolitan marriage for Lucrezia, once her divorce from Giovanni Sforza was obtained. Gandia's murder deferred the plan; Cesare left Rome six weeks after his brother's death, and the coronation of Federigo at Capua took place on 11 August. The King and legate then travelled together to enjoy the tainted pleasures of Naples: when Cesare returned to Rome on 5 September, Isabella d'Este's agent reported: 'Monsignor of Valencia has returned from the Kingdom after crowning King Federigo and he too is sick of the French disease [syphilis].' Even before he returned, Ascanio Sforza reported in a cipher letter to Ludovico that negotiations were going on between the Pope and the Prince of Salerno 'to give Dona Lucretia . . . to the son of the prince with certain conditions which, if true and put into effect, I believe will not result to the benefit either of the King or of Italy . . .'[23]

Lucrezia's second marriage was to be to Alfonso, natural son of Alfonso II of Naples and brother of Sancia, and merely a stepping stone to the realization of Cesare's new ambitions. Gandia's death had changed everything: now Cesare was to be the foundation of the family's earthly ambitions which, in 1497, focused on a marriage between him and Carlotta, legitimate daughter of King Federigo. In September a commission headed by two cardinals pronounced sentence of divorce between Lucrezia and Giovanni on the grounds of the latter's impotence.[24] The Borgias pushed hard to get Giovanni Sforza to agree to the divorce, and in order to accommodate the Pope the senior Sforza were prepared to abandon him. Throughout the autumn they pressed him relentlessly to sign a mandate agreeing to the Pope's terms, that is, of non-consummation. The wretched Sforza twisted and turned. He wanted the sentence nullifying the marriage to be based on grounds other than his non-consummation, as less offensive to his honour; he wanted the return of those of his possessions which were in the hands of Lucrezia, and to keep her dowry, with a clause agreed by the Pope and Lucrezia on behalf of herself and any future heirs guaranteeing its non-returnability.[25]

Apparently having already signed a mandate agreeing to the

divorce on the grounds of non-consummation he now wished
to substitute it for one simply nullifying the marriage.[26] Ludovico's
chancellor, Thomasino Tormelli, who had been sent to fetch 'this
blessed mandate' (*'questo benedetto Mandato'*, Sforza's signed state-
ment agreeing to the divorce) from Pesaro, told Ludovico in exas-
peration that if he were to present this form to the Pope, Alexander
would explode with fury and probably proceed to the sentence
without further delay anyway.[27] In response to a long wail from
Giovanni Sforza, Ludovico told him firmly on 12 December to
submit to the decisions of Ascanio in dealing with the Pope. On
21 December, Tormelli wrote to Ludovico informing him of the
Pope's joy at the settlement of the matter and the pronounce-
ment of the divorce the previous day, and of his great gratitude
to Ludovico for his intervention: 'The joy which you have given
him is as great as if you had given him 200,000 ducats.'[28] Alexander
had every reason to be joyful as he had obtained everything he
wanted – Giovanni Sforza's mandate attesting to non-consummation
(signed in Pesaro on 18 November) and the return of the dowry
of 30,000 ducats. A letter from a weary Ascanio Sforza revealed
the difficult negotiations behind the final settlement: all he had
secured for the 'small benefit' of Giovanni Sforza was the return
of jewels and things given by him to Lucrezia which, according
to the Pope, were worth several thousand ducats.[29] Lucrezia herself
seems to have had no regrets over her enforced separation from
her husband of more than four years. According to Taberna, she
appeared at the Vatican on 20 December 1497 for the promul-
gation of her divorce, when she made a graceful speech which
he described as worthy of Cicero in its eloquence. Within just
over six months she would be married for a second time.

4. The Tragic Duchess of Bisceglie

'We have entrusted to our beloved daughter in Christ, the
noble lady, Lucretia de Borgia, Duchess of Biseglia [sic], the office
of keeper of the castle, as well as the government of our cities of
Spoleto and Foligno, and of the county and district about
them. Having perfect confidence in the intelligence, fidelity and
probity of the Duchess . . . We trust that you will receive the
Duchess Lucretia as is your duty, with all due honour as your
regent, and show her submission in all things . . .'

– Alexander VI to the Priors of Spoleto, 18 August 1499

Alexander may have got what he wanted but the cost to Lucrezia's
reputation was high. Few believed that her marriage had not been
consummated or that Giovanni Sforza was impotent, since his
first wife had died in childbirth (his third wife would bear him
two children). The idea that Lucrezia was a virgin, so necessary
for her remarriage, was regarded as ludicrous. As Matarazzo, a
Perugian chronicler unfavourable to the Borgias, put it: '[it was]
a conclusion that set all Italy laughing . . . it was common knowledge that she had been and was then the greatest whore there
ever was in Rome'. Sforza's allegation that Alexander had taken
Lucrezia from him to sleep with her himself became common
currency. It may even be that he believed it. The closeness of the
Borgias made the accusation of incest feasible; even Juan Gandia
had been charged with sleeping with his sister. Both Alexander
and Cesare loved Lucrezia deeply: in fact it seems that she was
the only woman whom Cesare ever cared for.

Within months of the divorce Lucrezia was involved in further
sexual scandal. On 14 February 1498, the body of Pedro

Calderon, known as Perotto, a handsome young Spaniard who served in the Pope's chamber, was discovered in the Tiber. According to Burchard who in his position as papal master of ceremonies was well up in palace gossip, on the night of the 8th Perotto 'fell, not of his own will, into the Tiber . . . of which there is much said in the city'. And according to Marin Sanudo, the drowned body of Pantasilea, one of Lucrezia's women, was found with him. It seems likely that Cesare had them both killed for reasons intimately connected with Lucrezia, who was almost certainly having an affair with Perotto. Knowledge of this affair may well have been a reason for her seclusion in San Sisto at a time when her divorce from Sforza was being planned by Alexander and Cesare in June the previous year. Shortly before the discovery of Perotto's body in February 1498, Cristoforo Poggio, agent of the Bentivoglio family of Bologna, reported that Perotto had vanished mysteriously and was thought to be in prison 'for having got His Holiness's daughter, Lucrezia, with child'.[1] In March 1498, a report by the Ferrarese envoy to Duke Ercole alleged that Lucrezia had given birth to a child. Since at that very moment negotiations for a second marriage for Lucrezia were going on, Cesare had every reason to remove any evidence of misconduct on his sister's part by avenging himself on Perotto. Nothing and no one would be allowed to come in the way of his plans for Lucrezia which were so closely allied with his own.

The whole mysterious affair was complicated by the birth of a boy at around the same time. This was the notorious Giovanni Borgia, known as the *'Infans Romanus'*, who was certainly Alexander's child. Although his paternity was at first attributed to Cesare, Alexander later admitted it in a secret Bull of September 1502. The timing of the birth, however, led people to believe that he was Lucrezia's son, even, some said, fathered by the Pope. The fact that years later he was welcomed and well treated by the family of Lucrezia's third husband where he was known as her half-brother, makes these rumours unlikely. What happened to Lucrezia's child, if child there was – and the murders of Perotto

Strathcarron Hospice Retail Ltd

Grangemouth

Vat #: 971373211

Date: 6 March 2020 13:51
Transaction Ref: 017-2003-1660639
Served by: A volunteer someone like you

Sales

| 10000466 | 2 | £2.00 |
| Books | | |

Price Point: 1

TOTAL

SUB TOTAL	£2.00
VAT	£0.00
TOTAL	£2.00

TENDER

| Cash | £5.00 |
| Change | £3.00 |

and Pantasilea tend to support such a supposition – has never been revealed. It may, given Lucrezia's later history of difficult pregnancies, have died at or soon after birth.

The craziness, cruelty and danger of Roman life was illustrated by an incident at that time, recorded meticulously by Burchard:

In these days was imprisoned Cursetta, a certain courtesan, that is honest prostitute, who had amongst her household a Moor who used to go about dressed as a woman, who called himself Barbara the Spaniard and knew her carnally in I know not what manner, and for this they were both led through the city in scandal, [Cursetta] dressed in black velvet to the ground but not bound, but the Moor, in female dress, with his upper arms tied behind his back, and the skirts of his dress and shift raised up to his navel, so that all could see his testicles and thus his fraud was clear. Having made a circle of the city, Cursetta was set free; the Moor was thrown into prison, and on Saturday the seventh of this month of April, he was led out with two robbers from the Torre di Nona, preceded by a constable mounted on an ass bearing a cane to which was tied the two testicles cut off from a Jew who had copulated with a Christian woman, and taken to the Campo di Fiore where the two thieves were hanged. The Moor was placed on top of a pyre and tied to the pillory, the cord round his neck was twisted strongly behind the column, and the faggots set alight, but they would not burn because of the heavy rain, but his legs at last were burnt being closest to the wood.

Burning at the stake was normally the punishment for sodomy or heresy (at the end of that month of April 1498, for example, the fanatical reforming friar Girolamo Savonarola died at the stake in Florence). The manner of the Moor's death may have prompted Burchard's curious phrase '[he] knew her carnally in I know not what manner'. On the same day six peasants were put in 'the mitre' (presumably the stocks) after having been whipped through the streets, for a particularly disgusting fraud: they had sold olive oil to syphilis sufferers with which to bathe themselves in the hope of a cure; afterwards the vendors had put the oil back in their pitchers and sold it to unsuspecting customers.

Alexander willingly received Jews expelled from Spain by his extreme Catholic 'patroness' Queen Isabella; he regarded them not only as useful citizens but as a potential source of revenue. Large sums of money would be required to fund the Borgias' new plans for Cesare, and that summer there was a public conversion of three hundred Jews, or *marrani*, in the piazza of St Peter's, a grand occasion witnessed by Lucrezia and Sancia,[2] after which the 'converts' processed in scapulars marked with crosses to the church of Santa Maria sopra Minerva, where they deposited them. Sanudo certainly saw this as yet another money-raising move by the Borgia Pope: 'From letters I understand that the Pope ordered about 300 Spanish *marrani* dressed in yellow with a candle in the hand to proceed to Minerva . . . which was their public punishment. The secret one will be their money, as was done with the condemned Bishop of Calahorra [Pedro de Aranda, arrested and charged with heresy on 21 April 1498].'[3] Other sources of funds were the estates of dead or disgraced churchmen: when the papal secretary Bartolomeu Flores, Archbishop of Cosenza, was arrested on the charge of forging papal briefs,[4] Alexander confiscated his goods and his room in the Vatican with all its furniture and hangings which he gave to one of his confidants, Juan Marrades, and his archbishopric to another favourite, the chamberlain Jacopo Casanova. The Cardinal of Genoa died in March 1498: the Pope sent another of his Spanish chamberlains, Juan Ferrera, to take charge of his goods, and gave his archbishopric to a natural brother of Ascanio Sforza.

The archbishopric was probably the last favour the Sforza could expect from the Pope. Not only was Alexander contemplating a second marriage for Lucrezia into the Aragonese royal family of Naples, natural enemies of the Sforza, but on 7 April Charles VIII of France died at Amboise, an event which presaged further danger for both the Sforza and the Aragonese. Charles's successor, Louis XII, inherited not only Charles's claims to Naples but, in his own right, a valid claim to the Duchy of Milan. What is more he wanted a dispensation from the Pope to put aside his wife, Jeanne de France, and to marry his predecessor's widow, Anne de

Bretagne, in order to keep Anne's duchy of Brittany within the Kingdom of France. At that time the Pope and Cesare still saw their future with Naples but the needs and ambitions of the new French King would play a pivotal part in their policy.

That summer Alexander focused on Naples for his children's marriages, negotiating with King Federigo to marry Lucrezia to Sancia's brother, Alfonso, illegitimate son of the Duke of Calabria. His real goal, however, was to marry Cesare to Carlotta, the King's legitimate daughter. To the Pope's fury, Federigo made difficulties. Having obtained legitimization of his accession from the Borgias, he was far from eager to accommodate the Pope's bastards with further marriages, money and lands in his Kingdom. Ascanio Sforza watched nervously from the sidelines as the Neapolitan negotiations proceeded. Early in May he reported the Pope's anger with King Federigo's negative attitude to the marriages.[5] The King was not disposed to grant Alfonso a considerable estate and the Pope was enraged and humiliated at this slight, particularly since the affair had become public knowledge.[6] Alexander's reaction was to cover up by pretending that he intended to marry Lucrezia to Francesco Orsini, Duke of Gravina (who was to be executed by Cesare five years later).

He continued the pretence through the summer until, on 15 July, Alfonso arrived secretly in Rome. 'This morning Don Alfonso arrived here,' Ascanio reported to his brother, 'and although he came as far as Marino with 50 horse, from Marino to here he brought only 6 or 7, as His Holiness wished for secrecy. He dined with me in the Palace [Vatican] then he went to meet His Holiness who greeted him very warmly; this evening he lodges in the house of the Princess his sister [Sancia] under guise of secrecy.' In fact, Ascanio added, his arrival was widely known in Rome. The next day Cesare invited his future brother-in-law to his apartments with the most manifest display of affection and the following day the Pope welcomed him together with Lucrezia in the presence of Ascanio, the Cardinal of Perosa and Neapolitan representatives.

Finally, an agreement had been made between King Federigo

and the Pope, whereby the King would give Alfonso the Duchy of Bisceglie and the lands of Corato as security for Lucrezia's dowry,[7] while the Pope would give her a dowry of 40,000 ducats.[8] It was also agreed that Alfonso should stay in Rome for a year and that Lucrezia would not be obliged to go to Naples.

Once again Lucrezia was a political pawn: her marriage to Alfonso was simply a stepping stone to the more important marriage of Cesare to Carlotta of Naples, which would give him a foothold in the Kingdom. Within a comparatively short time her connection with Bisceglie, like her marriage to Giovanni Sforza, would be surplus to her family's requirements. She appeared happy, however, with her chosen husband, a good-looking youth of seventeen. The marriage took place in private on 21 July in the presence of cardinals Ascanio Sforza, Juan Lopez and Juan Borgia. In accordance with custom a naked sword was held over the couple by Juan Cervillon, the Catalan captain of the papal guard, but the celebrations were held behind closed doors. Burchard, who would have been in charge of the ceremonies had they been public, recorded only that Alfonso contracted marriage with Lucrezia in the Palazzo Santa Maria in Portico 'and then carnally consummated the marriage'.

However, there was an insider account. The celebrations enjoyed in the Vatican with huge exuberance by the Borgia inner circle were described in detail by Sancia, sister of the bridegroom, and now known to be Cesare's mistress. On Sunday 5 August a solemn nuptial mass was held in the Palazzo Santa Maria in Portico, with the couple flanked by Sancia and Jofre. Sancia described Lucrezia's magnificent dress at length; this stress on the richness of clothes and costly materials is a feature in every account of a period which laid such importance on *bella figura*, the display of beauty and wealth being considered an essential indication of the rank and importance of the person. Lucrezia's robes included a rich silken skirt of camlet with sleeves studded with jewels and a long robe in the French style of golden brocade with a pattern of black thread and crimson velvet trim; her belt was studded with pearls and other jewels, she wore a necklace of large, fine pearls round her neck, her 'very beautiful' hair hung down over her shoulders, and on her head she wore a cap embroidered with jewels and pearls and a band of gold wrought and enamelled. Alfonso was also splendidly dressed in black brocade lined with crimson satin; he wore a cap of black velvet with a brooch given him by Lucrezia: a gold medallion with a unicorn as a device and a jewelled golden cherub. Lucrezia was attended by three ladies, and by Geronima Borgia, sister of the cardinal, and her household all splendidly dressed.

The company remained in the palace all day and feasted there until, at the twenty-third hour, the Pope sent his courtiers to escort them to a hall in the Vatican, known as the Room of the Pontiffs, where, with the Pope enthroned and with Lucrezia, Alfonso, Sancia and Jofre at his feet, the order was given for the ladies and gentlemen to dance. At Alexander's command Lucrezia first danced alone and then with Alfonso. Afterwards they dined, with the Pope by himself at a high table, and at another Lucrezia, Alfonso, the cardinals Borgia and Perusa, the protonotary Capellan and Geronima Borgia. Sancia was given the signal honour of serving the Pope wine. Then the cardinals Borgia of Monreale and Perusa, with Don Alfonso, served the Pope's table before themselves sitting down to eat. The highest ranking courtiers acted as pages and after dining, which took three hours, the Pope presented Lucrezia with a magnificent silver service and the cardinals followed suit with gifts of silver and jewels. After this the Pope and his party withdrew to the Borgia Apartments where Cesare had set up magnificent tableaux – a fountain richly worked with depictions of cobras and other poisonous snakes, while in another room there was a wood in which wandered seven mummers dressed as animals: Jofre, quaintly, as a sea goose; the prior of Santa Eufemia (Ludovico Borgia), brother of Cardinal Borgia, as an elephant; and other gentlemen of Cesare's dressed as a fox, a stag, a lion and a giraffe. Cesare himself appeared as a unicorn. They were all dressed in satin according to the colour of the animal they represented and came in one by one, dancing before the Pope. At last Cesare asked permission to dance with Lucrezia, after which each of the mummers danced with the ladies. And so it continued until dawn was breaking when they had a collation served as before, and at sunrise the Pope ordered Lucrezia and Alfonso home, attended by all the company except Cesare, who remained with his father.

That day, Monday 6 August, was spent sleeping and on the Tuesday Cesare gave a party in the great loggia of the Villa Belvedere in the Vatican gardens (built by Pope Innocent VIII and decorated with frescoes by Mantegna). Cesare, seated beside Alexander, wore lay dress, splendid in a doublet of crimson satin and white brocade in the French style, white buskins or half-boots, a cape and a bonnet of black velvet with golden tassels and a white plume, adorned with a gold medallion showing a woman's head. Lucrezia, Cesare and Sancia danced together, then the others danced and at one hour of the night they brought in the table for supper. Cesare, who had changed his clothes once again, acted as master of ceremonies to the Pope while the principal men of his household carried out the service of the table. Others acted as pages bearing flaming torches, including Cesare's henchman, the sinister Don Miguel de Corella. Afterwards the company watched 'some buffoons who performed many tricks'. Then Cesare danced another dance with Lucrezia, and another eight with Sancia; then the Pope ordered Cesare, Lucrezia and Sancia to dance together, followed by general dancing, after which the company retired to rest. At sunrise the Pope got up and went to the loggia where they were all served with a collation of sweetmeats, with Cesare again acting as master of ceremonies. There were one hundred dishes of sweetmeats and conserves. Then came 'diverse and very beautiful inventions' – sugar statues presented by Cesare with diverse motifs. One placed before the Pope was in the figure of a woman with an apple in her hand signifying his mastery of the world; for Alfonso there was a cupid with verses in his hand; for Lucrezia a woman supposed to be the Roman matron Lucretia; for Cesare – significantly – a knight with arms given to him by the goddess of battles. Jofre was given a statue of a sleeping man, possibly a teasing reference to his role as his brother's cuckold; and Sancia, less suitably, a unicorn, the symbol of chastity. At the end of the collation the Pope sent Alfonso, Lucrezia and the others to their lodgings once more, at which point he again retired to his own rooms with Cesare.

That was not the end of the Borgia celebrations masterminded by Cesare and in which he played the dominant role. On 12 August, the following Sunday, in the park of Cardinal Ascanio's villa, he organized a bullfight; attended by ten thousand spectators, its most notable feature was a magnificently decorated platform draped with tapestries and lengths of silk for the guests of honour, Lucrezia and Alfonso, Sancia and Jofre and their retinues. Cesare appeared on the field on foot with twelve knights: his clothes (some of which she had presented to him that day) excited Sancia's admiration so much that in her record of events she even included a description of his horse, a white Barbary steed, with its jewel-studded harness and white brocade caparison the most beautiful she had ever seen. In one hand Cesare carried a fine lance worked in silver and gold which Sancia had also given him that day, and in the other held the reins of eight fine horses equally beautifully caparisoned. Two mounted pages holding lances bearing banners embroidered with a golden sun accompanied him, and he was preceded by twelve boys dressed in his livery of yellow satin halved with carmine, and twelve horsemen all wearing livery given to them by Cesare. In the course of the afternoon Cesare killed all the bulls. The party then feasted and the horsemen held races until nightfall when the party rode to Sancia's palace where they supped and passed six more hours in 'singing and other pleasures'.[9]

But even as Lucrezia and Alfonso exuberantly celebrated their wedding, the tide was already turning. Cesare's ambitions and Alexander's international policies had taken a new turn that summer. Since the death of Charles VIII, it had become obvious that there would be a conflict in Italy between Ferdinand of Aragon and Louis of France. This time Alexander saw more advantage to be drawn from the French King than from his old patron, Ferdinand. Ferdinand had placed obstacles in the way of

Alexander's plans for Cesare: supporting King Federigo of Naples in his refusal to give Cesare his legitimate daughter, Carlotta; opposing Cesare's intention to give up his cardinalate so that he could pursue his secular ambitions; and refusing to allow the late Juan Gandia's lands in Valencia to pass to Cesare. France, on the other hand, offered to accommodate Alexander in every way in order to obtain the dissolution of Louis's marriage with Jeanne de France and a dispensation enabling him to marry his predecessor's widow, Anne de Bretagne. Late that summer a secret agreement was signed between King and Pope, by which Louis promised to support Cesare's marriage to Carlotta of Aragon (who was at the French court at the time), to give him the counties of Valence and Diois, the former to be raised to a duchy, with revenues of 20,000 gold francs, the financing by Louis of a large force of nearly two thousand heavy cavalry to operate on Cesare's orders in Italy or elsewhere, a personal subsidy to Cesare of 20,000 gold francs per annum, the lordship of Asti for Cesare upon the French conquest of Milan, and finally his investiture of France's highest honour, the Order of St Michel.

On 17 August 1498, Cesare put off his cardinal's robes. A magnificently wrought parade sword he had had made earlier that summer symbolized his new personal ambitions for it was decorated with scenes from the life of Julius Caesar with whom Cesare identified. Cesare, who always signed himself 'Cesar', the Spanish form of his name and the one closest to the Roman original, was later to adopt as his motto '*Aut Caesar aut nihil*': 'Either Caesar or nothing'. That same day Louis's envoy, Baron de Trans, arrived in Rome bearing the letters patent that would entitle the former Cardinal of Valencia to call himself duc de Valentinois. For Italians, the two foreign titles sounded almost the same: Valencia became 'il Valentino'. There was general outrage at the blatant cynicism of the Borgias: Cesare had made his announcement to a sparse audience on 17 August, even the Spanish cardinals having thought it prudent to be out of Rome. Relentlessly Alexander rounded them up: five days later, at another consistory, he obtained all the cardinals' votes. Cesare's power in Rome had already been recognized – 'he has the Pope in his fist', an envoy had written two years before. Cesare held not just the Pope but the Pope's castellans in Rome and the surrounding territories in an iron grip.

His departure for France on 1 October was yet another public demonstration of Borgia power and splendour paid for by 200,000 ducats, raised, it was said, from the confiscation of the goods of Pedro de Aranda, Bishop of Calahorra, lately condemned for heresy, and from the three hundred Jews whose conversion Lucrezia had earlier witnessed in the piazza of St Peter's. Roman supplies of rich stuffs, jewels, gold and silverware had been exhausted so that additional luxuries had to be brought in from Venice and elsewhere. Cesare had requested Francesco Gonzaga and Ippolito d'Este to send him horses 'not unworthy of French esteem' from their famous stables. These coursers were to be shod with silver; Cesare even took with him a princely travelling privy 'covered with gold brocade without and scarlet within, with silver vessels within the urinals'. No expense was spared in an effort to impress the French and perhaps some of it was intended to offset the discomfort Cesare felt at his appearance. For the blotches under the skin associated with the second stage of syphilis now showed on his handsome face. The significance of his departure for France on a French ship, destined for a military career, was not lost on the watching envoys of the Italian powers. As the Mantuan Cattaneo wrote with wry foreboding: 'The ruin of Italy is confirmed . . . given the plans which father and son have made but many believe the Holy Spirit has no part in them . . .' Nor would the Holy Spirit have any part in Cesare's plans for Lucrezia, still happy and content in the Palazzo Santa Maria in Portico with her new young husband.

That autumn after Cesare's departure, Lucrezia was first in her father's attentions, courted particularly by Ascanio Sforza who was anxiously aware of which way the Pope's alliances were inclining. On 23 October, Sanudo reported that Ascanio was in Rome, though not invited to the Vatican by the Pope, but that he 'has been with the daughter of the Pontiff and attends to nothing else'.[10] At the end of the year, a confidant of Ludovico reported that Lucrezia, with the cardinals of Capua and Borgia, were the three people of influence with the Pope.[11] On the surface, all had seemed well; at a ceremony in the Vatican, Paolo Orsini's son, Fabio, married Geronima Borgia, sister of Cardinal Juan Borgia the younger, on 8 September, when Lucrezia's husband held the naked sword over the couple.

But even Lucrezia, now pregnant with her first child by Alfonso, could not avert the shadows gathering around him. In late December ambassadors arrived from Spain for a stormy four-hour interview with Alexander during which they complained of his negotiations with the French, returned to the old charges of simony concerning his election to the papacy and threatened a Council of the Church to depose him. They tactlessly raised the death of Gandia as God's punishment for his sins – to which Alexander angrily retorted that God had also punished the Spanish sovereigns with the death of their son.[12] They reminded him of his pledge (made in the immediate aftermath of Gandia's murder) to reform the papacy and send away his children. This Alexander steadfastly refused to consider: during another fierce row with the envoys in the Sala del Pappagallo the following month in the presence of six cardinals, when they petitioned him to recall Cesare from France and restore him to the cardinalate, Alexander, according to Sanudo, threatened to throw them into the Tiber.

In February, Lucrezia suffered a miscarriage. Running down a hill in a 'vineyard' on a beautiful Roman spring day she fell, and the lady following her fell on top of her, as a result of which she lost a baby girl. She was soon pregnant again but politics – and Cesare – would make a settled life with her husband impossible. On 23 May a special courier arrived in Rome with the news that Cesare had contracted – and consummated – marriage, not with Carlotta of Aragon, who had resolutely refused to consider it, but with a cousin of the French King, the sister of the King of Navarre. Charlotte d'Albret, three years younger than Lucrezia, was an acknowledged beauty – even the critical Italian envoys called her 'the loveliest daughter of France'. King Louis reassured the Pope that the marriage had been consummated, Cesare's performance in bed even surpassing his own wedding night with Anne de Bretagne: 'Valencia has broken four lances more than he, two before supper and six at night,' reported Cattaneo after all the letters from France had been read out on the orders of the delighted Pope. Alexander – and the Spanish, Milanese and Neapolitan party – had been on tenterhooks as to the outcome of Cesare's French adventure. The result spelled danger for the dynasties of Sforza and the Aragonese of Naples.

To celebrate her brother's marriage Lucrezia lit a fire outside her palace but it is unlikely that her jubilation was shared by her husband or her sister-in-law. It was not long before the outcome became clear: as commander of a squadron of heavy cavalry Cesare was to accompany Louis to Italy. By mid July as the news filtered through to Italy, the casualties of the Borgias' pro-French policy fled Rome. Ascanio was the first to go, leaving precipitately on 13 July for the Colonna stronghold at Nettuno. A week later Ludovico captured one of Cesare's servants en route from Rome to Lyons with secret letters from the Pope. Ascanio immediately fled Nettuno for Milan to join his brother. On Friday 2 August Alfonso, now, as the chronicler put it, 'an unwelcome guest', 'secretly left the city before daybreak . . . to go to the lands of the Colonna and thence to the Kingdom of Naples without the licence, knowledge or will of the Pontiff'. He left Lucrezia six months pregnant and in tears. There seems to be little doubt that they loved each other: from Genazzano, Alfonso wrote to her begging her to join him. He should have known the Vatican intelligence system better: the letters fell into the Pope's hands and Alexander forced Lucrezia to write back asking him to return. For greater security, the Pope sent Lucrezia out of Rome to act as Governor of Spoleto. Lucrezia was only nineteen but her appointment was far from being a cynical joke; later in life she was to demonstrate that she had inherited her father's administrative ability. With Cesare in France, Alexander regarded her as the only one whose ability and loyalty he could trust: Jofre had been placed in the Castel Sant'Angelo after incurring his father's wrath for involving himself with the city police in a brawl in which he had been wounded. Alexander's anger had extended to Sancia when the fiery princess defended Jofre. As a potential spy in the Vatican, she was dispatched to Naples in Alfonso's wake.

Lucrezia's appointment as Governor of Spoleto was intended to demonstrate a Borgia presence in the Papal States north of Rome and to provide Lucrezia with an independent power base with rich revenues. Jofre, who accompanied his sister as she left the city, was clearly considered inadequate to fulfil that role. Alexander made his trust in Lucrezia plain in a letter he wrote to the Priors of Spoleto:

We have entrusted to our beloved daughter in Christ, the noble lady, Lucretia de Borgia, Duchess of Biseglia [sic], the office of keeper of the castle, as well as the government of our cities of Spoleto and Foligno, and of the county and district about them. Having perfect confidence in the intelligence, fidelity and probity of the Duchess, which We have dwelt upon in previous letters . . . We trust that you will receive the Duchess Lucretia as is your duty, with all due honour as your regent, and show her submission in all things . . . collectively and severally, in so far as law and custom dictate in the government of the city, and whatever she may think proper to exact of you, even as you would obey Ourselves, and to execute her commands with all diligence and promptness.[13]

Lucrezia arrived in the great castle of Spoleto with a train of forty-three carriages loaded with goods designed to display her gubernatorial magnificence. Meanwhile Alexander, perhaps in fulfilment of a promise he had made to her before she left Rome, sent Juan Cervillon, one of the Borgias' most trusted henchmen, to Naples to persuade the King to send Alfonso back. 'And they will have a hundred matters to discuss, each seeking to fool the other,' the Mantuan envoy reported,[14] 'but the Pope will not trust the King, nor the King the Pope.' There was a mysterious killing in Rome of a Spanish constable of the guard, one of

Cesare's most favoured followers who had been 'involved with him in many matters'. He was found drowned with a cord round his neck, his hands tied, in a sack weighted with a stone. The body was meant to be found, as it had been attached to posts in a vineyard on the river bank, probably as a warning to the Borgias and to Cesare, now in Lyons with the French army destined for Italy, that they had powerful enemies. The Mantuan envoy, always ready to embroider a crime or a mystery, added 'it is presumed he knew too much'.[15]

King Federigo, however, perhaps unwilling to offend the Pope in these critical times, now agreed to send Alfonso back to Lucrezia. Avoiding Rome, the young man was reunited in Spoleto with his now heavily pregnant wife. With Jofre they joined Alexander on 25 September at the powerful fortress of Nepi, strategically situated between the two main roads, the Via Cassia and the Via Flaminia. Alexander had taken the castle from the absent Ascanio Sforza and fortified it; he now handed it over to Lucrezia, together with the city and its lands. Lucrezia was now mistress of two key castles and territories in the Papal States north of Rome, but she did not stay there long. On 14 October she returned to Rome with Alfonso and Jofre to be greeted by, among others, mummers and jesters of the Pope's household. Nearing her time, she retreated to her Palazzo Santa Maria in Portico. The Vatican was crowded with armed men and there was a palpable air of excitement and fear. On 11 October, Louis XII had entered Milan in triumph and splendour; riding close behind him was Cardinal Borgia, and two ranks behind him Cesare with Duke Ercole d'Este, followed by the Marquis of Mantua. A few days later, the Pope deprived the Malatesta lords of Rimini, the Riarii of Imola and Forlì, Varani of Camerino, Manfredi of Faenza, and Guidobaldo da Montefeltro, of their status as papal vicars on the grounds of non-payment of the census. Among them was Giovanni Sforza of Pesaro. The way was now open for a Borgia takeover of a large portion of the Papal States, the Romagna and the Marches, by Cesare acting in the name of the Church, backed by French troops and a loan of 45,000 ducats from the Commune of Milan, guaranteed by cardinals Borgia and Giuliano della Rovere.

On 1 November, Lucrezia gave birth to a son, named Rodrigo in honour of her father. He was christened in St Peter's on the 11th, St Martin's Day, amid great pomp. The entrance to Lucrezia's palace was hung with silks and brocade. As a mark of great favour, Juan Cervillon carried the baby, who was dressed in a robe of gold brocade trimmed with ermine, into the basilica to the sound of trumpets and oboes. The child was attended by the ambassadors of the Empire, England, Naples, Venice, Savoy and Florence. He was delivered by Francesco Borgia, Cardinal of Cosenza, to be baptized in the great silver gilt shell, commissioned by Pope Sixtus IV, by Cardinal Caraffa, who stood as his godfather. Underlining the reconciliation between Orsini and Borgia, Paolo Orsini carried the child back to Santa Maria in Portico. Startled by the noise of the trumpets the baby Rodrigo, who had been silent during the whole ceremony, began to cry.

As yet, the baby's father, Alfonso, had no reason to feel insecure, protected as he was by the high favour in which Lucrezia was held by the Pope. As of that moment, Cesare's attention was turned on the Romagna where, with Louis's political and military support, he anticipated an easy campaign. Almost without exception, the lords of the Romagna were a worthless lot, detested by their subjects, whom they shamelessly exploited. As Machiavelli later wrote in the *Discourses*: 'Before those lords who ruled it were driven out by Pope Alexander VI, the Romagna was a nursery of the worst crimes, the slightest occasion giving rise to wholesale rapine and murder. This resulted from the wickedness of these lords, and not, as they asserted, from the disposition of their subjects. For these princes being poor, yet choosing to live as if they were rich, were forced to resort to cruelties innumerable . . .'

For Cesare, as for Alexander, politics was the art of the possible: a Venetian report of a mission by Cardinal Borgia on Cesare's behalf illustrates his thinking: '. . . he did not want Ferrara since it was a great state, and its lord old and loved by the people, and has three sons who would never leave him in peace if he had it; however he wanted Imola, Forlì and Pesaro, an undertaking which would be easy . . .'

Even before he reached Forlì, Cesare was forced to make a secret dash to Rome on 18 November. The ruler of Forlì, Caterina Sforza Riario, a famous beauty who was also a warlike 'virago', had attempted to pre-empt Cesare's attack by poisoning the Pope. That afternoon Cardinal Riario suddenly left Rome on the pretext of going hunting and did not return, while Burchard revealed that one of Jofre Borgia's musicians, a native of Forlì, and an accomplice, had been taken to the Castel Sant'Angelo because they had planned to murder the Pope by means of letters steeped in poison which they intended to present to Alexander under the guise of a petition. Another version had Caterina Sforza wrapping the letters in a cloth taken from the body of a plague victim. It was a vain attempt and Cesare rode north again three days later to continue his campaign; Caterina's cities gave themselves to him 'like whores', as Sanudo put it. Only Caterina in the citadel of Forlì held out.

While Cesare was campaigning in the Romagna, Lucrezia was shocked by the murder in mid December of another Borgia intimate – Juan Cervillon, the man who had carried the infant Rodrigo to his baptism the previous month. As with so many crimes at the time, his death was imputed to Cesare but, as Burchard recorded, he had 'many enemies' and the murder could have been carried out by any of them. Cesare was, in fact, the least likely candidate.

Lucrezia's life in Rome at this time remains a mystery. While her father and brother were intent on their complicated plans for Cesare's advancement, she is barely mentioned. She is recorded as having ridden to the Lateran in procession with Alfonso and one hundred horsemen, including Giulia Farnese's husband, Orsino Orsini, as a part of the celebrations of the Holy Year of 1500 inaugurated by Alexander on 24 December. But she remained a part of Alexander's plans for the family, this time at the expense of the Caetani family whose lands at Sermoneta and other territories south of Rome he expropriated from the head of the clan,

Guglielmo Caetani, who happened to be Giulia Farnese's uncle. In February 1500 Lucrezia became ruler of Sermoneta in addition to her lands north of Rome. Five months later Guglielmo Caetani died of poison. Did Lucrezia close her eyes to the terrible things which were taking place? Probably. Did she protest? Almost certainly not. It was only when the atmosphere of violence touched her own circle that she finally rebelled against the ruthlessness of her father and brother.

As before, Lucrezia's fate and that of those close to her was closely bound up with Cesare's plans and ambitions. Cesare had returned to Rome in triumph in the last week of February, his arrival a carefully stage-managed spectacle which galvanized the city, already full of pilgrims and foreign visitors enjoying the spiritual and other less worthy benefits of Holy Year. Even before the appearance of the principal character, the event compared favourably with the excitement of a Roman triumph. Down the wide Via Lata (now the Corso) from the Porta del Popolo marched the city dignitaries and officials of the Vatican Curia in their finest robes, the cardinals riding in purple and ermine, with their households in rich livery, and the ambassadors from every country in the Christian world with their retinues. The organization of the procession outside the Porta del Popolo had driven the ever-precise papal master of ceremonies, Burchard, almost to despair. People had joined the company from every village it had passed through, forming a disorderly group with no more regard for papal protocol than Cesare's Swiss and Gascon mercenaries. These, in five companies under standards bearing his arms, refused to acknowledge Burchard's authority and 'indecently' occupied places in the procession to which they were not entitled. The more orderly part of the official entry comprised Cesare's baggage wagons, the mules caparisoned in his colours of crimson and gold, then two heralds, one in the colours of France, the other in Cesare's livery, then one thousand infantry in full campaign armour, and a hundred of his personal guard with 'Cesar' emblazoned in silver letters on their chests. Fifty gorgeously dressed gentlemen of his household preceded the cavalry headed by

Vitellozzo Vitelli, a renowned *condottiere*. Then came Cesare himself, flanked by cardinals Orsini and Farnese and followed by Alfonso Bisceglie and Jofre.

Cesare wore a simple robe of black velvet, his only ornament the golden collar of the Order of St Michel, the symbol of his new high rank. The stark cloth set off his looks more dramatically than the flashy silks he had worn on his departure for France almost eighteen months before. From now on, with a growing confidence in himself, black, with its connotations of outward drama, inner narcissism and introversion, was to be his preferred colour, a reflection of his increasingly dark personality.

Alexander was beside himself with paternal pride. At Cesare's reception in the Sala del Pappagallo ambassadors recorded him as so moved that he cried at one moment and laughed the next. He embraced Cesare tenderly and even welcomed his son's captive, Caterina Sforza, the woman who had tried to have him poisoned, and lodged her comfortably in the Vatican. (When she refused to sign away her rights and those of her children to Imola and Forlì, she was moved to less agreeable quarters in the prisons of the Castel Sant'Angelo.) When, the next day, Cesare staged an allegorical procession representing the Triumphs of Caesar, the Pope was so delighted with it that he insisted it pass twice before his windows. On 29 March he gave Cesare the Golden Rose and invested him with the insignia of Gonfalonier and Captain General of the Church. To the watchful envoys, this nomination could signify only one thing – a complete Borgia takeover of the Church. With the father wielding the spiritual and temporal authority of the papacy, the son in control of the papal forces and the beginnings of a Borgia state taking place in the Romagna, the future was pregnant with potential danger.

The Borgias' plans were put into a temporary state of suspension by the brief return on 5 February 1500 of Ludovico to Milan and the defeat of the French in Lombardy; without the help of the French, Cesare was not yet strong enough to pursue his conquest of the Romagna. But on 10 April, il Moro was decisively defeated by the French at Novara, taken prisoner and immured in the fortress of Loches in Touraine, where he died eight years later. It was a sad end for the once magnificent Duke of Milan, born for his own ruin as much as that of his country. Leonardo da Vinci recorded in his notebook an epitaph on his former patron: 'The Duke has lost fortune, state and liberty, and not one of his works has been completed.' The news was greeted with cries of 'Urso [Orsini]' and 'Francia' by the many Orsini partisans in the city and fires were lit outside the Orsini palace of Montegiordano and in the piazza outside the Pantheon. Ascanio was also captured and imprisoned in Bourges. The Pope, who had given 100 ducats to the messenger who had brought the news of Ludovico's downfall, rewarded with the same sum the tidings of the downfall of Ascanio, his old ally. According to Burchard:

The Pope has had from him [Ascanio] very pitiful, plaintive letters, in which he recounts how he has lost in three days, his brother, his State, his honour, his possessions and the liberty of his person, beseeching His Holiness that, in whatever manner it may seem best to him, he should deign to consider his liberation, signing himself: infelix et afflictus Ascanius ['unhappy and afflicted Ascanio']. The College [of Cardinals] has discussed it, and the Pope keeps the matter to himself, and shows himself well content with this matter or not, according to the person with whom he is speaking: moreover he shows no compassion . . .

Far from showing compassion, Alexander immediately took advantage of Ascanio's misfortune, seizing his art treasures and giving away his benefices to new allies, such as Giuliano della Rovere.[16]

With the Sforzas out of the way, the Borgias' hopes rested with France and Louis XII who, having regained his Milanese duchy, now looked to assert his rights to his Neapolitan kingdom. In this event, the Aragonese, including Alfonso Bisceglie, would be swept away just as the Sforzas had been. A decision handed down by Alexander at the beginning of April had indicated which way the wind was blowing when he gave sentence against Alfonso's relation, Beatrice d'Aragona, Queen of Hungary, daughter of King Ferrante, whose husband, Ladislaus Jagiello, had repudiated her, asking for an annulment. The line-up of the powers in this case was significant: the Emperor, the Kings of Spain and Naples and the Milanese interest supported her; the French and Venice took the opposite side. Alfonso Bisceglie complained bitterly of the Pope's decision, as Antonio Malegonelle reported to the Signoria of Florence: 'It seems to me of great significance this sentence against the Queen of Hungary, concerning which sentence as it happens, I being in the Camera del Pappagallo, heard the Duke of Bisceglie condoling greatly with the Ambassador of Naples, not noticing that I overheard him . . .'[17]

Alfonso's sister Sancia made her feelings clear when a Burgundian and a Frenchman quarrelled over a banner and the Burgundian challenged the Frenchman to a duel. When Cesare heard of it, he offered the Burgundian 20 ducats, brocade clothes and a new banner if he would give up the fight. The Burgundian refused and won the duel, which took place on 9 April. As a gesture of defiance to Cesare, Sancia had dressed twelve of her squires in livery bearing the cross of St Andrew in honour of the Burgundian. 'It was said,' Burchard wrote, 'that he [Cesare] would rather have lost 20,000 ducats than see the Frenchman beaten.' The affair between Cesare and Sancia was long over: that summer he took up with a beautiful, rich and intelligent courtesan, the Florentine Fiammetta de'Michelis. Fiammetta owned three houses in the city, including one on the piazza named after her near the Piazza Navona, and a country villa, or *vigna*. She was typical of the high-class courtesans of her time who liked to show off their intellectual abilities. Fiammetta spoke Latin, declaimed Ovid and Petrarch from memory and sang delightfully, accompanying herself on the lyre. Her relationship with Cesare was so well known that her will in the city archives was headed 'The Testament of la Fiammetta of il Valentino'. Lucrezia, however, sided with the husband she loved and with his sister. She was not prepared to change her loyalties to follow her father and elder brother and, conscious of her father's continuing favour, was confident of her power to protect Alfonso.

At the end of June 1500 the Borgia party in Rome was shaken by the Pope's near fatal accident when a whirlwind struck the Vatican, causing the roof of the Sala dei Papi where he was sitting to fall in. The Sienese banker Lorenzo Chigi, with whom he was conversing, was killed outright; the Cardinal of Capua and Gaspar Poto, the Pope's secret chamberlain who were in the room, saved themselves by standing in the window niches. Alexander escaped death only because the canopy over the papal throne protected him, but he was struck on the head and rendered unconscious. In his apartment beneath, Cesare had left the room shortly before-hand, but three people who had been there with him died. Rumours spread that the Pope was dead and armed men crowded the Vatican but despite being bled of thirteen ounces of blood, Alexander recovered quickly. Sanudo, the first outsider to visit him following his accident, found him in the bosom of his family – Lucrezia, Sancia, Cesare and Jofre. If Alfonso Bisceglie was there, the diarist did not mention him; he did, however, record that one of Lucrezia's ladies, 'the Pope's favourite', was at the seventy-year-old pontiff's bedside.[18] The young Borgias realized only too well how their fortunes depended on the Pope's life. Despite his tremendous vitality, Alexander was subject to fainting fits and fevers which suggest high blood pressure, bad enough to be public knowledge among Vatican observers.

Just over two weeks later, on Wednesday 15 July, Alfonso Bisceglie was attacked on the steps of St Peter's by 'persons unknown'. Francesco Cappello reported to Florence the next day:

Yesterday evening at three hours of the night [he] left the Palace and was going to his house which is beside St Peter's on the Piazza, and being on the steps of St Peter's, under the balcony of the Benediction, accompanied by only two of his grooms because he was unsuspecting, four men attacked him very well armed and dealt him three blows: one on the head, very deep; and one across the shoulder, either one of which could be mortal: and another small one on the arm: and by what is known the wounds are of a gravity that he will be in need of God's help: and this evening now they have examined his wounds, they say he is very ill. Who may have wounded him, no one says, and it is not obvious that diligent inquiries are being made as they should be, nor is it much spoken of. Indeed around Rome it is rumoured that these things are amongst their very selves, because in that Palace there are so many hatreds both old and new, and so much envy and jealousy both for reasons of State and others, that it is necessary often to hide similar scandals. It is said that the wounded duke was taken back into the Palace, and the Pope got up and went to see him, and Madonna Lucrezia was in a dead faint.[19]

According to Burchard, the attackers then fled by the steps of St Peter's to where around forty horsemen awaited them, with whom they rode out through the Porta Pertusa. Cattaneo wrote to Isabella d'Este that the assailants were dragging Alfonso away, possibly to throw him in the river, when they were surprised by the guards. According to him, the Pope was distressed and had his wounded son-in-law carried up thirty steps to apartments above his own. Three days later Lucrezia was reported as ill of a fever because of her anguish.

Once again, as in the case of Gandia, the attack on Bisceglie, 'a lord who was nephew of a late king, son of a present king and son-in-law of the Pope', was said to have been ordered by someone very powerful – 'someone with more power than him'.[20] Sanudo reported, 'it is not known who wounded the said Duke, but it is said that it was whoever killed and threw into the Tiber the Duke of Gandia . . .'[21] Fear now ruled the city: Cesare issued an edict forbidding the carrying of arms in the Borgo between Sant'Angelo and St Peter's. Suspicion was rife but people dared not name names. Alfonso's former tutor, Raphael Brandolinus Lippi, who received a stipend from the papal court, wrote to Ferrara on the day following the attack: 'Whose was the hand behind the assassins is still unknown. I will not, however, repeat which names are being voiced, because it is grave and perilous to entrust it to a letter.'

One name, however, was being voiced within twenty-four hours of the attempt on Bisceglie – that of Cesare. On 16 July, Vincenzo

Calmeta, poet and papal secretary, wrote his former patroness, the Duchess of Urbino, a detailed account of it, ending: 'Who may have ordered this thing to be done, everyone thinks to be the Duke Valentino.' Alfonso's wounds should not prove fatal, he said, adding significantly, 'if some new accident does not intervene'. Others saw the hand of the Orsini in the affair, since Alfonso was in league with the pro-Neapolitan Colonna. Although the Orsini were the most likely authors, or rather bunglers, of the assassination attempt, it is feasible to consider that Cesare might have had foreknowledge of it – he had his own reasons for wishing his brother-in-law out of the way – and he, rather than the Orsini, would have had intimate information as to Alfonso's movements. He is reported to have said: 'I did not wound the Duke, but if I had, it would have been no more than he deserved.' The one factor which might be seen to exculpate him from the actual planning of the attack was the bungling of its execution: his own henchmen never failed to carry out his orders, as events were soon to show.

Lucrezia and, apparently Alexander, were taking no chances. Only the doctor sent by the King of Naples was allowed to attend Alfonso while Lucrezia prepared his food herself for fear of poison. On 18 August, almost exactly a month after the attack, Alfonso, much recovered, was sitting up in his bed in his room in the Torre Borgia, talking and laughing with his wife, his sister, his uncle and the envoy, when sudden violence erupted. According to Brandolinus:

. . . there burst into the chamber Michelotto [Miguel da Corella] most sinister minister of Cesare Valentino; he seized by force Alfonso's uncle and the royal envoy [of Naples], and having bound their hands behind their backs, consigned them to armed men who stood behind the door, to lead them to prison. Lucrezia, Alfonso's wife, and Sancia, his sister, stupefied by the suddenness and violence of the act, shrieked at Michelotto, demanding how he dared commit such an offence before their very eyes and in the presence of Alfonso. He excused himself as persuasively as he could, declaring that he was obeying the will of others, that he had to live by the orders of another, but that they, if they wished, might go to the Pope, and it would be easy to obtain the release of the arrested men. Carried away with anger and pity . . . the two women went to the Pope, and insisted that he give them the prisoners. Meanwhile Michelotto, most wretched of criminals and most criminal of wretches, suffocated Alfonso who was indignantly reproving him for his offence. The women, returning from the Pope, found armed men at the door of the chamber, who prevented them from entering and announced that Alfonso was dead . . . The women, terrified by this most cruel deed, oppressed by fear, beside themselves with grief, filled the palace with their shrieking, lamenting and wailing, one calling on her husband, the other on her brother, and their tears were without end.

This time there was no doubt as to who had ordered the crime: Michelotto, an illegitimate son of the Count of Corella and a close confidant of Cesare, was well known to be Cesare's 'executioner'. From the first assault, Francesco Cappello had diagnosed its cause as 'a matter between themselves, because in that Palace there are so many old and new hatreds, and so much envy and jealousy for political reasons and others . . .' An internal power struggle between the partisans of France and those of Aragon had been waged in the Vatican for some time past, the ultimate prize being the mind of the Pope. There is little doubt that while Cesare was away in France the Aragonese party round Alfonso and Sancia had tried to win back Alexander to his old allegiance to Spain and the house of Aragon from which Louis's promises for Cesare had weaned him. When Cesare returned to Rome after his prolonged absence, he was quick to sense an undercurrent within the family circle in opposition to his interests. Sancia and Jofre, Alfonso and Lucrezia had lived on terms of the closest intimacy since Alfonso had rejoined the family in Spoleto the previous autumn and Sancia had been allowed to return to Rome some time during the winter. This close-knit clique would clearly have had Aragonese sympathies: Jofre, a cipher, in the absence of his elder brother was dominated by his strong-willed wife, while

Lucrezia, who had wept so bitterly when Alfonso left Rome, had clearly been much in love with him.

With his fiercely competitive nature and overriding ambition, Cesare was not a man to brook opposition within his own family circle, above all when it threatened his own interests, not only his political commitment to the French alliance, but also his personal position within the Vatican and his two closest relationships with his father and sister. At this stage in his career, dependent on his father as the source of his power, he was determined that Alexander should follow the path which suited his interests, and that no one should come between them. As far as Lucrezia was concerned, his intense love for her was well known, and while he may have feared that her pro-Aragonese sympathies might have influenced her father, who doted on her, jealousy of her evident feeling for her husband would have fuelled his hatred for Alfonso. Thus Cesare saw Alfonso as a threat to himself which must be eliminated and, in the political context of a French campaign against Naples, as an embarrassment whose removal would be an advantage. He may well initially have made use of the Orsini to attack Alfonso and, when they bungled it, waited to see if his brother-in-law would die of his wounds. When it became obvious that Alfonso was recovering, Cesare took direct and brutal steps to finish him off.

The excuse given out for this cruel murder was that Alfonso had attempted to kill Cesare with a crossbow shot as he walked in the garden. It was necessary to persuade Alexander, who had originally been very upset by the assault on Alfonso, that his son-in-law had deserved to die. Alexander seems to have accepted it but almost no one else did. Brandolinus gave the majority verdict on the murder of Bisceglie: it was, he wrote, motivated by 'the supreme lust for dominion of Cesare Valentino Borgia'.

Lucrezia, however, did not accept it. She grieved for Alfonso and raged against her father and brother. Her grief irritated and displeased Alexander and early in September she was packed off to Nepi to mourn out of sight. On 4 September, Cattaneo reported to Mantua that the Pope 'has sent away his daughter and his daughter-in-law and everyone except Valencia because in the end they were wearisome to him'. Cesare, ostentatiously guarded, visited Lucrezia the day after the unfortunate Alfonso had been privately and hastily interred, as Cattaneo reported: 'Valentia goes about very strong and heavily guarded now and the second day after Don Alfonso was most privately buried, this Valentia went to visit his sister D. Lucretia in her house which adjoins Valentia's apartments. From the Palace he entered her antechamber in the midst of one hundred halberdiers in full armour, and seems to have great suspicion of the Colonnesi and the King of Naples, it seeming to him that there can be no more friendship between them.'[22] Whether Lucrezia forgave him for murdering her husband, there is no way of knowing. It seems a proof of the extraordinary affection between them that Cesare could contemplate visiting her so soon. Perhaps he attempted to excuse himself on the grounds of Alfonso plotting against him; perhaps he also revealed to her his future campaign which would include the destruction of her first husband, Giovanni Sforza of Pesaro. He may even have told her of the plans he and Alexander had for her. On the day Lucrezia left for Nepi, her father was reported as already contemplating a third marriage for her, collecting money for her dowry with the nomination of further cardinals.[23]

The murder of Bisceglie, a deliberate act of terror, had had its effect. The Borgias, and Cesare in particular, were now regarded with fear and horror. As the Florentine Francesco Cappello wrote in a cipher letter reporting Bisceglie's death to his government: 'I pray Your Lordships to take this for your own information, and not to show it to others, for these [the Borgias] are men to be watched, otherwise they have done a thousand villainies, and have spies in every place.' That autumn, the Venetian envoy Polo Capello made a long report to the Senate concerning the Borgias. The Pope, he said 'is seventy and grows younger every day. Worries never last him a night: he loves life, and is of a joyful nature and does what suits him.' As Pope, his power in Rome was absolute: 'The Cardinals without the Pope can do zero'; only Giuliano della Rovere was marked down as a dangerous man. Alexander's resilience was indeed remarkable: neither his recent escape from death nor the murder of his son-in-law, not even his daughter's grief, affected him. Giulia Farnese, whose husband had been killed by a falling roof that August, had returned and was once more by his side. Capello's picture of Cesare was far more sinister: 'the Pope loves and fears his son who is twenty-seven, physically most beautiful, he is tall and well made . . . he is munificent, even prodigal, and this displeases the Pope'. As early as July the acute Cattaneo had diagnosed the scope of the Borgias' ambitions for Cesare. 'The Pope plans to make him great and king of Italy, if he can,' he wrote, 'nor am I dreaming but everything can be described and written down, and so that others will not think my brains are disordered, I will say no more . . .' Capello expressed similar opinions: 'He will be, if he lives, one of the first captains of Italy.' But while admitting Cesare's talent and physical beauty, Capello went on to depict him as a sadistic murderer, stabbing Perotto as he cowered under the Pope's cloak so that the blood spurted up in Alexander's face, ordering the death of Gandia and wholesale assassinations: 'Every day in Rome one finds men murdered, four or five a night, bishops, prelates and others . . .'

Capello continued, further accusing Cesare of incest with Lucrezia: 'And they say this Duke [sleeps with] his sister.' Apart from the charge of incest, Lucrezia escapes the general censure: formerly the Pope's favourite, she is 'wise and generous, but now the Pope does not love her so much and sends her to Nepi, and has given her Sermoneta which has cost 80,000 ducats, although the Duke has taken it from her, saying "She is a woman, she could not keep it."' Incestuous or not, there is no doubt that Cesare and Lucrezia loved each other above anyone else and remained loyal to each other to the end. Lucrezia was the only exception to Cesare's dismissal of women as irrelevant. To Bishop Soderini of Florence, discussing the brave, cruel and sexually insatiable Caterina Sforza, a remarkable woman by any standards, whom he was accused of abusing, he said later 'that he took no account of women'.

The murder of Bisceglie had indeed struck terror into the hearts of the Italian aristocratic families. Cesare's ruthlessness and his power made them wonder who he might strike next. The Gonzaga made fruitless attempts to enlist the protection of the Emperor Maximilian, comparing themselves and their fellow *signori* to condemned men who watch their friends hanged one by one without being able to help.[24] Earlier, as an insurance policy against attack by Cesare, the Gonzaga had begun negotiations for the marriage of Cesare's legitimate daughter by Charlotte d'Albret, Luisa, with their infant son and heir, Federico. A letter Isabella d'Este wrote to her husband, Francesco Gonzaga, on 29 July after the attack on Bisceglie shows the extreme nervousness with which they approached Cesare: she doubted the wisdom of sending an envoy to 'Valentino' to discuss his daughter's possible dowry, 'because he [Cesare] has little respect for me and even less than he has for Your Lordship. It has been agreed to use the means of the Illustrious Lady Lucrecia, as the Duke of Urbino reminds us . . .'[25] Only Lucrezia, it seems, was seen to have any influence with Cesare.

On 2 October, Cesare, accompanied by his personal staff and the customary signorial retinue of poets, singers and musicians, rode out of Rome northward up the Via Flaminia bound for his second campaign of conquest. Ahead of him marched his army of some 10,000 men – 700 men at arms, 200 light horse and 6,000 Spanish, Italian, Gascon and Swiss infantry, with an artillery train under the *condottiere* and lord of Città di Castello, Vitellozzo Vitelli. His captains were Spanish professionals – Miguel da Corella 'Michelotto', Juan de Cardona, Ugo de Moncada – his Italian *condottieri*, Paolo and Carlo Orsini, Gian Paolo Baglioni and Ercole Bentivoglio waited for him in Umbria and the Romagna. On his way north he stopped off to visit Lucrezia in exile in the fortress of Nepi.

5. Turning Point

'To speak clearly to His Majesty [King Louis XII of France] we will never consent to giving Madonna Lucretia to Don Alfonso [d'Este]: nor will Don Alfonso ever be induced to take her'

– Duke Ercole I d'Este of Ferrara, to his envoy at
the French court, Bartolommeo de'Cavalleri, 14 February 1501

From the citadel of Nepi in the two months of her exile there, October and November 1500, Lucrezia wrote a series of letters, some sad, some mysterious, to Vincenzo Giordano, her confidant, possibly her major-domo. The first was signed in her own hand 'the most unhappy princess of salerno', with the last three words, her title, crossed out, as if for greater emphasis. Written shortly after her arrival at Nepi, it was dated 15 September and its contents suggested that she had left in a hurry without many of the things she needed. Not surprisingly, given the suddenness of Alfonso's death, she was not sufficiently provided with mourning black either for clothes or furnishings. She specified 'our coverlet of black satin edged and striped in black velvet: with its [bed] furnishings'. She enclosed a list of other things she needed, including lye for laundering which should be sent as soon as possible because her supplies were exhausted. A later letter insisted that Giordano immediately send the black clothes she had ordered for '*la panderetta*' (possibly a slave) so that she could wear black 'for our present mourning'. In another letter she asked him to contact Cardinal Cosenza to arrange masses for the soul of Alfonso Bisceglie, paid for with the 500 ducats which she had given him.

By late October, some six weeks after she had left Rome,

Lucrezia's Borgia resilience had begun to reassert itself. Her letters to Giordano now had a practical tone which was both housewifely and commanding. In a letter of 28 October she ordered clothes and cloth for her son Rodrigo, now almost a year old, including '*tunicelle*' – little tunics, enclosing a design for them and ordering Giordano to see that they could be handed for delivery to Lorenzo, her groom, the bearer of the letter, as soon as possible. Acknowledging receipt of Rodrigo's *tunicelle*, she sent Giordano detailed instructions for elaborate bed hangings of black taffeta. She reproved him for having some clothes made up before she had had a chance to send the precise measurements; they would need letting out. 'We are amazed these things should be so costly, so much so that we tell you that when you compute the total that you write what you have computed . . . Do this for me so that you do and look well to everything so that we will know to give a good account of you . . .'[1] She wrote in great detail as to how the clothes and furnishings should be made up, seams should be covered with a strip of black silk, *capi* from one side to another should be garnished with fringes of black silk.

More interestingly, around that time her letters take on a secretive note, hinting at intrigues within the Vatican. In an autograph postscript to the letter to Giordano quoted above she enclosed a secret cipher letter for Caterina Gonzaga, the seductive lady of her letters from Pesaro in the summer of 1494, now apparently a close ally and perhaps even the 'favourite' of the Pope mentioned in the report of June 1500, asking him to request a written answer to the letter 'because it is very important'. Vincenzo, Lucrezia wrote, must not be surprised if the letter to Caterina was written in cipher 'because it is done for more secrecy and less scandal'. She was sending *capi* with the letter, wrapped in a paper which Lorenzo da Mila would bring to him: for some unexplained reason these caps were to be given 'secretly' to Caterina or to a certain Stefania.[2] A second letter is even more cryptic: 'The letter I have told you about for Caterina, give it to her secretly because it contains matters which should not be shown publicly. And I tell you that concerning this letter which you will give her say nothing to "*troccio*" [Francesco Troche, a confidential agent much employed by the Pope and Cesare, who was eventually murdered on Cesare's orders] for good reason. Send this messenger back quickly.'

Caterina Gonzaga, acting as Lucrezia's female contact in Rome, living in or frequenting the Vatican at the time, was equally mysterious, complaining to Giordano of the difficulty of communicating with Lucrezia. She had been so worried about the reception of her letters and parcels to Lucrezia that she was suffering from a quartain fever. She asked Giordano if he could come to the courtyard (*cortile*) in the Vatican where the Chancery (*cancelleria*) was, overlooked by the windows of the Pope's room. If he had received them (the letters and parcels) he should nod his head; if he did not do so she would take it that he had not.

This will be tomorrow, Monday, at the tenth hour, because our being at the window at that time and you being [there] I pray you so that I do not suffer more ... if you have had all seven advise me ... I have had one letter here for two days of much importance to the lady. I did not send it to her until I knew for sure that the letters had been received and as I said if you have not had these letters it will be necessary to reconsider as concerns this one I have. I will write to you how it can be certain that you have them, I will write to you on a piece of paper and put the letter in the packet in such a manner that no one will find it.

This was followed up by a reproof: 'vicenzo [sic], I can only marvel at you not having let me know as you should have if you have had the letters and what you have done with them ... Let me know as soon as possible ... if you have had two letters for Mons. De Venosa [the Bishop of Venosa, the Pope's doctor] and Corberan [a Borgia trusty] and one to our lady [Lucrezia]. For this may it be very soon [time] for me to leave Rome because I in this am with [sic] great danger ...'[3]

What danger threatened Caterina Gonzaga, who seems to have been a somewhat hysterical, foolish woman, the letters do not reveal. She appears to have faded from Lucrezia's life soon afterwards. Lucrezia was clearly angling for a return to Rome and on her own terms since, again emphasizing the need for secrecy, she expressed pleasure at the way Giordano's talks with 'Our Lord' [presumably the Pope] had been going and begged him to continue to advise her particularly on the proposals and answers which could not be entrusted to paper. She was sending with Lorenzo, the bearer of this letter, a letter for Caterina which she wanted him to give her as soon as possible. 'Also he brings a letter for the Cardinal of Capua [Juan Lopes] of the greatest importance concerning the matter you know of. Make sure you choose the way and the hour when he will not be with the Pope to give it to him or have it given him by Lorenzo as soon as possible and above all do not let this evening pass so that he can speak of it to the Pope because it is very important.' She had sent a letter for Cardinal Cosenza concerning the Spannocchi (the Borgias' Sienese bankers), and Giordano should for his own part speak to the cardinal about the necessities (presumably of paying for the goods ordered) which she had received.

Among her last letters was another mysterious missive to Giordano concerning her return to Rome, and her disappointment at not having heard from 'Farina' (Lucrezia's biographer, Ferdinand Gregorovius, hazards a guess that this could be Cardinal Farnese) and mentioning 'Rexa' (which Gregorovius thinks could be Alexander).

And as I wrote to you the other day with such melancholy so with as much greater pleasure I am writing you the present [letter] because Roble has arrived at this moment, safe and sound and as if by a miracle. It is true that he brought an order that I should not go to Rome. But I have remedied that by sending first this morning Messer Luis [?] Casalivio as I believe you have seen. Thus it seems to me that everything is going well there and that we have cause to thank God and his glorious Mother and thus I wish that as soon as possible I will have said the Masses of thanks. It seemed to be [good] to write to you all this for your consolation and to remove part of the fear that perhaps you felt.

Since things are going this way please see to it immediately that
they take up work on those things which you have ordered and to do
so in manner that at all costs they should be furnished in the time
promised and all the more because perhaps he will not return so soon
and I wish that you will get them there for Christmas Day.

I am sending you the enclosed letter which Roble brought for Rexa,
give it to him therefore quickly and tell him on my behalf that I thank
him greatly for the diligence he has employed for the coming of Roble
and that I am in such bad spirits and unease about my return to Rome
that I do not know how to describe it except that I weep continually
and that all these days seeing that Farina did not respond or write I
have not been able to eat or sleep . . . always in tears and that God
forgive Farina who could have remedied everything and did not do
so and that I will see if I can send Roble ahead before I leave . . . And
make sure that for no reason are you to show this letter to Rexa . . .

Lucrezia must have attached such importance to these mysterious letters from her time at Nepi that on her return to Rome
she took care to retrieve them and took them with the rest of
her important documents when she left Rome for her third
marriage. They were found among her papers in the Este archives
at Modena and, although referred to by Gregorovius (who,
however, mentioned neither Caterina Gonzaga nor the important Francesco Troche), are not mentioned by her principal
modern biographer, Maria Bellonci. The months Lucrezia spent
in Nepi after the murder of Alfonso Bisceglie marked a turning
point in her life. Whatever intrigue she might have been involved
in at the time, it is significant that she did not want Francesco
Troche to know of her letters, which suggests that she also wanted
to keep her father and brother in the dark. It seems likely that
in those lonely months she had determined she should take
control of her own life, which inevitably meant escaping from
the shadow of her father and brother. She talked of being 'in
such bad spirits and unease' about her return to Rome where,
once again, she would be involved in their plans.

In mid September, even before Lucrezia returned to Rome,

probably at the end of November or early December 1500, the acute Mantuan Gian Lucido Cattaneo had picked up rumours not merely of a third marriage but a very illustrious one, to Alfonso d'Este, son and heir to Duke Ercole of Ferrara.[4] This time the Borgias were aiming very high. The Este were one of the oldest and most prestigious families in Italy: of Lombard origin, they had ruled over various territories for nine hundred years, taking their name from the town of Este, south of the Euganean hills near Padua, of which they had been lords in the eleventh century. They had ruled Ferrara, their capital, as papal vicars since 1242 and subsequently acquired, as imperial fiefs, the lordships of Modena and Reggio. At their highest point their territory included the county of Rovigo between the rivers Po and Adige and their lands stretched across northern Italy from the Adriatic to the Apennines. Borso d'Este had acquired the title of Duke of Modena and Reggio from the Emperor Frederick III in 1452, and Duke of Ferrara from Pope Paul II in 1471. During the fifteenth century their court at Ferrara was one of the most splendid and cultivated of Renaissance Italy, while, unlike most of their contemporary rulers, their position as benevolent despots was secure with a loyal populace and a network of affiliated local aristocrats. The Este were accustomed to making the most splendid dynastic marriages: Alfonso d'Este's mother, late wife of the present Duke Ercole, was Eleonora d'Aragona, daughter of King Ferrante of Naples; his sister Isabella was married to Francesco Gonzaga, Marquis of Mantua, while his late sister, Beatrice, who died in 1497, had been the wife of Ludovico Sforza, Duke of Milan. The Este arms proclaimed their royal and imperial connections: to the original white eagle of the Este were added the French royal fleur-de-lis granted by Charles VII of France and the black crowned double-headed imperial eagle conferred by the Emperor Frederick III. Beside all this, the Borgia grazing bull was a humble creature. But in this, as in Lucrezia's other marriages, the power of her father and brother to affect international issues was to be crucial. And, once again, Lucrezia's marriage was designed to help Cesare's career.

It could be inferred from Lucrezia's mysterious correspondence with Rome that Cesare, on his way north to the Romagna early in October, had discussed with her the possibility of the Este marriage. By mid October he had chased her ex-husband, Giovanni Sforza, from Pesaro and the tyrant Pandolfo Malatesta out of Rimini with consummate ease. He was already lord of Imola and Forlì in the Romagna: the fall of Faenza would only be a matter of time. Bologna was within his sights. The state of Ferrara, on the northern border of the Papal States which Cesare intended to make his kingdom, would provide a useful buffer between his territories and those of powerful, aggressive Venice. While Ercole d'Este looked to France for protection, the international situation was once again swinging in favour of the Borgias. On 11 November a secret treaty was signed between Louis XII and Ferdinand of Aragon, partitioning the Kingdom of Naples between them: Louis XII was to be King of Naples, the Terra de Lavoro and the Abruzzi, Ferdinand was to take Puglia and Calabria with the title of Grand Duke. Both were to hold their lands in fief from the Church; the Pope, therefore, was to be a principal player. In the circumstances the King of France would have greater need to please the Pope than he would to accommodate the Duke of Ferrara.

There is no doubt that Lucrezia was as eager as her father and brother to achieve this marriage. To be the Duchess of an important state like Ferrara was certainly the highest position she could have aspired to – far beyond a mere Countess of Pesaro, or Duchess of tiny Bisceglie. Like Alexander and Cesare she was ambitious, clever and a realist. Rome had become oppressive to her, her surroundings a constant reminder of things she would rather forget. This was her chance to establish herself for life, to be no longer the pawn in Alexander and Cesare's high games. Like Cesare, she was aware that her chances of making such a marriage depended on the life of her father and the twists of international politics.

While Lucrezia was probably still in Nepi, the Pope had made it known to Ercole d'Este that he proposed a marriage between

Lucrezia and Alfonso. Ercole was appalled: not only were the Borgias a family of upstart foreigners, pushing to marry the illegitimate daughter of a pope into his illustrious family, but Lucrezia's reputation was of the worst kind. It was the Ferrarese envoy who had first reported to Ercole the birth of an illegitimate child in March 1498, and the Duke was well aware of the circumstances of her divorce from Giovanni Sforza and, indeed, of the murder of Alfonso Bisceglie. At just twenty, she was a woman with a shocking past. Ercole twisted and turned in his efforts to avoid the Borgia embrace.

Perhaps still unaware of the secret treaty between Ferdinand of Aragon and Louis XII, the horrified Ercole pressed for a French marriage for Alfonso. In December his envoy at the French court, the aged Bartolommeo de'Cavalleri, reported in his crabbed hand a discussion with the King who expressed a desire to have Don Alfonso at court where he would find him a suitable bride. Cavalleri suggested to Ercole that there were two good prospects for Alfonso, the daughter of the recently deceased Count of Foix, who later married Ferdinand of Aragon, and Marguerite d'Angoulême, sister to the heir to the French throne, the future Francis I.[5] In February 1501 Alexander made another attempt to press Lucrezia's suit. Ercole, not wishing to offend the Pope, had responded to the initial request by saying that the matter was out of his hands, that it was the responsibility of the King of France. Ercole began to press Cavalleri to prove the truth of what he had told Alexander: '. . . because we do not want His Majesty to govern himself according to the desire of the Pope, we would consider it a singular grace that he should show himself having already deliberated and decided for another matrimony'. He instructed Cavalleri to strain every nerve to ensure that the King would not compel him to give his son to Lucrezia: 'for to speak clearly to His Majesty we will never consent to giving Madonna Lucretia to Don Alfonso: nor will Don Alfonso ever be induced to take her'.[6]

Ten days later he reiterated his sentiments to Cavalleri, telling him the Pope had sent the Bishop of Elna, his nephew and

apostolic commissioner at Cesare's camp, to him to urge the
marriage. The King of France, he argued, should not seek to gratify the Pope in this because the Pope had more need of him (for
troops and money for Cesare) than Louis of the Pope. He urged
Cavalleri to do all he could so that the King would act 'to liberate us from this threat and peril'.[7]

Louis, in fact, was no keener on the marriage of Alfonso and
Lucrezia than was Ercole. In trickery, if not in skill, he was
Alexander's equal and in principle he saw no advantage to himself
in strengthening the Borgias' position which might give them an
advantage in negotiations with himself. In March he told Cavalleri
that he thought Ercole would be unwise to consider the Borgia
marriage since the Pope could die any day, and promised to give
Alfonso any bride he chose.[8] Through April and early May the
King kept Ercole's hopes of an advantageous French marriage
alive, while the Borgias piled contrary pressure on the unfortunate Duke of Ferrara. Giovanni Ferrari, Cardinal of Modena, was
deployed by Alexander to write Ercole letters stressing the advantages of the Borgia marriage because of the protection offered
by the friendship of the Duke Valentino in Romagna as well as
the friendship of the Pope.[9] Alexander also sent his most trusted
confidential agent, Francesco Troche, to the French court to ask
Louis to press Ercole to accept the marriage with Lucrezia; as a
result the powerful Cardinal de Rohan, who owed his cardinal's
hat to Cesare, told Cavalleri that he should write to his master
encouraging him to entertain the Borgia engagement.[10] Cesare
for his part kept up the pressure on Duke and King, sending
envoys to put the case for Lucrezia.

Ercole, still hoping that, if he could not have his first choice,
Mlle de Foix, who was apparently now promised to the King of
Hungary, Mlle d'Angoulême was still on offer, was overwhelmed
to receive Cavalleri's letter of 26 May which did not reach him
until 9 June. The news that the King now supported the Pope's
wishes threw him into paroxysms of rage and panic which he
expressed in a three-page letter to his envoy, repeating all his
previous arguments plaintively: 'And moreover having always

affirmed to the messengers of the pontiff that this matter of ours was in the hand of the most Christian King, trusting as we have said above: and now His Majesty writing to me according to the desire of the Pope: we are reduced to such perplexity that we do not know how to act: because since the beginning we have never been in favour of making this relationship with the pontiff. It does not seem to me to be apt to tell him absolutely that we do not wish it: because such a hostile response would make him most inimical towards us . . .' Ercole ended with a pathetic appeal for help to be transmitted to the King 'given that it matters most greatly to us . . .' In an anguished two-page postscript, he blamed Cavalleri for not preventing this, insisting he tell the King to inform the Pope that negotiations for a French marriage had gone too far and that the parties of the other part would not consent to their being broken off; therefore the marriage between Lucrezia and Alfonso was impossible. 'And this must be done immediately because we think that the Pope will not hesitate to send us the Royal Letters and to insist that we conclude the matter . . .' Cavalleri must act on the King so that the Pope 'will not become more inimical towards us than he is already . . .'[11]

In vain: on 13 June, a few days after this letter was written, Cesare was in Rome, conferring with his father as to how to push Ercole further. As evidence of his usefulness to the King of France, he was on his way with the French Marshal d'Aubigny to execute a brief, brutal and successful campaign to expel the royal house of Naples. The result of the Borgias' conference was immediately evident in Ferrara, where Ercole was subjected to a personal bombardment by representatives of the King, the Pope and Cesare, as he reported to Cavalleri: 'Yesterday the Archdeacon of Châlons, procurator of the King at Rome, arrived in Ferrara, sent by M. de Agrimont, the royal ambassador and Don Remolins first chamberlain of Duke Valentino and with him a messer Agostino, the papal commissary in [Cesare's] camp sent to Bologna by Duke Valentino, who presented us [Ercole] with letters from the King to the Duke Valentino and from M. de Agrimont, exhorting us to conclude the marriage [with Lucrezia] . . .'[12] Ercole was outraged that these messengers should appear before him in disguise — '*travestiti*' — as he complained to Cavalleri. Despite the pressure he was still determined not to give in over the Borgia marriage but equally he wanted Louis XII to take the responsibility for his refusal. He suggested a stratagem by which the King should write inviting Alfonso to the French court, upon which Ercole would immediately send him to find out the King's true mind on the matter. 'In this way time can be taken over this affair: the Pope will be kept in hope, knowing that Don Alfonso will have been called to France to discuss it. And His Majesty will be able to make use of the Pope, if at present he has need of him . . . and by this means perhaps God will inspire His Majesty to exercise some good and sound remedy to liberate us entirely from this difficulty in which we find ourselves.' The King must understand that if he would not do this 'the Pope will immediately become our enemy and always by every means will seek to ruin us and do us every evil he can . . .' In a postscript he insisted on a French marriage for Alfonso, if not to either of the ladies suggested, then to another. Anyone, in short, but Lucrezia Borgia. And in a second alarmed letter of the same day he urged, 'His Majesty should not reveal this to the Pope or to his own people . . . so great is the danger we run if the Pope understood what our disposition was . . . we are in very grave fear . . .'

Again, Ercole's pathetic pleas were to no avail. On 22 June, Cavalleri sent a letter to Ercole more or less indicating that the game was up: Louis XII absolutely refused to write anything on Ercole's behalf, although he had written four lines in his own hand endorsing the Pope's messenger. The King riposted that Duke Ercole was old and wise and knew more while asleep than he [Louis] did while awake. His cynical advice was that if Ercole was really not minded to make this match, he should make such demands that the Pope himself would not want to go ahead with it. As a sweetener, Louis's envoy to the Borgias, Louis de Villeneuve, Baron de Trans, told Cavalleri that to encourage Ercole to make this marriage he was to get 200,000 ducats and absolution from the papal census, an estate for his second son, Ferrante, plus benefices for Cardinal Ippolito and support for Ercole's desire to regain his lost lands of the Polesine di Rovigo. The King, as if to underscore the difficulty of dealing with Alexander, pointed out that the Pope was asking 50,000 scudi in return for the investiture of the Kingdom of Naples for Louis, plus an income of 18,000 scudi for Cesare and a state for his 'nephews' – presumably Giovanni Borgia and Rodrigo Bisceglie. Furthermore, he said, he himself might die any day and his successor might have no interest in Italy, and the money Ercole was now being offered by the Pope would provide for his future security and that of his state. To Cavalleri, these seemed, as he wrote to Ercole, 'wise words' which he hastened to transmit.[13]

Ercole had by now realized that further resistance was impossible: his resigned response to Cavalleri's letter of the 22nd was that in view of Louis's need of the Pope, and in order to do his Christian Majesty a service, he was prepared to agree to the marriage.[14] Meanwhile Louis, involved in outrageously greedy negotiations with the Pope over the investiture of Naples, urged Cavalleri to advise Ercole to draw out the business with the Pope for as long as he could. On 7 July, Cavalleri reported that the Pope had told the King that he had given the Bull of Investiture to Cardinal Sanseverino and that in return Louis and the King of Spain had to pay 150,000 ducats within the space of three months. In order to keep up the pressure on the Pope, Louis repeated his advice to Ercole to prolong the marriage negotiations, even holding out the original prospect of Mlles de Foix and d'Angoulême for Alfonso. He excused his letter supporting the Pope in his pressure for the conclusion of Lucrezia's marriage because of his present need of the Pope's goodwill. If Don Alfonso came to France, Cavalleri added, he hoped 'everything would go well'.[15]

But the time for tergiversation was over: by early July, Ercole had lain down his arms and accepted his – and Alfonso's – fate. Cavalleri informed Louis that in the Duke's view 'the practical overcame the honourable', a sentiment which the King applauded, although he still held out the bait of a French bride should the

Borgia marriage not come about. Louis added that if Alfonso did marry Lucrezia, he would understand that Alfonso was doing it unwillingly. Haggling and trickery continued on all three sides: Ercole reacted angrily to the accusation that he had made 'impertinent demands' on the Pope. He ordered Cavalleri to bring the negotiations to a conclusion on the agreement of 100,000 ducats of dowry, leaving the fulfilment of the other proposals to the Pope. He added, with some justification, that had it not been for his wish to serve the King, the matter could have been resolved three months earlier.[16] Later that month Cesare's man, Remolins, one of the chief negotiators, returned from Ferrara with a portrait of Alfonso to be presented to Lucrezia.[17] The Mantuan envoy Cattaneo had already noted on 11 August that Lucrezia appeared to have abandoned her mourning (even though it was less than a year since the murder of Alfonso Bisceglie): 'Up to now Donna Lucretia, according to Spanish usage has eaten from earthenware and maiolica. Now she has begun to eat from silver as if almost no longer a widow.'[18]

Early in August, Ercole wrote a note to the person who perhaps most influenced him in his decision and whose enmity he greatly feared – Cesare Borgia: 'Your Lordship will have heard that we have come to the conclusion of the marriage between the Illustrious Madonna Lucretia, your Excellency's sister, and the Illustrious Don Alfonso, our firstborn . . .' This had been done, he said, because of the reverence he had for the Pope and the virtues of Lucrezia but 'far more still from the love and affection we bear Your Excellency . . .'[19]

The Borgias now knew that they had won. The marriage contract was drawn up in the Vatican on 26 August, with Alexander writing out the terms in his own hand.[20] The nuptial contract was concluded, and the marriage *ad verba presente*, took place in the Palazzo Belfiore on 1 September 1501. On 5 September Ercole wrote to Cavalleri to inform the King of the terms concluded for Lucrezia's dowry: 100,000 ducats in cash, plus the castles and lands of Cento and La Pieve with an annual income amounting to some 3,000 ducats. While Cento and La Pieve could not immediately be handed over since they were part of the diocese of Bologna, Cesare had pledged his castles in the territory of Faenza until the deal could be concluded. Any shortfall in income, meanwhile, would be supplemented by the Pope – no wonder Alexander commented that the Duke of Ferrara 'bargained like a tradesman'. Beyond this the Pope would reduce the census which Ercole paid the Pope for Ferrara and his lands in Romagna from 4,500 ducats to 100 ducats a year. Mentally rubbing his hands together, Ercole told Cavalleri that he estimated the total value of the deal at 400,000 ducats.

Nonetheless, Ercole wished it to be understood that only a desire to serve the King of France and preserve good relations between him and the Pope had induced him 'to condescend to such an unequal relationship', as he wrote to Cavalleri on 5 September.[21] Because of his loyalty to the King of France, he added, he had resisted the angry opposition of the Emperor Maximilian to the marriage, and he had underlined the reason for his agreement to the marriage in the nuptial contract by specifying that it was the wish of the King of France. In a later letter he admitted that fear of the Borgias had played its part: '. . . we would have made His Holiness our greatest enemy if we had refused, and having the Lord Duke of Romagna [Cesare], with a great and fine State beside ours, there is no doubt that His Holiness would be able to damage us greatly . . .'[22]

To Lucrezia he wrote a graceful if wry letter announcing the completion of the marriage '*per parola de presente*': 'We rejoice for this with you whom first we loved uncommonly for your singular virtues and for our reverence for The Holiness of Our Lord and as the sister of the Most Illustrious Duke of Romagna who we hold as an honoured brother: now we love you intimately as more than daughter, hoping that through you there will come the continuation of our posterity: and we will operate so that you should be with us as soon as possible . . .'[23]

Lucrezia no doubt took this letter in the spirit it was intended. She cannot have been unaware of the difficulties her father and brother had encountered in pressing the reluctant Duke into acceptance of a marriage to which he had an extreme aversion. She had been entrusted by her father with the administration of the Vatican in July, while he toured Sermoneta and the lands recently acquired from the Caetani.[24] As Burchard had reported: 'Before His Holiness, our Master, left the city, he turned over the palace and all the business affairs to his daughter Lucretia, authorizing her to open all letters which should come addressed to him . . .' This time she was no mere pawn in the process managed by her father and brother but an active participant in the negotiations for her proposed marriage, as Ercole himself acknowledged in a postscript to a letter he wrote her on 2 September: 'Lady Lucretia. Because in the instrument drawn up concerning your dowry a certain article has been remitted to your decision and judgement and that of the Most Illustrious Lord Duke of Romagna. We would urge Your Ladyship not to come to any declaration until you have first discussed it with our representatives who are on their way to you.'

The historian Guicciardini, no friend to the Borgias, gave his verdict on the marriage:

Although this marriage was most unworthy of the house of Este, wont to make the most noble alliances, and all the more unworthy because Lucrezia was illegitimate and stained with great infamy, Ercole and Alfonso consented because the French King, desiring to satisfy the Pope in all things, made strong importunities for this union. Besides this they were motivated by a desire for securing themselves by such means from the arms and ambitions of Valentino (if, against such perfidy, any security whatever were sufficient). For Valentino, now powerful with the monies and authority of the Apostolic See and the favour which the French King bore him, was already formidable throughout a great part of Italy, and everyone knew that his cupidity had neither limit nor bridle.[25]

6. Farewell to Rome

'His Holiness went from window to window of the Palace to catch
the last glimpse of his beloved daughter'

– Beltrando Costabili, Ferrarese envoy in Rome,
to Duke Ercole, describing Lucrezia's departure from
the city for Ferrara, 6 January 1502

The news of Lucrezia's marriage became public in Rome on 4
September 'around the hour of vespers', celebrated by the firing
of continual rounds of cannon from Sant'Angelo. The next day
Lucrezia, wearing a dress of golden brocade ornamented with
curled gold thread, rode from the Palazzo Santa Maria in Portico
to the church of Santa Maria del Popolo accompanied by three
hundred horsemen and preceded by four bishops and followed
by her considerable household. 'On the same day,' recorded
Burchard, 'from the hour of supper until the third hour of night,
the great bell of the Capitol was rung, and many fires and beacons
lit on the castle of Sant'Angelo and all over the city, and lights
on the towers of the castle and the Capitol and elsewhere, incit-
ing everyone to celebrate with joy. The next day, two jesters to
whom Lucrezia had given her golden dress worth 300 ducats and
other clothing, went about the city shouting 'Viva the most illustrious Duchess of Ferrara! Viva Pope Alexander!'

On 15 September, Cesare arrived back from the Naples
campaign; the next day the Borgia family celebrations in the
Vatican began in earnest. The Florentine envoy Francesco Pepi
reported on the 17th: 'Although yesterday and today I went to
the Palace to see the Pope, he has given audience to no one
because he was occupied all yesterday concerning the marriage

and dowry of Madonna Lucrezia, and in dancing, music and
singing . . .'¹ Alexander adored the sight of beautiful women dancing and of his daughter in particular. One evening he called the
Ferrarese ambassadors to him to watch her, joking 'that they might
see the Duchess was not lame'. Both Cesare and Lucrezia were
exhausted by the constant round of entertainments organized by
their indomitable father. On 23 September, Gherardo Saraceni,
one of the Ferrarese envoys, reported that Cesare had received
them fully dressed but lying on his bed: 'I feared that he was sick,
for last evening he danced without intermission, which he will
do again tonight at the Pope's palace, where the illustrious Duchess
(Lucrezia) is going to sup.' Two days later he wrote of Lucrezia:
'The illustrious lady continues somewhat ailing and is greatly
fatigued . . . The rest which she will have while His Holiness is
away will do her good; for whenever she is at the Pope's palace,
the entire night, until two or three o'clock, is spent at dancing
and at play, which fatigues her greatly.' Lucrezia may have inherited her father's mental resilience but not his physical robustness:
her health was never strong. Alexander on the other hand never
tired; one day when he was suffering from a bad cold and had
lost a tooth, he remarked to the Ferrarese ambassador: 'If the
Duke [Ercole] were here, I would, even if my face were tied up,
invite him to go and hunt wild boar.'

On 25 September, Alexander and Cesare left Rome to inspect
the fortifications at Nepi and Civita Castellana, north-east of
Rome. Once again Lucrezia was appointed her father's regent in
the Vatican. Saraceni and his fellow envoy Berlinguer visited her
constantly, attempting, they told Ercole, to find a way to present
themselves to the Pope through her. They reported her state of
health:

The illustrious Madonna persists still in her little indisposition, saying
that it is no more than weakness, nor for this nor otherwise because
of [taking] medicine will she cease to carry on her affairs: and she gives
audiences as she is accustomed to nor do we believe that this indisposition will last longer because in truth Her Ladyship looks after

herself very well and also we believe that the rest of these few days
. . . must do her good, because these times that Her Ladyship visited
the Pope, they spent in dancing and celebration until the eighth or
ninth hour, something that very much harmed Her Ladyship.[2]

Lucrezia had quite won over the Ferrarese who were impressed
by her constantly expressed desire to be in Ferrara: 'Her Ladyship
does not cease every day to ask when we believe that she may
be leaving here, because in truth one hour seems a thousand until
she is able to be at Ferrara to do reverence to Your Excellency
and find herself in the sight of the Most Illustrious Don Alfonso
. . . and here now seems a prison to her . . . so great is her desire
to come: and the fear of bad weather [which would delay her
journey], that she with most great affection seeks to know the
time which Your Excellency has established to send for [her] . . .'[3]
Lucrezia was only too aware that many things could go wrong:
she did not trust the Este, her marriage depended on the continuance in power of her father and her brother; she could not be
sure of the outcome until she was safely in Ferrara, her marriage
to Alfonso – who had resolutely remained distant and out of
touch – consummated. Ercole, however, was determined that she
should stay in Rome until he had got everything he wanted out
of the Pope. When she expressed herself as 'most impatient' to
leave Rome, the ambassadors told her that her arrival was much
desired in Ferrara but equally 'her presence in Rome was too
necessary to conduct to a good end all the conventions through
the great influence she has on the mind of His Holiness'.

One unspoken condition of the marriage was the most personally difficult for her. On 27 September, after dinner, Lucrezia
offered to show the envoys round the Vatican: her son, Rodrigo
Bisceglie, not quite two years old, was with her. When the envoys
tactfully raised the subject of his future, she replied, apparently
with no show of emotion, that he would remain in Rome with
an allowance of 15,000 ducats. It could be deduced that the Este
had indicated that they would prefer Lucrezia to come to Ferrara
with the appearance at least of a virgin bride and without any

of the baggage of her previous life. The spectre of the murdered Alfonso Bisceglie hung over his son as an unpleasant reminder of Lucrezia's scandalous past. It was terrible for Lucrezia to be parted from the son who had been with her since birth but as a realist, a Borgia and a woman of her time, she accepted it, apparently without question. The infant Rodrigo had his part to play in the Borgias' dynastic plans to consolidate their power around Rome at the expense of the local barons. That month of September 1501, the child was entrusted to the guardianship of Francesco Borgia, Cardinal Cosenza, and created Duke of Sermoneta with estates including the Caetani lands purchased by Lucrezia and some of the recently confiscated Colonna lands in a new Borgia duchy. Giovanni Borgia, born in 1498, had his part to play in this reshuffle of Borgia lands necessitated by Lucrezia's departure for Ferrara. He was legitimized in two successive Bulls, the first declaring him to be the son of Cesare before his marriage, the second acknowledging him as Alexander's son. As the Borgias' historian Michael Mallett has pointed out, the timing of these Bulls may have been designed to counteract the rumours that Giovanni Borgia was an illegitimate son of Lucrezia; copies of them were among the many documents that the careful Lucrezia took with her to Ferrara. Again to avoid awkward memories, the Pope had requested that Giovanni Sforza, despite being linked to the Este family, should not be present in Ferrara when Lucrezia arrived for the nuptials. Among the subjects raised with Lucrezia was that of the census which Ercole now wished to be remitted to his heirs in perpetuity, though the Pope had not wished to change the terms of the Bull. The envoys had appealed both to Lucrezia and Cesare to change Alexander's mind: 'The Duchess had spoken to him of this the previous evening but without result; and she thought it was necessary to put off the demand to another time.' The Pope had apparently told her that it would be necessary to pawn her jewels to raise the cash for her dowry since Ercole had refused to take them in lieu. But she said they would not be taken from her and she still hoped the Pope would find other means to raise the money. She cunningly told them that 'His Holiness increasingly believed her to be too zealous for the interests of the Estensi'.[4]

Lucrezia hastened to give Ercole the same impression, assuring him in her letters that she would do everything possible to serve him. 'As to the particulars to negotiate with His Holiness I will make every effort to execute justly my debt to you [and] with every reverence and swiftness to observe your orders as you will see at greater length in the letters of your ambassadors . . .' she wrote on 28 September, following it up with an even more ingratiating letter on 8 October. She was taking the opportunity of the departure of the messenger for Ferrara to send Ercole a few lines in her own hand in place of a visit in person: 'meanwhile with the help of God I will be able to revere and serve you as is my only desire: concerning the other things which are being negotiated, I am sure Your Illustrious Lordship will be informed by your most diligent envoys . . .'[5]

In return, Lucrezia received the most charming letter from her prospective father-in-law:

So great is the love and affection we bear Your Illustrious Ladyship and so pleasing is everything to do with you that, having received your letter of the 8th which you sent me in place of a personal visit which has brought us greater pleasure, delight and content than any visit, even personal which could be made by any other person, because reading Your Ladyship's letter so full of sweetness, it seems as if we were seeing you and talking to you whose presence we desire as much as anything else we have ever had to heart, to be able to welcome you and treat you in a manner suited to a most beloved daughter. And thus we as you see are not failing on our side to do everything necessary so that your arrival here should not be delayed . . .[6]

Behind the sweet words, however, the haggling between Pope and Duke continued. Lucrezia played her part, assuring Ercole that she was on his side. She had understood from the envoys, she wrote on 11 October, how great was his desire for the extension of the remission of the census beyond the third generation of his descendants:

So desirous as your devoted and most obedient daughter to do all I possibly can in everything . . . I have recently with great insistence besought His Holiness Our Lord [about this] and although I understand it to be a somewhat difficult matter yet Your Excellency can be certain that for my part here I will endeavour to work on His Holiness so that you will recognize how great is my desire to serve and to please you: for this reason I have today been with the Cardinal of Modena who is most devoted to you and begun to set the matter in order: so that I hope that on the return of the aforesaid Holiness, I will be able to do something pleasing to Your Excellency, whom I again beseech to be of quiet and tranquil mind.[7]

Engaged in preparations for the bride's sumptuous reception in Ferrara, Ercole sent to Rome asking for details of the Borgia ancestry to be used in the customary welcoming orations at the wedding festivities.[8] A fake genealogy was hastily cobbled together representing the Borgias as descendants of Don Pedro de Atares, feudal lord of Borja and pretender to the throne of Aragon. The claim was entirely baseless since Don Pedro died without successors, although this was either not known or not admitted at the time.[9] The ambassadors had to report that, although in Spain the house of Borgia was certainly most noble and ancient, they had had trouble finding outstanding deeds by their forebears and suggested that the oration should concentrate on the achievements of Popes Calixtus and Alexander. Since tales of high deeds and chivalric romance (such as Ariosto's *Orlando Furioso* featuring the house of Este) were considered an essential part of the history of noble families, the Borgias' failure to produce anything better than a dubious relationship to the shadowy Don Pedro de Atares was of particular embarrassment, emphasizing the difference in social standing between their family and the Este.

While wrangling continued through the medium of the envoys on such subjects as whether the dowry was to be calculated in '*fiorini di camera*', as the Pope wished, or *ducati larghi*, as the Duke demanded, Lucrezia found a new way in which she could earn Ercole's gratitude. Ercole was extremely pious and his hobby was collecting nuns. And of all nuns, those who showed the sign of the stigmata, or Christ's wounds on their bodies, were the most prized. Whatever modern Catholics may think of the phenomenon, to deeply religious people such as Ercole they were a new manifestation of Christ's passion: 'These things,' he wrote, 'are shown by the Supreme Craftsman in the bodies of His servants to confirm and strengthen our Faith, and to remove the incredulity of impious men and hard of heart.'[10] Such nuns were considered a badge of honour, even a tourist attraction in their local towns. The three most famous women of the time were Sister Columba of Rieti, who lived in a convent in Perugia, Sister Osanna Andreassi of Mantua and Ercole's particular target, Sister Lucia Brocadelli of Narni, at the time in a convent in Viterbo. He had even tried to persuade his daughter Isabella d'Este to bring Sister Osanna (who was later to predict, to everyone's satisfaction, that Cesare's rule in the Romagna would be 'like unto a straw fire') to Ferrara, a request which Isabella cunningly evaded. He had, however, after a series of cloak-and-dagger episodes, succeeded in having Sister Lucia smuggled out of her Dominican convent in Viterbo and brought to Ferrara on 7 May 1499. Less than a month later, he had laid the first stone of the convent he had promised to build for her and on 29 May 1500 he had obtained from Alexander a Bull enabling him to establish for Lucia a convent of sisters of the third order of St Dominic, followers of St Catherine of Siena, and conferring special privileges and chief authority upon 'our beloved daughter in Christ, Lucia da Narni . . .' By the summer of 1501, the fame of Sister Lucia had spread even to the French court where the Queen sent messages to Ercole asking him to obtain Sister Lucia's prayers to God to give her a son.[11] In order to make Lucia happy, Ercole had resolved to get some of her former friends, nuns from Narni and Viterbo, and had sent his emissary Bartolommeo Bresciano for the purpose, only to meet with an absolute refusal from the prior of the Dominicans. In this impasse, Ercole turned to the one person he knew to have influence with the Pope – Lucrezia.

Bresciano was sent on to Rome to Lucrezia with a letter from

Ercole of 28 September asking her help. When he arrived on 11 October he was deeply impressed with Lucrezia and her eagerness to help: 'In truth this Lady has taken up this thing with all her powers to gratify Your Lordship, and I find her so well disposed to you that she could not be more. I hope that Your Excellence will be well satisfied with the most Illustrious Madonna, for she is endowed with so much graciousness and goodness that she continually thinks of nothing else, save how to serve you.'[12] The affair took on the aspect of comedy as the two nuns Bresciano had brought to Rome then absolutely refused on the feeblest of excuses to be sent to Ferrara, while the authorities in Viterbo and Narni in turn refused to let the women whom Sister Lucia had requested go. Lucrezia gave them a good scolding and the heads of the Dominican order, intimidated by the will of the Pope's daughter, instructed them to give way. In a stream of impassioned, almost hysterical letters, Ercole implored Lucrezia's help, which she, intent on her marriage and anxious to please her father-in-law, willingly gave. She had taken up his case with the Pope, she soothed him on 28 October, and she was sure that he would give Ercole entire satisfaction in this matter. 'Be of good heart,' she adjured him, 'because in this and every other affair concerning you I hope to achieve what you desire.'[13] By December the nuns Ercole had requested were on their way to Rome to be sent on to Ferrara: his letters to Lucrezia were effusive with gratitude: 'We have heard . . . that all the sisters we have requested are now in Rome with the intention of being brought here,' he wrote on 28 December. 'We have received singular pleasure and content from this [and] incredible satisfaction: and we could not thank Your Ladyship more, seeing that with your prudence and favour you have brought this matter to this end . . .'[14] She could have found no better way to win his heart.

From all the reports of the Ferrarese envoys in Rome to Ercole, it is clear that Lucrezia herself handled the negotiations and that the Ferrarese, rather than speaking directly to the Pope, generally used her as their intermediary. This cleverly underlined her importance in the eyes of the Ferrarese, as it was made clear that

any concessions made by the Pope were gained by her intercession. Indeed, Alexander and Cesare were out of Rome on two
occasions that autumn – in late September visiting Nepi, Civita
Castellana and other Borgia fortresses and from 10 to 17 October
touring the former Colonna properties – Lucrezia being left as
regent in the Vatican.

Lucrezia was involved in every aspect of the discussions, from
Ercole's demands for the archbishopric of Bologna for Ippolito
d'Este, which necessitated her writing to Giuliano della Rovere
asking him to renounce the archbishopric in Ippolito's favour, to
the wrangling over income of the Romagna castles to be given
as pledges for the eventual consignment of Cento and La Pieve,
and the financial agreements over the dowry. Saraceni and
Berlinguer reported to Ercole the extreme difficulty they were
having over the banker Jacopo de'Gianuzzi's absolute refusal to
deliver a sum of money to Ferrara. Then, they said, Lucrezia
stepped in to resolve the situation: 'When the Illustrious Lady
heard of the difficulties over this matter, and understanding that
perhaps this could delay her departure [for Ferrara], she sent for
Messer Jacopo and spent a long time in discussion with him.' The
upshot was that the banker agreed to provide the cash within
three days of presentation of the letters of exchange in agreed
places without taking any commission. There was a discussion
over jewels: the Pope asked in jest what he could expect to see
from Ercole so that perhaps he would not have to provide them
himself. The envoys replied in the same vein, that with the jewels
she already possessed, those the Pope intended to give her and
those which Ercole would give her 'she will be the best-equipped
Lady with jewels in Italy'. Alexander questioned the richness of
the brocade which the Ferrarese intended to give her, considering that he would send her with four most beautiful lengths of
golden brocade. 'Thus the Pope was laughing and joking along
these lines for a very considerable time,' the envoys reported,

and in truth His Holiness being very splendid and high-spirited enjoyed
this exchange because from every honour that has been done and will

be done to the aforesaid Lady [Lucrezia] he derives as much joy as it
is possible to describe, and thus holds it most dear that in all things
she should be the chief, and moreover at the same time having said
something about the investiture of Ferrara [the census] and the confirmation of matters relating to the bishopric of Ravenna, His Holiness
said how the aforesaid Lady had spoken to him of them, and that everything will be done in good form, saying give the letters to the Duchess:
because she is your good procurator [representative].[15]

Alexander never missed an opportunity to impress the Ferrarese
with Lucrezia's qualities. When they complained that they had
not been able to obtain an audience with Cesare, the Pope sympa-
thized with them, saying that Cesare had left the envoys of Rimini
waiting for an audience for two months. 'He lamented that [the
Duke] turned night into day and day into night, comporting
himself in such a manner that it left room for doubt that if his
father died he would be able to keep what he had conquered.
He commended the Duchess Lucrezia as the opposite for her
prudence and willingness to receive [people] benevolently, praising the way in which she had governed Spoleto, and the way in
which she could capture the heart of the pontiff in every matter
she dealt with him . . .'[16] On another occasion he praised her
again as beautiful and prudent, comparing her with the Duchess
of Urbino and the Marchioness of Mantua, both of whom were
famous for their intelligence and culture.

Minute observers of Lucrezia's life as they were, none of the
four Ferrarese officials in Rome mentioned an extraordinary
episode recorded by Burchard, of an orgy which he said took
place in the Vatican on 30 October, five days after the Pope and
Cesare returned from the tour of inspection of the Borgia fortress
of Civita Castellana:

On Sunday evening, the last day of October, there took place in the
apartments of the Duke Valentino in the Apostolic Palace, a supper,
participated in by fifty honest prostitutes of those who are called courtesans. After supper they danced with the servants and others who were

there, first clothed, then naked. After supper the lighted candelabra which had been on the table were placed on the floor, and chestnuts thrown among them which the prostitutes had to pick up as they crawled between the candles. The Pope, the Duke and Lucrezia, his sister, were present looking on. At the end they displayed prizes, silk mantles, boots, caps, and other objects which were promised to whomsoever should have made love to those prostitutes the greatest number of times . . .

That Cesare did at least give a party that night in the Vatican is attested by another source, the Florentine envoy Pepi, who reported on 4 November that the Pope had not attended mass in St Peter's or the papal chapel on the days of All Saints' and All Souls' because of an indisposition which, he added cautiously in cipher, 'did not impede him on Sunday night, the vigil of All Saints', from spending the night until the twelfth hour with the Duke who had brought into the palace that night singers, courtesans, and all the night they spent in pleasures, dancing and laughter . . .' Of the two accounts of the notorious 'Chestnut Supper', Pepi's sounds the most plausible. Courtesans of the first rank, like Cesare's Fiammetta, were an essential part of a lively, informal party in early sixteenth-century Rome; whether Lucrezia was actually there, Pepi does not say. As a Borgia, she was unshockable, and equally loved parties, dancing and singing, as the Ferrarese accounts of finding her worn out by Alexander's late evenings attest. Hot chestnuts are traditional at that particular time of year but when it comes to nakedness and sexual contests the only witness is Burchard who must have had one eye to the keyhole and the other on posterity.

Just over two weeks later Burchard had another 'incident' to report, again heavily spiced with sexual connotations and specifically involving Lucrezia. A peasant had brought mares loaded with wood into the city through the Porta Viridaria near the Vatican:

When the mares reached the Piazza San Pietro, some of the palace guard came up, cut through the straps and threw off the saddles and the wood in order to lead the mares into the courtyard immediately inside the palace gate. Four stallions were then freed from their reins and harness and let out of the palace stables. They immediately ran to the mares, over whom they proceeded to fight furiously and noisily among themselves, biting and kicking in their attempts to mount them and seriously wounding them with their hoofs. The Pope and Madonna Lucrezia, laughing and with evident satisfaction, watched all that was happening from a window above the palace gate.

Although Burchard clearly disapproves, most people of the time had an earthy sense of humour and would have found it funny – if, indeed, it did occur. It found an echo with the rabidly anti-Borgia chronicler Matarazzo of Perugia, whose bloodthirsty lords, the Baglioni, had every reason to hate the Borgias. Matarazzo found it necessary to spice it up: 'And as if this were not enough, [the Pope] returning to the hall, had all the lights put out, and then all the women who were there, and as many men as well, took off all their clothes; and there was much festivity and play.'

At about this time a vitriolic attack on the Borgias, apparently originating in Venice where several of Cesare's enemies had taken refuge, circulated in the form of a letter to Silvio Savelli, one of the expropriated Roman barons. It accused them of being 'worse than the Scythians, more perfidious than the Carthaginians, more cruel than Caligula and Nero'. It included every charge hitherto levelled against them including murder – of Bisceglie and Perotto – and incest. Burchard's chestnut supper and rutting stallions were included (whether the anonymous author got these from Burchard or Burchard appropriated them to liven up his text one can only speculate). The terms used to describe Alexander and Cesare were particularly bitter:

His father favours him [Cesare] because he has his own perversity, his own cruelty: it is difficult to say which of these two is the most execrable. The cardinals see all and keep quiet and flatter and admire the Pope. But all fear him and above all fear his fratricide son, who from being a cardinal has made himself into an assassin. He lives like the Turks, surrounded by a flock of prostitutes, guarded by armed soldiers. At his order or decree men are killed, wounded, thrown into the Tiber, poisoned, despoiled of all their possessions.

It was typical of Alexander that this vicious diatribe made him laugh, and when Silvio Savelli came to Rome a year later he received him with the utmost amiability. Cesare, however, was far less relaxed than his father when it came to insult. In the first week of December, shortly after the publication of the letter, a man who had been going masked about the Borgo uttering scurrilous rumours about him was arrested on his orders and thrown into the Savelli prison where his right hand and part of his tongue were cut off and exposed at the window with the tongue hanging from the little finger. Alexander liked to contrast his own tolerance with his son's vengefulness: 'The Duke,' he told Beltrando Costabili, 'is a good-hearted man, but he cannot tolerate insults . . . I could easily have had the Vice-Chancellor [Ascanio Sforza] and Cardinal Giuliano della Rovere killed: but I did not wish to harm anyone . . .' It was a curious remark for a pope to make.

In the wake of all this, the Ferrarese envoy Gian Luca Pozzi felt obliged to reassure Ercole d'Este as to the virtuous character of his future daughter-in-law:[17] 'Madonna Lucrezia is a most intelligent and lovely, also exceedingly gracious lady. Besides being extremely graceful in every way, she is modest and lovable and decorous. Moreover she is a devout and god-fearing Christian. Tomorrow she is going to confession, and during Christmas week she will receive communion. She is very beautiful, but her charm of manner is still more striking. In short, her character is such that it is impossible to suspect anything "sinister" of her . . .'

Finally, after endless delays instigated by Ercole who had originally sent the list of personnel to be included to the Pope for approval in October, the wedding escort left Ferrara on 9 December. It was headed by Ercole's fourth son, Cardinal Ippolito d'Este, who with the ducal chancellor Giovanni ('Zoanne' in Ferrarese dialect) Ziliolo, took with him caskets of jewels for the bride, and an inventory signed on each page by Ercole the previous day. The remaining Este jewels were not to be given to Lucrezia until she actually reached Ferrara, and even the handing over of those to be delivered to her by Ippolito in Rome was to be governed by strict instructions based on Ercole's mistrust of the Borgias.

The Borgias' riposte to the Este was a display of astonishing richness. Lucrezia's trousseau of dresses and jewels surpassed in splendour the most lavish of recent years, that of Bianca Maria Sforza to the Emperor Maximilian I in 1495. Recently, a papal chamberlain had died, leaving 13,000 ducats in money and goods; Lucrezia had asked for and obtained it as an addition to her funds. It was obvious from the Inventory of her Wardrobe made in Ferrara in 1502–3 that she had kept her wedding presents as well as her dowries from her previous marriages. Among the goods mentioned which she took with her to Ferrara was the magnificent silver service presented to her by Ascanio Sforza on her marriage to Giovanni in 1493, when her dowry of 30,000 ducats was supplemented by 10,000 ducats' worth of dresses, jewels, plate, ornaments and 'things for the use of illustrious women'. Her dowry at her marriage to Alfonso Bisceglie had been 40,000 ducats, half of which Alexander had given in kind – jewels, dresses etc.[18] Lucrezia was a woman of her time in her awareness of the power of display, and her clothes, jewels and possessions were designed to impress the Este with her family's wealth and prestige.

She had ordered more than fifty underdresses of the richest materials: gold brocade lined with turquoise taffeta, and sleeves in the French style lined with crimson satin; one of cloth of gold striped with violet satin and lined with half-turquoise and half-green taffeta, the wide French-style sleeves again lined with violet (satin); another was made of black velvet sewn with golden toggles linked by gold cords with lining and sleeves of turquoise damask; others were made of '*tabi*' – watered silk – of black velvet striped with grey satin. Then there were basques, underskirts, robes, tabards, capes, among which two were particularly notable for their magnificence – one of violet satin, lined with ermine and adorned with 84 balas rubies, 29 diamonds and 115 pearls, the other of crimson satin, also lined with ermine and embroidered with 61 rubies, 55 diamonds, 5 large pearls, 412 medium-sized pearls and 114 small ones. There were trunks of enamelled gold ornaments, elaborate bed hangings, valances and canopies, richly embroidered tablecloths, bedcovers of crimson satin, cloth of gold, azure velvet, embroidered with gold and silver thread, *dozieri* (cushioned backrests), wall hangings, tapestries and door curtains depicting biblical scenes, great cushions in valuable materials for seating, and tapestries of flowers and trees. Harness for horses and mules included elaborate cloths of velvet and caparisons of silver and gold, including one with twenty-two little hanging bells, fans – one of which contained one hundred ostrich feathers – elaborate coffers and chests, shoes in velvet and satin, including twenty-seven pairs imported from Valencia in gilded leather, emblazoned crystal cups with gold feet and covers, huge quantities of silver and silver gilt (some of it bearing Ascanio Sforza's arms), flasks, dishes, candlesticks and candelabra, sweetmeat dishes, a salt with the arms of Aragon (presumably from her marriage to Alfonso Bisceglie). There were lavish furnishings for her private chapel, including a great crucifix in crystal with the figures of the Virgin and St John, mounted on silver, porphyry reliquaries, golden chalices, pyxes, ampoules and bowls; altar cloths, cushions, two missals on vellum in velvet covers with silver and gold clasps and holy paintings.

Lucrezia took with her a small private library. This included a Spanish manuscript with gilded miniatures, covered in crimson velvet, with silver corners and clasps, in a case of red chamois leather; a printed volume of the letters of St Catherine of Siena bound in azure leather with brass corners and clasps; a printed book of letters and gospels in Italian; a book in the Valencian language entitled 'the twelve [principles] of the Christian'; a manuscript volume of Spanish songs by various authors, beginning with the proverbs by Diondigi Lopes, bound in red leather with brass trimmings; a printed romance of chivalry entitled *L'Aquila Volante*, by Leonardo Bruni; a world history, the *Supplementum Chronicarum*, by Jacobus Philippus de Bergamo; a book in Italian entitled *The Mirror of Faith*; a volume of Dante with commentary bound in violet leather; a book of philosophy in Italian; a book of the legends of the saints in Italian; a copy of St Bonaventure; a Latin school book, the *Donatus*; a Life of Christ in Spanish by Ludolphus de Saxonia; and a small manuscript Petrarch on vellum, bound in red leather. These were her own treasured books: at the Vatican and at Ferrara, where the Este library was celebrated for its size, range and magnificence, she would never be short of reading matter. And, as we know, she took with her significant family documents, including the Giordano letters.

The Florentine envoy Pepi was, or pretended to be, shocked by the Borgias' extravagance: 'The things that are ordered here for these festivities are unheard of: and for a minor feast the shoes of the Duke's staff-bearers are made of gold brocade, and the same for the Pope's grooms: and he and the Duke vie with each other in producing the most magnificent, the latest, and the most expensive things . . .' When Cesare rode out to meet the Ferrarese procession headed by Alfonso's brothers Ippolito, Ferrante and Sigismondo, he put on a show of armed power with four thousand immaculately equipped men, horse and foot. He rode a 'most beautiful strong horse, which seemed as if it had wings . . . and [its] trappings were estimated at 10,000 ducats because one could see nothing but gold, pearls and other jewels'.[19] The Ferrarese noted that Cesare's horsemen indulged in a good deal of showing off, caracoling and sidling sideways and backwards. Cesare greeted Ippolito, whom he knew as a fellow cardinal, then the other two Este brothers; after a two-hour ceremony of welcome with the orations considered necessary for Renaissance ceremony (which must have been exceedingly tedious in the cold), the procession, swollen by the retinues of nineteen cardinals and the ambassadors of France, Spain and Venice, marched across Rome to the deafening sound of oboes, drums and trumpets. At the bridge of Sant'Angelo leading to the Vatican the noise of bombards from the castle was such that it frightened the horses. After being welcomed by Alexander in the Vatican, Cesare led the Este brothers across the piazza to Lucrezia's house.

From the moment the Ferrarese delegation met Lucrezia we have minute descriptions of her dress and behaviour, demanded by Isabella d'Este of her brothers and of her particular spy, known as El Prete, a gentleman in the retinue of the poet and courtier Niccolò da Correggio who was part of the Este contingent. According to Ferrante, whose descriptions tended to be shorter and sketchier than those of El Prete (who had promised Isabella that he would follow Lucrezia 'like the shadow does the body'), Lucrezia came to meet them at the foot of the stairs leading to her apartments. She was wearing a dress in her favourite colour, mulberry (*morello*), with tight sleeves slashed in the Spanish mode – 'in the fashion of ten years ago,' sneered El Prete – with a mantle of gold brocade lined with sable over her shoulders, her blonde hair covered with a little cap of green netting bound with a fillet of gold and two strings of pearls, and others decorating her cap.[20] Round her neck she wore a string of large pearls with a pendant balas ruby ('not very big and not a very fine colour', commented El Prete). For greater effect and to set off her dress and jewels, she leaned on the arm of an elderly gentleman dressed in black velvet lined with sable and wearing a gold chain. 'She is a sweet and graceful lady,' El Prete admitted. Lucrezia then offered them what Burchard described as a 'beautiful collation and many presents'.[21] Wearing a long Turkish-style robe of gold brocade she attended Christmas mass in St Peter's with the Este brothers, at which time the sword and biretta destined for Alfonso were blessed by the Pope.

Lucrezia's last Roman carnival began the day after Christmas, on Alexander's orders. Cesare and the Este rode about the streets masked where, according to El Prete, 'one sees nothing but courtesans wearing masks'. Rome was known politely as '*la terra da donne*', 'the City of Women', although in *I Ragionamenti* Pietro Aretino put it more bluntly: 'Rome always has been and ever will be . . . the town of whores'. The rich courtesans, splendidly equipped at their lovers' expense, often dressed as boys and rode through the streets throwing gilded eggs filled with rose water at the passers-by and indulging in every kind of prank until the

twenty-fourth hour when, by law, they were forced to retire.
Courtesans' lives were precarious: they risked revenge mutilation
by the *sfregia*, or face slashing, which destroyed their beauty and
their livelihood. Equally horrible, if not more so, was revenge by
multiple rape – the *Trentuno* – carried out by thirty-one men,
and the *Trentuno reale*, involving seventy-nine.

On the 26th, Lucrezia gave an informal ball at her palace,
closely observed by the dutiful El Prete:

A nobleman from Valencia and a lady of the court, Niccola, led the
dance. They were followed by Don Ferrante and Madonna [Lucrezia],
who danced with extreme grace and animation. She wore a *camorra*
[robe] of black velvet with gold borders . . . Her breast was covered
up to the neck with a veil of gold thread. About her neck she wore a
string of pearls, and on her head a green net and a chain of rubies
. . . Two or three of her women are very pretty . . . one, Angela [Borgia,
an illegitimate cousin of Lucrezia] . . . I picked out as my favourite.

Over the following days there were the traditional races in
various categories – for wild boar, buffalo, prostitutes, Jews, young
men, old men and boys. Then there were races for three different breeds of horses – Barbary horses imported from Morocco
via Naples, much prized for their speed, light 'Spanish' horses and
the heavy *corsieri*, cavalry chargers. As usual there was a good deal
of violence and cheating, notably by Cesare's stable.

On 30 December, to the sound of trumpets and other musical instruments, Lucrezia, dressed in a long robe of golden brocade
with a train carried by her damsels, and accompanied by Ferrante
and Sigismondo, walked across to the Vatican for the ceremony
of the giving of the ring, performed by Ferrante, 'with the greatest reverence and elegance', followed by a tedious oration by the
Bishop of Adria which Alexander ordered to be cut short. Then
Ippolito ordered a table to be brought forward for presentation
of the jewels to Lucrezia: 'Our Reverend Cardinal,' wrote Pozzi
and Saraceni, reporting the ceremony to Ercole,

made the presentation of the jewels with the greatest grace so that the aforesaid Holiness said the present was fine, but that His Reverend Lordship had made it most beautiful, and in that presentation His Lordship was very well assisted by Zoanne Ziliolo, treasurer, who in all that was necessary used singular expertise and diligence and it was done very well [in order to] enjoy the preciousness and greatness of the gift. Thus by His Holiness Our Lord and the Most Reverend Cardinals and also by the Most Illustrious Madonna Lucrezia it was praised, and was estimated at some 70,000 ducats according to the Most Reverend Cardinal of Santa Praxede, and also the Most Illustrious Don Ferrante took the utmost trouble to demonstrate the presentation and goodness of the Jewels, and above all the Most Illustrious Madonna Lucretia commended the ornaments and the work surrounding the Jewels, there not being such good masters of the art here . . .

According to Burchard, Ippolito presented Lucrezia with 'four rings of great value, a diamond, a ruby, an emerald and a turquoise'. He then took out of a box a cap or head ornament studded with fourteen diamonds, as many rubies and about a hundred and fifty large pearls, four collars similarly decorated with jewels and pearls, many bracelets, four of which were of very great value, a pendant for the breast or head made of larger jewels, four long strings of large pearls, four beautiful crosses made of diamonds and other jewels, and finally another cap similar to the first.

All was not as it seemed, however. Ippolito had received previous instructions from his father to the effect that he should use a certain form of words which Gian Luca Pozzi would provide for him, so that in case Lucrezia was unfaithful to Alfonso the jewels would remain with the Este. In the envoy's long report of the ceremony on the 30th it was stressed 'concerning the said *deponatione* [handing over] there has been made an instrument in which it is said that the wedding ring is given and no mention is made of anything else which may be given: and for this the affair has passed off . . . according to the intention of Your Excellency that it should not be written nor that there should be any idea of a donation, and there is no need for Your Excellency to be suspicious of it'.[22]

After the presentation of the jewels, in which Alexander had gleefully participated, passing the jewels through his hands and showing them off to his daughter, he and Lucrezia withdrew to the window to watch the games in the piazza beneath; these included the mock siege of a castle defended by eight gentlemen against a similar number of combatants, during which five of them were wounded. Afterwards the company went up to the Sala del Pappagallo for a party which lasted until five in the morning. Lucrezia was splendidly dressed in a robe (*veste*) of curled cloth of gold in the French style with wide sleeves down to the ground, a cloak of crimson satin lined with ermine slashed deep on the left-hand side showing a rich fringe and jewel-studded embroidery. Round her neck she wore a string of pearls with a pendant comprising an emerald, a ruby and a pendant pearl and on her head she wore a cap worked in gold, her floor-length plait bound with a black cord and a covering of gold-striped silk.[23] At the Pope's request, Lucrezia danced with Cesare and then her damsels danced in pairs. Two eclogues were recited, 'one very boring' and the other more lavish, ordered by Cesare with woods, fountains and hills, animals and shepherds and featuring two young men who represented Alfonso and Cesare, each dominating their lands on different sides of the Po. There was a ballet – a '*moresca*' – and general dancing.

The Roman carnival that year, the Ferrarese reported, was more splendid than the usual celebrations. There was a parade of armed and mounted Romans and thirteen triumphal cars with representations of Caesar, Hercules and Scipio Africanus. The piazza was barricaded off for the next two days for bullfights and at night the Borgias, the Este and their guests danced and feasted in the Vatican.

Behind the gracious smiles and words and splendid ceremony, the business dealings went on. The Bull of Remission of the Census was 'very fine', drawn up with all of Ercole's suggestions, sealed with the papal seal and undersigned by all the cardinals present at the consistory ready to be taken to Ferrara by Lucrezia.

The dowry was also all in order, the Ferrarese reported, 'except the 8,000 ducats and because they are lacking that sum here, there is some difference over the payment, which will be made without doubt; and if it is not we will not leave here'. The fault, they considered, lay not with the Pope but with his ministers. They were still wrangling at the beginning of January as to how the dowry should be paid. The Pope got his way with a sweetener for the Este in the form of the promise of a bishopric for Don Giulio and the archbishopric of Bologna for Ippolito.[24] All was now sweetness and light between Ercole and the Borgias – for the moment.

Yet, in an interview with Gian Luca Pozzi on the eve of Lucrezia's departure, Alexander experienced last-minute anxiety as to how his beloved daughter might be treated by the Este once she was out of his sphere. At Ercole's instance, Pozzi had raised the subject of the marriage between the Gonzaga heir and Cesare's daughter by Charlotte d'Albret. Alexander put him off, saying that Cesare would do nothing about this at the moment without the permission and goodwill of the King of France, and that he had discussed this with Lucrezia. He then went on to tell Pozzi that he 'loved the aforesaid Madonna [Lucrezia] far more than he did the Duke [Cesare] because she was virtuous and prudent and had always been most obedient to him: and that if she would be well treated in Ferrara, nothing they could ask him would ever be in vain'.[25]

The sixth of January 1502, the Feast of the Epiphany, was the date of Lucrezia's final departure from the city she had known all her life to face her new future in Ferrara. She spent a long time kneeling at her father's feet in the Sala del Pappagallo where the two of them spoke alone before Alexander summoned Cesare. There was no mention of Lucrezia's farewell to Rodrigo, now just two, which must have been heartbreaking for her, nor of Vannozza, who as always seemed to play little part in her life. Once the Pope had given her leave to go, Lucrezia left the Vatican escorted by Ippolito and Cesare. She was dressed, according to Ferrante, in a robe of curled cloth of gold cut with crimson thread and over it a cloak of cloth of gold lined with ermine. She wore a hat of crimson silk with a golden cap ornament with a large pendent jewel on one side and a necklace of large pearls. At the foot of the steps of the Vatican she mounted a 'very fine mule, harnessed very richly with beaten gold and a long wide cloth of mulberry velvet'.[26] It was snowing as she left, followed by her huge company. As she did so, Alexander went from window to window of the palace to catch the last glimpse of his beloved daughter.

PART TWO
Duchess of Ferrara
1502–19

7. The Road to Ferrara

'She kept always to her room to wash her hair but also because she
is rather solitary and remote by nature'

– The Ferrarese envoys accompanying Lucrezia to
Duke Ercole describing her embarrassing experience in
finding herself in her former city of Pesaro

A list preserved in the archives at Modena details Lucrezia's
company on the long hard journey northwards. She rode either
her mule or a white jennet, or, when she was tired, in a handsome litter provided by her father. She was accompanied by her
old friends and relations, Geronima Borgia, Adriana de Mila and
her ladies, each with her personal servant. Headed by the beautiful Angela Borgia, always known as Dona Angela, they included
'Elisabetha senese [of Siena] and her daughter, Elisabetha perusina
[from Perugia], Catherina Spagnola [from Spain], Alexandra,
Geronima [who later married Lucrezia's favourite doctor,
Lodovico Bonaccioli], Nicola [who married into the Ferrarese
aristocratic family of Trotti], Camilla, Catherinella negra [a
favourite black slave], four chambermaids, la Napolitana [the
Neapolitan] with two daughters, Samaritana, and Camilla greca
[the Greek] and two handmaids ['*ancille*'], and a 'Madonna Joanna'
(possibly Juana de Moncada, married to one of Alexander's
nephews), with four personal servants. Unmentioned in the archive
list or in the list provided by the Ferrarese chronicler Zambotti
was a woman named Drusilla, reputed to be Cesare's lover. The
only evidence for this Drusilla is an epigram by the poet Fausto
Evangelista Maddaleni entitled 'On the sorrow of Cesare for the
departure of Lucrezia Borgia and Drusilla'.[1] Cesare's biographer,

Gustavo Sacerdote, hazards a guess that this Drusilla may have been the mother of his two illegitimate children, Girolamo and Camilla, who followed Lucrezia to Ferrara.

While Ippolito had returned to Rome, Cardinal Cosenza was to accompany Lucrezia as far as Gubbio. Three bishops rode with her household, one of whom, the Bishop of Venosa, was Alexander's favourite doctor. Also among the party were the major-domo, or master of Lucrezia's household (bearing the sword and biretta destined for Alfonso from the Pope); 'Messer Christoforo' Piccimini, her secretary; *il bacilliere*, an obscure title, literally meaning 'the bachelor', i.e. a graduate, who was probably designated to read to her during her journey or possibly also to compose gracious speeches for her; her master of ceremonies; two chaplains (who may also have been chapel singers); her master of the stables; 'Vincentio guardaroba' (probably the same Vincenzo Giordano of her letters from Nepi); Sancho, her *scalco* (steward); her master of horse; and Baldassare, her cup-bearer. Also in the party were the man in charge of the knives; the *credenciero*, responsible for her plate; the undercup-bearer; the doorkeeper; 'Martin who reads the book'; ten pages; ten grooms; the man in charge of her chapel; the candlemaker; the *spenditore* who oversaw the expenses of her kitchen; the tailor; upholsterer (*repostero*); the dispenser of her cellar; two cooks; Alonso, the goldsmith; stable boys; coachmen; the locksmith; the saddler, 'mastro Alvisi da cremona'; and Navarrico, the Spanish Borgia henchman who featured as a trusted messenger in the Vatican correspondence of 1494 and remained with Lucrezia at Ferrara. For this household alone, she travelled with one hundred and fifty carriages and mules and fifty muleteers.

Eight squires in the service of the Pope, almost all of them Spaniards, also accompanied her, and a party of Roman barons (those not yet dispossessed by Alexander), including Francesco Colonna of Palestrina and his wife, Giuliano Orsini di Stabia, Guillen Ramón, a nephew of the Pope and captain of the papal guard, and Ranuccio degli Ottoni, shortly to be deprived of his property in Macerata by Alexander in favour of the infant

Giovanni Borgia. In addition there were four Roman ambassadors; eight Roman noblemen; more than thirty of Cesare's gentlemen, including the gallant Yves d'Alègre, Ugo de Moncada, Cesare's right-hand man, Juan Castellar, Remolins, Juan Marrades, and many distinguished Italian noblemen such as the Genoese Ottaviano Fregoso (who featured among the cast of characters in Castiglione's *The Courtier*) accompanied by thirty trumpeters, six jesters and 'Nicolò the musician'. Sanudo computed the Borgia contingent as 753 people, 426 horses and 234 mules.

The five-hundred-strong Ferrarese party, headed by Ferrante and Sigismondo d'Este, included many Este connections, such as Annibale Bentivoglio who was married to Duke Ercole's illegitimate daughter, Lucrezia; Ercole d'Este, son of the Duke's brother, Sigismondo; Niccolò da Correggio, whose mother was an Este (as was the mother of Lodovico Pico della Mirandola); Uguccione dei Contrari, the leading Ferrarese nobleman, married to Diana d'Este, daughter of the elder Sigismondo; and many of the nobility with whom Lucrezia was to become familiar and who were to become part of her new life, both Ferrarese and local lords, bound to the Este not only by ties of kinship but by the gift of lands and city palaces, offices and military service. The party included the two Ferrarese envoys Gian Luca Pozzi and Gherardo Saraceni.

Ippolito d'Este, whom both Cesare and Lucrezia had known as a young cardinal, had remained behind in Rome. The third son of Ercole by his wife, the Duchess Eleonora d'Aragona, and just a year older than Lucrezia, he was the cleverest of the Este brothers and the most ruthless. Like Cesare, he had been destined for the Church from an early age: at only three he was given the abbey of Casalnovo *in commendam*, an early start even for those days. Aged seven, thanks to his aunt, Beatrice d'Aragona, Queen of Hungary, he was given the rich archbishopric of Esztergom in Hungary, with an annual income of 50,000 ducats. Created cardinal in his absence in Hungary by Alexander in 1493, he later spent some time with Ludovico Sforza in Milan where he landed the archbishopric worth 5,000 ducats a year. He also acted as

Governor of the city in the absences of Ludovico, but spent most
of his time hunting and feasting outside the city. Like Cesare, he
was clearly unsuited to the ecclesiastical life and, like him, preferred
the exercise of arms and political intrigue to his priestly duties.
His father Ercole had frequent occasion to reprove him for wearing armour instead of his priestly robes and for his generally
unsuitable behaviour. In 1493 he had adjured the fifteen-year-old
cardinal 'to bear yourself in such a way that you be reputed a
wise and prudent Cardinal . . . to give evidence of the virtue of
your disposition and of the constancy that a prelate of your rank
should have, and one raised to such a dignity as is the Cardinalate'.[2]
The news that Ippolito had ordered a suit of white armour from
Milanese craftsmen in order to fight for Ludovico in 1499 had
horrified his father who commanded him 'to desist from these
warlike ways, and to strive to live like a good Archbishop and a
most reverend Cardinal'.[3] Proud, insolent and voluptuous, but
gifted with great personal charm and the family passion for music,
Ippolito was to prove a good friend and counsellor to Lucrezia
in Ferrara.

Ferrante d'Este, Ercole's second son by Eleonora, was born in
Naples in 1477, when Giuliano della Rovere stood as his godfather. In 1493 he had been dispatched by his father to take service with Charles VIII of France at the French court and was sent
there richly equipped with four noble companions and eighty
horse. Anxious that his son should make a good impression, Ercole
told him he should present perfumes, '*cose odorifere*', to the King
and Queen and the important personages of the court and
dispatched a courtier to him bearing grains of musk and 'two
horns of civet'. Ferrante, however, vain, idle and dissolute, soon
disappointed his father by not showing enough diligence in serving the French King, preferring to lounge about and enjoy
himself. 'We know that you have plenty of talent and that you
know what your duty is, and that, if you wish, you can do yourself credit,' the anxious father wrote.[4] Ercole, however, spoiled
his son; in return for repeatedly sending him money, he received
news of the French court, but when later that year Charles VIII

invaded Italy, instead of showing keenness Ferrante merely dawdled in his wake and remained in Rome enjoying himself instead of following the French army to Naples. Ferrante's excuse was that he could not afford to go as Charles had not paid his allowance. A furious Ercole sent one of his secretaries to haul Ferrante off to Naples to see the King and supplied him with a letter of credit for 500 ducats. He also sent a stern letter: 'All these things,' he wrote,

have proceeded from your own negligence, and from your wishing to give yourself to idleness and avoid labour; because if you had followed the Most Christian King, as was your duty and our intention, you would have got your allowance sooner . . . But you wanted to stay at Rome and take a holiday where you have spent more than you would have done in following the King. If, by your laziness and negligence, you lose the support of the Most Christian King, you will repent of it with time . . . If by your own fault you lose this opening, do not hope for anything from us, save a bad welcome and harsh treatment . . .[5]

Thus adjured, Ferrante followed the French army to Naples and endeavoured to ingratiate himself with the King, receiving a good report from the ducal secretary. Ercole wrote praising him for having 'begun to behave yourself well and with diligence . . . you must continue in being diligent and assiduous in the services of that King, and be prompt and ready at that Court . . .' While Alfonso d'Este remained with Ludovico Sforza, now part of the League against the French, Ferrante was forced to follow Charles so that Ercole could keep in with both sides. He fought with him at the battle of Fornovo and only returned to Italy two years later, in 1497. He then obtained a *condotta* from Venice for her war against Pisa but, as usual, he was unhappy with his treatment and complained about lack of money, threatening to leave the Venetian service and earning himself another angry letter from his father. Despite all the evidence, Ercole continued to have faith in Ferrante's charm and his future at the French court and took him with him and Alfonso to Milan to meet Louis XII in 1499. Ferrante singularly failed to

live up to his father's expectations: he had piled up such a mountain of debt while at the French court that poor Bartolommeo
de'Cavalleri, Ercole's ambassador there over the Borgia marriage
negotiations, could get no credit and was forced to appeal to Ercole
for funds. Louis himself formed a very poor opinion of Ferrante,
whom he described as 'acute but idle and irresponsible'.
(Sigismondo d'Este, Ercole's youngest son, born in September 1480,
the least troublesome and ambitious of Ercole's children, played
only a small part in Ferrarese life. Like Alfonso and Ferrante he
had contracted syphilis in 1496–7 but while the other brothers
seem to have recovered he was so incapacitated by it that he became
increasingly unable to live a normal life.)

Progress by the vast cavalcade was extremely slow, the pace
being set by Lucrezia who found the horrible winter conditions
and the bad roads extremely tiring. The Ferrarese envoys Pozzi
and Saraceni, deputed by Ercole to get the bride to Ferrara by
the desired date, were in despair. From Foligno a week after their
departure from Rome they reported to Ercole:

From Narni we wrote to Your Excellency that we would travel from
Terni to Spoleto and from Spoleto here without stopping anywhere:
nonetheless the Illustrious Duchess finding herself and her ladies very
tired when they arrived at Spoleto, decided to rest for an entire day at
Spoleto and then another here so that we will not leave here until
tomorrow. And we will not arrive in Urbino before next Tuesday which
will be the 18th, because tomorrow we go to Nocera, Saturday to
Gualdo, Sunday at Gubbio, Monday at Cagli, then Tuesday at Urbino
where we will stay another whole day, that is all Wednesday, and from
there we go to Pesaro on the 20th, and then from city to city as we
have told Your Excellency. But we are certain that the Duchess will
rest many entire days in many of those places so that without doubt
we will not arrive in Ferrara before the last day of this month or the
first of the next, or even the second or third.

They warned Ercole that he might have to put off the grand
reception at Ferrara for a day or two and asked him to let them

know what to do: 'The reason I am led to believe what I have said above is that the Illustrious Madonna Lucrezia is of a delicate complexion and not accustomed to ride and neither are her ladies: and we can understand that she does not wish to arrive at Ferrara exhausted and undone by the journey.'[6]

Everywhere she went, Lucrezia was received with huge acclaim and rejoicing. At the gate of Foligno, the town of which she had briefly been an absentee Governor, was a trophy depicting the Roman Lucretia with her dagger in her hand and verses declaring how she gave way to this Lucrezia, being far outdone in chastity, modesty, prudence and constancy. Near the piazza was a triumphal car with a cupid in front of it and on it stood Paris with the golden apple of the Hesperides in his hand, declaring that he had given the apple to Venus but since Lucrezia was so far superior in beauty, wisdom and riches to the three goddesses, he had withdrawn it in her favour. Finally, in the middle of the piazza an armed galley with Turks in Turkish robes had advanced to meet her; standing on the prow of the galley one of them declaimed rhyming verses to the effect that their Great King knew how powerful Lucrezia was in Italy and how she could be a good mediator for peace, and therefore he was offering her that Christian territory which he held. 'We did not bother to take down the words of the verses, as they were not exactly those of Petrarch,' one envoy commented, 'nor did the representation of the ship seem of much importance or consequence.' However, they were both impressed by the appearance, four miles outside Foligno, of the entire Baglioni clan of Perugia gathered to do Lucrezia honour, doubtless, although he did not say so, more from fear of her brother than respect for herself.

Lucrezia, the envoys reported, persisted in her desire to travel by water from Bologna to Ferrara to escape the discomfort of riding and the roads. The Pope was so careful of Lucrezia's wellbeing 'that every day and every hour he wanted to hear of her progress: and she has to write in her own hand from each place to tell him of her wellbeing: which confirms what I have told

Your Excellency previously that His Holiness loves her more than any other person of his blood . . .'7

On the 18th they were at Urbino, having been greeted two miles outside Gubbio by Elisabetta, the Duchess of Urbino, whom Lucrezia had known while she was married to Giovanni Sforza, and lodged in the palace there, arriving by the light of torches. The arms of the Pope, the King of France, of Borgia and Estense united, and Lucrezia's own arms were displayed everywhere. At Urbino, Lucrezia and the Este party were lodged in the magnificent ducal palace of the Montefeltro while the Duke Guidobaldo and his Duchess themselves stayed outside the city.

Elisabetta Gonzaga da Montefeltro, Duchess of Urbino (1471 -1520) was one of the most celebrated women of her age. Sister of Francesco Gonzaga and sister-in-law of Isabella d'Este, to whom she was extremely close, she was much praised for her saintliness in enduring a sexless marriage to Guidobaldo who was both impotent and for much of his life crippled by what was described as 'gout' but was probably rheumatoid arthritis, which deformed his body from a young age. According to the archivist Luzio, despite his impotence (which was kept secret until 1502) Guidobaldo was extremely erotically inclined, so that Elisabetta was in a state of suspense every day in case he might fall upon her and have a relapse. Elisabetta was the heroine of *The Courtier* which described a sophisticated symposium at her court supposedly held over four days in the year 1507. She was accompanied, as always, by her faithful companion, the witty, high-spirited Emilia Pia, daughter of Marco Pio of Carpi, married to an illegitimate brother of Guidobaldo.

Elisabetta Gonzaga had little reason to love the Borgias, both because of Alexander's treatment of Guidobaldo, his captain in the Orsini war, whom he had refused to ransom and left to languish in captivity and, still more recently, because of the outrageous behaviour of Cesare who, just over a year earlier, had abducted one of her protégées, Dorotea Malatesta, wife of Giovanni Battista Caracciolo, a Neapolitan captain of infantry in the service of Venice. The incident had caused widespread scandal.

Dorotea, the twenty-three-year-old natural daughter of Roberto Malatesta of Rimini, had been brought up at the court of Elisabetta at Urbino where her marriage had been celebrated by proxy. She had been travelling under Venetian protection, and with an armed escort provided by Cesare at the request of Venice, to join her husband, when she was seized just after her company had crossed into Venetian territory. Everyone accused Cesare, who remained as arrogant and plausible as ever, blaming one of his captains, Diego Ramires, who, he said, had had an affair with Dorotea during carnival at Urbino. Letters of protest rained down upon him from Venice, the Pope, the King of France, even Francesco Gonzaga on behalf of his sister. But Cesare did not punish Ramires, nor did he restore Dorotea, and the evidence is that he kept her. At the end of December 1502 Sanudo reported: 'With the Duke when he left Imola was the wife of our captain of infantry.' Cesare's escapades can hardly have helped Lucrezia's relations with the Duchess of Urbino. And, close as she was to Isabella, Elisabetta was under no illusions as to her contempt for her Borgia sister-in-law.

Ferrante d'Este had obviously received a sharp rebuke from Isabella for failing adequately to describe Lucrezia's clothes. He hastened to write from Urbino that truthfully on the journey he had not seen much change in her wardrobe, but after the ball given by the Duke and Duchess in Lucrezia's apartments in the ducal palace he was able to satisfy her with more detail. Lucrezia, he said, 'appeared in a dress of black velvet in her own style decorated with raised stripes of drawn gold running down the robe from head to foot, a little necklace of jewels which we gave her round her neck, cap or coif with stripes of beaten gold and a diamond in the veil above her forehead, and a girdle of beaten gold with large tassels of gold and white silk. The whole outfit being so striking that I thought I should describe it to you.'[8] When she danced she was followed by two Spanish jesters shouting, 'Look at the great lady, how pretty her face is and how well she dances, rarely but excellently.'

The Ferrarese envoys remarked on the abundant hospitality

offered by Guidobaldo and Elisabetta, both soon to be rudely
ejected from their paradise by the bride's brother. This time they
were writing to Ippolito, 'because knowing how much you love
Our Illustrious Duchess, we are sure it will be very pleasing to
you to hear the particulars of everything, adding that our Lady
Duchess is well and travelling in good spirits; and if sometimes
Her Ladyship has been left weak from riding, the next morning
she is always gay [*gagliarda*] . . .'[9] On the same day they wrote a
long letter to Ercole projecting the time of arrival at Ferrara. As
to whether they would travel the final stage from Bologna by
road or water, Lucrezia told them the decision awaited the Pope's
answer. Although she would prefer to travel by water, 'she defers
so much to His Holiness in every little thing because she is most
obedient to him and because she is discreet, respectful and prudent
in a manner that she does not want her own way but follows
the wish and opinion of those superior to her or greater than
her'.[10]

Lucrezia and Elisabetta travelled on together from Urbino in
the splendid litter provided by the Pope, which seemed infinitely
preferable to riding on horseback through the mud. This was
prompted by a difficult, muddy two-day journey which left not
only Lucrezia and the ladies tired but the horses and mules
exhausted when they finally arrived in Pesaro. It must have been
a curious sensation for Lucrezia to enter the city of which, as
wife of Giovanni Sforza, she had once been countess; now she
was there as an honoured guest of her absent brother who, when
he was in the city, was accustomed to occupying Giovanni Sforza's
rooms. A hundred children in Cesare's colours of yellow and red,
with olive branches in their hands, greeted her with cries of
'Duca, Duca, Lucrezia, Lucrezia'. The highest ranking ladies, her
former subjects, greeted her warmly in her former palace, 'with
so great a demonstration of affection and respect that one could
not wish for better', noted the envoys of this disloyal or, rather,
cynical behaviour. Lucrezia permitted her ladies and damsels to
dance with the Pesarese in her antechamber but she herself was
not present, clearly feeling a certain reserve about the situation.

'She kept always to her room,' the envoys wrote, 'to wash her hair but also because she is rather solitary and remote by nature.'[11]

Lucrezia was now passing through Cesare's duchy of Romagna, staying in palaces from which he had rudely dislodged their former lords – Giovanni Sforza, bitter in exile in Venice; Pandolfo Malatesta of Rimini; Caterina Sforza of Imola and Forlì, now released from the dungeons of Sant'Angelo, greatly aged by her ordeal at the hands of the Borgias but living in comfort in the Villa Medici in Fiesole as the widow of Giovanni de'Medici; and Faenza whose young lord Astorre, after putting up a gallant defence against Cesare, had also been lodged in Sant'Angelo, an experience he would not survive. The shadow of Cesare lay across her path wherever she went. From Cesena on 24 January the envoys reported Ferrante's alarm at a rumour that Caracciolo was in the area and a kidnap attempt might be made on her, in revenge against Cesare for his part in the abduction of Dorotea.[12] In every city of the Romagna through which Lucrezia passed, on Cesare's orders crowds of children greeted her dressed in Lucrezia's livery of yellow and mulberry and waving olive branches; in all the palaces in which she stayed, so recently vacated by their former lords, the halls were extravagantly decorated and the local grandees lined up to meet her. At Cesare's orders, Don Ramiro de Lorqua, his sinister Governor of the Romagna, had had the roads levelled and repaired; the entire cost of the passage of her huge company, some 8,000 ducats, was borne by her brother. At Imola, Lucrezia once again insisted on spending a day to wash her hair before facing the Bentivoglio at Bologna in another situation complicated by Cesare's manoeuvres. The previous summer he had made threats against Bologna, where the Bentivoglio had only saved themselves by invoking the protection of the King of France, while Ginevra Bentivoglio, wife of Giovanni, lord of Bologna, was Giovanni Sforza's aunt. The envoys were in despair at Lucrezia's decision to linger in Imola. 'With Your Excellency's letters of the 25th we have renewed our insistence with the Illustrious Duchess so that we can leave this place tomorrow and arrive in the Borgo San Luca [outskirts of Ferrara]

by the last day of the month, as YE desires . . . She answered us
that she was always willing to conform to Your Highness's will
but it was necessary for her to remain here tomorrow, for the
reasons already given and because the Duchess of Urbino also
wanted to wash her hair which it seemed to her could not easily
be done in Bologna . . .'[13]

If there seems to have been much made of Lucrezia's practice
of washing her hair, it is worth commenting that this was an
important part of the Renaissance woman's beauty procedures.
Marinello, the sixteenth-century authority on health and beauty,[14]
gives five pages of recipes for colouring the hair blonde with
various waters, including ashes of vine stocks boiled in water with
barley straw, liquorice root cleaned of its outer bark and chopped,
and cedar smoothed with a knife; used to wash close to the head
and left to dry this 'will make the hair shine and glitter like gold
thread'. Other ingredients included saffron, shavings from horses'
hooves, cumin, myrrh and rock alum. Foreheads were to be kept
high, white and serene by hair removal, by applying a paste of
mastic overnight. Perhaps the most revolting beauty treatment for
whitening the skin of the face, neck, hands and other parts of
the body 'whiter than alabaster' was this, also from Marinello:
'Take two young white doves, cut off their necks, pluck them
and draw out their innards, then grind them with four ounces
of peach stones, and the same of washed melon seeds, two ounces
of sublimate of mercury, a spoon of bean flour and ground pebbles
which have been infused for a day and a night in milk: two young
cabbages: a fresh cheese made that day or hour, fourteen whites
of fresh eggs, half an ounce of camphor and an equal amount of
borax; and four bulbs of the white lily, ground together and mixed
together, put in a glass vial [*labico*] and mix with water and use
at your pleasure.' He continued with a further eight pages of
recipes for whitening skin, considered so necessary for the appearance of beauty. No wonder the ladies needed an entire day for
their beauty treatments.

Finally, on 29 January, Lucrezia and Elisabetta, flanked by
Ferrante and Sigismondo, made a grand entry into Bologna. Three

miles outside the city she had been greeted by Giovanni Bentivoglio's four sons, then two miles outside by the Lord Giovanni himself, who paid her the signal honour of dismounting to take her hand. The windows overlooking the streets she passed through were crowded with spectators, the walls decorated with the papal arms surmounting those of the Commune of Bologna, those of the King of France, the Este, Borgia and Duke of Romagna. That evening, Giovanni Bentivoglio gave a magnificent ball attended by many of the most beautiful women in Bologna in his palace where Lucrezia and her suite were lodged. By the end of the day Lucrezia, the cynosure of all eyes, was exhausted: so much so that the next day she slept late and, as Pozzi reported to Ercole, he had not the heart to waken her when the courier arrived with Ercole's letters and instructions.[15]

Lucrezia was aware that she was under close inspection every day and hour of her journey. Ferrante may have been dilatory in his reporting but Isabella's other correspondent, El Prete, was not. At Cagli he had even managed to see the room where Lucrezia had slept and to examine her nightclothes. He wrote that Lucrezia was assiduous in her change of toilettes, even down to the harness of her horses and mules. He sent intimate reports of her entourage of ladies whom he described as *'galante dame'*: 'the first is Madonna Hieronyma [or Geronima] Borgia, sister of the Cardinal, who they say has the French disease, the other is called Madonna Angela [Borgia] who I think will please you because she is my favourite, and she is the natural sister of Madonna Hieronyma, there is a Catalina from Valencia whom some admire and some do not, a girl from Perugia who is beautiful, another Catalina, two Neapolitan girls, one called Cintia, the other Catalina, who are not very good looking but graceful, and a Moor, the most beautiful woman I have ever seen, and gay and well dressed, she wears bracelets of gold and pearls . . . I understand she is the lady's dearest favourite.' El Prete became ever more impressed by Lucrezia, no doubt to Isabella's distaste. Like everyone else who met her he found her quite different from the villainess and whore of her earlier reputation: 'I can tell you that the bearing of this lady is modest, from her head which has no curls and her breast covered, as indeed is the case with all her damsels. Every day she makes a better impression on me; she is a lady with a very good mind, astute [so that] you have to keep your wits about you with her. To sum up, I hold her to be a wise lady, and this is not only my opinion but that of all this company . . .'[16]

All these enthusiastic reports of his bride excited the curiosity of Alfonso d'Este who until now had held himself resolutely aloof, indeed angry, 'con la moscha', at having to marry her. On 31 January, Lucrezia and the Este rode to Bentivoglio, intending, according to the Pope's decision, to go by water to Ferrara, in boats to be provided by Ercole.[17] At Bentivoglio on 31 January, Alfonso arrived unannounced shortly after the arrival of Lucrezia's party.

This evening at the 23rd hour, the Illustrious madama Duchessa having arrived shortly before, the Illustrious Don Alfonso arrived unexpectedly, so that he had already mounted the stairs of this palace before the Duchess had notice of it. The Magnificent Messer Hannibale [Annibale Bentivoglio, Ercole's son-in-law] was the first [to know] and announced it and immediately all through the palace there was huge applause and everyone crying 'Alfonso'. The Duchess, although she was astonished by the unexpected arrival of Don Alfonso, nonetheless received His Lordship with so much reverence and good grace that it must not have displeased her. We cannot describe the joy which all her company experienced, and Don Alfonso in person and manners could truly not have comported himself in every way with more kindness and naturalness which pleased everyone.[18]

In a second letter of the same day, the envoys added that as a result of the conversations which Lucrezia and Alfonso had enjoyed together 'on diverse and pleasing subjects', they had commissioned Pozzi and Saraceni to say that they had decided that it would be best to travel from there to Ferrara by land, because the road was good and if they took the water route they would arrive very late. 'This decision appeared a very necessary one to us,' the long-suffering envoys added, 'given that only with the greatest difficulty is it possible to get these duchesses to leave on time.'

Lucrezia was enchanted by this unexpected arrival, a romantic gesture on the part of Alfonso who hitherto had given every impression of distaste for their forthcoming marriage. He was four years older than her, born in 1476 at Ferrara, the eldest son of Ercole by Duchess Eleonora and named Alfonso after his maternal great grandfather (*bisavolo*). Alfonso was described by his contemporary biographer and secretary Bonaventura Pistofilo as tall, long-faced, 'of a grave and lordly aspect, more melancholy and severe than happy and joyous'. From the portrait medal engraved for his wedding, he appears somewhat heavy-faced and, increasingly unusual for those days, beardless. He was a man of few words and kept his own counsel but beneath his reserved appearance he was capable of strongly emotional reactions. He was physically powerful and well-built, fit from the physical exercise in which he took great pleasure, which included boating and swimming in the lake in the castle garden at Ferrara (in winter he would put the boat on a sledge and skate over the ice) and tennis. Hunting was also a passion, as it was for most of his contemporaries, and he was a good judge of arms, birds and horses. Less articulate and courtly than his father, he was physically courageous and a skilled leader of men, qualities which were to stand him in good stead during the years of war which were soon to engulf Ferrara. He was a widower, his first wife, Anna Sforza, having died in childbirth in November 1497, when Alfonso, so the Ferrarese chronicler recorded, was so disfigured by syphilitic pustules on his face that he had been unable to attend her funeral. He liked whores and low companions but, although uninterested in letters and humanism, he had his father's passion for music and architecture, and was a skilled player on the viola. In the years of peace he indulged his interest as a collector of antiquities and patron of Bellini and Titian. He had practical skills, learned to use a lathe and had foundries in his garden where he practised the fusion of bronze and made cannon with his own hands; he would become the most skilful deployer of artillery of his generation. His device, suitably, was an exploding grenade. He also made terracotta vases and plates which he used for his own table. He was shrewd, with knowledge and experience of foreign affairs, and proved dexterous in guiding his state through the treacherous currents of war and international politics. He was not gregarious and disliked crowds but was kind and pleasant to his household. He was not, in short, the kind of man to whom Lucrezia was naturally attracted; she would not be faithful to him, nor he to her, but over the years of their marriage a mutual respect would develop and, on Alfonso's side at least, a deep love.

In Rome, meanwhile, Alexander was tortured about his possible mistreatment of Lucrezia. Beltrando Costabili, the Ferrarese ambassador who had remained at Rome to continue final negotiations with Alexander, reported to Ercole a disquieting conversation he had had with the Pope: 'The Pope had heard that Don Alfonso did not sleep with his first wife; and let it be understood that he would experience the most profound displeasure if he heard that he did not share his bed with the Duchess Lucrezia . . .'[19] Since Alfonso's first wife had died in childbirth this outburst must have been prompted by the old fear of non-consummation which had agitated him at the time of Juan Gandia's marriage. Probably he suspected the Este might try to wriggle out of this marriage on these grounds, as indeed he himself had done with Giovanni Sforza. Concern for Lucrezia's wellbeing in what was in truth a forced marriage was evidently still in his mind. Three days later, in discussions with Costabili over Cento and La Pieve, Alexander 'speaking afterwards of his family links with the Estense, had declared that if they would treat Duchessa Lucrezia well, he would think of ways of making them great . . .'[20]

In the end, Lucrezia and the Este travelled to Ferrara not by road but along the waterways in a ship, a bucentaur (*bucintoro*), provided by Ercole. The most usual means of travelling in the region, the Val Padana, was by water. At the time a system of rivers and canals linked most of the important cities of Lombardy, the Emilia and the Veneto. Bologna, Modena, Argenta and most of the Este villas could be reached by water from Ferrara, and the Po was the most important artery for travel across northern Italy. The bucentaur was equipped with a mast and a sail as well as oars, and in shallower waters would be drawn by horses. Its superstructure contained several rooms magnificently decorated, painted by artists and hung with tapestries.

The anxious ambassadors had actually succeeded in getting the party off before dawn the next day in order to keep to the schedule planned by Ercole. At Malalbergo, Lucrezia was met by her new sister-in-law – one of the most famous and formidable women in Italy, Isabella d'Este, Marchioness of Mantua, wife of Francesco Gonzaga. Neither of the women was looking forward to the encounter. Lucrezia was intelligent enough to be aware that Isabella did not welcome her. Isabella was seething throughout these days of celebration when Lucrezia, not herself, would be the centre of attention. Indeed, she had written to her husband the previous day that 'to my great displeasure' she would have to get up early to go by boat to meet the bride. At twenty-eight, Isabella was six years older than Lucrezia and had already been married twelve years. She was of middle height with a tendency to plumpness and had dark eyes and an abundance of fair hair with a reddish tint. She was extremely intelligent and well informed and a passionate, even rapacious, collector of antiquities and works of art. She was cultivated and well read, sang and accompanied herself on the lute and was accustomed to praise from the great men of literature of the day. Niccolò da Correggio called her '*la prima donna del mondo*' – the first lady of the world. She patronized the leading artists of the time – even Leonardo da Vinci sketched her. She was very conscious of her high birth, as the eldest daughter of the Duke of Ferrara and of Eleonora d'Aragona, daughter of King Ferrante of Naples, and her pride was cut to the quick at the thought of the upstart Borgia occupying the place of her royal mother as Duchess of Ferrara. Like most aristocrats of her day but more so, Isabella was a tremendous snob. An inscription round the courtyard near her *studiolo* proclaimed her status as granddaughter of a king, daughter of a

duke, and wife of a marquis. She was conscious that Lucrezia as
Duchess of Ferrara would outrank her. Mantua was a small and
relatively unimportant state which could not be compared in
territory or wealth with Ferrara; indeed, Isabella resented the fact
that her revenues could not keep up with her expensive tastes.
Francesco Gonzaga supplemented his income by making his name
as a *condottiere*, working under contract to the various powers in
Italy. Her letters to Francesco (who was not at the wedding as
he had been advised not to attend by Ercole, probably because
of the Pope's loud complaints against him for harbouring Cesare's
enemies, such as Giovanni Sforza) were redolent of her distaste
for the Borgia marriage.

Isabella was accompanied by Giulio, the handsomest of the
Este brothers, and Ercole's illegitimate son, born in 1478 from
a relationship with one of his wife's (married) ladies, Isabella
Arduino. As Isabella described it to her husband, Francesco
Gonzaga, the two sisters-in-law greeted each other with
embraces and happy faces before continuing down the canal
to Torre de Fossa where Ercole, with the entire court, was waiting on the river bank to greet Lucrezia. When she disembarked
he took her hand and kissed her, although she attempted to
kiss his hand first. Then they embarked on the great ducal
bucentaur which was already crowded with the ambassadors of
all the powers, among whom Isabella and Lucrezia were seated.
Alfonso and Ercole were on the poop, amusing themselves by
listening to the jesters who, in Ferrarese dialect and Spanish
rhyme, eulogized Lucrezia and the Este. The party arrived to
the sound of trumpets and artillery at the house of Ercole's
illegitimate brother, Alberto d'Este, where Lucrezia was to spend
the night before making her ceremonial entry into Ferrara. 'I
will not describe her to you because I know you have seen
her,' Isabella wrote to Francesco, before then going into great
detail about her clothes: Lucrezia wore a robe of drawn gold
garnished with crimson satin with sleeves in the Castilian style
and a cloak slashed with mulberry satin lined with sable, and
a necklace of large pearls with a pendant spinel, pierced with

a pendant pear-shaped pearl. She wore a gold headdress without a veil.[21]

For Lucrezia this was the first sight of the father-in-law she had so assiduously courted. At seventy-one Ercole was tall, with strongly marked features, an aquiline nose and a thin, forbidding mouth. He was born in October 1431, the son of the Marquis Niccolò III by his third wife, Ricciarda da Saluzzo, but had spent most of his early life, from fourteen to the age of almost thirty, at the court of Naples where he and his brother Sigismondo had had a humanist education with the future King Ferrante. They had in fact been exiled to keep them out of Ferrara so that their illegitimate half-brothers, Leonello and Borso, could succeed. From the time Ercole grew up he had spent his time as a leading *condottiere*, first for the Aragonese and then the Angevin factions in Naples and finally for Venice. He was devious and ruthless, having engineered his own succession as Duke in 1471 in place of the chosen heir, Niccolò, whom he then plotted unsuccessfully to have poisoned. Five years later, when Niccolò attempted to take over Ferrara, Ercole had him beheaded privately in the *cortile* of the Castello and then, for reasons of family pride, had his head sewn back on and the body dressed for burial in gold brocade. The history of the ancient Este family was as blood-stained as most of the great Italian families, a record of plot and counterplot, executions and torture, as Lucrezia herself was to discover. The plots were customarily among themselves and not takeover attempts by outsiders, a pattern of behaviour which was to repeat itself with tragic consequences early in Alfonso's reign.

Ercole was an astute and cautious ruler but, as the historian of Ferrara has remarked, hardly one to be trusted.[22] In Naples he betrayed the Aragonese in favour of their predecessors, the Angevins, then married Eleonora, daughter of the childhood companion, Ferrante, whom he had betrayed. He then betrayed the Venetians who had helped him secure the duchy, an act of treachery which resulted in the disastrous war of Ferrara (1482–4) and the loss of the Polesine of Rovigo. Ercole was absolute master of Ferrara and popular with his people, although in recent years the extravagance with which he had indulged his passions for building, music and musicians and the theatre had led to administrative abuses such as the sale of offices. His greatest achievement as ruler had been his success in involving the citizens of Ferrara in the identity of the Este, with theatrical spectacles, jousts, tournaments and religious and charitable ceremonies. Bernardino Zambotti, the not-unprejudiced author of the *Diario Ferrarese*, wrote of him: '. . . this Duke of Ferrara in wisdom, shrewdness, experience and goodness was the first man of Italy, and thus more faithful and discreet, and loved by all the governments of Italy, except by the Venetians, who barely wished to hear his name mentioned'.[23] Since the death of Lorenzo the Magnificent in 1492, the defeat of Ludovico il Moro in 1500, and the destruction of the Aragonese in Naples, Ercole was indeed the pre-eminent prince in Italy. Altogether, despite his defects, his indecision and inattention to administration, Lucrezia's future father-in-law, soberly dressed in black as was his wont, was an impressive figure.

The Ferrara which Lucrezia saw across the River Po from the house of Alberto d'Este on the opposite bank was a glittering city, with walls, towers and battlements frescoed with chivalric scenes or painted in the Este colours of red, white and green. In the centre of the city, the grim fourteenth-century dark red brick Castello (the Castel Vecchio, or Old Castle), with its moat, four towers, and below-ground dungeons dominated its surroundings. It was linked by a covered way with the Palazzo del Corte, the Court Palace, a graceful building with arches and loggias of white Istrian stone in the style of the Doge's Palace in Venice, overlooking the cathedral and the main square, the theatre for public events – jousts, tournaments and, less pleasantly, executions. To the north of the Castello, a whole new quarter known as the Terra Nova was Ercole's creation, with new streets, a piazza, palaces, gardens, churches and monasteries built over the last twenty years. The city was well defended with ramparts, redoubts and another castle, the Castel Novo, overlooking the Po. The Este dukes had created an impressive setting for the display of their power and prestige and, under their initiative, fifteenth-century Ferrara had become one of the major centres of Renaissance theatre, music and the decorative arts. The court was one of the most splendid in Italy, the palaces richly furnished with tapestries, silk hangings, oriental carpets, alabaster and painted and frescoed rooms. Its splendours rivalled Florence of the Medici, far outstripped those of the contemporary papal court, certainly the provincialism of Pesaro and even the magnificent ducal palace at Urbino. Outside the city, Este wealth and power were demonstrated by a number of magnificent villas and hunting lodges. All this was to be the state of Lucrezia Borgia, bastard daughter of a Spanish pope.

8. A New Life

'She is most beautiful of face, with vivacious, laughing eyes,
upright in her posture, acute, most prudent, most wise,
happy, pleasing and friendly'

– The Ferrarese chronicler Bernardino Zambotti, describing
Lucrezia's arrival in Ferrara, 2 February 1502

Ferrara, a northern river city on a flat plain ribboned with water-ways and marshes, could hardly have been more different from Rome, some two hundred miles to the south. In the autumn heavy rains drenched the streets: now in winter, with chilling mists rising from the surrounding waters and the canals that bisected the town, its gaily painted battlements and gilded towers took on the appearance of a medieval miniature. And on 2 February 1502, the day appointed for Lucrezia's formal entry into the city which was to be her home for the rest of her life, the scene was a blaze of colour.

The arrival of the bride destined to be the next Duchess of Ferrara had been the occasion for months of preparations intended to impress not just Lucrezia and her suite but also the envoys of all the powers represented and the citizens themselves with the ducal magnificence of the Este. Lucrezia crossed the bridge over the Po into the city through the fortified gate of Castel Tedaldo, where doctors of the University of Ferrara waited to hold a canopy of white silk over her. She was mounted on a splendid horse caparisoned in cloth of gold with gilded harness, and accompanied on foot by eight of Alfonso's courtiers. This was fortunate for, a few moments later, the horse, startled by a shot, threw her and she had to be helped to her feet, laughing, and remounted on a mule which Ercole had thoughtfully provided. Riding beside her under the canopy in the place of honour was the ambassador of the King of France, signifying his approval of the marriage.[1]

The bridal procession then wound through the streets headed by seventy-five of Alfonso's mounted crossbowmen in his red and white livery, wearing white plumed caps in the French style, followed by eighty trumpeters and twenty-four musicians playing woodwind instruments, then the Duchess of Urbino's company, in black satin and velvet, with Alfonso and his brother-in-law, Annibale Bentivoglio, bringing up the rear. Alfonso rode a great bay horse, with trappings of purple velvet glittering with plates of beaten gold in high relief. He himself wore a tunic of grey velvet all covered with scales of beaten gold, a black velvet beret on his head, with laces of beaten gold and white plumes, and short boots of soft grey skin made from unborn calves. Behind him marched Lucrezia's company, ten Spanish arquebusiers dressed in gold brocade and black velvet, followed by five bishops and the Ferrarese gentlemen and courtiers marching two by two with the Italian ambassadors. Lucrezia rode behind, then Ercole and the Duchess of Urbino side by side, followed by Geronima Borgia and Adriana de Mila, then Lucrezia Bentivoglio in a carriage covered with gold brocade and, following her, in twenty court carriages decorated in gold brocade and white silk drawn by white horses, the Ferrarese and Bolognese gentlewomen and damsels allotted by Ercole to attend the bride.

Lucrezia herself sparkled, her dress carefully noted by Isabella d'Este in one of her daily reports to her absent husband, Francesco Gonzaga. She wore a robe with long sleeves in the French style lined with ermine and decorated with interwoven stripes of cloth of gold and violet satin and over it a cloak of drawn cloth of gold open on one side to reveal its ermine lining. Bitterly, Isabella noted round Lucrezia's neck a diamond and ruby necklace which had belonged to the Duchess Eleonora and on her head the headdress which Ercole had sent to Rome for her,[2] also undoubtedly a part of the family jewels since it was loaded with spinels, diamonds and sapphires and other precious stones, including very

large pearls. 'The jewellers,' wrote Bernardino Zambotti, 'estimated its worth at 30,000 ducats.' Zambotti was equally impressed
by Lucrezia's baggage train of seventy-two mules caparisoned in
her livery of yellow and mulberry and carrying her rich trousseau
worth at least 200,000 ducats beyond the 100,000 in cash. He
was very taken with the bride's appearance (he gave her age as
twenty-four although she was still only twenty-two – since other
authorities overestimated her age, Lucrezia must have looked older
than she actually was). 'She is,' he wrote, 'most beautiful of face,
with vivacious, laughing eyes, upright in her posture, acute, most
prudent, most wise, happy, pleasing and friendly.' The people were
pleased by her, he said, hoping therefore for help and good government from her and beyond that great benefit to the city, particularly by the authority of the Pope, 'who loves this daughter of
his above all things, as he has demonstrated with the dowry and
the castles (Cento and Pieve) which he has conceded to Don
Alfonso'. Lucrezia's prize for completing the final part of her
journey to Ferrara was another valuable consignment of Este
family jewels presented to her that day, including a silver gilt
mirror surrounded by rubies and diamonds.[3]

Winding through the streets of the city, past platforms of citizens declaiming the praises of Lucrezia and the Pope, the procession reached the piazza in front of the cathedral and the Palazzo
del Corte, where two acrobats swung down on ropes from two
towers to arrive simultaneously at the cathedral door, to the great
amazement of the crowd. As soon as Lucrezia had dismounted
at the palace, in the customary division of spoils Ercole's crossbowmen seized the baldachin and fell to squabbling with Alfonso's
men over her mule, an argument won by Alfonso's servants. At
the head of the marble staircase (which still exists) she was greeted
by Isabella, with Lucrezia Bentivoglio, three bastard daughters of
Ercole's brother Sigismondo d'Este, including one of the principal courtiers, Diana, Countess Contrari, and the ladies of the
court, and taken through the Great Hall (*Sala Grande*) decorated
with cloth of silver and gold and precious silks, and featuring
two gilded giants with maces in hand. From there they proceeded

to Ercole's apartments in the Palazzo del Corte which had been specially prepared for the bridal couple, while Ercole himself retreated to newly decorated rooms in the Castel Novo.

After a short while Lucrezia and Alfonso were left alone together for the first time. Forced marriage or not, Alfonso found Lucrezia sexually attractive: that night, according to the report of Isabella's chancellor to Francesco, he made love to her three times ('*ha camminato tre miglia*').[4] He continued to spend every night with her. What he did during the day was another matter, returning to his former 'Prince Hal' life of whores and low tavern companions. Lucrezia's father, however, was characteristically delighted by the news, 'particularly understanding that they continue to sleep together at night', Beltrando Costabili, the Ferrarese envoy at Rome, reported, 'although he has heard that Don Alfonso takes his pleasure in diverse places as a young man, His Holiness says that he does very well'.[5]

Although Ercole reported happily to the Pope that Alfonso and Lucrezia 'gave each other pleasure', that did not mean they loved each other. It was a marriage of state, eagerly entered into by the one, reluctantly by the other. Lucrezia was not attracted by Alfonso's rough ways and manners and reserved character, but she had achieved her ambition and she was determined to make a success of her career as Duchess of Ferrara. She used charm and tact to consolidate her position. She had already won over the Este men; she even attempted to win over Isabella herself, but here she met with a polite, well-concealed rebuff. Isabella's family pride was offended by this young cuckoo in the Este nest, resentful that anyone with Lucrezia's background should occupy her mother's place. She had her spy in the Este chancellery, Bernardino di Prosperi, a devoted follower who gave her daily news of Lucrezia's progress, and whose letters, running into thousands, provide the best and most continuous contemporary account of Lucrezia's life in Ferrara.

Isabella's letters to her husband, describing the post-marriage festivities which took place during those carnival days at Ferrara, make clear her resentment. She was not, she made it plain, enjoying

herself. There had been no boisterous *matinata* with the family
and favoured courtiers waking the newly-wed couple with lewd
jokes. Perhaps, since the bride could by no stretch of the imagination be described as a virgin, it was considered inappropriate
by the Este. Lucrezia, reportedly 'tired from her night's engagement with her husband', kept to her apartments with her household the next day and did not leave them until Isabella and her
ladies came after dinner to take her into the Sala Grande for
dancing. Lucrezia, with Isabella, the Duchess of Urbino, and
Lucrezia's company of Roman and Ferrarese ladies, sat on a tribune decorated with cloth of curled gold and tapestries. Isabella
complained that the hall was so crowded that dancing was almost
impossible and after two dances Ercole paraded 110 actors in their
costumes for the five comedies by Plautus which were to be
enacted over the following days. The party then went by covered
way to the Palace of Justice (the Palazzo della Ragione) nearby,
where there would be more space for plays. A stage was set up
with painted wooden houses and castles and the company disposed
themselves on specially constructed rows all around the room.
The comedy the *Epidicus* was presented, interspersed with *moresche*
– dancing tableaux – including a mock fight of gladiators. Isabella,
like her sister-in-law and close friend Elisabetta da Montefeltro,
the latter nine years older than Lucrezia, must have felt their noses
out of joint at the younger woman's glamour and her position
at the centre of attention; they did not enjoy themselves. The first
play, the *Epidicus*, always had been mediocre, Isabella told
Francesco, although she went into detail about the four *moresche*,
which featured soldiers, Moors and mock battles. There was no
time to describe the variety and number of changes of Lucrezia's
dresses, she said, and complained of the numerous pickpockets
operating there – one thief had been found hiding under the
bed in the Palazzo Schifanoia and had robbed Cesare's envoy of
a valuable gold chain, for which he was hanged the next day as
a deterrent to others.[6]

A tone of rancour and disparagement of Lucrezia ran through
all accounts by Isabella and her entourage of the wedding

festivities. The Marchioness of Cotrone wrote a letter of breath-taking sycophancy to Francesco Gonzaga featuring his wife as the star of the proceedings: on the day of Lucrezia's entry, she wrote, Isabella overshadowed everyone in her 'beauty and elegant appearance ... grace and everything', so much so that had Lucrezia been aware of this she would have made her entry accompanied by blazing candelabra. On the night of the ball, she reported, 'As soon as your illustrious consort appeared in the room, all eyes turned where she went, and when she arrived among the ladies, she appeared as the sun does obscuring with its rays all the stars ... Throughout this court one hears the two jesters, finely dressed in clothes given them by the Marchesana [Isabella] shouting out the royal behaviour of the Marchesana. In fact, my lord, the praise of all these feasts will be all for my excellent patroness and conse-quently of Your Excellency . . .'[7]

Isabella was infuriated by the time it took Lucrezia to rise and dress herself in the morning, as she complained to Francesco:

Yesterday we all had to remain in our rooms until the twenty-third hour because Donna Lucretia takes so long to rise and dress herself . . . and, it being Friday, there could be no dancing so at the twenty-third hour there began the comedy, *Le Bachide*, which was so long and tedious and without fine *intermezzi* that more than once I wished myself in Mantua to which it seems a thousand years before I will be able to return – both to see our little son and to get out of here where there is no pleasure at all. Your Lordship should not envy me for your not being here at this marriage because it is of such a coldness that I envy anyone who remained in Mantua.

She used the same words in a brief note to her brother-in-law, Sigismondo Gonzaga, the same day.[8]

Isabella was never backward in singing her own praises to Lucrezia's detriment. She did not have a moment to write in her own hand as she would have liked, she told her husband, because the whole day her brothers never left her alone nor did the gentle-women who courted her because they could not see Lucrezia until she came down to the hall. 'At the fifth hour of night we meet, at the seventh and eighth we go to bed. Just think how much pleasure I take from this and have pity on me.' Just to underline the superiority of her own behaviour as compared with that of her new sister-in-law, she added a proud postscript: 'I cannot refrain from saying in commendation of myself that I am always the first up and dressed.'

'Coldness' was again the theme of her next report: 'Saturday passed with this coldness: the bride did not make herself visible, having spent the day washing her hair and writing letters . . .'⁹ This sin was compounded in Isabella's eyes by Lucrezia's making a private presentation that evening to Ercole of the papal brief rescinding the census. Isabella and Elisabetta amused themselves, meanwhile, by touring the city with Ferrante, Giulio and Niccolò da Correggio, returning to entertain the French ambassador who had invited himself to dine. After dinner the ladies and 'some Frenchmen and Spaniards sent by the Lady' danced *il ballo del capello* (the hat dance) and finally, by general request, she said, Isabella sang, accompanying herself on the lute. On Sunday in the cathedral the Pope's representative presented Alfonso with the sword and cap blessed by the Pope at Christmas, and that evening Isabella and Elisabetta, with the Este brothers, fetched Lucrezia to the Sala Grande to dance for two hours, during which time Lucrezia danced some *basse francese* with one of her damsels 'very gallantly', as even Isabella admitted. There was yet another comedy, the *Miles Gloriosus*, and *intermezzi*. The following day, from the balcony of the Torre di Rigobello of the palace, Lucrezia and the company watched a joust in the piazza between a Mantuan knight and a Bolognese, in the course of which the Bolognese's horse was killed. This, according to Isabella, was a victory for the Mantuan, who shouted '*Turco! Turco!*', the Gonzaga battle cry. This bloodthirsty spectacle was followed by another comedy, the *Asinaria*, and a Mantuan composition by the celebrated singer and composer Tromboncino, who again performed an *intermezzo* to the comedy *La Cassina* the next day, when a *barzelleta* in honour of the bridal couple was sung. Later six violas were played, one of them by Alfonso himself. That morning, 6 February, Ercole presented Lucrezia with what Isabella described as 'almost all the remaining jewels', including diamonds, rubies, turquoises and pearls set in gold or fashioned into head ornaments.[10] Following this the ambassadors had given her their wedding presents – rich pieces of cloth, crimson velvet cloaks from the Venetians, curled cloth of gold from the Florentines and two silver vases from the Sienese.

Isabella described *La Cassina* as 'lascivious and immoral' although she enjoyed the sight of Alfonso and Giulio taking part in almost all the *intermezzi*. But she remained bored and distant from the festivities, as she told Francesco: 'I am more than certain that you will have derived more pleasure from my letters than I have from these festivities because I have never been in any place with more tedium than I have here . . .'[11] On Saturday without fail she would leave for Mantua accompanied by Elisabetta. All the ambassadors were leaving the following day, except the Roman ladies who had come with Lucrezia, because the Pope had written telling them that they should stay for the present – perhaps, she thought, so that they could be sent to France to fetch Cesare's wife, Charlotte d'Albret. (Charlotte never arrived, but her brother, Cardinal d'Albret, did, and 'being young' amused himself greatly taking part in the dancing.) 'How much this pleases my father your lordship can imagine,' she added sarcastically. The Gonzaga secretary, Benedetto Capilupo, was deliberately malicious when he compared the style and grace with which Isabella and Elisabetta responded to the formal farewells of the Venetian ambassadors with Lucrezia's performance: Isabella replied to the ambassadors' speeches 'with such great eloquence and prudence that it would have sufficed for every consummate orator', he wrote to Francesco, but as for Lucrezia, 'although she has had more experience of men than either your wife or your sister, she got nowhere near their prudent replies . . .'[12]

Now that it was Lent and the festivities were over, there was little to do. Inseparable, Isabella and Elisabetta wandered the streets of Ferrara looking for amusement before going to dine with

Lucrezia in the late Duchess Eleonora's apartment in the Castello which she and Alfonso now occupied. As usual, there were complaints about her tardiness: it was the twenty-third hour and she had only just finished dressing. On 11 February, Ercole paid Lucrezia the great compliment of taking her and Isabella to see his cherished Sister Lucia: 'She was in bed in a trance,' Isabella reported, 'because of the passion she had suffered the previous night and did not recognize anyone, even her relatives from Viterbo, a stupendous thing.'[13]

A few days later Ercole, who was truly charmed by his daughter-in-law and their shared interest in nuns, went personally to fetch Lucrezia from the castle and again took her to visit Sister Lucia, with the additional treat of seeing a nun who had been brought from St Peter's in Rome after being walled up there.[14] Whatever his daughter and her courtiers might have thought, he was pleased with his daughter-in-law, as he wrote to Alexander:

Before the most illustrious Duchess, our common daughter, arrived here, my firm intention was to caress her and honour her, as is fitting, and not to fail in anything pertaining to singular affection. Now that Her Ladyship has come here, she has so satisfied me, by the virtues and worthy qualities that I find in her, that not only am I confirmed in this good disposition, but the desire and intention to do so have greatly increased in me; and so much the more as I see your Holiness, by a brief in your own hand, lovingly suggests this to me. Let Your Holiness be of good cheer, because I shall treat the said Duchess in such a wise that your Beatitude may know that I hold her Ladyship for the dearest thing that I have in the world.[15]

Lucrezia, whose 'remote and solitary nature' had already been remarked upon by the envoys who had accompanied her to Ferrara, kept herself to herself in her apartments in the Castello. She was aware of being watched, spied upon and judged in comparison with the Este women, not so much Isabella as her royal predecessor, the Duchess Eleonora. Ugly, clever and an excellent administrator, Eleonora had been popular and admired for her abilities and her piety. Even after death she would be the yardstick against which Lucrezia would now be measured. Accustomed as she was to the labyrinthine life of the Borgia court at Rome, where hostile outsiders spied on their every move, Lucrezia knew she had to tread warily and trust no one. Similarly, she was regarded with suspicion and hostility by many of the court who knew her and her family only too well by reputation. Di Prosperi noted that the wife of the Venetian *visdomino* and some other gentlewomen had visited her – 'but few in number, however'. 'Madonna Leonora, Countess of La Mirandola', had called but not been received and had returned affronted and annoyed, according to reports. Di Prosperi had, however, spoken to Lucrezia for the first time on 18 February and his impression was, he said, that she was of great goodness and prudence, far more than had been reported. And according to Madonna Theodora, a leading lady at court, she was most kind and very patient with those who served her. 'And I believe,' he added, 'that she will make herself more at home the more she understands our ways.'

It was a difficult time for Lucrezia, whose household was being dismissed by Ercole and replaced by Ferrarese of his choice. Di Prosperi struggled to find out for Isabella exactly what was going on but largely in vain. He believed that they were awaiting final instructions from Alexander but it seemed that many had left and certain others were preparing to leave. Lucrezia had been visited in the *camerino dal pozzolo*, the room with the balcony, by several noble ladies but very few men, he said.[16] A week later he was able to tell her that Geronima Borgia and the beautiful Catherina had left with two women singers 'and therefore the greater part of those Spaniards of her household'. Adriana de Mila and Angela Borgia were still there, as well as the two Neapolitan sisters and their mother.

As if to compensate for the difficulties she was experiencing, Lucrezia's relationship with Alfonso and Ercole was serene. Alfonso took her to watch him hunting in the Barco, the huge hunting ground and lake developed by Ercole behind the castle: falcons were flown, a hare was chased down and killed by '*pardi*' (leopards, possibly cheetahs) and a wolf by dogs, something di Prosperi concluded, probably incorrectly since Lucrezia's father and brother were such keen huntsmen, she had never seen. On her return, Ercole himself went to the gate of the Barco and accompanied her back into the castle, while the next day he took her in a carriage to see the nuns of the Estes' favoured convent, Corpus Domini, and again the following day to mass at San Vido. 'His affection and honour for her with such demonstrations is a great thing,' di Prosperi commented. Moreover Alfonso never failed to sleep with her at night and to do everything to make her happy. 'Yesterday he had decorated the *Zardino del bagno* where she could eat and wash her hair and [his favourite] il Barone, who is always with His Lordship and eats with him at table, accompanied her to the Castle.'[17]

This is a reference to the rooms and garden formerly occupied by Eleonora and later by Alfonso. Giovanni Sabadino degli Arienti, the Bolognese writer and scholar who had presented Ercole with a beautiful manuscript celebrating the marriage of Alfonso and Lucrezia, has left an enchanting description of this garden by the Castello where Lucrezia enjoyed a suite of bathrooms, with warming rooms and a necessarium furnished with marble benches on which to sit and marble steps leading down into a bath which would be lined with linen cloth for greater comfort. Bathing was a social occupation as well as a beauty treatment. Lucrezia and her ladies could spend long hours either bathing or sitting chatting in the warm room heated by a stove. Apart from the water drawn from the earth beneath the city, barrels of mud and water from spas near Padua at Abano and San Bartolommeo were brought in for health treatments. The garden itself enclosed an orchard, shrubs surrounded by box hedges, and a central pavilion surmounted by a gilded statue of Hercules, its lead roof resting on sixteen white marble columns, and a floor of inlaid coloured marble. Gilded bronze lions' heads issued water into a marble basin surrounding the pavilion; four paths leading from it were paved in terracotta and shaded by roses growing on

frames of crossed willow. Outside in the garden there were orna-
mental fruit trees, tall cypresses and jasmine; the walls were lined
with vines growing out of borders of rosemary. There was a
potager for vegetables and herbs, a flower garden planted with
lilies, violas, carnations and white privet and a fishpond. Under
a white marble loggia in summer tables would be placed for
dining, decorated with flowers and herbs.[18] That winter, however,
Lucrezia occupied rooms which had been specially redecorated
for her in the Torre Marchesana of the Castello, while one of
Alfonso's rooms in the Torre San Paolo had been designed to
make her feel at home with roundels containing the arms of the
Pope, Cesare and the King of France; a ceiling featured the devices
of Alfonso and Lucrezia on an azure ground.[19]

Even in these delightful surroundings Maria Bellonci has
nonetheless represented Lucrezia as resentful and rebellious over
the replacement of many of her former household. This seems
unlikely for it was normal practice at the time for local servants
and courtiers to replace the large contingent of 'foreigners' accompanying the bride. A core of her household, and, more importantly for her, her ladies, remained with her, including her cousin
Angela Borgia, her favourite Nicola, the much-loved Catherinella
negra, Elisabetta senese, and others who accompanied her from
Rome. They were, according to her wardrobe accounts, still with
her in 1507,[20] while Zambotti lists no fewer than twelve of the
women – ladies and servants – who accompanied her from Rome
and remained with her in Ferrara.[21] Of the male members of her
staff from Rome, no fewer than twenty remained with her. These
included such important people as her secretary, Messer
Cristoforo; her chaplain, the Bishop of Orta; Vincenzo Giordano,
the master of her wardrobe; Sancho, her steward, the master of
ceremonies at her table; and such officials as her *credenciero*; stable
master; *il bacilliere*; her tailor and her cook, while Navarrico also
remained. The men allotted to her by Ercole included two gentlemen in waiting, *compagni*, and the distinguished Jacobo Bendedei
who acted as her seneschal, cooks, doctors and table officials, a
financial controller, doorkeepers, pages, serving men and others.[22]

Six Ferrarese women were recruited to her household and twelve '*donzelle*', or damsels, aged under eighteen, who included the daughters of local aristocrats, merchants and craftsmen. The list names 'the daughter of Ercole, goldsmith, formerly a Jew', and La Violante also 'formerly a Jew'. Lucrezia's court was to be a finishing school for these girls, where they were taught embroidery, dancing, courtly skills and Christian principles. Lucrezia looked out for husbands for them, often pursuing recalcitrant fiancés beyond the city limits. Her household in total comprised 120 persons, or '*boche*'.[23]

Di Prosperi, who was certainly not prejudiced in Lucrezia's favour although he was gradually won round to her, specifically denied that she made any fuss about the changes imposed on her. Talking of the new household arrangements he told Isabella: 'And as far as I understand, Her Ladyship speaks as modestly as it is possible to describe [concerning this] nor has she ever shown any discontent or dislike and has even said that she is pleased that some of her own people remain and as far as the rest is concerned she has always wished for no more than what should please the Duke and her husband, in a manner that she has, they say, demonstrated goodness and prudence, and that her kind way of speaking has ensured the retention of her people.'[24] Subtle and intelligent as she was, Lucrezia knew perfectly how to achieve her purposes by the use of charm rather than confrontation.

Angry confrontations, however, did take place between Alexander and Ercole over the amount of Lucrezia's annual allowance. As was her wont in difficult times, Lucrezia retreated to the convent of Corpus Domini, ostensibly for Holy Week preceding Easter, while Alfonso went to the Certosa. From Rome, Alexander showered Lucrezia with papal indulgences for her and her household, while exchanging furious letters with Ercole over her income. Di Prosperi reported that Lucrezia's allowance would probably be established at 10,000 ducats a year to cover the expenses of clothes, subsistence and salaries for her household. Alexander demanded 12,000 ducats while Ercole, typically, started the bidding at 8,000, arguing that that had been the sum allotted to his daughter Isabella.

By the end of March there were rumours that Lucrezia was pregnant, evidenced by her poor appetite: 'She eats almost nothing and for this reason she rarely eats in public and rarely goes out, although the members of the family and the men and women of good family visit her,' di Prosperi reported to Isabella on 2 April. She found the antics of the clown La Fertella, who ate at her table, extremely diverting and went out on occasion to dine with the rich Rizo del Tartufo and with Ferrante d'Este, one of her favourite brothers-in-law. She also gave a dinner for Ercole at which she exhibited the splendours of her *credenza*, a dresser displaying silver, and was well enough to watch the Corpus Christi procession, which was diverted to pass by her windows, and later the traditional races for St George's Day. She continued, however, to be unwell, and the cautious Ercole did not inform the Pope of her pregnancy until 21 April.

On 3 May, Alfonso, accompanied by Sigismondo, was ordered by Ercole to go to meet the King of France and receive his prize, the county of Cotignola, donated by Louis as a sop to the Este for swallowing the Borgia marriage. On his departure Lucrezia also left Ferrara for Belriguardo, the magnificent Este villa which was to become one of her favourite retreats. As she told Ercole on 4 May, the day after her arrival, she had found it 'much more beautiful than I could have imagined . . .' Eight miles south-east of Ferrara, Belriguardo, of which little remains today, was one of the most celebrated palaces in Italy. It was huge, and had cost Ercole, according to Sabadino, 'a mountain of gold'. It featured stabling for five hundred horses, secret passages, stately halls, marble loggias, box-lined gardens and a chapel painted by the celebrated Cosimo Tura within its battlemented walls. It contained a succession of vast frescoed halls, one lined with portraits of wise men, another with a painting of Ercole and his courtiers with their names and arms, and another room showing Ercole in Triumph, with what could be described as a veritable *Who's Who* of the Herculean circle in the early 1490s. In one adjoining room he was depicted as a member of the Order of the Garter, again surrounded by his principal courtiers; the most famous room was the Sala di Psiche with its series of huge murals of the Roman myths. 'And seeing the *broilo* [box garden] with its fruiting plants all in order and the huge garden, each enclosed by high and fine walls with their white battlements and red crenellations by this enormous and beautiful palace with its glazed and iron-grilled windows, I should think that a circuit of the place . . . would be more than a mile,' Sabadino marvelled.[25]

Lucrezia was accompanied to Belriguardo by Ferrante, the idle but amusing brother of whom she was extremely fond – 'how much we laughed over your letters', she was later to write to him. She also received regular reports from Sigismondo on his and Alfonso's progress to France (Alfonso himself was a poor correspondent). Replying to thank him, she apologized for only being able to write him a postscript in her own hand – 'the cause being my pregnancy . . .'[26]

Despite her friendly letters, Lucrezia was not only feeling increasingly unwell but also relieved to be out of Ferrara and away from the constant observation of courtiers like di Prosperi who criticized her for remaining away. 'She has not moved from Belriguardo,' he reported on 9 May, 'and stays there very willingly.' Worse, she only seemed to enjoy herself with such intimates as Angela Borgia who had been ill and stayed behind, but had joined Lucrezia, her '*patrona*', 'who only lets herself enjoy herself much unless with her and her other Spanish ladies as she has always done since she came here. And also I understand that in these days Messer Nicolo da Correzo [Niccolò da Correggio] was there wishing to visit her and was told that she was sleeping and he could not see her then. If these things are reported in such a way, I leave it to your ladyship what to think.' Di Prosperi's comments on '*la patrona*' became increasingly critical:

So that Your Ladyship can understand what is happening here and the difference it makes between one *patrona* [the Duchess Eleonora] and another [Lucrezia] you must know that on Tuesday around the twenty-second hour, His Lordship your father mounted his horse and with a great part of the court and crossbowmen rode to the bridge of San Giorgio to meet Madonna who, returning from Belriguardo had dismounted at Cogomaro to eat at the house of Antonio Guarnero so that . . . it was the twenty-fourth hour before she arrived and then he accompanied her to the Zardino del Castello to the apartments of Don Alfonso where she now lodges. Yesterday after vespers he came to take her from her apartment and accompanied her to Sor [Sister] Lucia. I let Your Ladyship imagine in what a state we now are . . .

Ercole and the male members of the Este family were as charmed by Lucrezia as clearly as Isabella d'Este was not. Lucrezia's early attempts to establish a relationship with her formidable sister-in-law, whom she knew to have considerable influence with her brothers, fell on stony ground. Writing to Lucrezia, whom she addressed as 'Lady Lucretia Borgia', as if unwilling to grant her the Este name, Isabella reported her safe arrival back in Mantua and the 'convalescence' of Francesco Gonzaga (who had clearly used illness as an excuse for his absence from the wedding). It was a polite, even gracious, but distant letter, unlike the one of the same date she wrote to Lucrezia's cousin, Geronima Borgia, in which she gushed about 'the love and friendship they had contracted' and expressed the hope that Geronima would write to her 'so that our mutual benevolence should not pass into oblivion'.[27] Lucrezia replied to Isabella with a graceful, ingratiating letter, signing herself, significantly, 'Lucretia esten de borgia'. In May, still at Belriguardo, she wrote to Isabella recommending a certain 'Jo. Jacomo Sculptore', recently arrived from Rome, and asking her if she would let him make a portrait bust of her for Lucrezia's pleasure.

But on her return to Ferrara, Lucrezia, possibly encouraged by Alexander, appeared to be digging her toes in. Ill and pregnant, conscious that she might be carrying the longed-for Este heir, she was proving rebellious, as her late arrival and keeping Ercole waiting reported above by di Prosperi showed. Accustomed to the Borgia courts, she well knew how to play her game and, as far as the core friends of her household were concerned, she succeeded. On 26 May, di Prosperi followed up his account of her arrival in Ferrara with the news that four people – 'the first and the best' – assigned to Lucrezia's service had begged Ercole to let them leave her. He replied that they should await the return of Alfonso. 'This,' di Prosperi wrote, 'proceeds from their being badly looked on and worse treated. Only the Spaniards find favour with her so that I suspect few of our people [i.e. Ferrarese] will stay with her, remembering as they do a greater Lady than her [Duchess Eleonora] and having been kindly received . . .'

Lucrezia was longing to leave Ferrara again, this time for the Este villa at Medelana, but her departure was delayed by the dangerous illness of her beloved Angela Borgia. So she remained, staying in the beautiful Palazzo Belfiore on the north-eastern confines of Ferrara, probably because of redecorations to her apartments in the Giardino del Castello. Belfiore was mostly used as a summer residence away from the unhealthy heat and, no doubt, smells, of central Ferrara. Only four displaced marble columns remain of this building, which once stood on an island in the Barco. It was described by the Bolognese writer Giovanni Sabadino degli Arienti as 'a habitation of the most splendid and marvellous beauty, and of the most beautiful architecture that ever could be built by the engineer's art'. There are now no traces of the loggiaed central courtyard with its cycle of enchanting frescoes showing Alberto d'Este and his court hunting and feasting in the meadows then surrounding what was his hunting retreat but now enclosed within Ercole's new quarter. Other rooms showed more hunting motifs with stags, lions and boar; there were scenes from Ercole's life, even a representation of an elephant which had apparently visited Ferrara; but the most notable series glorified the life of the Duchess Eleonora and her court, playing chess, dancing to the sounds of drums and pipes and feasting. Eleonora's formal entry into Ferrara as a bride and her marriage ceremony were depicted there, all reminders to Lucrezia of Este expectations.[28]

Lucrezia was still there in June when Cesare made another

violent demonstration of his Borgia nature in a lightning strike on Urbino, surprising Guidobaldo who was expecting him to attack Camerino more than one hundred miles to the south, and who just had time to flee without any possessions before Cesare marched into Urbino on the morning of 21 June. News of Cesare's taking of Urbino sent a shock wave through the courts of Italy, not least in Mantua and Ferrara. With only four horsemen as companions, Guidobaldo had a nightmare journey to Mantua where Elisabetta was still staying, stopping only to consult Ercole who was at his villa of Monastirolo. As di Prosperi wrote to Isabella, 'the sad news of the Illustrious Lord Duke of Urbino has caused such wonder among all the people [here] that it was two days before anyone believed it, but confirmation from all sides has left the populace in the greatest sadness and displeasure that you can imagine'. Lucrezia, he said, was most distressed, bearing in mind the honour and welcome she had received in Urbino from Guidobaldo and pitying the Duchess. 'I do not believe her reaction is simulated,' he added, 'because the case merits condemnation unto the gates of hell: and these Spaniards of hers do not disagree.'[29] Writing on the same day to her sister-in law Chiara Gonzaga, Isabella reported the arrival there of Guidobaldo 'in his doublet' having only just succeeded in escaping with his life. Calling Cesare's attack 'unthought of and cursed', she said they had all been 'so shocked, confused and grieved [by it] that we ourselves hardly know where we are'.

Isabella was panic-stricken that she too might share her sister-in-law's fate. The fact that she had provided shelter, even briefly, for the family of the Duke of Urbino, was bound to arouse Cesare's ever-alert suspicions. The arrival of an envoy sent by Cesare, named only by Isabella as 'Francesc' but probably Francesco Troche, who was intimately concerned in Cesare's plans, frightened her further. Convinced he was a spy, she wrote immediately to Francesco Gonzaga who had left to join the French court, asking him to send a letter favourable to Cesare which she could show to this man. Gonzaga as usual had dawdled and then produced what Isabella considered to be an inadequate epistle.

She therefore drew up another one and forwarded it to him, entreating him to keep the fact that she had done so a secret. This time she included Lucrezia as well as Cesare in her suspicions: 'so that knowledge of it should not come to the ears of either the Duchess or the Duke, so that they should mistrust those words which I artfully inserted in the letter to give greater hope [of our loyalty] to il Valentino'.[30]

Only Machiavelli, in Urbino with a Florentine delegation for his first interview with Cesare on 24 June, was impressed, taking away an idea of the twenty-five-year-old leader which he later transmuted into his famous Chapter VII of *The Prince*: 'This Lord is truly splendid and magnificent, and in war there is no enterprise so great that it does not appear small to him; in the pursuit of glory and lands he never rests nor recognizes fatigue or danger. He arrives in one place before it is known that he has left another; he is popular with his soldiers and he has collected the best men in Italy; these things make him victorious and formidable, particularly when added to permanent good fortune.'[31]

For Lucrezia, Cesare's coup was profoundly embarrassing, adding to the suspicion with which she was regarded by the Ferrarese and, indeed, the Gonzaga. Yet no doubt she was secretly proud of her brother's daring successes which, far from undermining her own position, actually enhanced it. Her existence guaranteed the safety of Ferrara, but it must also have increased her sense of isolation and her dependence on the Spanish core of her household. Alfonso was with the King of France, Ercole was making his way there and she was having a difficult pregnancy. As the summer wore on, her health grew worse; in mid July an epidemic of fever reached Ferrara, and in her weakened state Lucrezia became seriously ill. On 11 July, di Prosperi reported that the previous Saturday after eating a little she had vomited and had a fever and that 'this evening there was great disquiet about her'. Ercole and Alfonso were informed. 'God preserve her because it would not be to anyone's purpose that she should die for now,' he added cynically. From Belfiore on 13 July she wrote to Ercole, thanking him for his letter written from Piacenza en route to join Louis XII in Milan. 'If anything could give me swift relief from this my present indisposition,' she wrote, 'it has been your most welcome letter.' Since the previous Saturday she had been overtaken by fever and had felt too ill to write to inform him of her illness, certain that Gian Luca Pozzi (who was always with her, hoping for her help in obtaining a cardinal's hat from her father) would inform him.[32] She suffered a severe paroxysm, then another, this time less severe. Alfonso arrived to console her, closely followed by Sigismondo.[33] By 24 July she was still suffering paroxysms accompanied by fever and the doctors were doing everything they could both to cure her and to save the baby. Alfonso slept every night in a room next to hers and was always there when she took food.[34] Francesco Troche paid her a call en route from the King of France to the Pope. The Pope sent his favourite doctor, the Bishop of Venosa, from Rome, while Francesc Remolins, known to the Italians as Remolino, came from Cesare's camp for the latest news.[35]

Doctors were ordered to her side by Ercole, the Pope and Cesare, and with their help she would try to get well, she told Ercole on 28 July. In Rome Alexander characteristically made use of her illness in his negotiations with Ercole over her allowance, telling Costabili that it had been caused by the deficit in her allowance which should be made up from 10,000 to 12,000 ducats so that she could pay her debts.[36] Cesare's contribution to his sister's health was to write her a letter from Urbino on 20 July announcing the imminent surrender of Camerino and its lords, the Varani, yet another family connection of the Este. The fact that he could do this is an indication that Lucrezia was far from being as shocked by his aggressive coups as she pretended to be:

'Illustrious Lady and dearest Sister,' he wrote:

I know nothing could be better medicine for Your Excellency in your present illness than the good news which I have to impart. I must tell you that I have just had information that Camerino will yield. We trust that on receiving this news your condition will rapidly improve, and that you will inform us at once of it. For your indisposition prevents us from deriving any pleasure from this and other news. We ask you to tell the illustrious Duke Don Alfonso, your husband, our brother-in-law, at once, as, owing to want of time, we have not been able to write to him direct.

Your Excellency's brother, who loves you better than himself . . .

But this cheering news did not cure Lucrezia whose condition over the following days deteriorated. On 31 July, di Prosperi reported that she was very weak and the general opinion was that both she and her child would die. She suffered a severe nose-bleed but seemed better to the extent that she expressed a wish to go to Belriguardo but this the doctors would not consider. Many of her ladies, di Prosperi reported, were also ill, and Madonna Cecharella mortally so. But by the time both Cesare and Alfonso rushed to her bedside on 3 August, she was well enough to lie dressed upon her bed where she received them, as she reported to Ercole three days later. Disguised as a knight of St John, Cesare was on his way with three other horsemen (including Troche and Remolins) to see Louis XII, with whom he had a secret and vital agreement, in Milan where the King was surrounded by Cesare's enemies. Alfonso arrived shortly afterwards and, according to Lucrezia, the three of them enjoyed 'pleasant conversation' for two hours. The next day the two men left in the direction of Reggio.

Lucrezia, however, recovered only briefly at the sight of her brother and husband. She suffered a relapse and the fever and the 'flux' continued, although her brave letters to Ercole gave no indication of the danger she was in. Many of her doctors too were sick, Francesco Castello grievously so, while another, Francesco Carri, later died. By the beginning of September she was seriously ill, suffering fits of sweating interspersed with chills every day. Francesco Castello told Ercole that only giving birth would relieve her; the Bishop of Venosa wrote unsympathetically to Rome of '*accidenti di animo*' (fits of the spirit) and hysterical phenomena. On 3 and 4 September her fits were so severe that Castello could only recommend her to God's grace; then, on the evening of the 5th, she was seized with a convulsion which caused her to arch her back, as screaming, she gave birth to a stillborn, seven-month-old daughter. Puerperal fever consumed her and the doctors despaired; two days later, at dawn on 7 September, Cesare made a sudden appearance, having ridden furiously from the French court at Milan, accompanied by his brother-in-law the Cardinal d'Albret and thirteen gentlemen. Later that morning the doctors took the decision to bleed Lucrezia; to distract her Cesare held her foot and told jokes, even succeeding in making her laugh, but that night her condition deteriorated. Castello did not sleep, not daring to leave her, and in the morning she was given communion. However, as the morning went on she seemed better and an exhausted Castello told the inquiring di Prosperi that if things went on in this way until the next day he believed she would survive.[37] Cesare, hoping for the best for his adored sister, left as swiftly and as secretly as he had arrived. Couriers rode furiously between Ferrara and Rome bearing the latest news of Lucrezia. In Rome on 8 September, Costabili reported that Alexander had heard 'with great grief of the stillbirth of his daughter Duchess Lucrezia, but concluded that the grief would have been considerably greater if the child had been a boy'.[38] Saraceni, who had also seen the Pope, added that 'he much praised the prince Alfonso for his great tenderness towards her'.[39] Ercole, however, as a letter dictated by Lucrezia of 4 September reveals, had not ceased to press her over his hopes for a cardinal's hat for his favourite, Gian Luca Pozzi. Yet on the news of her stillbirth he had rushed to her side from Reggio where he had been conferring with il Valentino.

Lucrezia had failed in her duty to provide the Estes with a male heir and her sufferings were by no means over. On 13 September she had yet another relapse, so severe apparently that she felt her own pulse and exclaimed, 'Oh good, I am dead.' She added a codicil to her will which she had brought with her from Rome, to the benefit of Rodrigo Bisceglie. Rumours ran through the courts of Italy that she had been poisoned, the theory being that her failure to provide the Este with an heir had caused them to wish to rid themselves of the hated Borgia. This was unfair; not only had both Alfonso and Ercole expressed the greatest concern for her but Alfonso had vowed that, if Lucrezia survived, he would make a pilgrimage on foot to the shrine of the Madonna di Loreto. In the event, he changed his mind and went more comfortably by boat with Alexander's specific dispensation from his original vow. By early October, Lucrezia was considered cured; while Alfonso left for Loreto, she took her court to the convent of Corpus Domini where, for three or four days, she intended to fulfil, out of the public eye, a vow made during her illness to wear only grey.[40]

Elsewhere in Italy, Lucrezia's family was approaching the zenith of its power. As the year came to a close Cesare committed one more great act of terror which has resounded down history, dubbed by his contemporaries 'a most beautiful deception'. No one knows whether Lucrezia, sick as she was in the summer of 1502, had been aware of Cesare's plans to extend and consolidate his position in Italy, nor of the incredible risks he had knowingly run. The danger lay in his own success in the takeover of the lands of the Church, planned from the day he was made Gonfalonier. By the end of June 1502 most of the former vicariates north of the Campagna were in his hands, Camerino was about to fall and Sinigallia, a small town on the Adriatic, was marked down for destruction. Around Rome all the lands of the Roman barons except those of the Orsini, his allies for the moment, had been taken over by the Borgias. Within the Papal States, Cesare's chosen area of operation, only Bologna, Perugia, Città di Castello and Fermo remained outside his control and, as such, obvious targets. Cesare's lightning attack on Urbino had marvellously concentrated the minds of the lords of these cities – most of whom were paid captains of Cesare's – on the fate that could befall them too. At a meeting at Lake Trasimene, shortly after Guidobaldo's overthrow, between Vitellozzo Vitelli of Città di Castello and Gian Paolo Baglioni of Perugia (both of them Cesare's captains), grand words were spoken about the 'great betrayal' (of Urbino) executed by the

Duke (Cesare) and they began 'to recognize his *marrano* faith more clearly'.[41]

Once again the key for the Borgia advance was the French King's desire for the Kingdom of Naples. Throughout July and August, while in Rome Alexander talked openly and ominously of the Orsini and Vitellozzo Vitelli, and Cesare, as secret and as elusive as ever, went hunting with leopards in the hills round Urbino, his face covered with thin silk against the flies, Francesco Troche was working to persuade Louis to abandon his protection of the Orsini and the Bentivoglio of Bologna in return for Borgia support for his Naples campaign. Isabella d'Este, far more politically acute and cool-headed than her husband, had wind of this and warned Francesco to be careful:

It is generally believed that His Most Christian Majesty has some understanding with Valentino, so I beg of you to be careful not to use words which may be repeated to him, because in these days we do not know who is to be trusted. There is a report here . . . that Your Excellency has spoken angry words against Valentino before the Most Christian King and the Pope's servants . . . and they will doubtless reach the ears of Valentino, who, having already shown that he does not scruple to conspire against those of his own blood [a reference to the death of Gandia], will, I am certain, not hesitate to plot against your person . . . it would be perfectly easy to poison Your Excellency . . .[42]

Isabella herself was more cynical in her reactions to Cesare's 'nefarious' crime against Guidobaldo and Elisabetta: the day before she wrote this warning letter to Francesco she had written to her brother Ippolito in Rome asking him to intercede with Cesare to help her acquire for herself two statues of Venus and Cupid which had been in the palace at Urbino. Cesare, who was in the process of packing up all Guidobaldo's treasures, including his father Federigo's celebrated library, and sending them to the Rocca di Forlì, instantly obliged, sending a special messenger to deliver the statues to the cupidinous Isabella.

Cesare's unexpected arrival at the King's court at Milan and the ostentatiously friendly welcome accorded him by Louis, frightened his enemy lords gathered there. Even Francesco Gonzaga who, on the day of Cesare's arrival, had unwisely boasted to the Venetian envoy that he would fight a hand-to-hand duel with 'that bastard son of a priest', hastened to make his peace with il Valentino. 'Today we have caressed and embraced each other, offering each to the other as good brothers, and thus together with the Most Christian Majesty we have spent all this day dancing and feasting . . .,' he reassured Isabella.

Cesare's next objective was to be the Bentivoglio, the Este in-laws and rulers of Bologna, another papal vicariate. While Cesare laid plans for the next campaign, in Rome Alexander was intent on his long vendetta to avenge the death of Juan Gandia. On 25 September, Giulio Orsini told him to his face that the French had warned Cardinal Orsini at Milan that it was the Pope's inten-tion to ruin the house of Orsini. The next day the clan gathered for a family conference at Todi which could not bode well for the Borgias. This was followed by a meeting at Cardinal Orsini's castle of La Magione, attended not only by the principal members of the Orsini family (one of whom, Paolo, was in Cesare's employ), but a powerful group of Cesare's captains who feared for their states, namely Vitellozzo Vitelli of Città di Castello, Oliverotto of Fermo and Gian Paolo Baglioni of Perugia, while the lords of threatened or surrendered cities – Guidobaldo da Montefeltro, Giovanni Bentivoglio and Pandolfo Petrucci of Siena sent repre-sentatives. Baglioni warned the conspirators that if they did not take preventive action against il Valentino they would be 'one by one devoured by the dragon'. The situation was fraught with danger for Cesare: on 7 October the revolt against him of the key fortress of San Leo in Urbino jolted the men at La Magione into action and on the 9th a League was signed against Cesare.

Machiavelli was at Imola with a Florentine delegation to Cesare when the news of the League of La Magione arrived. He had the support of the King of France, Cesare told him, boasting that 'events would show what kind of men they are and who I am'. He moved swiftly, raising troops and negotiating separate agreements with his conspiring captains who even agreed to help him regain Urbino. Guidobaldo, who had returned to Urbino following the revolt of San Leo, scarcely had time to gather up the few possessions Cesare had left him before going on the run again, this time to Venice. He also moved on Camerino, where the eighty-two-year-old Giulio Cesare Varano was strangled and his lordship then bestowed as a duchy by Alexander on his son, Giovanni Borgia. He made separate agreements with the Bentivoglio, Orsini and the other captains, all of whom agreed to continue fighting for him. Machiavelli sized up the sinister situation with his usual perspicacity:

As to the suggested understanding . . . I do not augur well of it. For when I consider the . . . parties concerned, I see on the one hand Duke Cesare, vigorous, courageous, confident in his future, blessed with exceptional fortune, backed by the favour of the Pope and King . . . Confronting him, we have a group of lords who, even while they were his friends, were in anxiety for their possessions, and fearful of his growing power; and now, having thus injured him, and become his declared enemies, naturally more defensive still. So that I fail to understand how, on the one part, such injury can be expected to find forgiveness . . .[43]

But Machiavelli, acute observer though he was, failed to penetrate the secrecy of Cesare's intentions before il Valentino rode out of Imola in heavy snow to spend Christmas at Cesena, the capital of his province of Romagna. There, on Christmas morning, people were shocked to see the decapitated body of Cesare's former Governor of the Romagna and long-standing follower, Don Ramiro de Lorqua, displayed in the piazza, his black-bearded head impaled on a lance beside it. The ostensible reason given for his death was that Ramiro had been demoted by Cesare as a result of his unpopular treatment of the people of the Romagna and was being made an example of; but the real reason for his execution, as Alexander confessed later in Rome to the Venetian envoy, was that Cesare considered him a traitor for plotting with the conspirators against him. Once again it was an effective,

deliberate act of terror. Cesare knew that the time had come for
the final round in the contest with his *condottieri* and had already
set the stage at Sinigallia, which his captains had agreed to take
in his name from Guidobaldo's sister, Giovanna, who ruled as
regent in the name of her son, Giovanni Maria della Rovere.

On 26 December, Cesare set off with his personal guard down
the Via Emilia to meet his captains there, having sent small bodies
of troops southward to mislead the conspirators into underesti-
mating the strength of his forces. He had ordered them to with-
draw their troops from the town so that he could quarter his
own guard there, and that all but one of the gates should be
locked. Outside the town the *condottieri* came to meet him, nervously surprised to see that he was wearing full battle armour
although fighting was not expected. Cesare greeted them
cordially, riding with them into Sinigallia past the drawn-up lines
of his heavy cavalry. Behind them the gates were quietly closed.
Nervous but unsuspecting the conspirators accompanied Cesare
into a house specially selected for the purpose by Michelotto on
the pretext of a meeting. There the conspirators were seized as
they sat in their chairs round a table, their hands bound behind
them. At two o'clock on the morning of New Year's Day,
Oliverotto and Vitellozzo, seated back-to-back on a bench, were
garrotted on Michelotto's orders. Cesare took the three Orsini –
Paolo (father-in-law of Geronima Borgia), Francesco, Duke of
Gravina (once considered a possible husband for Lucrezia) and
Roberto – with him to meet a similar fate on the road to Rome,
strangled at the castle of Sarteano on 18 January 1503. As he left,
Cesare caught sight of Machiavelli. 'This,' he told him, 'is what I
wished to tell at Urbino, but I never trusted the secret to anyone,
thus the occasion having come to me, I have known very well
how to use it . . .' In Rome, encouraged by Cesare's success,
Alexander arrested the aged Cardinal Orsini along with other
family connections, including Rinaldo Orsini, Archbishop of
Florence, and sent them to Sant'Angelo.

Throughout Italy Cesare's coup was regarded not only as a
justifiable punishment for treachery but as a masterstroke.

Machiavelli called it an 'admirable deed', the King of France 'an act worthy of a Roman hero', a later anti-Borgia historian, Paolo Giovio, 'a most beautiful deception'. Isabella d'Este hastened to congratulate him with exaggerated expressions of affection, sending him a hundred carnival masks 'because we believe that after the strains and fatigues which you have undergone in these your glorious undertakings, you should also find time to amuse yourself'.[44] She was still deep in negotiation over the projected marriage between her son, two-year-old Federico (born 17 May 1500), and Cesare's daughter Luisa, of exactly the same age. But her real sentiments were echoed by di Prosperi in a cautious reference written on 6 January 1503 to 'the sad news from the Romagna'.

In Ferrara no one remarked upon any reaction from Lucrezia whose existence had protected the Este from her brother's depredations. She and Alfonso danced and feasted through the first days of carnival. The Borgias were now at their apogee and Cesare's successes underlined the necessity of propitiating them. For Lucrezia this had a satisfactory material outcome: the vexed question of her allowance had at last been settled to her satisfaction.[45]

9. The Heavens Conspire

'Furthermore, although you have now lost your very great father . . .
this is not the first blow which you have suffered at the hands of
your cruel and malevolent destiny . . . you would do well not to
allow anyone to assume, as some might be led to infer in present
circumstances, that you bewail not so much your loss but what may
betide your present fortunes . . .'

– Pietro Bembo to the grieving Lucrezia on
the death of Alexander VI, 22 August 1503

Young (she was still not quite twenty-three), beautiful and now
restored to health, Lucrezia, with her close group of ladies, Angela
Borgia, Nicola and Elisabetta senese, were the focus of court life.
Since Ercole was a widower, she was already known as '*la duchessa*'
and she was the centre of attention in Ferrara. With renewed
confidence in herself and a strong sense of having returned from
the brink of death, Lucrezia set out to enjoy life. Duke Ercole
had given in over the question of her allowance: on 10 January,
di Prosperi reported that she was to have 6,000 ducats for herself
and 6,000 for the clothing and salaries of her household – the
12,000 ducats which Alexander had been insisting upon. She felt
free to enjoy herself, often occupying the place of honour as she
did on 19 February when she and Ercole presided over a comedy
by Plautus in the Sala Grande. Seated alone with Ercole in front
of two tribunals, one occupied by gentlewomen, the other by
gentlemen and citizens, she was described by the local chronicler as 'most richly dressed with great jewels'.

Isabella's principal spy, El Prete, was in Ferrara for carnival that
year, apparently accompanying his master, Niccolò da Correggio.

e was adept at telling Isabella what she wanted to hear, usually
o Lucrezia's discredit. She had appeared at a ball in the house of
the Roverella, apparently in a bad temper, 'which it seems she is
always in nowadays'. She was always in conversation with Don
Giulio, perhaps her favourite, as he was his father's. She danced
the torch dance, '*ballo da la torza*', with Ferrante, and then Giulio,
and her last dance with Alfonso. El Prete liked to make out how
difficult Lucrezia was, dining alone with her beloved Angela Borgia
and being disagreeable to her Ferrarese ladies. On one occasion,
he said, two of them refused to put on masks: 'she rebuked them
so that they were reduced to tears'.[1] More honest and less sycophantic than El Prete, di Prosperi reported earlier on Lucrezia's
efforts to familiarize herself with Ferrara and its ways. She had
dined at the monastery of San Giorgio and at the Certosa: 'and
I understand that every Saturday she wishes to visit one of our
convents to see the places and enjoy our town better than she
has up till now'.[2] Even Isabella's sister-in law, Laura Bentivoglio,
married to Giovanni Gonzaga, gave her a good report: 'Her
manners and comportment seem to me all gracious and friendly
and happy,' she wrote, adding that Lucrezia had expressed herself
as anxious that Isabella should write to her sometimes 'and behave
in a more intimate manner than hitherto'.

Strangely enough, the charge of being too formal had been
levied against Lucrezia by Isabella the previous year − 'there is no
need to use such terms of reverence [to me] being your cordial
sister'[3] − but the rivalry between the two, especially in terms of
clothes, remained. Lucrezia questioned Laura Bentivoglio closely
about Isabella's wardrobe and particularly the manner in which
she dressed her hair. Isabella spent a fortnight at Ferrara that
spring, in anticipation of which, according to a malicious later
report by Cattaneo, Lucrezia had pawned some of her jewellery
to pay for splendid clothes to dazzle her sister-in-law and had
asked her father to give her the year's income of the bishopric
of Ferrara.[4] Lucrezia welcomed her sister-in-law to Ferrara with
a great show of graciousness, organizing Spanish dances to the
sound of tambourines, and a keyboard competition between

Vincenzo da Modena and the Duke's organist, Antonio dall'Organo; and with her she attended a series of elaborately staged miracle plays ordered by Ercole to be performed in the Duomo. After Isabella returned to Mantua, Lucrezia wrote her a letter of exaggerated friendliness: 'It would be difficult for me to express the supreme pleasure and consolation which I recently received from your most welcome letter,' she wrote on 17 May, 'particularly for the news of your most pleasant journey and . . . safe arrival', going on to insist on how much she missed Isabella, particularly now that Alfonso had 'left for Marina'.

But, far from feeling bereft and lonely in the absence of Isabella and, more significantly, Alfonso, Lucrezia as the beautiful young Duchess had become the focus and inspiration of a court of literary young men. Ercole was now old, and devoted rather to music and the theatre, while Alfonso, despite a humanistic education, inclined to the visual arts and was uninterested in literature. On the announcement of her betrothal, Giovanni Sabadino degli Arienti had composed *Colloquium ad Ferrarem urbem* in honour of the wedding and sent two magnificently illuminated copies, one to Ercole and one to Lucrezia, the previous November. Lucrezia's arrival in Ferrara and her marriage had been the occasion for the most extravagant epithets by poets, including Ludovico Ariosto, who had composed an epithalamium for her marriage and was later to complete his masterwork, *Orlando Furioso*, the romantic epic poem on the Este which featured Lucrezia. Her arrival had also been celebrated by the Latin poets, father and son Tito and Ercole Strozzi, and her circle included the disreputable poet Antonio Tebaldeo (then in the service of Ippolito but who later became her secretary), and expanded to include the great Venetian printer Aldus Manutius (who at one point made her the executor of his will) and the celebrated humanist Giangiorgio Trissino. Lucrezia took their eulogies, which included describing her as 'most beautiful virgin' and comparing her with the swan in the famous frescoes in the Palazzo Schifanoia, with a large pinch of salt, but she developed a close friendship with Ercole Strozzi and through him a passion-

...e relationship with one of the most famous young writers in Italy, Pietro Bembo.

Ercole Strozzi was a member of the Florentine banking family exiled by the Medici and now established in Ferrara. Despite being so lame that he had to walk with a crutch, he was an intense womanizer and a natural romantic, with a taste for dangerous love affairs. He had been in love for ten years with a woman who was not only married but also had a lover described by contemporaries as '*vir magnus*', a powerful man. Strozzi was captivated by Lucrezia and soon became her closest male confidant in Ferrara and the facilitator of her love affairs, a dangerous course which may have led to his violent death five years later. Ercole had succeeded his father (who had made himself deeply hated by the populace for his extortions) as *Giudice dei XII Savi*, leader of the principal administrative council of Ferrara, and as such was a prominent citizen with easy access to the court.

Strozzi became indispensable to Lucrezia; like her he adored extravagant clothes and, although coming from a rich family, was perennially short of money. On frequent visits to Venice (still, after the fall of Constantinople, the main source of textiles from the Ottoman Empire) he acquired wonderful materials for her wardrobe, as witnessed by repeated entries in her wardrobe account books, beginning as early as July 1502, when he provided lengths of the much-prized white '*tabi*'.[5] Despite the lavish trousseau she had brought with her from Rome, Strozzi's contributions feature on almost every page of her wardrobe accounts for the years 1502–3. Encouraged perhaps by Ercole's concessions over her allowance, she was generous in providing clothing: on 19 June 1503 she had four doublets for Cesare's lute players made up, and a robe for 'Zoanmaria the Jew', one of his musicians. Two yellow velvet doublets were made for woodwind players (*piffari*) to be sent to Cesare that year. There were skirts and other clothing for Angela Borgia, Girolama, Nicola, Catherinella and Camilla. On 9 August 1502, two capes in purple (*paonazzo*) satin were ordered for Giovanni Borgia and Rodrigo Bisceglie. From the same source it is apparent that Lucrezia in return loaned Strozzi money.

On 15 January 1503, Ercole Strozzi gave a ball for her, and it was at this ball that she renewed her brief acquaintance with the most famous of her lovers, Pietro Bembo. A member of a distinguished Venetian family, Bembo was well known in Ferrara, where his father Bernardo had acted as *visdomino*, or co-ruler, a deeply resented office imposed on the Ferrarese after they lost the war with Venice in 1484. Pietro had stayed on in Ferrara for a while after his father returned to Venice; the cultivated atmosphere of Ercole's court suited his temperament better than the stern, hard-headed mercantile Republic. Bembo's closest friend in Ferrara was Ercole Strozzi from whom he had heard about Lucrezia long before he met her. Since October 1502 he had been staying in Strozzi's villa at Ostellato and had briefly entertained her there in mid November, writing afterwards to Ercole that he wished she had stayed longer, describing her as 'such a beautiful and elegant woman who is not superstitious about anything'.[6] After the ball in January, he boasted to his brother Carlo of how many compliments '*la duchessa*' had paid him. 'Every day,' he added, 'I find her a still worthier lady, seeing she has far excelled all my expectations, great though they were after hearing so many reports of her and most of all from Messer Ercole . . .'[7] Ercole's reports to Bembo about Lucrezia, which Bembo called 'the Lucretian letters', continued after Pietro left again for Ostellato. According to one authority[8] Bembo was inspired to write verses in praise of Lucrezia which were secretly passed to her by his literary friends in Ferrara, Ariosto and, particularly, Ercole Strozzi.

Strozzi deliberately fanned the flames of Bembo's passion; romantic adoration for Lucrezia became a cult between the two young poets. Very possibly he urged Lucrezia on in the relationship; romantic intrigue excited him and, as later became obvious, there was little love lost between him and Alfonso. Lucrezia entered into the teasing of Bembo with delight: on 24 April she addressed a letter to him in her distinctive hand but when he opened it there was only another letter from Strozzi. A month later, on 25 May, Lucrezia copied out in her own hand a love poem by the fifteenth-century Aragonese poet Lope de Estuniga,

o piense si me muriese . . . The poem barely translates into English,
a language with so different a rhythm:

> I think were I to die
> And with my wealth of pain ·
> Cease longing,
> Such great love to deny
> Could make the world remain
> Unloving.
> When I consider this,
> Death's long delay is all
> I must desire,
> Since reason tells me bliss
> Is felt by one in thrall
> To such a fire.

Bembo responded with a poem of his own, in Tuscan, the
language of his hero Petrarch, in which he described himself as
caught in the beauty of Lucrezia's blonde hair, which in his presence she let down loose on her shoulders and then with 'two
hands of immeasurable beauty' bound up again and with them his
heart. Three hundred years later, viewing what he called 'the prettiest love letters in the world' in the Biblioteca Ambrosiana in
Milan, Lord Byron stole a blonde thread from the lock of Lucrezia's
hair which she must have sent Bembo in response to this passionate poem. With this and another sonnet, Bembo sent Lucrezia the
first volume of his famous prose poem *Gli Asolani*, 'which I received
this very hour'.[9] Lucrezia's response was to ask him to suggest a
motto for a medallion which she was thinking of having made
featuring flames 'according to that most subtle and most apt suggestion you gave me', '. . . nothing can prevent me from ever ador-
ing your name', Bembo replied by courier that same day. 'As for
the fire on the gold medallion which your Ladyship has sent me
with the request that I should devise a motto for inscription, I
can think of no nobler location than the soul. Wherefore you
might have it thus inscribed: EST ANIMUM . . .'[10]

Passionate but still apparently platonic: some time after the letter was written Bembo went to Ferrara to meet Lucrezia where they had an intimate conversation and may have exchanged declarations of love. This might be interpreted from Bembo's subsequent letter written on 19 June from Ostellato: 'Gazing these past days into my crystal [heart] of which we spoke during the last evening I paid my respects to your Ladyship, I have read therein, glowing at its centre, these lines I now send to you . . .'[11] The sonnet *Poi ch'ogni ardir* was an expression of physical passion, still apparently unfulfilled. Lucrezia's reply mirrored his: 'Messer Pietro mio. Concerning the desire you have to hear from me regarding the counterpart of your or our crystal as it may be rightly reputed and termed, I cannot think what else to say or imagine save that it has an extreme affinity of which the like perhaps has never been equalled in any age . . . And let it be a gospel everlasting.' The situation was clearly becoming serious, even dangerous; from now on her name was to be 'f.f.' Bembo's reply was passionate: 'Now is my crystal [heart] more precious to me than all the pearls of the Indian seas, and surely you have acted most mercifully in granting parity such as you have given it, and such company. God knows no human thing could be so dear to me as this certainty . . .'[12] There has been much unresolved speculation, as to the precise meaning of 'f.f.' Two years later Lucrezia had a portrait medallion struck with, on the reverse, a blindfolded cupid bound to an oak tree and with the motto 'FPHFF'. All that can be ascertained with any degree of certainty is that the need to use a pseudonym reflected the increasing depth of the relationship and perhaps also the dangers which this implied for both in Ferrara where the Este were all-powerful.

For the poet, unattached, ardent and living in the luxury of the Strozzi villa among the waterways and flat fields of Ostellato, twenty-five miles from Ferrara, there was no impediment to romantic dreams. But for Lucrezia, living in the enclosed circle of the court and constantly spied upon, life was more complicated. And in the distance, but always dominating the Italian political scene, were her father and brother. In his next letter written from Ostellato in late June, Bembo refers specifically to Lucrezia's 'vexations' and 'distress' and 'these present cares.'[13] It is unclear from this whether these may have been connected with Alfonso's return to Ferrara (he had been away in May) or to Lucrezia's own family situation.

At the beginning of 1503 Cesare's fortunes, which seemed so bright, were actually on the cusp. Where his success had rested on his alliance with Louis XII, the King now blocked his path. Cesare had grown too powerful and Louis was unwilling to allow him to extend his dominion over either Bologna or, more particularly, Florence. Venice and the French-held Duchy of Milan obstructed his expansion northward; Cesare's only real option was to turn southward. And, as always, the Kingdom of Naples loomed large in his calculations; here it was now Spain which was calling the shots. In a series of victories in April, the French in the Kingdom were routed by the Spanish forces under their brilliant commander, Gonsalvo da Cordoba; on the 13th Gonsalvo entered Naples. Alexander, Iberian at heart, had never really liked the French alliance, nor, rightly, had he trusted Louis. To the Bolognese envoy he made it plain that the French could not rely on the Borgias to win the Kingdom back for them: 'We are resolved not to lose what we have acquired,' he said, adding piously, 'because we see that it is God's will that the Spaniards have been victorious; and if God wills it thus, we must not wish it otherwise.'[14]

Unlike his father, Cesare kept his counsel as he considered his future. As Machiavelli was later to write of him in *The Prince*: 'When the Duke had become very powerful and in part secure against present perils, since he was armed as he wished and had in part destroyed those forces that, as neighbours, could harm him, he still, if he intended to pursue his course, had before him the problem of the King of France, because he knew that the King, who too late had become aware of his mistake, would not tolerate further conquest. For this reason the Duke was looking for new alliances and wavering in his dealings with France . . .' The first public sign of the way Cesare's thoughts were tending came with the nomination of the new cardinals early in May:

five of the nine were Catalans, either close relations or depen-
dants of the Borgias. There was not one Frenchman.

Lucrezia naturally had her own sources of information in the
Borgia camp, although it is unlikely that she was ever consulted
by Cesare, now totally dominant in the partnership with his father.
In February she had a new source of information in Cardinal
Ippolito d'Este, recently returned from Rome where he had
enjoyed an affair with Sancia, now once again unaccountably
confined to Sant'Angelo by Alexander. There were rumours, as
always with il Valentino, that Ippolito had fled Rome from fear
of Cesare although it is unlikely that Cesare would have cared
what Sancia did, powerless as she was but still his sworn enemy.
Moreover, Alexander specifically expressed his delight at Lucrezia's
friendship with Ippolito: 'She spends the night with Don Alfonso
and the day with the Cardinal d'Este, who was with her all day
and accompanied her wherever she went,' he declared proudly
to Costabili, adding that the three of them were 'three bodies
and one sole mind'.[15]

Lucrezia formed a close alliance with Ippolito, as she had with
all the Este brothers, a key factor in the dangerous situations
which surrounded her. The first public sign of trouble came with
the murder of the hitherto most trusted Borgia henchman,
Francesco Troche. On the night of 8 June, Troche was strangled
on a boat moored on the Tiber. According to Costabili's account,
Cesare interviewed the prisoner and then 'His Excellency plac-
ing himself in a spot where he could see and not be seen, Troche
was strangled by the hand of Don Michele . . .' (Michelotto). It
was all too reminiscent of the murder of Alfonso Bisceglie. Count
Lodovico Pico della Mirandola, then one of Cesare's captains,
wrote in a letter to Francesco Gonzaga that Troche's crime was
to have revealed to the King of France the Borgias' negotiations with Spain. As Troche was known to be pro-French he
was now expendable and, with his intimate knowledge of
Cesare's affairs, positively dangerous.[16] Cesare then compounded
the effect of this act of terror by executing at dawn on the same
day a leading Roman nobleman, Jacopo di Santa Croce, whose

body was exposed on the bridge of Sant'Angelo. No explanation for the execution was given, but since he had been arrested with Cardinal Orsini and the others at the time of Sinigallia and confined with them to the Castel Sant'Angelo the probable reason was that Cesare suspected him of conspiring with the Orsini against him.

For Lucrezia, knowing Cesare as she did, and well informed through the Este envoys at every court, the future seemed perilous. The Borgias, father and son, had been raising huge sums for the coming campaign. In secret consistory on 29 March, Alexander had created eighty new official posts to be sold to candidates at 760 ducats apiece. Cesare himself had set the rates for the new cardinals' nomination. Driven on by the fear of being caught in the coming clash between France and Spain, the Borgias resorted to poisoning wealthy victims, a means which was, as Guicciardini admitted, an Italian rather than a Spanish custom. For this reason Italians were wont to attribute the deaths of prominent people to poison whereas they were usually down to some virulent fever caused by food poisoning; the number of cardinals who died during Alexander's papacy did not proportionately exceed the average number of deaths under previous pontificates. Cesare's normal method of disposing with enemies was the Spanish garrotte, or swift strangulation. The method now used was probably *cantarella*, white arsenic, and one case – the death on 10 April of Cardinal Giovanni Michiel, Bishop of Porto and Patriarch of Constantinople – was almost certainly the result of deliberate poisoning. As soon as Alexander heard of his death, Giustinian reported, he had Michiel's house plundered. 'The death of this Cardinal gives him more than 150,000 ducats.' In early July, Alexander issued a Bull conferring the vicariate of Vitellozzo Vitelli's Città di Castello on Cesare and requested the Perugians to offer him their lordship in place of the Baglioni. Negotiations with the always impecunious Emperor Maximilian for the investiture for Cesare of Lucca, Pisa and Siena were well under way. Everyone north of Rome expected some lightning move by Cesare but as July wore into August, il Valentino had still not made a move. In reality, the 'son of Fortune' was in an agony of suspense. In Gaeta the French, under Cesare's old companion-in-arms Yves d'Alègre, still held out against the Spaniards while in Lombardy a large French force was massing to march south to the rescue.

By mid July, as Cesare waited in Rome, the romance between Bembo and Lucrezia became ever more intense, on the poet's side at least. He was in Ferrara, as ardent as ever and, it would appear, led on by Lucrezia:

I rejoice that each day to increase my fire you cunningly devise some fresh incitement, such as that which encircled your glowing brow today [presumably a jewelled head ornament perhaps representing flames]. If you do such things because, feeling some little warmth yourself, you wish to see another burn, I shall not deny that for each spark of yours untold Etnas [Bembo's first printed work was entitled *De Aetna*] are raging in my breast. And if you do so because it is natural for you to relish another's suffering, who in all justice could blame me if he but knew the reasons for my ardour? Truly I can do no sin if I put my faith in such a gospel and in so many miracles. Let Love wreak just revenge for me, if upon your brow you are not the same as in your heart.[17]

Four days later, on the verge of leaving Ferrara, he was still burning with passion: 'I am leaving, oh my dearest life, and yet I do not leave and never shall . . . If likewise you who stay were not to stay, I dare not speak for you, but truly "Ah, of all who love none more blest than I!" . . . All this long night, whether in dreams or laying awake, I was with you . . .' He entreated her to read *Gli Asolani* which he was leaving with her and to discuss it with 'my dear and saintly Lisabetta'. 'My heart kisses Your Ladyship's hand which so soon I shall come to kiss with these lips that are forever forming your name . . .' After their parting, he could not resist one final note: 'Not because I am able to tell you what tender bitterness enfolds me at this parting do I write to you, light of my life, but only to entreat you to cherish yourself most dearly . . .'[18]

After he left, Lucrezia, whom he had suspected was unwell when he left Ferrara, suffered two bouts of tertian fever but recovered sufficiently to charm Ariosto who was, Bembo told her, 'deeply inflamed by Your Ladyship's surpassing qualities, indeed all afire'. Apparently she had also praised his *Gli Asolani* both in a letter to him and to Ariosto: 'Messer Lodovico [Ariosto] writes to me saying that he feels there is no need for it [*Gli Asolani*] to be brought out and read by all the world in order to gain glory, for more than it enjoys already could never come its way . . .'[19] By early August he was back in Ferrara, very sick with fever and too ill to visit Lucrezia who bravely did him the signal honour of visiting his bedside and spending what he described as 'a long while' with him. 'For the truth is your visit has altogether dispelled every trace of my grievous illness . . . and that vision alone and the merest pressure on my wrist had been enough to bring back all the health I had before. But to this you appended those dear sweet words so full of love and joy and the very quick of sympathy.'[20]

Even as Pietro Bembo wrote this, Lucrezia was about to face the most dangerous crisis of her life. On 11 August, her father had celebrated the eleventh anniversary of his elevation to the papacy but observers noted that he was far from in his usual spirits. He had been greatly depressed by the death on 1 August from fever (probably malaria) of his nephew Cardinal Juan Borgia-Lanzuol, Archbishop of Monreale (known as Juan Borgia 'the elder' to distinguish him from his younger brother of the same name). The cardinal had been excessively corpulent and as his funeral procession passed below the windows of the Vatican, Alexander, thinking of his own heavy body, had remarked, 'This month is fatal for fat men.' August was indeed a dangerous month to be in Rome – three of Alexander's predecessors, Calixtus, Pius II and Sixtus IV, had died in the month of August and Innocent VIII at the end of July – and the August of 1503 was exceptionally hot. Alexander had remained in Rome because of the difficulties of the political situation, with Gaeta still holding out and a huge French force nearing Rome. Normally the papal court would have left the city for the cool of the Alban hills and to escape the threat of *malaria perniciosa* borne by the mosquitoes bred in the swamps of the Roman Campagna and the Tiber itself. The sickness struck without warning, accompanied by vomiting and bouts of fever which could raise a man's temperature in a few hours to over 106 degrees Fahrenheit. On Saturday 12 August, Alexander was seized with a fit of vomiting and fever; Cesare, who had been planning to leave Rome on the 9th to try to come to terms with the French, fell ill the same day with the same symptoms.

The envoys circled the Vatican trying with little success to pick up scraps of information. It was two days before Costabili could even inform Ercole of the Pope's serious illness – it was only on the 13th that he learned what had happened the previous day. The doors of the Palace were shut and no one was allowed out. 'All this court is in considerable fear as to the illness of His Holiness and much is said,' he reported. 'All the same I try every way to find out the truth: but the more I investigate, the more I am told that it is not possible to understand anything for certain because the doctors, pharmacists and surgeons are not allowed out. But there is great suspicion that the illness is grave. The Illustrious Duke of Romagna is still, I understand from a good source, dangerously ill with "*due tertiane*" and "vomiting".'[21] Two days later he could report only that the Pope seemed better and Cesare worse; the Spaniards had retreated from Gaeta and Cesare's troops were near Perugia, but there was no news of the French. On 18 August, at the hour of vespers, Alexander died. Writing to Ercole that evening Costabili was still unaware of it, noting only that the Palace was locked and more heavily guarded than usual. Lucrezia was better informed: her favourite, Cardinal Cosenza, and her '*Magiordomo*' (possibly the Sancho Spagnolo frequently mentioned as being in her service) were both in the Vatican and knew the truth. Not only had she lost her beloved father but, unless Cesare, gravely ill, could somehow extricate himself from the dangerous situation, the Borgia era would be over, with all the implications that that might have for her own future.

On 21 August, Bembo found Lucrezia prostrate with grief at the Este villa of Medelana, not far from Ostellato, where she had gone with her household to escape the plague then raging through Ferrara. He had gone there to offer her consolation but '. . . as soon as I saw you lying there in that darkened room and in that black gown, so tearful and disconsolate, my feelings overwhelmed me and for a long time I stood there unable to utter a word, not knowing even what to say . . . my spirit in turmoil at the pity of that spectacle, tongue-tied and stammering I withdrew, as you saw, or might have seen . . .'

Wisely he counselled her to compose herself and demonstrate the self-control that people had come to expect of her:

I know not what else to say but to ask you to recall that Time soothes and lessens all our tribulations, and it would more become you, from whom all expect a most rare self-possession in view of the daily proofs you have given of your valour on every occasion and at every mis-adventure, not to delay such a time but rather to prepare for it resolutely. Furthermore, although you have now lost your very great father . . . this is not the first blow which you have suffered at the hands of your cruel and malevolent destiny. Indeed your spirit ought by now to be inured to shocks of fate, so many and so bitter have you already suffered.

'And what is more,' he added, 'you would do well not to allow anyone to assume, as some might be led to infer in present circum-stances, that you bewail not so much your loss but what may betide your present fortunes . . .'[22]

Lucrezia was isolated, well aware that apart from the Borgia partisans no one would mourn her father's passing or her brother's ill fortune, and that the latter group would certainly include her husband's family. Ercole's letter to Giangiorgio Seregni, his envoy in Milan (then under French control), made it plain what he felt: 'Knowing that many will ask you how we are affected by the Pope's death, this is to inform you that it was in no way displeas-ing to us', adding with singular ingratitude:

there never was a Pope from whom we received fewer favours than this one . . . It was only with the greatest difficulty that we secured from him what he had promised, but beyond this he never did anything for us. For this we hold the Duke of Romagna responsible; for although he could not do with us as he wished, he treated us as if we were perfect strangers. He was never frank with us; he never confided his plans to us, although we always informed him of ours. Finally, as he inclined to Spain, and we remained good Frenchmen, we had little to look for either from the Pope or His Excellency. Therefore his death caused us little grief, as we had nothing to expect from the above-named duke . . .

Seregni was to show this letter to Chaumont (the French Governor of Milan) as evidence of Ercole's true feelings but otherwise to speak cautiously on the subject and return the letter via Gian Luca Pozzi. Ercole was still uncertain which way to jump in case Cesare might regain or increase his power. He was telling Louis, however, what the French King wanted to hear.[23] He did not visit Lucrezia although he was at Belriguardo, not far from Medelana.

Early in September, Bartolommeo de'Cavalleri, Ercole's envoy with Louis in Macon, reported the French King's significant reaction: 'His Most Christian Majesty asked me if I had news of any reaction Madonna Lucretia had shown on the death of her father. I replied no and then he added, "I well know that you were never content with this marriage." I answered that that was true and that if His Most Christian Majesty had attended to what he promised me not to write to Your Excellency to make the said marriage, it would not have been made. He answered that everything has been for the best, saying that Madonna Lucretia was not the true wife of Don Alfonso . . .'[24]

Lucrezia's situation was indeed precarious. As di Prosperi wrote significantly to Isabella: 'I understand that the Lady is very upset and in truth it affects her in various respects, as Your Ladyship may imagine . . .'[25] The Pope, the source of any power and influence she might have, was now dead. Her brother was gravely ill and could not help her and, although as lord of the Romagna he was still a factor in the Este considerations, no one could predict what his position might be on the election of a new pope. And as far as her own position as Alfonso's wife was concerned, the reasons of state which had pushed the Duke of Ferrara into making this marriage no longer existed and the King of France had turned against Cesare. Moreover, everyone knew that her divorce from Giovanni Sforza on the grounds of non-consummation was a farce and it could have been argued that, as Louis had said, her marriage to Alfonso had no legal basis. Worst of all from her point of view was her failure to bear the Este a male heir. For the time being, uncertainty as to Cesare's future helped her but, in the end, the fact that the Este made no attempt to dissolve the marriage is a tribute to her own character and the position she had managed to establish for herself in Ferrara. The Este — with the notable exception of Isabella — liked and appreciated her. There is no indication that they ever considered getting rid of her; had they done so they would have had to give back her vast dowry but whether this was a factor or not, the subject was never raised. According to di Prosperi, the Este did not desert her in her time of trouble: Ippolito had ridden out to Medelana to give Lucrezia the news of her father's death and, even if Ercole did not visit her immediately, Alfonso did before going on to Belriguardo, no doubt to consult with his father.

Lucrezia may or may not have known the sad and revolting details of her father's death and burial. Rumours of poison were rife; some even held that the Borgias had poisoned each other by mistake at the dinner held on 5 August by their friend Adriano da Corneto, recently created cardinal. Cesare and Alexander, the story ran, had intended to poison their host and seize his possessions, but there was a mix-up over the jugs of wine and they too drank the poison intended for their victim. It is an indication of the extraordinary atmosphere surrounding the Borgias that this farcical scenario was widely believed. Francesco Gonzaga, at the French headquarters at Isola Farnese outside Rome, sent Isabella an account of Alexander's death which included a Faustian pact with the devil:

When he [Alexander] fell sick, he began to talk in such a way that anyone who did not know what was in his mind would have thought that he was wandering, although he was perfectly conscious of what he said; his words were, 'I come; it is right; wait a moment.' Those who know the secret say that in the conclave following the death of Innocent he made a compact with the devil, and purchased the papacy from him at the price of his soul. Among the other provisions of the agreement was one which said that he should be allowed to occupy the Holy See twelve years [actually eleven], and this he did with the addition of four days. There are some who affirm that at the moment he gave up his spirit seven devils were seen in his chamber. As soon as he was dead his body began to putrefy and his mouth to foam ... The body swelled up so that it lost all human form. It was nearly as broad as it was long. It was carried to the grave with little ceremony; a porter dragged it from the bed by means of a cord fastened to the foot to the place where it was buried, as all refused to touch it. It was given a wretched interment, in comparison with which that of the cripple's dwarf wife in Mantua was ceremonious. Scandalous epigrams are every day published concerning him.[26]

That a sophisticated aristocrat like the Marquis of Mantua should believe such stuff about pacts with the devil is an indication of how close medieval superstition lay to the surface of the supposedly humanist, classical Renaissance. The gruesome facts of the burial were to some extent, however, confirmed by Burchard who was in charge of organizing it. As soon as Cesare, lying weak but conscious in the room above the Pope's, was made aware of his father's death he sent Michelotto and a squad of armed men to secure the Pope's apartments and remove silver, jewels and cash to the value of 300,000 ducats (in their haste they missed another cache of valuables but what they managed to find was enough to finance Cesare's immediate future). The papal servants then plundered the apartments and wardrobes

1. Pope Alexander VI (Rodrigo Borgia), Lucrezia's father. Detail from a fresco by Pinturicchio in the Borgia Apartments in the Vatican painted shortly after Rodrigo's accession to the papacy in 1492.

2. Vannozza Cattanei, Lucrezia's mother. Also known as Giovanna de'Cattaneis. The beauty which fascinated Lucrezia's father is hardly evident in this portrait, executed in her later years by an unknown artist.

3. Subiaco. The Rocca, or stronghold, traditionally Lucrezia's birthplace, still dominates this small town in the hills south-east of Rome.

4. Lucrezia Borgia. Traditionally held to be a portrait of the teenage Lucrezia depicted as St Catherine in the fresco *The Disputation of Saint Catherine* by Pinturicchio in the Sala dei Santi in the Borgia Apartments in the Vatican, 1492–4.

5. Cesare Borgia. Always – almost certainly correctly – held to be a portrait of the dangerous 'il Valentino' at the height of his power. By Altobello Melone.

6. Sancia d'Aragona and Jofre Borgia, depicted at the time of their wedding in Naples in May 1494. Sancia, wearing a coronet, rides in front of her natural father, King Alfonso II. She is immediately preceded by Jofre, recently created Prince of Squillace.

7. Juan Borgia, Second Duke of Gandia. Detail from *The Disputation of Saint Catherine*. Juan's arrogance and his fondness for exotic clothes emerge in this depiction painted presumably before his departure for Spain in August 1493 to marry Maria Enriques.

8. Giulia Farnese, known as 'Giulia la Bella', Alexander VI's teenage mistress and the wife of Orsino Orsini. Her brother Alessandro Farnese, created cardinal by Alexander, later became Pope Paul III. Detail from *The Transfiguration* by Raphael painted *c.* 1519–20 and therefore years after the events described in this book.

9. Giovanni Sforza, Count of Pesaro. Lucrezia's first husband whom she divorced on the grounds of non-consummation.

10. Alfonso d'Aragona, First Duke of Bisceglie, natural son of Alfonso II and brother of Sancia. Lucrezia's second husband. The upper illustration shows him riding behind the musicians, wearing a dark cloak and escorting the Spanish general Gonsalvo de Cordoba (centre) into Naples after the defeat of the French at Ostia. In the lower illustration he is in the foreground riding into Naples in May 1497.

11. Ercole I d'Este, Third Duke of Ferrara, Lucrezia's father-in-law by her third marriage to Alfonso d'Este, heir to the dukedom. By Dosso Dossi.

12. Ferrara: Castello Estense, also known as the Castel or Castello Vecchio, the moated castle in which Lucrezia spent most of her married life in Ferrara. She occupied rooms in the Torre Marchesana, on the right, connected to Alfonso's celebrated *Camerini* in the ravelin on the extreme right of the picture. In Lucrezia's day the space immediately to the north of the castle, now occupied by relatively modern buildings, was a huge garden and beyond it stretched Ercole's new quarter of Ferrara.

13. Alfonso I d'Este, Fourth Duke of Ferrara, Lucrezia's last husband. He is shown, typically, in armour against a battle scene. His military skills, particularly in the field of artillery, saved Ferrara. By Dosso Dossi.

14. Ippolito d'Este. The cleverest and most ruthless of Alfonso's brothers, a cardinal who liked nothing better than to wear armour and fight his brother's enemies.

15. Courtly pastimes. Ladies embroidering, weaving and gossiping. One of a series of fifteenth-century frescoes of *The Months* by Francesco del Cossa and others.

16. Ferrara as it looked at the time of Lucrezia's arrival in 1502. The River Po is in the foreground. The Palazzo del Corte is on the left of the broad street in the centre of the picture with, beyond it, the four towers of the Castel. Opposite the Corte is the Duomo. Late fifteenth-century woodcut.

17. *Left*: Isabella d'Este, Marchioness of Mantua. Alfonso's only legitimate sister and the wife of Lucrezia's lover, Francesco Gonzaga. Famous for her culture and patronage of the arts, sycophantic admirers called her 'the first lady of the world'. By Leonardo da Vinci.

18. *Right*: Francesco II Gonzaga, Marquis of Mantua. Husband of Isabella d'Este and lover of Lucrezia. Contemporary portrait bust by Gian Cristoforo Romano.

19. *Left*: Pietro Bembo. The famous poet at the time of his love affair with Lucrezia, painted by Raphael in 1504–6.

20. *Right*: Ercole Strozzi. The poet and friend of Lucrezia who not only eulogized her but acted as go-between in her romances, a role which probably cost him his life.

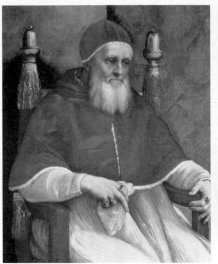

21. Pope Julius II (Giuliano della Rovere). Portrait of the Borgias' old enemy by Raphael.

22. Pope Leo X (Giovanni de'Medici) with cardinals Luigi de'Rossi and Giulio de'Medici. By Raphael, 1518.

23. Engraved silver plaque showing the thirty-two-year-old Lucrezia presenting her son and heir, Ercole (b.1508), to San Maurelio, protector of Ferrara. Note that Lucrezia and one of her ladies carry the latest fashion accessory, a sable or ermine pelt. The plaque was executed by Giannantonio da Foligno to commemorate the victory of the French and Ferrarese forces over the papal and Spanish armies at the battle of Ravenna in 1512.

leaving only the papal thrones, some cushions and hangings. At four o'clock in the afternoon, they opened the doors and announced that the Pope was dead. Burchard, arriving to supervise the laying out of the body, found the Vatican more or less deserted and not a cardinal in sight. He had Alexander's body clothed in red brocade vestments and covered with a fine tapestry, laid on a table in the Sala del Pappagallo, scene of so many Borgia festivities. Two tapers burned beside it but no one kept vigil. The next day it was borne on a bier by the customary group of paupers to St Peter's where fighting broke out as the guards tried to seize the valuable wax tapers from the monks accompanying the body. In the confusion the Pope's body was abandoned. Burchard and a few others dragged the bier behind the railings of the high altar and locked the grille for fear that Alexander's enemies might try to desecrate his body.

During the next day, as Gonzaga described, the body began to decompose in the great heat. Burchard found a horrific sight: 'Its face had changed to the colour of mulberry or the blackest cloth, and it was covered in blue-black spots. The nose was swollen, the mouth distended where the tongue was doubled over and the lips seemed to fill everything. The appearance of the face then was more horrifying than anything that had ever been seen or reported before . . .' At the burial it was found that the coffin was too short and too narrow; six porters making blasphemous jokes about the late Pope and his hideous appearance 'rolled up his body in an old carpet and pummelled and pushed it into the coffin with their fists. No wax tapers or lights were used and no priests or any other persons attended his body.'

Hundreds of miles to the north, Lucrezia, as Bembo had pointed out, could not afford to be seen destroyed by grief for long. As a Borgia, she was resilient and she saw that she had to act quickly to salvage what remained of Borgia power: that meant Cesare. Despite his weakness, Cesare played his cards with his usual skill and deception. He was still the major Italian force in terms of money and troops, a factor which could decide the balance between France and Spain. Most of his lands in the Romagna still held firm for him. Equally importantly, both the French and the Spanish believed that Cesare, with the numbers of cardinals at his command, could swing the result of the election of the next pope, critical in the circumstances. And, whatever Ercole d'Este might have privately felt, he was sincerely apprehensive as to what his old enemy, Venice, might do should Cesare's power in the Romagna crumble. Cesare at first feigned to make an agreement with Prospero Colonna and the Spanish side, then double-crossed them by making an agreement with the French, and took the road to Nepi. On 5 September the French dispatched letters in his favour to the Romagna to the effect that the Duke Valentino was 'alive, well and the friend of the King of France'. This had the effect of stemming the tide running against him in the Romagna where Guidobaldo had returned to Urbino, Gian Paolo Baglioni to Perugia and the surviving Vitelli to Città di Castello. Venice had occupied Porto Cesenatico on 1 September, sent Giovanni Sforza back to Pesaro on the 3rd, and Pandolfo Malatesta to Rimini on the 6th. Attempts against Cesena, Imola and Faenza failed, the Venetians drew back and the cautious Ercole wrote to Cesare offering his congratulations on his recovery and his wisdom in turning to the French.

Lucrezia acted resolutely to help her brother: Sanudo reported on 27 September that she was raising troops in Ferrara and paying 20 ducats each to twenty bombardiers.[27] On 7 October he wrote that she had sent fifty cavalry to help Cesare at Faenza and Forlì, and on the 20th that Cesare's captain at the Rocca di Forlì had left Ferrara with a force including 150 Germans, the greater part of them sent by the Duke of Ferrara in Lucrezia's name, and gone to Cesena.

Cesare, however, was not the only Borgia Lucrezia had to be concerned about. In the dangerous times following Alexander's death, the two little Borgia children, Rodrigo Bisceglie and Giovanni Borgia, were sent for safety to the Castel Sant'Angelo, to be followed later by Cesare's illegitimate children, Girolamo and Camilla. Alexander's last child, named Rodrigo, born of an unknown mother in the last year of his papacy, is not mentioned, possibly because he was young enough to be left with his mother. On 2 September when Cesare left for Nepi he took with him Vannozza, the Borgia children and Jofre who had shown considerable courage after Alexander's death. Sancia who, for some unexplained reason had been in the Castel Sant'Angelo since October 1502, was released and departed for Naples with Prospero Colonna, whose mistress she soon became. On 3 October, Cesare returned to Rome with his family, determined to confront his enemies and to exert his influence over the recently elected pope, the old and ailing Cardinal Francesco Piccolomini, now Pius III. Cardinal Cosenza and Ippolito d'Este had been appointed guardians of the two elder boys; at this juncture Cosenza apparently wrote Lucrezia a letter, which has not survived, suggesting that Rodrigo should be sent to Spain for his own safety, the implication being that while Giovanni and the other little Borgias might be acceptable to the Este, poor Rodrigo, whom Lucrezia had not seen for well over a year, would not be. In an anguished letter which has hitherto not been published, Lucrezia, often accused of being a thoughtless mother where Rodrigo was concerned, appealed to Ercole for his opinion, enclosing Cosenza's letter. To send him so far away seemed to her very hard to bear as a mother:

Knowing it to be my duty to communicate to you as my father and only benefactor all my affairs and particularly of such importance to me as the interests of don roderico my son, I am writing this to you now.

It is the opinion of the Most Reverend Cardinal of Cosenza for reasons which Your Lordship will understand from his enclosed letter that Don Roderico [Rodrigo] be transferred to Valencia. As to which although it seems to me so far away as to be most hard for a mother [to bear] however I will accede to your most wise counsel, given the fact that the death of His late Holiness Our Lord happened so suddenly that he [Rodrigo] could not establish an appropriate state and that little which he did have will be taken from him, for this I pray Your Excellency that not only will you consult me as to your opinion but hold him recommended in everything you know might preserve and profit him: which will be among the other obligations I have to you of eternal benefit . . .[28]

Ercole replied, in an affectionate, thoughtful, almost fatherly letter, that he considered the cardinal's advice sound, and that Lucrezia owed Cosenza a debt of gratitude

for the demonstration and proof of so much cordial love that he clearly bears to you and to the most illustrious Don Roderico your son, who, one can say, has been preserved in life by his means. And although Don Roderico will be somewhat severed from Your Ladyship, it is better to be so far away and safe, than near with the danger in which he evidently would be; nor, because of this distance, will the love between you be at all diminished. When he has grown up, he will be able according to the condition of the times to decide on his own course, whether to return to Italy or to stay.

He thought the cardinal's suggestion that Rodrigo's Italian property should be sold to provide for his support a wise one (since, following the death of Alexander, the dukedom of Nepi would be taken away from him, leaving him only with his father's estates in the Kingdom of Naples). 'Nevertheless,' Ercole ended, 'if to your Ladyship, who is most prudent, it should seem otherwise, we yield to your better judgement.'[29]

Lucrezia's maternal feelings led her to reject the advice of both Ercole and Cosenza. She could not bring herself to send her first-born – and at that time only – child to Spain. A compromise was reached whereby Rodrigo was to be brought up by his father's relations, first in Naples, probably by Sancia, his aunt, and then after her death in c.1506 by his father's half-sister, Isabella d'Aragona Sforza, Duchess of Bari, the legitimate daughter of Alfonso II. He would keep his Neapolitan estates. This last decision may possibly have been prompted by a solemn promise made by the Catholic Kings, Ferdinand and Isabella, on 20 May 1502 confirming Cesare, Jofre, Juan Gandia's son (also named Juan), in the possession of all their Neapolitan estates, an impressive document which Lucrezia had taken care to bring with her from Rome since it still exists among her papers in the archives at Modena.[30] Although apparently not allowed to have Rodrigo with her at Ferrara, Lucrezia continued to care for his welfare and there are many entries in her wardrobe accounts for clothes for 'Don Rodrigo'. Lucrezia's baby half-brother, also called Rodrigo and born in the last year of her father's life, was apparently brought up in Naples, while Giovanni Borgia and Cesare's two illegitimate children were brought to Carpi, not far from Ferrara.

Just at this time Lucrezia and Pietro Bembo had a quarrel in the course of which she seems to have accused him of wavering in his devotion to her and leaving her to go to Venice. Bembo's affair with Lucrezia was described by his biographer as 'the most ambitious and memorable, but also the most risky and anguished' of his life. It seems probable that his father, well acquainted with the situation in Ferrara, had put pressure on him to return to Venice for his own sake and indeed planned (unsuccessfully) to get him out of the way by obtaining a post for him with an embassy to France. Poor Bembo was anguished. On 5 October he wrote:

Firstly . . . I would rather not have come by some great treasure than hear what I heard from you yesterday . . . although – as our sworn affinity deserved – you might well have let me know it earlier. And secondly, that as long as there is life in me my cruel fate will never prevent the fire in which f.f. and my destiny have placed me from being the highest and brightest blaze that in our time ever set a lover's heart alight. It will soar by virtue of the place where it burns, bright with the intensity of its own flame, and one day it will be a beacon to all the world.

She had completely misjudged him, he told her.

Now think me false as much as you will, believe the truth as little as you please, but like it or not, the day shall come when you must acknowledge how far you judged me wrong. There are times I fear this is not so much how others would have you believe, it is your very own opinion. And if this be so, then I hope that the motto I read among your papers a few days ago will prove to be true: *quien quiere matar perro ravia le levanta* (he who would kill a dog must work himself up a rage). Make a merry blaze of all my other letters . . . and this alone I beg you to deign to keep as pledge for what I write . . .[31]

During the time Lucrezia had been at Medelana and Bembo at Ostellato, the two had enjoyed romantic meetings, as he recalled in a letter from Venice on 18 October. In the eight days since he had parted from Lucrezia not one hour had passed without his thinking of her: 'Often I find myself recalling . . . certain words spoken to me, some' on the balcony with the moon as witness, others at that window I shall always look upon so gladly . . .'[32] But Lucrezia had been right in her diagnosis of her lover's waning ardour, or more probably his increased concern for his own safety. Bembo's surviving subsequent letters for that year are no less ardent but full of excuses for not seeing her. On 25 October he wrote to 'f.f.' from his father's villa at Noniano that he had to go to Venice for two days, after which, as he had promised her, he would return:

to see once more my own dear half without whom I am not merely incomplete but nothing at all, she being not simply one half of me but everything I am and can ever hope to be. And there could be no sweeter fate for me on earth nor could I win anything more precious than to lose myself like this, living the rest of my life in one thought alone, which, if in two hearts one and the same purpose thrives, and one single fire, may endure as long as those hearts wish, no matter what the heavens conspire. And this they can all the more readily accomplish because strangers' eyes are unable to discern their thoughts and no human power can bar the road they take since they come and go unseen . . .[33]

But Bembo was being overoptimistic: the heavens were indeed about to conspire against the lovers. In November 1503 Bembo had taken refuge in Ferrara with Strozzi even though Lucrezia was still in Medelana 'because at Ostellato, as I told you, there are no provisions on account of the visit of His Lordship Don Alfonso's court . . .', a feeble excuse which suggests that Bembo was unwilling to incur Alfonso's anger by being seen in Lucrezia's vicinity. Although Lucrezia was in Ferrara from at least mid December, there was time for only one last meeting before Bembo was called back to Venice to find that his brother Carlo had died on 30 December. The need to comfort his elderly father and, one might well speculate, the instinct that he was not welcome in Ferrara once Lucrezia's husband had returned, led him to decide to stay in Venice and send for his books, which indicated that his stay would be a long one. He would always, he assured her in words that have an almost valedictory ring, 'be that faithful Heliotrope to whom you alone and for ever remain the sun'.[34]

10. The Dark Marquis

'If during this period you chance to find your ears are ringing it
will be because I am communing with all those dark things and
horrors and tears of yours, or else writing pages about you that will
still be read a century after we are gone'

– Pietro Bembo to Lucrezia, 25 July 1504

During the high summer and autumn of 1503 the plague had
raged through Ferrara; all those rich enough to escape had left,
and the Este with their various households had retreated separately to their country villas. The poor and the *artisanelli* – literally 'little artisans' – had been the principal victims and some 850
had died. By November the disease had spread to the countryside: on 1 November, di Prosperi reported that he had heard that
fifty-seven members of Lucrezia's household were sick. Both
Lucrezia and Alfonso remained outside the city, Lucrezia at
Medelana, Alfonso at Ostellato.

Meanwhile, an event had occurred in Rome which was to
have serious consequences for Cesare, the Este and indeed
Lucrezia herself. On the night of 17 October the gentle, kindly
but infirm Pius III died after a reign of only twenty-six days.
Pius had protected and favoured Cesare; on 8 October, the day
of his coronation, he had confirmed him as Captain General of
the Church and Gonfalonier. Cesare had been preparing to leave
for the Romagna as his enemies – the Orsini, Gian Paolo Baglioni
and Bartolommeo d'Alviano – gathered in Rome. Even the
Colonna joined them. Cesare tried to break out but the Orsini
got wind of his plans and after a ferocious fight Cesare was forced
to retreat to the Vatican for safety. Even there he was not secure

as the Orsini and their allies raged through the Borgo, shouting, 'Let us kill the Jewish dog!' Protected by the cardinals and the castellan of Sant'Angelo, a Borgia partisan, Cesare fled along the covered way to the castle with his family – Rodrigo Bisceglie, Giovanni Borgia and his two illegitimate children. Two days later Pius died, leaving Cesare at bay in the Castel Sant'Angelo. News of his predicament caused the final crumbling of his states in the Romagna where, by the end of the month, he held only a few cities and castles. In Rome he still hoped to gain something by bargaining the support of his Spanish cardinals in the conclave to elect the new pope. But in reality there was only one candidate: the Borgias' lifelong enemy, Giuliano della Rovere.

On 1 November 1503, Giuliano became pope, taking the title Julius II; Cesare had made an agreement with him over the election but the long-term prognostication for their relationship was not good. The former Giuliano della Rovere was sixty years old when he attained the papacy, the object of his lifelong ambition. Men said of him that he had the soul of an emperor and his appearance was as imperial as his manner was imperious. He was a man of volcanic temperament: when he acted it was with dynamic energy and he was given to fits of violent temper, often fuelled by too much wine. Guicciardini wrote of him that he was notoriously difficult by nature and formidable with everyone; that he had spent his long life in restless action, in great enmities and friendships and constant intrigues. The Venetian envoys Lippomano and Capello described him as extremely acute but tempestuous: 'It is almost impossible to describe how strong and violent and difficult to manage he is. In body and soul he has the nature of a giant.' He had the reputation of being a man of his word, which even the Borgias believed, but in fact he was subtle, devious and ruthless in pursuit of his aims. And Cesare had seriously misjudged him, as Machiavelli, always the acute observer, commented: 'He does not love il Valentino, but nonetheless strings him along for two reasons: one, to keep his word, of which men hold him most observant, and for the obligations he has towards him, being recognizant to him for the good part of the Papacy; the other, since it seems to him, that His Holiness being without forces, the Duke [Cesare] is better placed to resist the Venetians.'[1]

Cesare's predicament caused strains in the relationship between Lucrezia and her husband. Alfonso was not enthusiastic about her support for her embattled brother. While Ercole had taken the view that Cesare in charge in the Romagna would be less dangerous to Ferrara than a powerful Venice, Alfonso was more circumspect and courted Venice through the medium of the Venetian envoy, della Pigna. According to Sanudo, on 21 October Alfonso complained to della Pigna that the Venetian Signory 'do not wish him well and he does not know why if it were not for the men sent by madonna Lucretia to help Valentino, and he has not given him a penny, etc . . .' The envoy concludes that 'it would be good to act together with Don Alfonso, who wishes evil to Valentino . . .'[2] Ercole, eager to keep in with the new Pope, had dispatched Ippolito to Rome with Ferrante, the Pope's godson, for Julius's coronation on 3 November.

Whatever their differences over Cesare (and it is possible that Alfonso was playing games with the Venetians) and Alfonso's distaste for Lucrezia's literary circle, he was strongly physically attracted to his wife; from the first year of her marriage to the end of her life, Lucrezia was almost continually pregnant and getting her in that condition seems to have been almost an obsession with him. Numbers of children were associated with virility: Alfonso's grandfather, Niccolò III, had so many children, legitimate and otherwise, that official genealogists gave up after sixteen, adding after the sixteenth, Baldassare, 'and many other bastards'. Ercole himself had fathered eight children. On 17 November, di Prosperi reported to Isabella that Lucrezia was said to be unwell due to a new pregnancy; her condition was confirmed by the end of the month. It was only just over a year since the stillbirth of her daughter when Alfonso had promised her another child. Her hopes were high but some time the following year she miscarried; the only written evidence is in a letter to her from Bembo of September 1505 which talks of 'the cruel disappointment and vain hopes of last year'.[3]

Meanwhile, in Rome things were going from bad to worse for Cesare. Julius II was a warrior pope with vast ambitions. Like Alexander he was determined to have the States of the Church under his control, and even to extend them further than Alexander and Cesare had done. Cesare was merely a temporary instrument to be discarded once his usefulness was past. For some months the Pope played a cat and mouse game with il Valentino, intent upon gaining the surrender of Cesare's remaining fortresses in the Romagna. On 1 December news came that Michelotto and Cesare's cavalry had been captured near Arezzo. This report, according to Machiavelli, threw the Pope into ecstasies, 'since it seemed to him that by the capture of that man he had the chance to uncover all the cruelties of robberies, sacrileges and other infinite evils which over the past eleven years . . . have been done in Rome against God and man'. Julius told Machiavelli gleefully that he was looking forward to interviewing Michelotto 'to learn some tricks from him, so as to enable him to better govern the Church'. Devastated by the capture of Michelotto, Cesare promised to render to Julius certain fortresses in the Romagna. However, when the papal messenger arrived at Cesena, Cesare's castellans, the Ramires brothers, beat him and hanged him from the castle walls, and sent an insolent message to the Pope. Julius fell into a rage and on 20 December confined Cesare to the Torre Borgia, the very room in which Michelotto had murdered Alfonso Bisceglie three years before.

Early in January 1504, Cesare suffered another blow when two wagonloads of his possessions destined for Ferrara were seized, one from Rome by the Florentines in Tuscany, the other coming from Cesena, by Giovanni Bentivoglio, as it passed through Bolognese territory. The latter contained many of the goods taken by Michelotto from Alexander's room on the day of his death, including the jewel-studded mantle of St Peter, altarpieces and cups of gold and precious stones, eighty huge pearls and 'a cat in gold with two most noble diamonds as its eyes'.[4] They had been travelling in the name of Ippolito, an indication that under Lucrezia's persuasion the Este were still prepared to help him.

Ippolito and Lucrezia were acting to help Cesare, as is evident from a letter of 10 April 1504 written by Juan Artes, commandant of Cesare's galleys, addressed to Ippolito but mentioning Lucrezia; he gave them what he described as 'the good news' that an agreement had been reached whereby Cesare's castellans in the Romagna would hand over his fortresses to the Pope's representative, after which Cesare would be freed from the fortress at Ostia, where he now was, to go safely to Naples.[5] However, at Naples, Cesare, the great deceiver, was himself the victim of a double-cross from the quarter he least expected it, Gonsalvo da Cordoba, 'the Great Captain'. On 26 May, the eve of his departure by ship for Tuscany, he went to take leave of Gonsalvo only to find himself arrested, despite the safe conduct he had received from him. He was the victim of an international intrigue between the Pope, who was afraid of what il Valentino might do once freed, and the King and Queen of Spain, who wanted two things from the Pope and were therefore desperate to please him – a dispensation enabling Catherine of Aragon to marry her dead husband's brother, the future Henry VIII of England, and their own investiture with the Kingdom of Naples. Moreover, it was reported that Juan Gandia's widow, convinced that Cesare had murdered her husband, pleaded in person with the Spanish sovereigns to bring him back to be tried for his crime. In August, Cesare lost his last possession in the Romagna when his loyal castellan, Gonsalvo de Mirafuentes, rode out of the Rocca di Forlì, lance held high.[6] With this, Cesare had lost everything for within the Rocca di Forlì was stored the loot he had stolen from Urbino, including the famous library. With tears in his eyes Guidobaldo retrieved his possessions; the Pope's agents seized the rest. A few days later Cesare was shipped as a prisoner to Spain.

To Lucrezia, in despair over Cesare's fate, Ercole wrote a letter which showed how much she had captured his affections: 'Be of good heart, for even as we love you sincerely and with every tenderness of heart as our daughter, so we shall never fail him, and we wish to be to him a good father and good brother in everything.' But there was little in fact that Ercole could do beyond the pious exhortation to 'hope in Our Lord God who does not abandon whoso trusts in him'.[7]

Indeed, at the moment when Artes's letter had arrived with its message of false hope, Lucrezia had had no one to turn to beyond her father-in-law, now in failing health. Alfonso embarked on 13 April on a protracted tour of the European courts, in the course of which he visited Paris, then Brussels, where he met the future Charles V, and England where he was welcomed by Henry VII and 'much caressed and honoured'.[8] Ippolito had managed to quarrel both with his father and the Pope. A messenger had been sent by Julius to Ippolito to deliver a brief concerning the surrender of some of his benefices which the Pope wished to confer on someone else. Ippolito fell into a rage and had the unfortunate man soundly beaten. When an outraged Ercole ordered him to write a letter of apology to the Pope, he rudely refused and was exiled to Mantua, whereupon there was an exchange of angry letters between father and son. 'Since you have been disobedient and ungrateful towards us, you need not wonder that we have dismissed you from our State; because behaving yourself as you do, we do not think you are worthy to be near us,' Ercole wrote on 14 April in reply to an insolent letter from Ippolito.[9] That day Francesco Gonzaga arrived by barge down the Po to effect a reconciliation between Ercole and Ippolito; his intervention was successful and the cardinal was back in Ferrara for the annual St George's Day races, when Isabella's horse won the *palio* prize.

Despite the valedictory note of Bembo's letter to her of 5 January 1504, Lucrezia continued to correspond with him. Although Bembo still wrote her occasional romantic letters from afar, referring to her as 'f.f.', he did not visit her, pleading 'indisposition'. In late May she was also 'indisposed'; she may even have miscarried then. In July he was planning to visit her in Ferrara but procrastinated so that she had gone to Modena at the time he was to arrive. Instead he went to his Paduan villa 'so that I may finish those things which I began for you'. 'If,' he told her, 'during this period you chance to find your ears are ringing it will be because I am communing with all those dark things and horrors and tears of yours, or else writing pages about you that will still be read a century after we are gone . . .'[10] This is prob-ably a reference to *Gli Asolani* with its dedicatory letter to Lucrezia dated 1 August 1504 – although it was not published by Aldus Manutius until March 1505. Ercole Strozzi was still acting as a go-between on lightning visits to Venice and they were still in touch through him and Lucrezia's ladies – Nicola, now the wife of the Ferrarese aristocrat, Bigio dei Trotti, Elisabetta senese and Madonna Giovanna. They also now had another friend of Bembo's, Alfonso Ariosto, a relation of Ludovico, who acted as a private messenger. Alfonso Ariosto, Bembo wrote, 'comes to you deeply desiring to render you homage and make your acquain-tance, already afire with the flame that the rays of your great qualities have kindled in his breast, having heard them praised so many times . . .' Towards the end of September, Lucrezia sent Bembo a poem by their mutual friend Antonio Tebaldeo, now acting as her secretary. In October, Bembo wrote that he had planned to come to Ferrara to see her but that he had heard that the Gonzaga would be there on account of Duke Ercole's seri-ous relapse, which would prevent him from paying his respects to her 'as unhurriedly as I would desire'.

A long and most interesting letter from Venice dated 10 February 1505, addressed to 'Madonna N' (Nicola dei Trotti) but intended for Lucrezia, seems to indicate that somehow Bembo had succeeded in seeing her and that their passion had been reignited. 'As long as I live,' he wrote, 'I cannot recall ever receiving a letter as gratifying as that which your Ladyship gave me upon my depar-ture and in which you proved to me that I abide in your favour . . . you must know the first hour I saw you that you penetrated my mind to such a degree that never afterwards have you been able to quit it . . .' There is a great deal in the 'star-crossed lovers' vein which was, no doubt, part of the attraction for both: his ill fortune is 'more than ever arrayed against me now', he tells her,

yet I have no fear, for it could never make me so afraid that I could cease to love you and not count you the one true mistress of my self and my life, ever serving you with the purest and warmest loyalty that a valiant and steadfast lover can offer the woman he loves and honours above all things human. I do beseech you never to alter and never to lose heart in this love, though there are so many things which oppose and obstruct our desires . . . But endeavour rather to be ever more deeply inflamed with love the more arduous you see your resolve become . . . in spite of ill fortune I love you and . . . nothing can take this from me and I fancy, if there be likewise nothing that can make you not love me, in the end the day must come when we two shall triumph and vanquish ill fortune . . . and when that day comes it will be so lovely and precious for us to recall that we were staunch and constant lovers . . .

There is no doubt that Bembo was deeply concerned at the possibility that their correspondence might be discovered – presumably by Alfonso. 'Above all,' he implores her, 'I beg you to take care that no one may know or discover your true thoughts lest the paths which lead to our love become even more restricted and thwarted than they are at present. Do not trust anyone, no matter whom, until I come to you, which in any case will be soon after Easter if I am alive . . .' She could trust the bearer of this letter and reply via him. 'Indeed I beseech you to do so, for since we can talk so little face to face please speak at length with me in letters and let me know what life you lead, and what thoughts are yours and in whom you confide, which things torment you and which console. And take good care not to be seen writing, because I know you are watched very closely.' After kissing 'one of those prettiest and brightest and sweetest eyes of yours which have pierced me to the soul, first and lovely cause, though not the only one, of my ardour', he begged her to accept his favourite medal, an Agnus Dei: 'Out of love for me sometimes please deign to wear at night the enclosed Agnus Dei which I once used to wear upon my breast, if you cannot wear it in the day, so that your precious heart's dear abode, which I should gladly stake my life to kiss but once and long, may at least be touched by this roundel which for so long has touched the abode of mine . . .'[11]

Bembo, it seems, did see her, as he promised, once again when he passed through Ferrara in April en route to take part in a Venetian embassy to Rome. He may even have seen her on his return journey early in June when he went on to Mantua to be presented to Isabella. He never saw Lucrezia again thereafter, although they were in touch sporadically until the end of her life. Bembo spent six years at the court of Urbino where he featured as one of the characters in a dialogue on love in *The Courtier* before spending the rest of his life in Rome, becoming secretary to Pope Leo X.

Lucrezia, or 'f.f.', had taken an enormous risk with this relationship even if it was romantic in the fashionable tradition of 'courtly love' rather than actually physical. Several people knew about it – her ladies Nicola and Giovanna, Ercole Strozzi and Alfonso Ariosto. The Este had a reputation for ruthlessness in similar circumstances. The Torre Marchesana, one of the four towers of the Castello in which Lucrezia's apartments then were, had been the scene of a grim ending to a tragic love affair, that of Ugo and Parisina. In the dungeons of this tower just eighty years earlier, on the night of 21 May 1425, Alfonso's grandfather, Niccolò III d'Este, had ordered the beheading of his second wife, Parisina Malatesta, and of his favourite, illegitimate son, Ugo Aldobrandino, for committing adultery together. Danger, however, was something to which Lucrezia, as a Borgia, had become inured; she may even have derived a certain thrill from risk – as long as that risk was something which, with her experience and charm, she could control and circumvent.

Yet even as her romance with Bembo was on the wane, Lucrezia had embarked on another very different and more long-lasting relationship. She had first met Francesco Gonzaga when, as the hero of the battle of Fornovo, he had passed through Rome in March 1496 and called upon her and Cesare when she was still – just – Countess of Pesaro. Born in 1466 in Mantua, the son of Federico I, the third Marquis of Mantua, and Margherita of Wittelsbach, he had succeeded his father aged not quite eighteen and married Isabella d'Este, aged sixteen, in 1490. He was not handsome: the bust by Gian Cristoforo Romano in the Palazzo Ducale at Mantua shows a man of exuberant carnality, with overblown, sensual lips, protuberant eyes and thick, wiry hair. Although he protected and helped Andrea Mantegna, whose greatest paintings were executed for the Gonzaga family, he was no intellectual. His overwhelming passion, apart from sex, was his stable of horses which was famous throughout Europe and won every race in Italy. Like most aristocrats of his time his chief preoccupations beyond the practice of arms and political survival were horses, hunting dogs and falcons. Beyond his undoubted military skills and extreme untrustworthiness, Francesco's sexual overdrive was his most significant characteristic. Until at least 1497 he had openly kept a mistress, Teodora Suardi, by whom he had three illegitimate children, often accompanying her in public to the mortification of Isabella. His sexual interests were certainly not confined either to his wife or his mistress – young girls, who could be married to complaisant husbands, and young boys were equally desirable. Lodovico 'Vigo' di Camposampiero, with whom he carried on a scabrous correspondence for some years and who was with good reason hated by Isabella, acted as his pimp. One of his functions was to provide boys for Gonzaga. In October 1506 when Gonzaga was campaigning in leisurely fashion against his friends and connections, the Bentivoglio of Bologna, di Camposampiero wrote to him from Rome that he was sending him a boy: 'As you are at war up there you will not be able to have all your usual comforts . . . you may not find him as beautiful as he has been depicted, but nonetheless he is at your command . . .'[12]

He revelled in the Rabelaisian, often actively pornographic letters of the distinguished Bolognese jurist Floriano Dolfo. The theme of many of Dolfo's letters was sodomy, whether homosexual or heterosexual; Dolfo himself liked boys and despised women. He particularly enjoyed retailing the notorious practices at the Baths of Porretta near Bologna. He delightedly described an incident concerning Battista Ranuzzi, lord of the locality, 'who, the other night, going to the baths with a nun, wanted to sodomize her in the water, and having placed his penis in her arse, both of them seated, he raised himself slightly to penetrate her further and both of them slipped right under the water; but thanks to the goodness of God who never inflicts an unjust punishment, knowing that this sin merited fire not water, both escaped the peril . . .'[13] 'The love of boys,' Dolfo wrote, was 'less wearisome, less dangerous and less expensive than the servile love of women.'[14] Although careful not actually to say anything to the detriment of Isabella, he could not resist scurrilous fun at her expense. Condoling with Francesco that their firstborn, Eleonora, was a girl, he 'comforted' him, saying that as a girl her birth would have brought 'less pain to the Most Illustrious Marchioness, and less stretching to her quim when she will have brought you a benefit and greater pleasure in your communal embraces, so that you won't find such a large chamber that it would be like a dried pea in a rattle or a clapper in a bell'.[15] Sodomy with either sex was not only a sin but a crime punishable by death by burning; only the rich, like Francesco's brother Giovanni, married to Laura Bentivoglio but nonetheless a practising homosexual, might escape by paying a hefty fine. Unsurprisingly given his relentless sexual activity, Francesco, like Alfonso, Cesare and even the Pope, Julius II, had syphilis; the disease eventually killed him.

Francesco had charm and a powerful sexual magnetism; he liked to flirt with women and knew how to talk to them. To Lucrezia he was far more like the men she had loved – her father and Cesare – than the refined, eloquent Bembo. Biographers have called her relationship with Bembo 'the great love of her life' but a study of the relevant documents indicates rather that Francesco was her passion. The fact that he was Isabella's husband can only have added spice to the affair. Francesco admired his wife for her cool and subtle political instinct, so necessary in restraining his own impulsive temperament and capacity for getting himself into trouble. He was proud of her as a celebrated collector of antique statues and works of art, her patronage of the arts, her skill and accomplishments in entertaining and her taste in dress, all of which passions cost him more than he could afford on his income from Mantua, even supplemented by his successful career as a *condottiere*. There was no question that intellectually Isabella was far his superior but physically, over the next few years, his interest in her waned and after she had borne him eight children, including the longed-for heir, Federico, in May 1500, their relations ceased. Increasingly her bossiness and vanity irritated him as did her coldness towards her daughters, particularly Eleonora, and perhaps also a little her passion for their son, of whom she once wrote that she hoped he would not inherit the vices of his father.[16] Francesco and his brother-in-law Alfonso shared a mutual contempt which gave an affair with Lucrezia additional piquancy.

Lucrezia's first letters to Francesco date from the spring of 1502: and, unlike her letters of the same period to Isabella, they are written, not by a secretary, but in her own distinctive, legible, spiky hand. Her first letter, written on 11 April of that year, has a distinctly flirtatious note and, since she refers to a letter he has written her, they were already in correspondence. 'My illustrious lord,' she wrote,

being on the verge of the confessional, I received a letter from you for which I kiss your hand and ask your pardon for the tardiness of my answer although it was caused by not wishing to disturb Your Lordship in your devotions in these Holy Days [a reference to Easter Week] and because of this I make my reply about 'your falcon' as brief as possible. I am advised that he is very well, and better, to judge by appearances, and is often examined by others who had heard from the confessor some things which have happened, although I understand that all this may be said without offence to God . . . because I desire as much as my own health to hear that Your Lordship is renewed from now on in the fear and service of God: and as a good son of San Francesco, as am I, although unworthy, and a Patron of so many excellent friars as much as of their religion. I want in every way to do honour to such as a father [*padre*]. I know that Your Lordship ridicules me and my preaching which is the fault of Sister Eufrosina and Sister Laura who want me to spite the world by becoming a preacher and martyr. I thank Your Lordship for the other particulars of your letter which Count

Lorenzo [Strozzi] has told me in person at greater length and which have given me the greatest pleasure. But the too kind terms which you use to write to me [*cum suportatione de quella*] I regret that it does not seem suitable to me, holding Your Lordship as Lord and brother as I do . . .[17]

This altogether mysterious letter was clearly intended to be properly understood only by Francesco; for important people to write personal letters to each other was a risky business. Strozzi, one could assume, would have provided the key, which centred on the 'falcon'. Indeed, Lucrezia's second letter of the same date was a passionate recommendation of Lorenzo, Ercole Strozzi's brother, and his affairs in Mantua, pleading with Francesco to continue his protection of Lorenzo: 'and to this end I am sending the present bearer to Your Lordship so that he may explain more fully my feelings towards the said count'. Lorenzo Strozzi, like Ercole, would act as go-between for Lucrezia and Francesco. Closely watched as they knew themselves to be, the letters Lucrezia and Francesco exchanged tended to be circumspect, and important messages would be delivered personally by trusted emissaries such as the Strozzi. Indeed, several letters of this period concern favours which she wanted Gonzaga to do for Lorenzo Strozzi. A letter to Francesco that year, written on 30 December, has a playful note:

May Our Lord God be thanked that we have here a pledge from Your Lordship that you will be constrained to let yourself be seen here sometimes for to tell the truth it has been too long since you have been here. I do not joke, My Lord, but I have not been able to be of more service to you than I have been. But it has not been possible for the reasons Count Lorenzo wrote to you: and if they are not enough to excuse me to you I ask a thousand pardons because certainly I desire to serve Your Lordship in everything possible. I thank you as much as I can for the good expedition you have given to the affairs of the said Count . . .[18]

From 1503 only one letter survives, written in a secretarial hand and asking Francesco to help a member of her household in his affairs at Mantua, while for the same year there are nine letters from Lucrezia to Isabella, all of an administrative nature; this is presumably because Francesco spent a great deal of his time that year with the French armies going against Naples, leaving Isabella in charge.

In the spring and summer of 1504, when Alfonso was on his travels and Duke Ercole was ailing, Lucrezia, following the example of the Duchess Eleonora, took a regular part in the *Esame delle Suppliche* (Examination of Petitions) and much of her correspondence arose out of the cases presented to her there. Many of the requests were for pardons or the release of prisoners held in Mantua. When Gonzaga did nothing about them, she repeated her requests firmly until he complied. While in Ferrara, he had promised to release to her a certain Bernardino della Publica, imprisoned for murder. When he failed to do so, she wrote insistently and several times, finally and sharply five months later: 'I beg you to fulfil your promise ... release [Bernardino della Publica] and send him to me as soon as possible . . .' Her competence must have impressed Francesco because in one letter she thanked him for all the kind things he had said about her to Duke Ercole which had been repeated to her.

Towards the end of April, Gonzaga (with Isabella) again visited Ferrara for the annual St George's Day races, inspiring flirtatious letters of regret on his departure from Lucrezia and her ladies. From the beginning, immediately after Gonzaga had left Ferrara, she and her ladies had entered into a conspiracy to seduce him. On 8 May 1504, her ladies wrote a collective lament for his absence, feeling themselves half alive, they said, for the lack of his 'benign, kind, sophisticated and divine presence', his 'divine virtues and exalted and angelic manner'. Angela Borgia and Polissena Malvezzi were particularly concerned to do his bidding, 'principally when we see the affection borne by our most excellent Duchess, who in all our conversations never ceases to hold the sweetest memories of you'. The letter was signed 'the most dedicated damsels of the most excellent Duchess'.[19] Polissena wrote the same day describing court festivities and adding, 'But every delight gave little pleasure to Her Ladyship or to me, her servant, since Your Illustrious Lordship was not present.'

Lucrezia was anxious to please her brother-in-law whenever the opportunity arose. Typically, Francesco was anxious to have some fine horses of Cesare's which were being kept in the Rocca di Forlì by the castellan, de Mirafuentes, as he had made clear during his May visit. Lucrezia immediately contacted de Mirafuentes, as she told Gonzaga in a letter of 11 May, enclosing the castellan's reply: 'I only beg of you to signify if there is anything else you need in this case and if I can be of help to you because I assure Your Excellency that you will find me always most prompt and well-disposed in this and in anything else you know that I can be of service to you.' At the end of July, responding to further requests from Francesco about the horses, she told him that she had written immediately and with the greatest urgency to the castellan and was sure that he would obtain what he desired.

As early as 1502 Lucrezia had taken under her protection the beautiful Barbara Torelli, maltreated wife of Ercole Bentivoglio, son of Giovanni, lord of Bologna. Barbara, a cultivated and intelligent woman of a noble family of Ferrarese origin, had taken refuge in Ferrara because of the Este friendship for her family and because she found the cultured Este court congenial. She seems to have been a difficult woman, and the nuns with whom she first lodged complained to Lucrezia that they did not wish to keep her, whereupon the compassionate Lucrezia had persuaded a Messer Alfonso Calacagnino to have her in his house.[20] Two years later Francesco Gonzaga took up the cause of Ercole Bentivoglio at the instance of his own brother, Giovanni Gonzaga, who was related to Bentivoglio through his wife, Laura. He sent a trusted servant, Marcantonio Gatto, to request Lucrezia that Bentivoglio's daughter, Costanza, be taken from her mother and sent to Mantua to Giovanni Gonzaga's house. Lucrezia replied in the beautiful hand of Tebaldeo that she had hastened to do as he asked, despite her status as Barbara Torelli's protector: 'And in this case she has shown herself somewhat difficult: nonetheless, to satisfy Your Lordship's desire, I have operated in such a manner that Madonna Barbara, her mother, has consented, albeit unwillingly. And so the girl will go with Marcantonio whom you sent here for this purpose . . .'[21]

As the summer months passed the tone of the letters became more intense and the two exchanged verses, mentioned by Luzio but which have since disappeared. On 10 July, Francesco wrote that he was sick from being deprived of 'the air of Ferrara which so suits me and of Your Ladyship's conversation which brings me such pleasure', excusing himself for not being able to write in his own hand or send the sonnets he had promised her.[22] 'I received your letter and understand that your tardiness in writing was due to your indisposition which grieves me,' Lucrezia replied, 'but there was no need to use such terms to me because I am certain of your feelings towards me, for which I will always be truly grateful. And I applaud Your Lordship for passing these tiresome times in pleasures and delightful pastimes as you describe to me. Of ours here, there is no need to describe them since Your Excellency well knows of what sort and quality they are. I am happy you should make fun of us if it gives you pleasure. I and the other ladies here think you are right, and thus Madonna Giovanna, Dona Angela [Borgia] and I myself kiss your hand . . .'[23] Five days later she was making plans to see him again: Ercole, who had been gravely ill in June, had been on a pilgrimage to Florence in fulfilment of a vow he had made. He had invited Lucrezia to meet him at the frontiers of Modena, on his return, which seemed to Lucrezia to provide a convenient opportunity to meet Francesco.[24] That she did indeed go to Modena is evident from a letter written from there on 25 July, but there is no mention of a meeting, only of thanking him for news of Alfonso who had written to her himself from Paris informing her that he would be returning to Ferrara on 12 August.

Francesco appears, however, to have made a tentative attempt to see her, according to a letter from Alfonso to Isabella of

3 October which reveals a little of the manoeuvres required. Isabella had written to him informing him that her husband desired to go to Comacchio, the villa in the Po delta used by the Este for hunting and particularly fishing. Apparently Francesco had said that he did not want to disturb Alfonso, who was in the midst of taking the water treatment (*'questa mia aqua da bagni'*), probably mud from Abano, but Alfonso said it would be a great displeasure for him not to accompany Gonzaga there; he had only not replied earlier, he said, because he had been waiting to see if Lucrezia wanted to go or not:

Yesterday morning she departed with our uncle Sigismondo and a goodly company of ladies and gentlemen to go to Comacchio which, with the journey, will be about ten or twelve days. As soon as she returns I will let you know so that you can tell the Marchese what day he can leave there [?Mantua] and come to Ferrara because I intend at all costs to accompany him [to Comacchio]. And in these few days I will finish my water treatment and His Lordship will be content to wait these few days in order to have the greater enjoyment. And to have better lodging than he could at present there because the people I have mentioned are there . . . Please remind him that the fewer people he brings the more comfortable he will be . . .[25]

Presumably Francesco had hoped to have Lucrezia to himself at Comacchio without her husband's surveillance; if so, he (and probably also she) was disappointed.

It is tempting to speculate that Alfonso had written to defer Francesco Gonzaga's journey to Comacchio in order that he should *not* see Lucrezia there. Certainly it would appear so from a letter Lucrezia wrote to Francesco on 28 October after she returned to Ferrara: 'Not having been able personally to see Your Excellency and speak to you on your journey to Comacchio as I greatly desired . . .', she was sending her 'major-domo' to him with the request she would have made him. The object of this request was a strange one: the release to Lucrezia 'in absolute freedom' of a certain Antonio da Bologna, a formerly trusted courtier of both Francesco and Isabella, who had been condemned by Gonzaga for abusing his position by ordering expensive clothes for himself while pretending that they were for the Marquis and his family. Gonzaga had apparently bluntly refused Lucrezia's request: she then wrote him, in her own hand, a passionate and imperious demand that he should do as she asked. Quite why she should have been so attached to Antonio da Bologna is a mystery; that he was a young man of charm and allure is, however, clear from other references. Gonzaga must eventually have released him because not long afterwards he secretly married (becoming her second husband) Giovanna d'Aragona, Duchess of Amalfi, the protagonist of Webster's drama, and was murdered in 1513 by a Gonzaga connection, probably on the orders of her brother, Cardinal Luigi d'Aragona, a cousin and intimate of the Este.[26]

Alfonso had in fact arrived in Ferrara on 8 August, earlier than expected, the reason for his hasty return being the severe illness of Ercole; there were rumours of rivalries among the Este brothers over the succession and mutual suspicions which were to erupt in violence over the next two years. Sanudo had reported on 7 June: 'From Ferrara the news comes that the Duke is ill; Don Alfonso is in France and is going to England, so that a messenger has been sent after him for him to return, because his father is in great danger; and if at his death he should not be found in Ferrara, the second brother, Don Ferrando [Ferrante], who is loved by the people, could be made Lord.'[27] Ferrante had returned from Rome, his head turned by the welcome given him there by the Pope, his godfather, whose favourable treatment of him had enraged his brother, Ippolito. This may well have given him ideas that he might have been invested with the Dukedom by the Pope in Alfonso's absence. Bernardino Zambotti also recorded that Alfonso hurried back, 'thinking that he was in danger of not succeeding to the lordship of Ferrara, if his father died in his absence'.[28] Speculation as to the succession was rife in Rome and in Venice, as the Venetian envoy in Rome, Giustinian, reported to the Doge on 29 June: 'It was said that there were letters from Ferrara that the Lord Duke had had a return of his malady and was in great danger of his life. As to what will happen in the event of his death, various judgements are passed, and all conclude that there must be great dissensions among his sons, and that the absence of Don Alfonso will be greatly to his disadvantage, since the Cardinal, who is popular with the people, is in Ferrara . . .'[29]

Lucrezia had clearly been relying on Francesco to help her if Ercole died while Alfonso was away and had obtained his promise to do so, as a letter to Francesco from Marcantonio Gatto makes clear. Gatto was one of the private messengers employed that year by Lucrezia and Francesco to convey letters and confidences too risky to be committed to paper. On 6 June, precisely at the time Ercole first fell ill, Gatto wrote to Francesco reminding him of the promise he had given to Lucrezia to go to Revere, within easy reach of Ferrara, should she have urgent need of him: 'Everyone has offered the Lady their support should the Duke die and to dedicate their souls and their lives to her service – and above all the Cardinal [Ippolito] . . . although most people do not trust him,' he wrote. 'Many other things I will keep to tell you personally that I do not dare to write confirming that all this city will be in favour of the Lady, when they intend however to cry "*Turco!*" in the piazza . . . Believe Gattino, [little cat] My Lord, that you alone can do more in this city than all the house of Este together . . .'[30] The story behind this last letter reflects the feverish atmosphere in Ferrara as Ercole's reign was clearly coming to its close. Gatto was a very minor player who was in reality no more than a messenger. It does, however, demonstrate Lucrezia's fears as to what might happen to her if Ercole, her principal protector, died while Alfonso was abroad, with Cesare out of the game and the Borgias' greatest enemy on the papal throne.

Lucrezia's last letter of that year, written on 17 December, was carried by hand to Mantua by Gatto. In it she asked Francesco to trust him as he would herself (the conventional formula for confidential messages) and 'hold him as the most faithful servant which he is', asking him to give effect to his promise that he would take him (Gatto) into his service. It was written when

Ercole was on his deathbed; the content of her message via Gatto can never be known but clearly related to the latest situation and its possible dangers. Gatto was a fool who had got into deep water; Lucrezia, compassionate and appreciative of loyal servants, thought it better that he should stay out of Ferrara under Gonzaga's protection. Ippolito for one would not have hesitated to eliminate him had he got wind of the gist of Gatto's letter to Gonzaga.

Less than ten days earlier, on 8 December, Giustinian had reported Lucrezia as taking an important political initiative to protect herself and Alfonso in the event of Ercole's death:

Letters from Ferrara announce that Duke Ercole is gravely ill, in imminent danger of death. On this occasion the Cardinal Regino told the Venetian orator that Donna Lucrezia, consort of Lord Alfonso, was his '*comare*' [literally meaning co-godparent, which in those days implied a closer relationship than it does now], and in all her affairs bows ['*fa capo*'] to your most Reverend Signory and that she serves you willingly, since she is a virtuous lady and well loved by him: with some other words spoken with considerable reserve and prudence, by which he tacitly wished to insinuate that, in case of the death of the aforesaid duke, she and her husband would be recommended to Your Serenity; saying, however, that she would not do otherwise, for her goodness and justice; . . . saying that it was almost common opinion among those who do not judge well of the affairs of Your Excellency from not understanding this, that she on the death of the Duke will be making some change in that state.[31]

Since the death of Alexander VI and the accession of Julius II, Ferrara was again a state suspended between the expansionist ambitions of the papacy on the one hand and Venice on the other. Julius II had made it clear in his dealings with Ercole that he was no friend to Ferrara and its ruling family; his favouring of Ferrante, which had led Ippolito to leave Rome in a rage, indicated that he might well cause trouble by using Ferrante as an instrument in any succession quarrels. Alfonso had chosen to placate Venice, the power on his borders, rather than the probably implacable papacy. In September he had made a journey to Venice with the specific aim of obtaining the support of the Signory. Now, as the crisis of Ercole's death approached, he was supported by Lucrezia who well knew how to exploit her still-powerful connections. As Christmas of 1504 approached, Alfonso was beginning to throw off his 'Prince Hal' image while Lucrezia looked forward to attaining the supreme position she had always wanted, as undisputed Duchess of Ferrara. For the first time, they were a true partnership and, once again, Lucrezia was pregnant.

11. Duchess of Ferrara

'Do not trust anyone . . . And take care not to be seen writing
because I know you are watched very closely . . .'

– Pietro Bembo to Lucrezia shortly after
her accession as Duchess, 10 February 1505

On Saturday 25 January 1505, Ercole died after days of fever and
shivering fits. Di Prosperi wrote to Isabella that on the Friday
evening he had had what appeared to have been a stroke, brought
on, it was thought, by the administration that morning of *auro
potabile* (water mixed with gold). From the hour that his state had
worsened, Alfonso and Giulio had never left his side and in the
morning he died peacefully, surrounded by his sons and brother.
Of the expected turbulence between the Este brothers, which
was to make the following year a dangerous one for the family,
there was no sign. Di Prosperi wrote of the death of Ercole and
the accession of Alfonso: 'For the one I condole with Your Ladyship
and for the other I congratulate you all the more having seen
everything come to pass in union, peace and love . . .'

On hearing of Ercole's death, the *Giudice dei Savi*, Trotti, ordered
the palace bell to be rung, and the people and the members of
the Council (*Savi*) summoned to his office. He had ready the
golden staff of office and the sword of justice for Alfonso's investiture. Having announced the death of Ercole and the elevation of
the new Duke, his eldest son, they proceeded to the Camera de
la Stufa Grande in Alfonso's apartments. There Alfonso, seated in
an armchair and wearing a mantle of white damask lined with
fur, a white cap and a collar of gold and jewels, was ceremonially invested with the office and insignia of Duke. After a speech

by the *Guidice dei Savi* he was presented with the *bacheta* (baton), the symbol of his sovereignty, and the sword for the defence and maintenance of the State, whereupon he made a speech of response promising to be a good lord to all his subjects in love and justice, followed by the cry 'Alfonso, Alfonso, Duca, Duca!' Afterwards, mounted on a great courser, he rode through the streets to the sound of trumpets, shouts, the ringing of bells, and *schioppi* (bursts of gunfire), through a violent blizzard of snow, with Ippolito on his right hand and the Venetian *visdomino* on his left, followed by Giulio and Ferrante. He dismounted at the cathedral where the *Giudice* and the *Savi* swore fealty.

Lucrezia, through all her troubles and indeed dangers, had finally succeeded to the secure position of Duchess of Ferrara. While Alfonso was being greeted as Duke by his people, Lucrezia, splendidly dressed in a *camorra* of crimson velvet and a gown of white *tabi* with long golden fringes and a jewelled headdress, received recognition as their Duchess by the leading gentlewomen of Ferrara. She had watched the acclamation of Alfonso and his progress through the piazza from the windows before going down to meet him. It was a triumphant moment for both of them when they met, both 'with happy faces' as di Prosperi described it. Bowing, Lucrezia made as if to kiss his hand but Alfonso raised, embraced and kissed her, and hand in hand they went to show themselves to the people; then she returned to her apartments while Alfonso remained to receive the plaudits of the populace, before going up to join Lucrezia with whom he dined, together with their court favourite, the jester, il Barone, 'in great joy'.

Ercole's funeral took place two days later, when his body was carried through the streets bearing the Order of the Garter given him by the King of England to his burial place in the church of Santa Maria degli Angeli. 'It is not too much to say,' Gardner, the historian of Ercole's court, wrote, 'that of all the Italian sovereigns in the epoch of the Borgia, Ercole d'Este is the one sympathetic, almost the only not ignoble figure.' Although, for all his piety, he could be time-serving, devious and untrustworthy, Ercole was undoubtedly the maker of modern Ferrara, almost doubling

the city in size, with an entire new quarter to the north, magnificent ramparts and broad new streets lined with palaces, rebuilt
churches and convents. He had employed artists of distinction,
such as Cosimo Tura, Ercole de'Roberti, and, as his principal
architect, Biagio Rossetti. The work was completed by the time
of his death; the 'city of silence' of today – its works of art, magnificently decorated palaces and colourfully emblazoned buildings a
pale shadow of Ercole's Ferrara, half obliterated by earthquakes
and the exile of the Este family – is still largely his creation. At
the time of Ercole's death, the Este court was the most cultured
in Italy, the centre of theatre and music. His household included
one of the largest companies of musicians and singers in Italy and
he had even begun a purpose-built theatre, the building of which
was discontinued by Alfonso. Ercole's children did not inherit his
extreme piety, and the mantle of protector of religion in the city
was to fall upon Lucrezia. Indeed, the principal loser by Ercole's
death was Sister Lucia whose downfall was immediate. Already
unpopular with her fellow nuns for the ducal favour she had
enjoyed, she was accused of artificially renewing the wounds of
the stigmata and deprived of all authority and precedence within
the convent. Then aged only twenty-nine, she was kept a virtual
prisoner by the other nuns until her death forty years later.

To all intents and purposes Alfonso had been in charge of
Ferrara since his return, while the dying Ercole consoled himself
with music, a choir of boy singers and the performance of a
keyboard player. As the new Duke, Alfonso immediately showed
skill and good grace in dealing with both his family and his
subjects, ensuring that his brothers had enough money to live in
style in the palaces with which their father had provided them.
More importantly he addressed the economic situation of Ferrara,
impoverished first by the war against Venice and then by Ercole's
great passion – the building of the new city, all of which had to
be paid for by increased taxation. Ercole's last years had been a
saga of maladministration. To raise money he had resorted to the
sale of offices and to commuting punishment to payment of fines,
to such an extent that Sanudo talked of extortion and gross

profiteering, while even the faithful di Prosperi wrote of 'enor-
mities worthy of being deemed corruption'. Alfonso abolished
many of his father's taxes and abandoned the system of the sale
of offices. Despite spending his mornings hawking and hunting
with his brothers, he directed most of his attention to the reform
of the state: 'The Lord thinks of nothing else but how to satisfy
his subjects to the best of his ability,' di Prosperi recorded.[1] He
sacked several officials and abolished various tax exemptions
granted by his father. He sent to Venice to buy grain to avert the
famine that was threatening, and made a state visit there in May,
accompanied by Ferrante and Giulio, where he was received with
signal honour by the Doge. From the beginning he had shown
respect for Lucrezia's administrative abilities by instituting on 31
January the *'Examine'* for private petitions under her charge,
assisted by Niccolò Bendideo, who was to become her secretary,
and Hieronymo Magnanimo. She carried out her office, according to di Prosperi, with 'intelligence and good grace'.

One of Alfonso's first acts was to have the ceiling raised on
the 'secret way', the *via coperta* built by Ercole as a passage between
the Palazzo del Corte and the Castello. This crossed the moat
from the eastern side of the palazzo over a small bridge to the
Ravelin, a tower with foundations in the moat, and from there
over a drawbridge to enter the castle. As a child, at the time of
the rebellion of Niccolò d'Este, Alfonso had escaped with his
mother from the palazzo through this passageway to the safety
of the castle. Now he was connecting new rooms in the Palazzo
del Corte to Lucrezia's apartments in the Castello to make
communication with her easier and more discreet, instead of
having to go to the castle outside by the 'via Courta'. This has
been represented by Lucrezia's biographer Maria Bellonci, who
persistently denigrated Lucrezia's relationship with Alfonso, as
inspired by jealousy, so that he could spy on Lucrezia and surprise
her at any hour. It was in fact designed not only for convenience
but to satisfy Alfonso's own desire for privacy. Alfonso, who to a
great extent shared his father's passion for rebuilding and
decoration, indulged it whenever he could during the few

untroubled early years of his reign. He modified the *via coperta* with a new roof and a new drawbridge, over which he built a colonnaded gallery, lit by many windows. On 4 February, di Prosperi reported to Isabella: 'I believe Your Ladyship will have heard about the passage being built above the via Courta for access between the Corte and the Castello, but also he [Alfonso] has ordered a '*lumaga quadra*' [a spiral staircase] by which His Lordship wishes to be able to descend into the piazzetta without going by the Corte or the Castello, by night and by day.' Far from making these improvements to spy on Lucrezia, Alfonso was making it easier to come and go to his whoring without drawing attention to himself.

In the wake of Ercole's death there was naturally a reorganization of the ducal households. There was, as usual, a swirl of rumour surrounding Lucrezia; di Prosperi, diligently but with only partial success as for obvious reasons he was held at arm's length by Lucrezia, attempted to divine what was going on for Isabella's information. On 1 January he wrote that as Duchess she would take on the living expenses of her court as she had at first 'because those of her household had proved themselves incapable of providing for their needs'. She had also disgraced Polissena Malvezzi and ordered her immediately out of the household: 'the cause no one knows but I believe she must have had good cause because she is known to be most wise'. Polissena, the woman who had entered so wholeheartedly into the flirtation with Francesco Gonzaga, turned out to be a malicious gossip and it was possibly on that account that Lucrezia so summarily dismissed her. Bembo's friends, Ercole Strozzi and Antonio Tebaldeo, whom he had specifically linked with Lucrezia in his dedicatory letter for *Gli Asolani*, were both, according to Gardner, given 'a severe fright' by Alfonso at the beginning of his reign. Isabella's secretary, Benedetto Capilupo, wrote to her on 3 February that Ercole Strozzi was in great danger because he had all the people against him and was out of favour with the Duke, and hinted that there was something more that he would tell her in person.[2] Early in April, a panic-stricken Tebaldeo wrote to Francesco, begging for a post in Mantua because 'this duke hates me, though I know not why, and it is not safe for me to stay in this city . . .' Possibly Lucrezia protected them – for the time being at least, since they remained in Ferrara. Bembo had written his long, passionate letter to Lucrezia on 10 February of that year, enjoining the utmost secrecy: 'Do not trust anyone . . . And take care not to be seen writing because I know you are watched very closely . . .' One possible spy may have been Girolamo da Sestola, nicknamed 'Coglia', principally a musician and dance teacher, but also, according to the historian of Ferrarese music, a 'courtier, horseman, dancer, musician, spy, newsmonger and emissary'.[3] Apart from choreographing the dancing for Lucrezia's wedding, he had acted at various times for Ercole, Alfonso, Ippolito and as an informer for Isabella. Another may have been a Gascon, Gian de Artigianova, a court singer known as 'Gian Cantore', who had recruited the famous composer Josquin Desprez for Ercole, and acted as confidant and pimp for Alfonso, and agent for the other Este. Bembo may also have been referring to members of the court, such as Beatrice de'Contrari, an intimate of Isabella.

Di Prosperi dropped repeated hints to Isabella about the changes in Lucrezia's household. In May he reported that one Benedetto, a pupil of Hieronymo Ziliolo, was to be in charge of Lucrezia's wardrobe (household accounts), 'and for this they say that all her Spaniards will have to go'. In June he wrote, 'It seems that it is the will of Our Lord that Madonna Elysabeth [presumably Elisabetta senese] and all the other foreign men and women who are in the Household of the Illustrious Lady his Consort should leave, including the Neapolitans and Samaritana Romana, whence they are all in a state which Your Ladyship may imagine. The causes of this I believe Your Ladyship will judge according to your own opinion. Above all, Count Lorenzo Strozzi has been deprived of the office of Seneschal [*Sescalcharia*] . . .' He added that Madonna Beatrice de'Contrari, a favourite of the Este (and particularly of Isabella), 'is said to be going to join Lucrezia's household and to live in the Palace . . . and that Tromb[onc]ino [the famous singer-composer] and d.Thebaldeo would be among the number of those forced to leave . . .'

Di Prosperi was not always totally reliable. Several of those mentioned by him as being dismissed were still members of Lucrezia's household a year later. Lucrezia was passionate about music and Bartolommeo Tromboncino, composer of *frottole*, lutenist and the most celebrated and highest paid of the court musicians, who had moved from the court of Isabella that year (no doubt much to the latter's disgust), was still with her in 1506–7 and remained with her until she could no longer afford to pay him during the years of war, when Ippolito took over his salary. Significantly he was the only Italian musician outside Rome or Naples to compose *frottole* with Spanish texts, something which must have been done to please Lucrezia. As a woman she was not allowed to maintain a chapel choir of her own, but she had other musicians for her secular entertainments. They included Dionisio da Mantova, 'Papino'; the fact that he was a Mantuan lutenist and composer (as was another of Lucrezia's musicians, Paolo Poccino, who joined her in 1505) probably further annoyed Isabella. Niccolò da Padova, the 'Niccolò Cantore' of Lucrezia's wedding company from Rome, was a lutenist, singer and composer of *frottole*. Then there was Ricciardetto Tamburino, a pipe and tabor player, and a woman singer, Dalida de'Putti, who eventually became one of Ippolito's mistresses. On 20 June, di Prosperi wrote that Lucrezia's Spaniards were preparing to leave but that for the moment nothing was known about her ladies. And on the 23rd he reported that Giovanni Valengo had replaced Lorenzo Strozzi, and that apart from him and Benedetto of the wardrobe, not one of Lucrezia's household would be permitted to live in the Castello, apart from the *credenciero* and some *staffieri* (squires). Later he reported that Ercole Strozzi had been removed from office 'and various things are said of him'. Apart from this, he and his brother Guido were said to be in dire financial straits.

In the letter quoted previously, Bembo referred to 'some solace to your anguish with my letter'. Lucrezia's anguish, indeed her central preoccupation, was connected with the fate of Cesare. Since he had

arrived in Spain towards the end of September 1504 – ironically at
the very same Valencian port, Villanueva del Grao, from which his
great uncle Alfonso Borgia, the future Pope Calixtus, had set sail
to found the Borgia fortunes in Italy – Cesare had been imprisoned in the fortress of Chinchilla, 700 feet up in the Valencian
mountains. Isolated as he was, he still had friends and supporters:
his Spanish cardinals, Lucrezia, and his brother-in-law, Jean d'Albret
(moved by the grief of Cesare's wife, Charlotte, his sister), continued to plead for his release with Ferdinand of Aragon, but the
shadows of Juan Gandia and Alfonso Bisceglie hung over him and
Queen Isabella was his implacable enemy. She, however, died at
Medina del Campo on 26 November 1504, an event which raised
the hopes of Cesare's partisans. Cesare himself made a fruitless
attempt to escape; early in 1505 unfounded rumours swept Italy
that he was free and well received at the Spanish court by Ferdinand
who hoped to make use of him in Italy for his own purposes.
Isabella d'Este learned of them from Benedetto Capilupo who
reported to her from Ferrara on 3 February.[4] Lucrezia had soon
discovered that these rumours were not true; she grieved for her
brother and persisted in her attempts to gain his release. Among
those she enlisted in her cause was Francesco Gonzaga, who was
in Ferrara for Ercole's funeral. A few days later, di Prosperi, on a
courtesy visit to Lucrezia in the Castello, found her lying on her
bed conversing with Stefano della Pigna, a distinguished Venetian
envoy, celebrated astrologer and friend of Gonzaga.

It was a horrible summer at Ferrara; it was very hot, the plague
had reappeared and there was widespread hunger. Early in May,
Lucrezia had written an urgent official letter to Francesco
Gonzaga asking him to speed through his territories the grain
and food supplies which Alfonso had ordered from Piemonte. In
July, di Prosperi reported that there was panic in the city because
of the plague, and that all the citizens who could had left, only
the poor and the merchants remaining: fifty to seventy corpses
were being buried every day. In August he wrote that there had
been 1,500 dead since the first outbreak of the plague and even
more of hunger. The Este scattered to their country villas and

palaces: Alfonso left for Belriguardo in mid June, returning briefly because of the grain crisis (and presumably to deal with Lucrezia's household changes). Ippolito was nearby at Vigoenza. Lucrezia went to Modena with Alfonso's uncle, Alberto d'Este, and her court. She was in frequent correspondence with Francesco Gonzaga, sometimes by private messages sent via Alberto Pio da Carpi, the humanist and bibliophile lord of Carpi, friend of Aldus, Bembo and Strozzi, with whom she had placed Cesare's son Girolamo. On 19 July she wrote to thank him for some caps – *scotie* – he had sent her 'by the present bearer', 'for which since they are most perfect, I thank you as much as I can and all the more because I recognize that in remembering me so often you give me more cause to be grateful to you every day . . .'

Plague had broken out in Modena too, but for Lucrezia help for Cesare was again in the forefront of her thoughts. After his failed escape he had been transferred from Chinchilla to the great keep, the Torre de Homenaje, of the castle of La Mota at Medina del Campo, in the heartland of Castile. It was considered impossible to escape from the castle with its central keep, four enceintes, single access gate and deep defence ditches, but from Cesare's point of view it had advantages. He was no longer isolated. Medina del Campo was the great emporium of Castile: fairs held there brought bankers, merchants and traders from all over Europe; it was also one of the seats of the Spanish court.

Lucrezia renewed her efforts to secure his release and Alfonso was prepared to help her. Two messengers arrived at Modena from Cesare asking her to help by sending an ambassador to Rome. She had asked Niccolò da Correggio when he left there to take this message to Alfonso. She received a speedy response: on 1 July she wrote to thank Alfonso with all her heart for the letter he had written to Beltrando Costabili, Ferrarese envoy at Rome, 'so that he can intercede for the liberation of the Most Illustrious Duke my brother. I have read the letter and it could not be better, according to my heart and desire. Then I sealed it with the impression of your seal which you sent me and forwarded it to Rome . . .'[5]

The letters she wrote to Alfonso were far more formal than those she addressed to Gonzaga. She wrote to him about business and administrative affairs, the appointment of a new *podestà* for Modena, whether or not she should condemn a man, local quarrels and the need for him to provide the nuns of the convent of Corpus Domini with food since the plague prevented them from begging. She reported to him about her fever and diarrhoea on 9 July, probably caused by the bad water and great heat, then thanked him for his concern and offer to send her a doctor, which she would not need because she was better. In another she retailed what she was doing to save 'Your Lordship's "Morro" [Moor]', whom he had left with her and who she was having treated by her favourite doctor, Lodovico Bonaccioli. Bonaccioli suspected Alfonso's 'Moor' had the plague: he had a high fever, a swollen left side and beneath his groin a huge swelling. Sadly the Moor later died. As a result, Lucrezia, being very pregnant, now moved from her present rooms to the former Rangoni house, but dared not leave the city for fear of causing panic. She received the envoy of the King of France and discussed with him the matter of Cento and La Pieve, still unresolved since the time of her dowry agreement, and now the subject of vituperative discussion between the Pope and Ippolito. Later the principal French commander, M. de Lapalisse,[6] visited her, accompanied by a gentleman of the French court, bringing extremely kind letters from the King and Queen of France for Alfonso and herself. At times Lucrezia felt it necessary to soothe Alfonso, begging him not to impose inquisitions and punishments on the couriers if certain letters did not arrive as quickly as he would like – 'I would be so grateful'. The tone of the letters might not have been passionate but they were friendly and affectionate: 'I pray God that he may keep you for many years in health and happiness: the comfort and encouragement you have given me with your good-hearted letters have given me incredible pleasure . . .' she wrote from Modena on 26 July.

In mid August she again asked Gonzaga for his help for Cesare. 'I have always recognized that Your Lordship through every twist of fortune has borne a singular love to the Duke my brother,' she wrote with a startling disregard for the facts.

And being well disposed towards everything that might be to his ease and honour as if you were his flesh and blood brother. [Therefore] with every faith in you I am asking your present favour for his liberation for which at the moment I am negotiating in Rome to send the Cardinal Regino to His Catholic Majesty with the licence and favour of His Holiness Our Lord. The Most Reverend Cardinal, on being asked if he would willingly go, has graciously answered that he would be happy to do so: all that remains is the permission and favour of the Pope. Whence, knowing the love His Beatitude bears Your Lordship, I earnestly beseech you to write to His Beatitude, pressing him to give permission to the Cardinal, and to write with such efficacy to the Catholic King that the Duke be liberated because I know for a fact that what His Holiness wishes will be done.

Poor Lucrezia was indulging in fantasy: the last thing the Pope would want was il Valentino at liberty to stir up trouble again, as he undoubtedly would. With an even more astonishing lack of reality she suggested that Francesco should write to the one man living whom Cesare had perhaps injured the most, Guidobaldo da Montefeltro, asking him to try to keep the Pope 'to this effect'. She begged Francesco to write these letters and send them to her by her courier so that she could forward them to Rome; also he might think it possible to write to one of his friends there who might be able to influence the Pope: 'the Illustrious Lord my brother and I will be beholden to you and remember this kindness . . .'[7] At the same time she wrote to Ippolito asking him to write to the Pope recommending Cardinal Regino's mission; Ippolito responded with a 'wonderfully satisfactory' letter which she sent on to Rome under her seal.[8]

Meanwhile, Lucrezia had sent her trusted and long-serving major-domo, Sancho, who had come with her from Rome, to Spain for news of Cesare. The difficulty of communication was such that she did not receive Sancho's reports from Segovia of

5 September until 10 October and even then all he could tell her was that he had been kindly received by the Duke of Alba and intended to go and visit Cesare.[9]

Lucrezia had moved from Modena to Reggio with her court on 14 August and it was there on 19 September in the citadel at the eleventh hour that she gave birth to a son, Alexandro, named in honour of his papal grandfather. Couriers were straightway sent to inform not only Alfonso but Francesco Gonzaga. An hour after the birth she felt cold in her legs which were wrapped in hot cloths; fever then came over her which lasted for five hours. Poor little Alexandro was a sickly child and unwilling to take the breast, Lucrezia warned Alfonso, who rushed '*per stafeta*' (by the posts or post horses) to see his wife and child before returning to Belriguardo.

From Venice, Pietro Bembo wrote a gracious letter of congratulations on Alexandro's birth: 'Especially precious and cheering was it for me since I cannot tell you how anxiously it was awaited in view of the cruel disappointment and vain hopes of last year.' This was evidently a response to the public proclamation of the birth but apparently Lucrezia was still close enough in touch to write personally to Bembo about it. On 30 September he replied saying how glad he was to hear that she and the baby were in good health. It is clear from this letter that Lucrezia and Bembo had parted for good, since he refers nostalgically to 'those days in my good Messer Ercole's Ostellato which often still keeps house for that only part of me which can dwell there now . . .'[10]

Less than a month later, the baby's condition had deteriorated to the point that Alfonso sent his finest doctor, Francesco Castello, to see him. On 13 October, Lucrezia wrote to Alfonso enclosing the doctor's report on their child. Her words sounded ominous; the arrival of Castello had been a great comfort to her and everything would be done 'for the conservation and health of our little son'. At the same time the pregnant Isabella was unwell at Mantua and asked for Beatrice de'Contrari and the *comatre*, who were at Reggio in attendance on Lucrezia and her child. Lucrezia, she told both Alfonso and Francesco, agreed to send Beatrice to Mantua accompanied by her nephew, Lorenzo Strozzi, but after consultation with Castello she felt she could not release the *comatre*: 'our little son has been gravely ill in these past days,' she wrote to Francesco, 'and although, thank God, he has begun to take the breast he is in such a condition that he will not be able to do without the Comatre . . .' Three days later Alexandro died having suffered several fits and convulsions. The loss of a second child by Alfonso within the space of three years caused Lucrezia profound grief, as she told Francesco, the more so in that this child had reached full term and been born alive, and that being male it would have been the Este heir. News of Alexandro's death did not reach Bembo until the end of November when Tullio, Bembo's manservant, brought him a letter from Lucrezia. As somewhat cold comfort he sent an astrological chart which he had had prepared for the baby in Venice 'by a man skilled in this art as soon as I received notice of his birth, so that Your Ladyship may discover some consolation in reflecting that we are truly in great part ruled by the stars . . .'[11] He did not write to her again for more than seven years.

For Lucrezia, too, the romance was in the past. Ten days after her baby's death, as soon as she had received a letter from Alfonso saying how much he would like to see her at Belriguardo, she was making plans to meet Francesco en route at Borgoforte.[12] According to Isabella's biographer, Luzio, who was not exactly prejudiced in favour of either Francesco or Lucrezia, Francesco was 'beside himself with joy at the news', writing on 25 October in a letter which has since disappeared, 'we would not wish to have acquired a great treasure . . .' than the news he had just received of her projected arrival.[13] Luzio dates Lucrezia's stay with Francesco at Borgoforte as the beginning of a declared love affair between the two, facilitated once again by Ercole Strozzi, an old friend of Gonzaga, who had just happened to issue on 27 October 1505 a humorous invitation to an eight-day wildfowling contest based at his villa at Ostellato. Luzio seems to have believed that the affair was platonic, given the difficulties the two of them had in meeting, but it is hard to credit that two people with the sexual records of Francesco and Lucrezia would not have taken advantage of any opportunity of having a physical relationship when it was offered. Despite all the difficulties it was to be a mutual and long-lasting passion. After spending the night at Borgoforte, where he offered a dinner for Lucrezia and her party, Francesco insisted on escorting her to Mantua despite her 'resistance', as she disingenuously informed Alfonso in a letter written from Borgoforte:

Your Excellency will see from this letter how the Most Illustrious Lord Marquis truly battled with me and forced me with such a vehemence and desire that I should go tomorrow to visit the Most Illustrious Marchioness: and how much resistance I put up. Nonetheless I was forced to obey and thus must go there tomorrow by all means. And he has sent for many court carriages and horses. And he says that he will secretly lead me into the castle and I will be there tomorrow in the company of the Marchioness and will lodge there with my ladies and in the morning he will send me in his bucentaur wherever I planned to go . . . that is via La Stellata and Bondeno, then to Monastirolo and Belriguardo . . . Here the Marchese has done me much honour and festivity and has lodged me very well in the house which belonged to Hieronymo Stanga . . . [14]

But as soon as she had arrived back at Belriguardo, where Alfonso joined her, she wrote formally to Francesco expressing her great gratitude for all the kindness he had shown her not only at Borgoforte but also at Sermide (on the border between Mantuan and Ferrarese territory) and on board the ship. [15]

Five days later she wrote to him again, thanking him for his kind letter as another example of the love and affection which existed between them. Among the subjects which they had discussed together had been, obviously, Cesare. Francesco told her that he would send an envoy to Spain; Lucrezia was delighted because the man would be able to take with him two letters which she enclosed, one to the King of Spain, the other to Cesare.

She was trying all means to have her brother released, suggesting that Francesco should also write to the King and to any people he might know 'with authority in that Kingdom'. Soon she hoped to return to Ferrara because for some days past 'things have been going well there'.

But things were not going well in Ferrara, at least as far as the Este family was concerned. After a miserable summer of heat, plague and famine, sibling rivalries had already surfaced and were about to plunge the princely family into one of the darkest episodes of its history, known as the '*Congiura*', the Conspiracy. The roots of the trouble lay in the proud, competitive temperament of the Este which extended to rivalry over musicians. Ercole's cherished stable of musicians, some of whom enjoyed the status of *cappellani* (chaplains) had included one Don Rainaldo who, at the end of 1504, was working for Giulio, the most musical of the Este, but who was coveted by Ippolito for his own '*cappella*'. Towards the end of 1504, as Ercole lay dying, Ippolito had approached Don Rainaldo, who agreed to join his household. Don Rainaldo subsequently disappeared and it was thought he was dead; in fact, he had been spirited away by Ippolito and secluded in the Rocca del Gesso, a stronghold which belonged to Giovanni Boiardo, Count of Scandiano and nephew of the famous poet Matteo Maria Boiardo, the author of *Orlando Innamorato*.

Some time towards the end of May 1505, Giulio, burning with resentment against his half-brother, the cardinal, had discovered the whereabouts of Don Rainaldo. Having asked both Alberto Pio da Carpi and Enea Furlano, nicknamed 'il Cavaliero', both members of Gonzaga's circle, for armed men and crossbowmen, without telling them the reason (or so Pio later testified), he went to stay with Ferrante at a place called Le Lame, near Carpi. From there he went to the Rocca del Gesso, took away Don Rainaldo and returned with him to Ferrante. Furious, Ippolito discovered what had happened and complained to Alfonso, whose right-hand man he now was. Alfonso then ordered Giulio to appear before him at Modena and exiled him from the Ferrarese state on the grounds that he had caused grave offence to Boiardo. Ferrante had also been summoned to Modena and ordered to stay there although not under arrest. According to the historian of the *Congiura*, Riccardo Bacchelli, it was at this point in August 1505 that Lucrezia had attempted to mediate, calling upon Giulio and Ferrante to hand over Don Rainaldo, and persuading the priest to take refuge in the fortress of Casalgrande. Alfonso then wrote Lucrezia a firm letter intimating that she should not meddle in this affair: Giulio had offended him deeply and as punishment Alfonso ordered that he should be exiled to Brescello, present himself each day to the ducal commissary there, and go no further than two miles outside the town. 'We wish that this our decision you will make known by Niccolò Bendideo, our secretary, warning Don Giulio to obey us, because, if he fails to do so, Your Ladyship may know that we will proceed to other means.' There was nothing more Lucrezia could do; the wretched Giulio was forced to comply. The loyal di Prosperi, as an old follower of the Este, was anguished by the situation, as he told Isabella; he was sure that Don Giulio would never think of doing anything to harm his brother the Duke. But Alfonso and Ippolito were very close at this time, the one at Belriguardo, the other at nearby Vigoenza, and seeing each other every day, a situation which could not bode well for Giulio.

Isabella had done her best to mend the rift, taking the occasion of the birth of Alexandro to write to Alfonso asking him to pardon Giulio in honour of the occasion and that he should not exclude from public amnesty 'a brother who not from malice but from lack of thought has fallen into error. This is no time,' she continued, 'to remember affronts and hatreds and if the Most Reverend Cardinal is of this way of thinking, I would remind him of the same.'[16] Francesco Gonzaga also intervened on Giulio's behalf, as Ferrante wrote gratefully to him on 24 September from Reggio. Del Forno (a member of the Modenese family who were very close to Alfonso and Ippolito) and il Barone had told him of the kind efforts he had made with Alfonso for Don Giulio for which he was most grateful. Now that Ippolito had arrived at Reggio, he begged Francesco to send a trusted emissary to bring a formal end to the feud between him and Giulio.[17] As a result of these efforts by the Gonzaga, di Prosperi wrote on 12 October that Giulio had been allowed to return to Ferrara and had been to Belriguardo, adding with an optimism which was no more than wishful thinking: 'I judge his case to be settled, thanks to the good offices of Your Ladyship.'

But matters were far from settled: the hatred and rivalry between the powerful cardinal and his reckless younger brother found a new cause which had nothing to do with chapel singers – Angela Borgia. Angela Borgia was the most beautiful and charming of Lucrezia's ladies, graceful and elegant, according to her many admirers. And among those admirers in 1505 were Ippolito and Giulio. Angela is held to have enraged Ippolito by telling him: 'Monsignore, your brother's eyes are worth more than the whole of your person.'

She was also the closest of all her ladies to Lucrezia, who was concerned about her; she was now eighteen years old and a good marriage was a necessity. Earlier that year, on 10 March, after Gonzaga's visit to Ferrara, Lucrezia wrote to him: 'After Your Lordship's departure from here I have spoken to Messer Cesari, the bearer of this letter, concerning some matters to refer to you about "*el negotio*" the business of Dona Angela . . .' It may have been that Angela and Giulio had begun an affair which might make the question of a marriage all the more pressing. Less than a year later, on 18 January 1506, di Prosperi reported that Angela Borgia 'had given birth on the ship' but did not indicate the precise date of the birth, which could well have been some weeks before news of it reached him. She was still unmarried and no father was named, but tragic intervening events indicated who he might have been.

Shortly after Lucrezia returned to Ferrara, on 3 November 1505, Giulio, returning from a pleasure excursion in the meadows by the straight road leading to Belriguardo, ran into an ambush laid by Ippolito and his servants. He was dragged from his horse and stabbed in the eyes. The official version given by Alfonso in a letter of 5 November to Isabella was that the *staffieri* had done it of their own accord 'perhaps to please their lord or perhaps because of some insult one of them had received from Don Julio . . .' In a postscript, however, he confessed the truth. Ippolito had been present and had ordered the assault: 'Don Julio returning from the fields as I have said, met the Most Reverend Cardinal, our brother, who had come there with four *staffieri* who he commanded "Kill that man: cut out his eyes".'There was no hope, they thought, for Giulio's left eye, and no one could be sure about the vision in his right.

Unwisely, Alfonso gave a hostage to fortune by writing the next day to Francesco, including both versions he had given to Isabella, telling him to burn the postscript and only to disclose the official version which blamed it all on the *staffieri* and did not reveal Ippolito's direct involvement.[18]

For a Renaissance prince to commit such damning information to paper is a measure of the shock Alfonso was feeling and his need for the support of his family and equals. It was quite out of character for a man normally so reserved and inclined to conceal his feelings and intentions. If either of these letters had fallen into the wrong hands – and couriers were frequently waylaid and spied upon – it could have caused him and his family enormous damage. As it was, the case intrigued Italy when the official version came out and was, of course, not believed to be the full story. In Rome Julius II was agog, embarrassing Beltrando Costabili with his acute questioning. Costabili wrote anxiously to Ippolito that the Pope was greatly desirous to know the cause of the attack on Don Giulio, asking the cardinal for instructions as to what he should say. On 14 November, Costabili reported that he had communicated the letters of Alfonso and Ippolito to the Pope who had found the case 'most audacious' and issued a brief for the capture of the delinquents should they be found in the States of the Church.[19] (The nineteenth-century transcriber of this letter for Lord Acton could not resist a comment: 'Marvellous impudence of the Cardinal Ippolito, who was the principal delinquent in the crime, having ordered his *sicari* [assassins] to carry it out, from envy of seeing Don Giulio preferred by a Lady.') Five days later, however, Costabili informed Ippolito that the Pope no longer believed in the exactitude of the account he had been given – 'that he was of the opinion that the case had happened in another manner than Your Excellency's account of it'. Needless to say, the guilty four were never brought to justice and it was rumoured that they had fled to Hungary.

Isabella and Francesco were outraged and sent Francesco's surgeon Messer Andrea and another physician to attend Giulio, who wrote pathetically thanking them for their kindness 'which has greatly alleviated my pain although it is most grave and almost insupportable'. Alfonso sent back the Mantuan doctors since the Gonzaga's son, Federico, was ill; Giulio could see with his left eye and there were hopes of some sight returning to his right. Two weeks later di Prosperi visited Giulio to report to Isabella that her brother could see the outlines of people and things but could still not open his eyelid without using his hand as the muscle was so damaged; with his right he could only distinguish darkness from light and he was still in great pain. 'God help him,' di Prosperi added, 'and from every side give that love and peace which there should be between good brothers for the good of their honour and of this Most Illustrious House . . .' Alfonso had decided that the wisest course of action would be inaction, particularly against Ippolito, but tension and suspicion remained in the family. Ippolito went to Mantua without warning to visit Isabella, as Francesco nervously informed Alfonso who replied that he was grateful for Gonzaga's firm determination not to receive anyone who might be unwelcome to him in Ferrara. But in the case of Ippolito, 'Your Lordship must know that you have in no way disturbed us in any way by receiving His Most Reverend Lordship because it is our opinion and goodwill that he can go and stay wherever he wants in our dominions at his pleasure. And moreover Your Lordship has done well to receive his visit since it has in no way displeased us . . .'

At around the same time an act of private violence occurred which was probably in some way connected with the undercurrents of bad blood between the senior Este brothers and Francesco

Gonzaga. Gonzaga's principal favourite at court, Antonio Regazzi da San Secondo, known as 'il Milanese', was murdered by Enea Furlano, the courtier known as il Cavaliero, who happened to be married to one of Francesco's illegitimate daughters. After a brief spell of imprisonment, he was released and exiled from Mantua. Bacchelli explicitly claims that il Milanese was killed on the orders or instigation of Alfonso and Ippolito.[20] Furlano was afterwards often seen in Alfonso's company and after Francesco Gonzaga's death even his sentence of exile was reversed by Isabella.[21]

Unperturbed, Alfonso continued his ducal business, receiving his secretaries but no one else except for his brothers and intimate friends. He and Lucrezia were occupied with the extension and redecoration of their rooms. He spent hours overseeing the planting and working of his garden. The city was filling up again as the plague was now over and the citizens returning. Lucrezia came and went between Ferrara and Belriguardo, supervising the work on her apartments. 'Yesterday I saw the Rooms which the Duchess is having made [in the Torre Marchesana of the Castello] which will be most beautiful,' di Prosperi reported on 6 December, 'as will a small salon where the balcony was: And from the rooms of His Lordship her Consort [the *camere dorate* in the Palazzo del Corte] you can proceed to Her Ladyship's rooms without being seen from the piazza or anyone being aware of their passage unless they wished it to connect their private rooms with each other's. For the present the Lady is staying in the rooms in the Castello where His Lordship was . . .' Giulio was installed in an apartment in the Corte rather than his splendid palazzo in the Via degli Angeli, presumably for better security. Antonio Costabili told di Prosperi that Alfonso thought it was time to settle the differences between Ippolito and Giulio and that the cardinal should return to Ferrara for this purpose. On 24 December, di Prosperi was able to report that a reconciliation between the two had taken place.

Alfonso had sent Antonio Costabili for Ippolito who arrived accompanied by Count Lodovico Pico della Mirandola and had supper with Alfonso in his *camerini*. Subsequently Alfonso sent Hieronymo Ziliolo to Giulio to tell him of his great desire that he and the cardinal should be reconciled, and that he hoped Giulio would accede to this. At their meeting, Alfonso spoke first of the repentance felt by the cardinal and of his regret and of the goodwill in which he would hold Giulio, 'whereupon the Cardinal added in most kindly and repentant words of how he would in future be a good and loving brother and other words of similar tenor'. Giulio then spoke a few words, addressing himself to Alfonso: 'My Lord, you see how I am', and then, turning to the cardinal, he said that he had to thank God and Our Blessed Lady who had granted him his sight. 'And although my case has been most cruel and inhuman and done to me with no fault of mine, nonetheless I pardon Your Lordship and will not cease to be to you that good brother I have always been', to which Ippolito replied pleasantly. Alfonso was seen to be deeply moved and 'incapable of many words except to say that he prayed them to love each other and to enjoy this State with him', warning them that if they did not do so he would be obliged to force them to comply. Unable to go on, he turned to Niccolò da Correggio to speak on his behalf. Finally, Ippolito and Giulio exchanged a formal kiss of peace. 'God grant that things go from good to better,' intoned the ever-optimistic di Prosperi.[22]

Lucrezia, who had been warned by Alfonso to cease any attempts at mediation that summer, had kept out of these Este family quarrels which were uncomfortably dangerous and still, as it was to turn out, far from settled. Her first year as Duchess of Ferrara had, apart from her romance with Francesco, not been a happy one. Her state of mind regarding her own fertility cannot have been enhanced by the news that Isabella had been safely delivered of a second son, Ercole, in November. And bitterest of all, perhaps, was her concern for Cesare's continuing captivity.

12. The *Congiura*

'May God put his hand in these things and discords'

– Bernardino di Prosperi to Isabella during the
unravelling of the Este Conspiracy, 24 May 1506

After the supposed peacemaking between Giulio and Ippolito, Lucrezia and Alfonso celebrated carnival with dancing at the Castello. It was noted that Alfonso was particularly gaily dressed, although the official year's mourning for Ercole was not yet over. He wore a long robe in the Turkish style down to mid-calf, lined with sable and wolf, a Spanish cape and an elaborately tailored tunic ornamented with silken strips, 'showing himself very gallantly and with more joy in his heart than usual', according to di Prosperi. It may have been that he was relieved that his difficult first year as Duke was over and the rift in his family apparently healed.

Di Prosperi, however, noted ominously on 6 January 1506 that since the reconciliation neither Alfonso nor Ippolito had spoken of or seen Giulio, 'nor had any more provision, considering his condition, been made for him than he had before'. Giulio, he said, resented this. Ippolito deigned to send his secretary to visit Giulio but did not go in person and Giulio, probably mortified by his disfigurement, kept to his rooms. Yet, di Prosperi reported, at court there were masques every day, 'as if they were in the greatest state of happiness in the world'. An eclogue was performed, composed by Niccolò da Correggio, with *moresche*. Lucrezia ordered comedies 'of three kinds of lovers', one of them based on Boccaccio's *Cento Novelle* and in di Prosperi's opinion 'very improper', and there was dancing till dawn in the castle.

There was a Battle of the Eggs on 13 February and in the piazza men with long staves and blindfolded competed with each other, to the sound of trumpets, to kill a tethered pig. 'The Gypsy', 'il Cingano', a favoured member of Alfonso's household, walked blindfolded with irons on his feet on a tightrope across the piazza. Lucrezia frequently rode round the streets masked, accompanied by il Barone or Niccolò da Correggio.

Lucrezia also had in her household a number of young Ferrarese girls of good family – *donzelle* – whom she trained and for whom she found husbands. New recruits must not have passed the age of twelve: 'And they will be brought up otherwise than the usual,' di Prosperi wrote, 'in work [embroidery] and in learning virtue.' The prospective husbands of these *donzelle* often proved recalcitrant and had to be dragooned by Lucrezia into keeping their promises. 'Today the marriage of La Dalara to the son of Hieronymo Ariminaldo should have been made public,' di Prosperi told Isabella, 'but the husband could not be found, perhaps as a young man he has repented of the word he had given the Lady Duchess. However, Her Excellency will not permit herself to be disobeyed. She has had the consent of both him and his parents and I understand this evening a Commandment will be sent to the house, by which he must appear to be married to the girl under pain of a fine of a thousand ducats.' Carnival, preceding Lent, was the time of year for Lucrezia to oversee marriages for her damsels, including the daughter of Federico Maffei and La Violante. 'And thus My Lady attends to find homes for her ladies,' di Prosperi wrote. 'Every day My Lady makes a marriage for one of her ladies,' he reported on 8 February, 'but she has not yet found anyone for La Napoletana.' Hector Berlinguer was dispatched to Francesco Gonzaga to negotiate the marriage of Ercole Bentivoglio's daughter by Barbara Torelli to Ercole Strozzi's brother, Count Lorenzo.

On 2 February 1506, Lucrezia busied herself with the marriage of the errant Angela Borgia to Alessandro Pio da Sassuolo, a minor local lord and faithful adherent of the Este family. There was the question of the dowry: after the death of Alexander the Borgia family fortunes were no longer what they had been. Lucrezia wrote to Angela's brother, Cardinal Ludovico Borgia, with meagre results; the Este had to top up Angela's dowry and Lucrezia to provide her with clothes, as she had generously done hitherto. It was an intimate, comical occasion: Lucrezia summoned the happy pair and had them shut up together to consummate the relationship ('*fare la copula*'), after which they emerged two hours later laughing. The marriage had to be kept secret, as the fate of Angela's unfortunate child had been. Alessandro Pio's domineering mother, a daughter of Giovanni Bentivoglio, would have opposed it and only learned of the affair when a formal 'marriage' took place in December. Angela meanwhile (and later) remained in Ferrara, where she was joined at the Palazzo del Corte by Alessandro Pio in May, taking part in Lucrezia's court life as she was accustomed to.

On 21 February another Pio of a different branch of the family, Alberto Pio da Carpi, came to Ferrara for carnival, bringing with him Cesare's son, Girolamo, who had been entrusted to him by Lucrezia. Lucrezia's choice of Alberto Pio da Carpi as guardian for Cesare's son was understandable. Alberto Pio was eminently suited to the guardianship of Girolamo Borgia. Apart from his intellectual and social standing, he was a member of Lucrezia and Francesco Gonzaga's circle and his mother was a Gonzaga. Lucrezia's friendship with Alberto Pio demonstrated the independence with which she chose her friends, for Alberto Pio was very far from being a friend of Alfonso's and later that year at times actively opposed him and intrigued against him. Indeed, for some years there had been a running feud between Alberto Pio and Lodovico Pico della Mirandola, who was related to the Este and protected by Alfonso. Alberto Pio tried to stir up trouble between Francesco Gonzaga and Alfonso, urging Gonzaga to write to Alfonso pointing out that his (Pio's) affairs were his business not Alfonso's: 'And show him that you do not want him to think that he can make himself cock of Italy, Your Excellency being older than him, a prince as he is and in military virtues and achievement worthy of comparison with him . . . and that

the duke is not the '*maestro di scuola*' [master of the school] in
these times, nor is Messer Niccolò da Correggio, his mouthpiece.'
Alberto Pio's objective was to declare independence from Ferrara
for Carpi, and for that he would need Gonzaga's support. Gonzaga,
however, was too wily to be drawn in; much as he despised
Alfonso, he did not intend to go to war with him on Alberto
Pio's behalf. In March 1506 trouble between Alberto Pio and
Mirandola escalated into open war. Alfonso sent a number of light
horse from the company commanded by Masino del Forno to
the aid of Mirandola while Gonzaga sent troops to Alberto Pio,
but in the end the differences between Pio and Mirandola were
settled through Gonzaga's mediation.[1] Rancour, however,
remained; later that summer Francesco Gonzaga's harbouring of
Giulio and prevarication about handing him over showed that he
had seen him as a weapon to use against Alfonso, as well as indicating his contempt for his ducal brother-in-law. In these complicated enmities and concealed hatreds, Lucrezia had chosen,
however secretly, to favour two men, Alberto Pio and Francesco
Gonzaga, who were no friends to her husband. During his carnival visit to Ferrara, Alberto Pio forged a closer link between Giulio
and Francesco Gonzaga, reporting on 23 February that he had
visited Giulio to assure him of Francesco's friendship and that
Giulio had sworn that he was more a servant of Gonzaga 'than
of the duke my lord and brother'. 'The most reverend cardinal,'
he added, 'has not yet visited him [Giulio] being day and night
occupied in pleasures and masking.'[2]

The Este carnival celebrations, taking place within earshot, but
in which he, with his ravaged looks and damaged sight, could
not take part, fuelled the wretched Giulio's resentment. He had
not forgiven Alfonso for his failure to punish Ippolito or for his
continuing favour towards him, any more than, despite the sham
reconciliation, he had forgiven Ippolito. Even as Alfonso and
Lucrezia enjoyed the carnival of 1506, Giulio became involved in
a fratricidal conspiracy, the *Congiura*, with Ferrante, who was motivated by ambition to succeed his brother. They were joined against
Alfonso and, to a lesser extent, Ippolito, by some minor lords,

Gherardo de'Roberti and Albertino and Roberto Boschetti, who feared losing their states. According to the subsequent interrogation of the conspirators, at the time of Alfonso's absence abroad in 1504 Gherardo de'Roberti had suggested to Ferrante, whose head had already been turned by ambition to succeed his father, that he should provide a band of assassins to waylay and kill Alfonso. A year later, Gherardo de'Roberti and Albertino Boschetti had proposed to Ferrante that they should assassinate Alfonso during the carnival of 1506. Also involved in the conspiracy was Alfonso's favourite singer, Gian de Artigianova (Gian Cantore): the singer's motives seem inexplicable unless he hoped for even greater favours from the passionately musical Giulio. Ferrante and de'Roberti visited Giulio in his apartments in the Corte: the idea was to kill Alfonso and replace him with Ferrante. Ippolito would also have to be disposed of. One suggestion was that Alfonso should be murdered while off guard in some whorehouse.

The plotters could not, however, agree among themselves and appeared singularly incompetent in executing their intentions. Ferrante wanted Alfonso killed first; Giulio preferred Ippolito. Gherardo and Sigismondo, son of Albertino, acting on information from the treacherous Gian Cantore, waited for the Duke with poisoned daggers by night in the streets of Ferrara. Twice they missed him and twice they lacked the courage to carry out their mission. Alfonso was a big man and skilled in the practice of arms; moreover, he wore chain mail beneath his doublet. The conspirators quarrelled among themselves, renewed the poison on their daggers, and prevaricated.

In April Alfonso left for Venice, apparently with the intention of informing the Signory of his plan to go on a pilgrimage to Compostela, and in the meantime to obtain their protection for his state. It was to be a short visit: he intended to leave later for Spain. Lucrezia was to be left in charge as Governor of the city, giving audiences and issuing orders, not merely attending to the examination of petitions. It was an indication not only of her administrative talents but a demonstration of trust. Otherwise, of all his relations, Alfonso confided only in Ippolito, who remained in Ferrara, and Niccolò da Correggio, who accompanied him to Venice. Moreover, said di Prosperi, Alfonso had told Lucrezia that he did not wish her to consult him about anything while he was away 'except for something of such importance that it bore on the maintenance and conservation of the State'. For greater security in Alfonso's absence, Lucrezia was to move into Alfonso's rooms in the Palazzo del Corte, while hired *lanzknechts* and men-at-arms were moved in to guard the Castello. On the day scheduled for Alfonso's departure, Lucrezia went to stay in Corpus Domini, as was her wont in Holy Week, and there she fell ill with a fever and chills. According to di Prosperi her illness developed into '*el terzo termine de terzana*' – the third stage of tertian fever – and Alfonso deferred his departure, as usual keeping everyone in the dark as to the day he actually planned to leave. He eventually left on 19 April, characteristically at dawn so as to avoid the attentions of the populace who would wish to kiss his hand. He returned at the end of the month to be greeted by Lucrezia and Ippolito who dined with him in his garden. He was off again in mid May to Venice and the Adriatic.

Giulio remained in his palace in the Via degli Angeli, observing experiments with poison on cats, dogs and doves. At the end of April, Lucrezia, who had been fond of Giulio, might have had some inkling of what was going on and, for this reason and perhaps for fear of what Ippolito might do to him, attempted, without success, to make Giulio leave Ferrara. Alfonso, perhaps at her prompting, also sent Gian Luca Pozzi to order him to leave but he again refused and was still there when Alfonso left in May. Di Prosperi, who had reported optimistically to Isabella that Alfonso was able to leave untroubled, 'because My Lady and your brothers are all disposed for the good', then curiously remarked of Giulio that he could come and go as he pleased but as yet had not ventured out by day, spending all his time in his palazzo, in his garden or with his horses.

Ippolito and his spies had indeed picked up some information as to what was going on. On 24 May, di Prosperi reported the arrest, on the cardinal's orders, of one of Giulio's servants, one

Hieronymo, 'a flycatcher – *pigliamosche* – of a sad sort'. He did not know the reason and was not going to try and find out, assuming that it was yet another episode in the enmity between the brothers – 'May God put his hand in these things and discords.' On 13 June it was reported that a servant of Don Ferrante, Andrea della Matta, had been arrested in the Romagna on Ippolito's commission and brought to Ferrara, while Giulio's servant Hieronymo had been sent to the Castello. 'May God, once and for all, place his hand on us with peace and love' was di Prosperi's despairing reaction. As well as Giulio's servant and Ferrante's Andrea, another man involved in the mechanics of the conspiracy, one Tuttobono, was arrested; both Andrea and Tuttobono were shortly afterwards released. The arrest of the latter, for some reason, had terrified Ferrante who wrote to Isabella pleading with her to get Giulio out of Ferrara to safety in Mantua. The historian of the *Congiura* suspected Tuttobono of being an *agent provocateur*, presumably of Ippolito, his function having been to spy on the conspirators. His release and that of Andrea were intended to lull Giulio into an illusion of security. On the 19th di Prosperi reported that crossbowmen had been sent to arrest Gian Cantore – 'the cause, I understand, being that he refused to go on the ship with the Duke, excusing himself on the grounds that the sea made him ill. And that he had fled without telling anyone, which disturbed the Duke. Others,' he added, 'judge that his flight proceeds from those troubles and discords between the cardinal and Don Giulio, which have reached such terms that I doubt that there can ever be love or peace between them.' It seems that Gian Cantore's original mission in accompanying Alfonso on his voyage had been to poison him: his nerve had, however, failed him and he disappeared for fear that the conspirators might try to silence him.

Meanwhile, Alfonso, having paid his respects to Venice, continued his journey on 15 May by boat down the canals, accompanied by Niccolò da Correggio, the doctor Francesco Castello, and a large company, with the intention of attending the annual fair at Lanciano, a rough event which included mock battles and appealed to his fondness for low life. At Lanciano he encountered two Venetian war galley captains (*soracomiti*), and, dismissing most of his party, continued his voyage down the Adriatic with them, keeping Lucrezia informed all the while. Having landed incognito at Trani in Puglia, he surveyed the surrounding countryside from a belltower before going on to Bari where his cousin, Isabella d'Aragona, the widow of Gian Galeazzo Sforza, now resided with Lucrezia's son, Rodrigo Bisceglie, in her care; whether or not Alfonso saw him there has not been recorded. Alfonso and his two Venetian captains next set off for Ragusa on the Dalmatian coast and then Corfu, pursuing some pirate ships in the hope of capturing them. In fact his true intention was almost certainly to familiarize himself with the situation of the Venetians in the Adriatic. Venice responded in fury, imprisoning the two captains and turning away Alfonso's envoy Niccolò da Correggio, sent there to plead innocence since Alfonso had been given (limited) letters of authorization. Alfonso's attempts to ingratiate himself with Venice had failed; he now had personal experience of the arrogance of *La Serenissima*. He decided to return to Ferrara, where he arrived on 2 July, moving with his usual swiftness and unexpectedness, so much so that Ippolito and Ferrante, who had gone to meet him at Monastirolo, missed him.

Yielding to Isabella's advice and, possibly that of Lucrezia, Giulio was by then safely out of the way at Mantua. But neither Ferrante, nor the co-conspirators, the Boschetti, seem to have been aware of imminent danger. Alfonso had written in a friendly manner to Boschetti, offering him unaccustomed favours. Suspicion appeared to be centred on Giulio: Isabella and Francesco sent Capilupo to Ferrara to see Alfonso on a mission of reconciliation, but Alfonso responded by demanding that Giulio return in person to Ferrara to explain himself, as he told Giulio in a written ultimatum on 22 July: 'If you do not return within two days we will judge that you do not wish to return and we will commence an investigation into your case.' Giulio replied indirectly to Niccolò da Correggio, refusing on the grounds that 'he had [as] good cause to fear returning to Ferrara as he had in leaving there' since many days before Isabella had been warned that 'certain evil' would have been done him if he did not. This warning, apparently, had been at the instigation of Ferrante at the time of Tuttobono's arrest.

Gonzaga then asked for safe conduct for Giulio or, at the very least, the raising of the two-day ultimatum. Alfonso replied in a letter of 25 July that he would certainly give Giulio safe conduct and that he would not be harmed by anyone, specifically mentioning Ippolito, but that he could not guarantee him a safeguard against justice should Giulio be found guilty of plotting against him.

Events were now moving swiftly and an inquiry had already begun on 22 July; on the 25th Albertino Boschetti was arrested and detained in the Castello, and on the 26th the craven Ferrante denounced Giulio to Alfonso, as he told Francesco Gonzaga in a panic-stricken letter pleading for his protection:

If Your Lordship does not help and save me I shall perish because, having been induced yesterday morning to reveal the conspiracy of Don Julio to my Illustrious Lord and brother and thus having facilitated Julio's escape although knowing him to merit every evil and punishment for conspiracy, nonetheless I earnestly pray Your Lordship that you will give up the person of Don Julio to the Most Illustrious Don Sigismondo, my brother, and Messer Antonio de Costabili, because thus Your Lordship will give me life since the Lord Duke will be content with that for all [despite] the punishment I might merit and however, once again I pray Your Lordship to have more respect for my safety than that of Don Julio and to grant me this grace . . .[3]

Gonzaga, however, refused to hand over Giulio to Costabili and Sigismondo, provoking an agitated letter from Alfonso who had taken to his bed with a fever caused by the anxiety of the case. There is no doubt that he had been horribly shocked by the revelations of his brothers' plot against him and, he told Gonzaga, more and worse facts against Ferrante had been discovered and he had therefore had him imprisoned in the castle. Naively, he still seems to have had absolute trust in the friendship and good faith of Francesco Gonzaga, reminding him of the obligations they had towards each other as heads of state – 'of being of one mind and will in every fortune'. Far from being trustworthy, however, two days later, Gonzaga wrote to the Pope's nephew, Galeotto Franciotti della Rovere, Cardinal of San Pietro in Vincula, asking him for his protection of Gian Cantore 'whom I have always known to be a good man and recognised as such by the Most Illustrious Duke Ercole, my late father-in-law'.[4] Gonzaga's reasons for doing this are hard to fathom; by this time the complicity of Gian Cantore and his gross betrayal of his patron, Alfonso, were known. Bacchelli attributes it to Gonzaga's hostility towards both Alfonso, for his pro-Venetian policy, and Niccolò da Correggio, promoter of that policy. That same policy had provoked a hostile reaction in Rome where the fratricidal conduct of the Este brothers had made the worst possible impression.

The trial of the conspirators began, on Alfonso's orders, on 3 August, in the privacy of Sigismondo d'Este's house and concluded with sentences against Albertino Boschetti, Gherardo de'Roberti and Franceschino Boccacci da Rubiera. The guilt of Ferrante and Giulio was pronounced on 25 August and 9 September. The judges (the *Savi*) were among the most distinguished men in Ferrara, and the executive sentence was given on 9 September by their leader, the *Giudice dei XII Savi*, Antonio Costabili. The involvement of the *Savi* showed that Alfonso was determined to keep to his oath of justice; there were to be no summary punishments even though the eventual fate of all the conspirators was to be cruel. Ferrante had been under arrest since 29 July when Alfonso had personally accompanied him to the castle and had him imprisoned in a room in the Torre Marchesana. After four days, the windows were blocked halfway up so that Ferrante could not see out.

On the same day Alfonso had had Gherardo de'Roberti brought from Carpi and taken through the piazza to the piazzetta where a great crowd waited to see him. From the windows of Alfonso's rooms in the *via coperta* the triumvirate of Alfonso, Lucrezia and Ippolito watched. Afterwards, Alfonso visited de'Roberti in the castle dungeon to interrogate him: enraged, he seized a baton and gave him such a blow that he almost took out an eye. De'Roberti was then consigned to the lowest dungeon of the Great Tower and shackled. The discovery of the plot, symbolized by the imprisonment of the two men, was greeted with the ringing of all the bells, and bonfires were lit that evening all over the city; this continued for three days. Lucrezia and the noblewomen of Ferrara attended solemn mass sung by the ducal singers in the cathedral, and afterwards thanksgiving processions wound through the city, attended by Alfonso and Ippolito with the noblemen and populace.

Lucrezia no doubt found the whole business hard to bear and the tension within the family and household excruciating. She had been fond of both Ferrante and Giulio: Ferrante had been her proxy husband at the Vatican ceremony and her companion on her wedding journey north. Giulio had frequently accompanied her on her forays to the Este villas and had been one of her favourite dancing partners. Ippolito was ruthless and unyielding, Alfonso bitter and emotional. On 19 August Lucrezia rode to Belriguardo for a few days to escape the atmosphere. Alfonso remained nervous and mistrustful. He gave orders that only his guards should have access to the Castello and, probably to her great annoyance, moved Lucrezia from her beautifully decorated apartments in the castle to the rooms in the Corte she had occupied during his absence. Di Prosperi reported:

The principal cause I believe is because His Lordship wishes to restrict access to the Castle by anyone except the guards and it seems that he has moved the Lady to the rooms in the Corte – The Lord keeping for himself his *camerini* with the two *camere dorate* [gilded rooms] above the piazzetta of the Castello, from which he can come to the small salon with the balcony and the Sala Grande. However every day he changes his mind but he has told Madonna that she cannot at the moment enjoy her beautiful Rooms and princely apartments which she had had decorated (and was still having done) and on which have been spent thousands of ducats.

As a show of force Alfonso held a review of his light horse and a new display of men-at-arms.

Still Francesco Gonzaga held out, refusing to return Giulio; Sigismondo d'Este and Costabili, now reinforced by Niccolò da Correggio with twenty-five crossbowmen, failed to persuade him to hand over Giulio and, after a blazing row, returned to Ferrara empty-handed. Gonzaga continued to demand humane treatment for Giulio and also for Ferrante, although, as Bacchelli remarks, the latter did not even have the excuse of bad treatment by Ippolito for his treachery. In Ferrara, however, the courtiers besieged Alfonso with advice as to how the prisoners should be punished, Antonio Costabili pointing out that in ancient Rome traitors were put in a sack with animals and thrown into the Tiber. Alfonso, however, promised Gonzaga that neither Giulio nor Ferrante should be personally harmed but that they would be imprisoned. Meanwhile, in the Castel Sant'Angelo in Rome, Gian Cantore confessed to papal and Ferrarese commissaries that he had been drawn into the plot by the Este brothers: he had not yet been handed over. Alfonso expelled the Boschetti family from their castle of San Cesario; in Mantua the unfortunate Boschetti daughter was forced into a convent. Giulio, now confined to his room in the castle at Mantua, his goods confiscated, had written a grovelling letter of apology to Alfonso, excusing his treachery by blaming Ippolito's attack on him and Alfonso's apparent alliance with the cardinal, an excuse unlikely to further his cause. Moreover, Ippolito was enraged by any attempt to lay blame upon him and was working cunningly behind the scenes to cover his tracks, even to the extent of instructing Ariosto, now his employee, not to mention the part he had played in the eclogue which Ariosto was writing about the *Congiura*.

Alfonso was determined to lay his hands on Giulio, and Francesco Gonzaga could no longer hold out. On 6 September, with two hundred light horse, crossbowmen and *stradiots* (the dreaded Albanian light cavalry brought to Italy by the Venetians), he arrived in Ferrara en route to meet Julius II, whose Gonfalonier he had been appointed, at Urbino preparatory to the campaign against the Bentivoglio. On the day of his arrival he was escorted by Alfonso to see Lucrezia in the Camera de la Stufa Grande where she was then lodged. He spent two days in the city, lodged in the Palazzo del Corte, leaving on the 8th. Giulio, in chains, was handed over to Alfonso's representative in Mantua on Isabella's orders on 9 September and taken the next day to Ferrara by the brothers Masino and Girolamo del Forno, trusted henchmen of Alfonso and Ippolito. He was imprisoned in the deepest dungeon in the Torre dei Leoni and shackled. He was only twenty-six years old.

The grisly punishment of the non-Este conspirators took place publicly: they were taken on a wagon from the castle to a tribune in the piazza where the process against them was read out. Franceschino da Rubiera was the first to suffer. Blindfolded, stunned with the executioner's axe and kicked as he lay on the floor, he was then dragged to a block, decapitated and then quartered. Boschetti and Gherardo suffered the same fate. Their heads were placed on lances on the tower of the Palazzo della Ragione, their butchered body parts above three gates of the city. On 8 October, Ferrante and Giulio were sentenced to death but pardoned by Alfonso and imprisoned in rooms on two floors of the Torre dei Leoni. Finally, Gian Cantore was brought to Ferrara, seated on a horse with his hands tied behind him and his feet bound together under the horse's stomach. Before him rode the executioner, holding a rope tied round the singer's neck, and as he was led through the streets the populace spat in his face, pulled out his beard and aimed blows at his ribs. He was imprisoned in the Castello until 6 January 1507, Epiphany, when he was put in an iron cage suspended halfway up the Torre dei Leoni. Dressed in thin rags, shivering in the cold, icy wind, he remained there subsisting on bread and wine until the night of the 13th when either he hanged himself or was hanged by his gaolers. His body was then stripped and dragged by the heels through the streets behind a cart, to be hung by the feet from the bridge of Castel Tedaldo above the Po, the same bridge by which Lucrezia had entered the city.

As far as the Este family was concerned, the story was over. Giulio and Ferrante were kept imprisoned in the Torre dei Leoni while court life went on as if they had never existed. Their goods were handed over to Alfonso's favourites with Niccolò da Correggio receiving the prize of Giulio's magnificent palazzo on the Via degli Angeli. Ferrante died in prison in February 1540, aged sixty-three, after spending thirty-four years without a visit from any of his family. Giulio was released by Alfonso's grandson, Alfonso II, on his accession, after fifty-three years' imprisonment. Aged eighty-one, Giulio emerged to astound the people of Ferrara, still dandified and, according to the chroniclers, 'a most handsome man' but a figure from the past with a long beard and clothes which had been made for him in the fashion of fifty years ago.

Julius II, meanwhile, had revived Alexander VI's campaign to bring the Papal States under the control of the Church. The Bentivoglio of Bologna, who had only escaped being taken over by Cesare in the name of the Church by very substantial bribes, were now a prime target. They were deprived of their status as papal vicars of the city, which was excommunicated as long as they remained there. On 14 October 1506, a copy of the papal interdict against Bologna had been nailed to the door of the cathedral in Ferrara. Under its terms anyone who killed a Bolognese would be granted remission of his sin and a papal indulgence, as well as the goods of his victim. Any priest who failed to leave Bologna would forfeit his benefices. The author of this Christian document, the belligerent, bibulous Julius II, was on his way north; having already received the submission of Gian Paolo Baglioni of Perugia, he was approaching Imola with his army which included Francesco Gonzaga. The Bentivoglio family had already been excommunicated. Alfonso and Ippolito, who were related by marriage to the Bentivoglio and who had already outraged the Pope by their treatment of his godson, Ferrante, hastened to Imola to pay reverence to him. On 28 October a relieved Lucrezia wrote to Alfonso to tell him of her delight at hearing he had been well received there by the Pope and cardinals. He was not, however, prepared to participate totally in the humiliation of his friends and on his return to Ferrara on 3 November he issued a proclamation to the effect that anyone who had taken cattle and other animals from a Bolognese should register them with the *Giudice dei Savi* on pain of payment of a fine or, if not, *tracti de corda*. (This particularly painful torture involved tying the victim's arms behind his back, then hoisting him up by cords tied around his wrists, thus dislocating his shoulders.) He also refused the Pope's invitation to accompany him on his triumphal entry into Bologna.

The Bentivoglio had scattered before the Pope's advance; Alfonso diplomatically retired to Belriguardo and Ostellato en route for Comacchio on 9 November, shortly before the arrival that afternoon of his half-sister Lucrezia Bentivoglio and her children, as refugees in Ferrara. Lucrezia, too, kept her at arm's length, as di Prosperi told Isabella on 12 November: 'Yesterday evening the Most Illustrious Madonna Lucretia [Bentivoglio] was to have been taken to see the Duchess, but Her Excellency was celebrating the feast of St Martin with the Cardinal and Messer Sigismondo and others.' That day with Niccolò da Correggio she received her half-sister-in-law for a lengthy conversation which, however, di Prosperi noted acidly, did not appear to have been of great consolation to Lucrezia Bentivoglio: 'I did not see her return to her lodging more comforted than before, not so much for her adversities, but for reasons I cannot write: Your Ladyship, I believe, will hear of this from her . . .' Lucrezia Bentivoglio's mother-in-law and sister-in-law arrived that day and lodged outside the city walls. They were clearly not invited in. Ippolito had not seen his half-sister Lucrezia since her arrival although he had called and been told that she was at table. Some of the leading noblewomen of the town had visited her but it was clear the ruling family could not risk incurring the Pope's wrath and possible excommunication by harbouring his enemies. On 11 November, Julius II made his formal entry into Bologna.

Meanwhile, what of Lucrezia in all these Este family affairs?

Apart from a brief intervention when she had been warned off by Alfonso, she seems to have kept herself apart, although undoubtedly aware of what was going on. Only one letter of that year from her to Alfonso has survived – assuming that there were more – and that, dated from Ferrara on 28 October, when the *Congiura* and its attendant horrors were over, refers to her pleasure at hearing from him of the good reception he and Ippolito had received from Julius II at Imola, where the warrior pope was on his way north to take Bologna. There is not one letter from her to Ippolito but since they were together in Ferrara for much of that year it is understandable. There are many letters to Francesco Gonzaga, some of them via trusted messengers such as Tebaldeo, Alberto Pio da Carpi and Hector Berlinguer, who transmitted her messages orally. Others, more explicit, were mainly of an administrative nature: requests for clemency for various subjects, asking him to take action concerning the reduction of water to their lands in Carpesana and their subjects there, caused by the construction of a watermill by a Mantuan citizen on the canal leading to their mills. She repeated Alfonso's request to him to return the situation to what it had previously been. She was a passionate defender of the interests of her citizens and friends; she took up the cause of one Messer Amato Cusatro, who had suffered greatly from losing Gonzaga's esteem and was now being unjustly persecuted by the *podestà* of Sermide in consequence: 'I pray with all my heart that Your Lordship will not deny me this favour, because the love that I bear Messer Amato is such that I would hold any injury done to him as if it were to my own person, having found him a rare and affectionate servant to my Illustrious consort and myself . . .' In December she wrote in her own hand asking Francesco to favour Ercole Strozzi: 'Your Lordship knows that affection I bear to Messer Hercule Strozza [sic] and the obligations I have to him for his singular virtues and merit. He is coming to ask you a favour, as he will explain to you. I recommend him with all my heart and pray you that you will for love of me do for Messer Hercule as I am sure you would do for myself, because for the reasons I have referred to no less do I desire his wellbeing and ease than my own: whatever favour you will do him I will receive as done to me . . .'

Angela Borgia's up-and-down erotic career appeared finally to have reached a happy conclusion, despite her contrary mother-in-law. In June, di Prosperi reported that Alessandro Pio had appeared in Ferrara and 'remarried' Angela. Early in December, he wrote to Isabella that Angela had had a row with her husband over a golden robe which she wanted and which he told her should be paid for out of her dowry. This quarrel was resolved: a few days later she was ceremonially accompanied to the rented house she was to share with her husband, in a carriage with Lucrezia and attended by Alfonso, Ippolito and all the court on horseback 'to the sound of trumpets'. She was dressed in brocade, richly adorned and her fine carriage covered with satin striped with black velvet which, di Prosperi gossiped, had 'cost her dowry but little'. There was a collation with plates of sugar confections, supper and dancing.

For Lucrezia, the great event of that extraordinary year was the news which reached her in the last week of November that Cesare was at liberty again. On the night of 25 October, he had made a dramatic escape from La Mota, injuring himself quite severely when the rope down which he was climbing was cut from above, precipitating him into the fosse. He made for Navarre and the court of his brother-in-law, Jean d'Albret, taking a tortuous route to evade capture, and reaching Pamplona on 3 December. Somewhere along the way he managed to get word to Lucrezia, who learned of his escape on 26 November and wrote immediately to Gonzaga, expecting him to share her joy. By the end of December, Lucrezia had learned where he was from his chancellor, Federico, whom she sent on to Gonzaga with the happy news and a letter from Cesare. (Cesare had also written to Ippolito; he did not, significantly, write to Alfonso.) 'I am sure,' Lucrezia wrote disingenuously, 'that this [news] will make you rejoice and you will derive from it as much content-ment as does the Duke [Cesare] . . . loving him as you do as a brother . . .'[5]

One other important person certainly did not share her joy: Julius II, now triumphantly ensconced in Bologna. As Federico passed through Bologna, the Pope had him seized. Lucrezia was distraught and wrote to Gonzaga asking him to intercede with Julius for his release, assuring him that Cesare intended no harm to the Pope, nor would she have allowed Federico to engage in any such activity, 'being a most devoted and faithful servant to His Beatitude together with my consort. I know that he is not here for anything other than to give me the news of his [Cesare's] liberation.' Such a detention could only do harm to her brother and herself, giving the impression that they were not in the Pope's good graces, therefore she begged Francesco to obtain Federico's speedy release. In fact Julius had little to fear from Cesare. Although il Valentino still signed his letters 'Cesar Borgia de Francia, duca di Romagna', these were but empty words. As Julius himself sneered, Cesare now had 'not one rampart in the Romagna'. He was practically penniless: Julius had sequestrated the money which his bankers had distributed around the leading Italian banks, and the treasure which Florence and the Bentivoglio had captured. Louis XII had refused his request for the restitution of his duchy of Valentinois and his offer to take service with him once again. Yet where the charismatic, driven Cesare was concerned you could never be sure that he was finished. As Ferdinand of Aragon's chronicler Zurita wrote, the news of his escape 'put the Pope in great consternation, because the Duke was such a man that only his presence was sufficient to raise new troubles in all Italy: and he was greatly loved, not only by the soldiery, but also by many people of Tuscany and the States of the Church'.[6] And in Ferrara he had his loyal and loving sister who would do anything to help him.

13. 'Horrors and Tears'

'The more I try to please God, the more he tries me . . .'

– Lucrezia's anguished cry on hearing of the violent death
of Cesare in Navarre in March 1507

The new year of 1507 began as the old year had ended, with
present-giving, balls and festivities. Lucrezia sent Isabella boxes of
salted fish and oysters from the lagoons – *valli* – of Comacchio,
while Isabella ordered for herself pounds of sweetmeats and the
Ferrarese speciality, sugared *cedri* (large lemon-type citrus fruit),
from Lucrezia's celebrated confectioner Vincenzo Morello da
Napoli, known as 'Vincentio spetiale'. Lucrezia gave balls for the
French commander de Lapalisse at which the torch dance ('*il
ballo de la torce*') was performed.

Lucrezia was pregnant again, as di Prosperi learned on 3 January,
from il Barone, who in turn had had confirmation from one of
Lucrezia's priests. Despite her history of miscarriages and difficult pregnancies, she threw herself into the carnival celebrations.
Francesco Gonzaga arrived on the 9th with two pleasure-loving
young cardinals, his brother, Sigismondo Gonzaga, and Alfonso's
cousin, Luigi d'Aragona, and immediately visited Lucrezia, accompanied by Alfonso. The Sala Grande was decorated with tapestries and silks in preparation for the carnival balls. Lucrezia's
enthusiasm proved fatal to her pregnancy: in mid January she
miscarried again. Alfonso was furious and despondent, the more
so because he blamed Lucrezia for bringing it on herself: 'it is
attributed to various causes,' di Prosperi reported, 'to remaining
on her feet for long hours, going about in carriages, and perhaps
some jaunts abroad in masks – also by climbing some steep stairs

which she has had made in the *camerini* above the *stuffeta
longa*, which she has turned into two *camerini* with two more
above them.' The foetus was so undeveloped that it could not be
discerned whether it was male or female – possibly six weeks
old, di Prosperi guessed. Lucrezia too was very upset by 'this disas-
ter of hers', as di Prosperi put it: at her failure at her third attempt
to provide an Este heir, and perhaps by the knowledge that her
own overexuberance in the presence of Gonzaga had been responsible for it. Adding to her pain was the fact that Isabella was
pregnant and nearing her proper term; she successfully gave birth
to a third son shortly afterwards, which she, perhaps defiantly,
named Ferrante. The concealed rivalry between the two women
continued.

With her usual resilience, however, Lucrezia quickly recovered
her spirits, although she kept to her rooms. By early February
she was well enough to go out and take part in the masking in
the streets, and in the evening there was dancing, singing and
concerts in her apartments, attended by Luigi d'Aragona and other
worldly cardinals including Cardinal Giovanni de'Medici, the
future Pope Leo X. She went out richly dressed in a carriage to
a supper at the house of Antonio Costabili and herself gave a
dinner, with dancing in her principal chamber. The cardinals,
having escaped from the less amusing court of Julius II, enjoyed
themselves every night until dawn until the end of carnival. By
the end of February, di Prosperi wrote that the masques and dancing had been put aside and 'now we all attend the sermons of
Fra Raphaele of Varese', whom Lucrezia had invited specially to
Ferrara. Despite her lighthearted enjoyment of conversation, dancing and singing, Lucrezia had a strong streak of genuine piety in
her nature and took her religion seriously. She enthusiastically
followed Fra Raphaele's sumptuary prohibitions but when orders
were issued to 'moderate the pomp of ladies' – forbidding the
wearing of rich materials and cosmetics (women used a white
paste as a foundation on which they dabbed a rouge made of
maiolica) – most people thought that she was going too far and
that they should be allowed to practise as they wished. Deep

décolletées were also proscribed. The ladies of Ferrara rebelled and Lucrezia and her preacher were forced to back down.

While Lucrezia and her friar were attempting to tame the ladies of Ferrara, Cesare Borgia was embarking on his last campaign, fighting for his brother-in-law, the King of Navarre, against a rebel count. At dawn on 12 March 1507 he was killed in an ambush outside the small town of Viana in Navarre; stripped of its armour, his naked body was left bleeding on the ground. Cesare was thirty years old; he had survived the lifespan, twenty-eight, he had set himself by just two years, dying three days short of the Ides of March which had been fatal to his hero, Julius Caesar.

Lucrezia remained unaware of what had happened for some six weeks after his death. Cesare's faithful squire Juan Grasica arrived in Ferrara with the news on 22 April. He went first to Ippolito who, knowing that, as one of Isabella's correspondents put it, Lucrezia 'loved her brother as much as if she were his mother', could not bring himself to tell her and deputed Fra Raphaele to do so. For Lucrezia, Cesare's death was the supreme sorrow of a life already full of tragedies. She apparently responded with an anguished cry: 'The more I try to please God, the more he tries me . . .', and shut herself away, 'torturing herself day and night' with grief, calling out his name, unable to conceal her pain. Di Prosperi opined that few people would dare condole with her 'because of her reserved nature'. In public, just as she had when Alexander died, she kept her self-control, as Sanudo reported on 22 April: '. . . the death of Duke Valentino was notified to his sister, madama Lucretia by Fra Raphael who preached there this lent; she showed great grief, nevertheless with a great constancy and without tears'.[1] Fortitude was a much admired quality in the Renaissance, as it had been during classical times. Alfonso was proud of her and grateful for Ippolito's tactful handling of the matter: 'We are beyond measure satisfied with what your most reverend Lordship has intimated to us, touching the notification of the fate of the Duke her brother to our most illustrious consort,' he wrote to Ippolito on 27 April from the camp at Genoa, 'it seeming to us that Your Lordship in this matter has proceeded according to your natural prudence and experience. Likewise we are much pleased that Her Ladyship, our consort, has borne this calamity so patiently as Your Lordship tells us . . .'[2]

It was not until the end of the month that she could bring herself to leave her bed and to receive the condolences of her own household; few others were admitted. Agapito da Amelia, the distinguished humanist who had long served as Cesare's confidential principal secretary, arrived from Bologna where he was now secretary to the papal legate, and remained many hours with her talking over the past. Beyond Angela Borgia, with whom she had dined during carnival in Ferrara and who returned from Sassuolo to comfort her, there was no one with whom she could truly share her grief; and, indeed, outside the remaining Borgia circle, no one mourned the death of the terrible Valentino. Alfonso, who was away helping Louis XII crush the rebellion at Genoa, tried to comfort her by writing that Cesare was 'victorious against the enemies of his brother-in-law' when he was killed.

Lucrezia's circle of poets now sprang into action: Ercole Strozzi wrote an epicedium on Cesare's death which he dedicated to 'the divine Lucretia Borgia', describing Cesare as 'The chief pride of thy race . . . thy brother, mighty in peace, mighty in war, whose arduous glory is equal both in deed and in name to the great Caesars . . .' 'And now all dare give rein to so great a sorrow,' he added with pardonable exaggeration. Geronimo Casio of Bologna, who had known Cesare, wrote equally histrionically, 'Cesare Borgia, whom all for force of arms and valour regarded as a sun, dying, went where sets the sun Phoebus, towards the evening, to the West.' Machiavelli saw Cesare's life in Renaissance terms, as an example of the extreme malignity of fortune, as he wrote in Chapter VII of The Prince, of which Cesare was the hero: 'So summing up all that the Duke did, I cannot possibly censure him. Rather, I think I have been right in putting him forward as an example for all those who have acquired power through good fortune and the arms of others. He was a man of high courage and ambition, and he could not have conducted himself other than the way he did; his plans were frustrated only because Alexander's life was cut short and because of his own sickness . . . If when Alexander died, he had been well himself, everything would have been easy for him.'

But Cesare's enemies mocked him and his famous motto 'Either Caesar or nothing'. In Mantua Isabella d'Este gleefully recalled Sister Osanna's prophecy that Cesare's dominion would be 'as a straw fire'. Some remembered him with sympathy: 'In war he was a brave man and a good companion', a French captain said of him. He has gone down in history as a monster which, to a certain extent, he was. He was a creature of darkness and light, ruthless, amoral, charming and brilliant. His soldiers loved him and those close to him remained loyal to the end. He was popular in his lands of the Romagna where he had begun to lay down a new administration of justice. History has not been kind to him: he made too many enemies and in the end he failed; but the single-minded drive and ability with which he pursued what he saw as his high destiny had the qualities of genius.

Lucrezia had loved her brother passionately: whether their relations had ever been incestuous or not, he was part of her and no man could ever replace him. In her anguish she turned for solace to the other two men in her life: her husband, Alfonso, and her lover, Francesco Gonzaga. Bembo, probably aware by the autumn of 1505, when he had last written to her, of her relationship with Gonzaga and of Alfonso's hostility, had removed himself to the court of Urbino. Lucrezia's dealings with men were as deft as the neat steps with which she executed the complicated choreography of the torch dance. She managed to keep the affection and respect of her husband while retaining the lifelong love of Gonzaga under the most difficult and dangerous circumstances, seemingly occupying a special place in the hearts of two men who were not generally known for their respect for women.

Bravely, Lucrezia had managed to bring herself to write almost daily to Alfonso, saying how pleased she was by his favourable reception by Louis at the camp before Genoa and that he was in good health and spirits. She received Gian Luca Pozzi, who gave her a long account of the events at Genoa, but it was not until 30 April that she received Alfonso's handwritten letter of the 27th about Cesare (which has not survived). In her grief she felt the need of his reassuring presence: 'I pray God continually for the preservation and good health of Your Lordship and that matters at Genoa are quickly and happily expedited so that Your Lordship can return home with a swiftness which I desire with all my heart.' In Alfonso's absence, she also had the presence of mind to correspond with Ippolito about the movements of the Bentivoglio, whom the Pope suspected of trying to recapture Bologna, and about the information she had received from the papal legate there and about his request that she should send a commissioner into the Modenese with orders not to facilitate their passage nor to provide them with supplies.[3] She wrote to no one else for several months in the period after Cesare's death – not even to Gonzaga – or if she did the letters have not survived. After the surrender of Genoa to the French King, Alfonso returned on 9 May but, although he visited her first, he did not spend long with her and went on to confer at length with Ippolito.

From the time of Cesare's death rumours that Lucrezia was pregnant were repeated and denied throughout the summer with increasing insistence by di Prosperi. On 18 May she was reposing in bed for most of the time 'to preserve her pregnancy' but by 2 August, when Alfonso left for Venice and Comacchio, she was in charge again: 'The Lady is Governor in the usual way which has clarified the fact that she is not pregnant,' he reported. Later in August, Lucrezia went to Modena while Alfonso busied himself with his artillery foundry in Ferrara and dined frequently with Ippolito. By 16 September, in a letter reporting the marriage of Ercole Strozzi to Barbara Torelli and the return to Ferrara of Angela Borgia and her husband to spend some months there, the inquisitive di Prosperi had found the Comatre Frassina in the Corte and asked her if the Duchess were indeed pregnant: 'It seems that there is some hope that she is.' This time it appears that the rumours were true: on 7 November the Comatre Frassina confirmed the pregnancy and that in four months a child would be born.

But in the summer of 1507, as she looked for consolation for the loss of her adored brother, Lucrezia's relationship with Gonzaga had become ever more passionate – and secret. Ercole Strozzi had again taken up the dangerous role of facilitator of romance between Lucrezia and her admirers, which he had played so effectively during her relationship with Pietro Bembo, and was now involved in her correspondence with Gonzaga. Gonzaga was an old friend and patron, Alfonso a man who both disliked him and had deprived him of his lucrative office. And Strozzi had a tenderness for Lucrezia, probably exaggerated by his biographer, Wirtz, into love. Under the pseudonym 'Zilio' (lily), Strozzi carried on a correspondence between 'Guido', the name of one of his brothers but actually referring to Francesco Gonzaga, and 'Madonna Barbara', who was not Barbara Torelli, the object of his affections, but Lucrezia herself. In a letter to Gonzaga dated 23 September 1507 announcing his own marriage to Barbara Torelli, Strozzi coyly referred to Torelli as 'my Madonna Barbara', sending greetings from himself and Lucrezia 'your Madonna Barbara'.[4] The master archivist of Mantua, Alessandro Luzio, however, found an earlier letter among the few surviving in the Gonzaga archives at Mantua, beginning in the summer of 1507: 'I have not sent back that messenger because I have been trying everything to get an answer to M. Guido's letter, if Madonna Barbara had not been suffering such mental travail [presumably a reference to Lucrezia's continuing mourning for Cesare], it would have already been done because Zilio never stops soliciting for it . . .'[5]

The situation was complicated for Lucrezia by the undercurrents of hostility of which she was well aware between Francesco Gonzaga and Alfonso. That September of 1507 in the official correspondence with Gonzaga which she had resumed in the absence of Alfonso she had felt it necessary to stress that Alfonso's letters and actions showed 'his excellent disposition towards Your Lordship'.[6]

Knowing that she was pregnant, Lucrezia had made preparations for the carnival of the new year of 1508 to be particularly joyful. The Sala Grande was hung with the most splendid of the Este tapestries. Everyone focused on the pleasures of going about masked: Lucrezia, her ladies and courtiers watched from the great window of the Sala Grande. A 'very gallant' ball was held in the Sala Grande. There was tilting at the quintain ('*Quintana*'), more feasts and more balls. Angela Borgia, who was rumoured to be pregnant, 'found it necessary to dance' but Lucrezia, wiser this time and without the stimulating presence of Francesco Gonzaga, did not. The carnival festivities went on unhindered despite the thunderings of a hellfire preacher. The young men of the court began practising for a great joust on the feast of St Matthew, and on 13 February an eclogue commissioned by Ippolito was performed in the Sala Grande where Alfonso and Ippolito, 'both masked', and Lucrezia with a good company of gentlewomen, sat on a tribune hung with tapestries. The eclogue was composed by Ercole Pio, brother of Emilia, one of the heroines of Castiglione's *The Courtier*, a dialogue of amorous shepherds praising the great ladies of Old Testament, Greek and Roman times and of three contemporary *grandes dames*, Lucrezia, Isabella d'Este and Elisabetta, Duchess of Urbino. This was followed by Ippolito's Slav acrobats executing prodigious leaps, a girl tightrope walker and the cardinal's lute players and singers singing the praises of the 'diva Borgia'. Incense was thrown on a sacrificial fire and the whole thing ended in a dance. The eclogues, separately commissioned by Alfonso and Lucrezia (from Tebaldeo) and performed on 8 March, were generally considered inferior, but the first performance of Ariosto's comedy, *La Cassaria*, ordered by Ippolito, was praised by di Prosperi as 'as elegant and delightful as any other I have ever seen played'. Described by Gardner as 'a rollicking piece of work', it was greatly appreciated by the court, as were the music and the scenery painted by the Duke's court painter, Pellegrino da San Daniele.[7] The joint presentation of the eclogues and comedy by the three symbolized the new unity of the Este family after the upheavals of the *Congiura*, but in the bowels of the Torre dei Leoni, Ferrante and Giulio lived their lives in isolation and silence.

For the moment, however, the Este were determined to enjoy carnival. There were jousts, and Ippolito and a companion were seen going about disguised in Turkish costumes of gold brocade ornamented with appliqué flowers of black silk, estimated to cost 200 ducats each. It was hardly a disguise, di Prosperi commented, since the pair stood out among the others for the richness of their clothes. Ippolito reacted with his usual violence to the impertinence of his chamberlain, one Alfonso Cestatello, whom he had ordered not to take part in the last evening's carnival celebration, for failing to provide some things necessary for the cardinal's masking. Cestatello had replied impertinently and gone there all the same whereupon he was seized by the hair by Masino del Forno, confined to prison and afterwards exiled to Capua for six months.

It was noticed that Lucrezia had not taken part in the dancing during the last days of carnival; she was reported to be seven months gone and to have engaged a beautiful young wet nurse. Both she and Angela Borgia were nearing their term, and both had ordered sumptuous cradles and preparations for their lying-in. On 25 March, di Prosperi estimated the birth to be imminent; people were storing away books and documents from the Palazzo della Ragione and public offices for fear of their being burned in an outbreak of rowdy celebrations at the birth of an heir. By the 29th, Angela Borgia had already given birth to a son while Lucrezia's delivery was daily awaited. Alfonso, who had had some misunderstanding with Venice, went there on 3 April with a fleet of boats to make his peace and he was there when, on 4 April, Lucrezia gave birth to a son, named Ercole in honour of his grandfather. The baby was fair-skinned, handsome and lively, with, according to di Prosperi, who saw him when he was three weeks old, 'a most beautiful mouth but a little snub nose and eyes [which were] not very dark nor very large'.

On 27 April, di Prosperi went to visit Lucrezia in her *camerini* and found her reposing on her bed in conversation with Ippolito. 'Her Ladyship is very well and from what I understand for these holy feast days she has gone to the loggia of the Chapel to hear divine service. I also saw her son who seemed to me even handsomer and more vivacious than before . . .' He described Lucrezia's apartments:

Yesterday I visited the Duchess's rooms . . . the decoration of the apartment is as follows. In the Salotto there is only a great carpet over the table, with a bench and a backrest; in the large Antechamber the upholstery of the bed is of mulberry satin which belonged to your mother [the Duchess Eleonora], embroidered with bunches of everlasting flowers, with very fine hanging [tapestries] of silk and wool around this room from the ceiling to the floor, among them the scene of the Judgement of Solomon. In the Camera de la Stufa Grande, the back hangings are fashioned in pavilion style [tent shaped], attached to the gilded cornice which surrounds this room.

In the first Camerino the hangings ordered by the Duchess Eleonora include a pavilion with curtains of crimson satin with the arms of the Este. In the Duchess Lucrezia's room, where she is now, there is a pavilion of cloth of silver with a deep fringe of gold thread, decorated with sheets of striped cambric . . . and round this Camerino are curtains of crimson mulberry velvet and cloth of gold, with the arms of the house of Este. In the Camera dorata next to these rooms the baby lies in a camp bed [*de bachete*], with a satin cover striped *alla morescha* in white, crimson and other colours; the room is hung round with satin cloth. Then there is the cradle placed in front of the bed in this room which is of such a splendour that I do not know how to describe it: it is made in a square six feet long and five feet wide with a mounting step covered with white cloth, and at each corner there is a square block in the antique fashion, above which rise four columns which sustain a most beautiful architrave with its cornice, and above the architrave is a carved garland which goes from corner to corner – all in gold without any colour, and it is hung with curtains of white satin, as is the canopy. In the centre of this square is a cradle . . . on a pedestal, all of it gilded. The cradle cover is of cloth of gold and its sheets of cambric and turnings of most beautiful embroidered linen.

In the outer rooms, Beatrice de'Contrari and the Comatre Frassina were in attendance, while il Barone sat on the floor with other court jesters.

Ercole Strozzi's ostensible role in corresponding with Francesco Gonzaga was to compose differences between Alfonso and Ippolito on the one side and Francesco on the other, petty but continuing disputes to which di Prosperi also referred. An optimistic letter of 2 January 1508 from Strozzi to Gonzaga was counteracted by an angry letter of 14 January from Francesco complaining that fugitive servants of his had been welcomed at Ferrara and another on 13 March, asserting that his brothers-in-law, under the cover of amicable protestations, continued in their intent to find new cause for controversy.[8] The efforts of Benedetto Brugi and Bernardino di Prosperi were equally optimistic and equally unavailing. According to Luzio, Alfonso's feelings against Francesco were such that when he had left for Venice just before Lucrezia's delivery of their son, he had ordered that Lucrezia was not to send news of the event to the Marquis of Mantua.

It was just before Alfonso's prohibition concerning the communication of the birth that the first surviving letter of the 'Zilio' correspondence of this year began. Naturally, pseudonyms were used: Alfonso was 'Camillo' and Ippolito 'Tigrino' ('little tiger'), an apt reference to his fierce nature. According to this letter, dated 23 March 1508, Francesco ('Guido') had obviously sent back the incriminating letters: Strozzi had handed Lucrezia her letter and burned the rest. Some of the letter is devoted to the cause of reconciliation between Gonzaga and the Este brothers; there had been a suggestion that Gonzaga should have come to Ferrara to effect it. From the text it is apparent that it was Lucrezia who made the running; Gonzaga hung back on the excuse that he was ill. Although he suffered from syphilis, this was a pretext which he frequently deployed to keep himself out of trouble and Lucrezia, it seems, saw through it: 'She regrets that you have been unwell, all the more that that sickness has prevented you from writing and even more from coming here. If you come here it will be as dear to you as 25,000 ducats and more: I cannot express to you the anger that has taken her because she was [so] willing to see you and because you have never answered her, which has made her anxious to know the cause.' Strozzi advised him to 'dissimulate' with Alfonso and Ippolito even if they had taken his servant (a page who had apparently fled Mantua and been received and protected in Ferrara by Ippolito).[9] If Francesco did not do this, 'they will seek every day to offend you in one way or another'. 'Madonna Barbara' had commissioned him to write on her behalf that he (Francesco) should follow Strozzi's advice: 'It cannot injure you and could profit you, and if it does not profit you in one way in another it will profit you with Madonna Barbara who I certify to you loves you: she is displeased by your lack of warmth but she is pleased that you are discreet, as well as many qualities she praises in you.' Nonetheless he repeated Lucrezia's surprise that Francesco had not written to her: 'if you agree, as my brother-in-law is coming here, it would be good to write to her and if you wish it she can send the letters back to you'.

Ercole Strozzi repeated Lucrezia's desire to see Francesco: 'she says you should do everything so that she can see you'. The next letter had been written on the eve of Lucrezia's giving birth to her son, a fact which greatly shocked Luzio, a committed partisan of Isabella. Gonzaga had sent a message to 'Madonna Barbara' that he had fever: she prayed him to let Strozzi know how he was and not to be so unfriendly. 'Every day we talk of you,' Strozzi wrote, 'and urge you to do everything you can to reconcile yourself with Camillo because from every point of view it is better to make peace.' Alfonso had gone to Venice the day before, he reported, although he did not mention 'Camillo's' instructions to his wife not to send Gonzaga news of her delivery. Lucrezia conveyed this in a message asking Francesco to forgive her if she did not advise him of her delivery and to believe in her 'good-will'.[10] Accordingly, Bernardino di Prosperi was sent officially by Lucrezia to Mantua to announce the birth of Ercole to Isabella, but to Isabella only. Alfonso wrote to Gonzaga from Venice to make the formal announcement the next day. Even di Prosperi thought it more than odd that he had not been commissioned

to take a letter to Francesco: 'From what I hear everyone is sorry
that I was not given a similar letter to the Most Illustrious
Marchese . . .'

Lucrezia, reckless and passionate, dictated a letter on 9 April
to Strozzi for transmission to 'Guido', complaining that both
Alfonso and Ippolito had indicated that they did not wish her
to announce the birth to him. She denounced them almost hyster-
ically and wanted Francesco to let it be known that he was
surprised at the omission so that she could officially send someone to him. She wanted to send Strozzi, who, according to his
letter to Gonzaga, had told her firmly:

It would not be good that I should go at present because it would
appear that I was going expressly for this purpose. You cannot believe
how she is displeased by such an error and perfidy on the part of
Camillo and wants you to understand that she is yours and not given
to flightiness and that you command her and she would see you very
willingly were it possible. She says that Camillo is going away tomorrow, posting to France, and recommends herself to you infinitely. This
is worthy of an answer concerning a visit [here] as I wrote to you in
my last letter and in this.

Alfonso had little time to enjoy his firstborn before he was off
again on another of his state missions, this time to the King of
France to reassure him of his loyalty, given that the award to him
of the Golden Rose by the Pope in April and his reconciliation
with Venice might have aroused Louis' suspicions. Gonzaga failed
to rise to the opportunity proffered by Alfonso's absence. He did
not visit Lucrezia; instead he hastened to use the occasion of little
Ercole's birth to make things up with Alfonso. The Gonzaga secretary Benedetto Capilupo was sent expressly to Alfonso to congratulate him, with protestations of cordial and fraternal friendship
which the goodhearted Alfonso told Capilupo he readily accepted.
Proudly he took Capilupo to see his son and had him changed
so that he could see that the naked baby 'was fine and well
equipped in everything'.[11] Strozzi transmitted renewed vows of

passion from Lucrezia and demands that Francesco Gonzaga should go to her. Instead, Gonzaga sent by one of his household a letter in his secretary's hand saying that his illness continued. He still did not wish to commit himself to writing in his own hand which in those days was considered a proof of intimacy, instead dictating to a secretary which would make it appear more formal to any spying eye in Ferrara. Even this innocuous document has disappeared, although there are numerous letters by Lucrezia to Francesco in the Gonzaga archives at Mantua. (Francesco's letters to her in the Este archives are limited to the years 1518–19.) 'I cannot tell you how great is Madonna Barbara's affection for you which could not be greater . . ,' Strozzi told him: 'she loves you to a considerable extent and considerably more than perhaps you think, because if you believed that she loved you as much as I have always told you, you would be warmer than you are in writing to her and coming to her wherever she might be . . .' Strozzi urged Francesco to make every effort to put a visit to Lucrezia in train: 'so that you will see how much she will caress you and then you will understand . . .'

Lucrezia had wanted to keep back the messenger so that she could write a letter to Francesco in her own hand, but childbirth had left her too weak to do so. She stressed that a reconciliation with Alfonso would be a good excuse for him to come to Ferrara and that before his departure Alfonso had said that such a move by Gonzaga would be welcome to him. She could hardly have made her feelings plainer: '[She] says you must do this [reconciliation] because you will soon be able to come to where she is.' Emotional and confused, Lucrezia at one moment wanted to speed Strozzi on his way, the next asked him to stay and keep her company. 'Write to her in any case so that it does not appear to her that you are cold,' Strozzi implored him.[12] This was Strozzi's last known letter: whether or not Gonzaga did respond is unknown. But, using sickness as a pretext, he did not in the meantime venture from Mantua, probably still wary of the Este. Alfonso might have been absent but the more ruthless and hostile Ippolito was still there and often visited Lucrezia. Alfonso made an astonishingly rapid return from the French court on 13 May, going straight to visit Lucrezia and his son.

Violence was never far from Lucrezia's life. Even as she rejoiced in her newborn son and the fulfilment of her duty as Duchess of Ferrara, which made her position impregnable, the murder of two people close to her reminded her of her Borgia days in Rome. On 5 June she wrote to Francesco Gonzaga: 'On Sunday night around midnight Don Martino, a Spaniard, formerly a *capellano* of the late Duke my brother who has been in my service, was treacherously killed by brutal wounds in the face and head by a jealous Moor . . .' Should the man, whom the bearer of the letter would describe, pass through Mantuan territory, she begged Francesco, according to the agreement he had with Alfonso, to arrest him and hand him over to her as 'a homicide and traitor'. This young priest, di Prosperi reported, was the one who had helped the Duke Valentino escape. Having dined in the Palazzo del Corte with Lucrezia's household, he was on his way to his room near the church of San Paolo when the attack occurred. The murderer was apparently never found.

That night of 5–6 June, three weeks after Alfonso's return, an even more sinister murder occurred. On the morning of the 6th, Ercole Strozzi's body was found in the middle of the road at the corner of the church of San Francesco, with twenty-two stab wounds in his body and his hair pulled out. His crutch lay beside him and he was wearing spurs, having ridden out on his mule to take a little fresh air and been ambushed by persons unknown. Despite his horrific wounds there was no blood on the ground: clearly he had been killed somewhere else and his body dumped by San Francesco. It was an obvious act of terror, of the kind which Cesare Borgia would not have hesitated to order, but why had it been committed? And by whom?

A week later di Prosperi was still uncertain as to the identity of Ercole Strozzi's killers. Strozzi's widow, Barbara Torelli, had also been the widow of Ercole di Sante Bentivoglio, with whom she had been on the bitterest of terms. Various names came up, including those of the Bentivoglio, who were hardly in a position to arrange such things at the time. Among them were Angela Borgia's husband, Alessandro Pio da Sassuolo, for no conceivable reason other than the fact that his fierce mother was a Bentivoglio, and even Giovanni Sforza's brother, Galeazzo, who had married one of Barbara's daughters and was involved in a quarrel with his mother-in-law over his wife's property in Bologna. 'Of the malefactors and authors of the death of Messer Hercule Strozzi there are those who point one way, others another, but no one dares to speak for fear of coming up against a brick wall and voicing a dangerous opinion . . .,' he wrote ten days later.

Ercole's brothers, Lorenzo and Guido Strozzi (the first of whom had married another of Barbara's daughters, Costanza), announcing his death on Barbara's behalf to Francesco Gonzaga, exhorted him to carry out a vendetta against the murderers of 'such a faithful servant' as Ercole had been to him. Barbara, recovering from the recent birth of her daughter by the murdered Ercole, also looked to Gonzaga for protection. Gonzaga had promised to stand as godfather to Barbara's child, but cautiously after Ercole's death deputed Tebaldeo to perform the office in his stead. It is noticeable that the Strozzi did not turn to the lord of Ferrara who, in the circumstances, could have been expected to institute investigation and punishment of the death of a man who, as a former *Giudice dei XII Savi*, had been a prominent administrator, a close friend of Lucrezia and a renowned poet and man of letters. Nothing happened, just as nothing had emerged after the deaths of Gandia and Bisceglie. Ercole Strozzi's biographer Maria Wirtz cites a letter written twenty-four days after the murder by one Girolamo Comasco to Ippolito d'Este naming Masino del Forno as the author of the crime.[13] Seizing a victim by the hair was a signature of del Forno's operations, as had been noted in his violent arrest of Ippolito's chamberlain, Cestatello, the previous year. Masino del Forno was one of the most loyal and ruthless of the senior Este brothers' henchmen: if he was involved so were they, a fact which would explain the failure even to search for the killer. Two years later, in June 1510, Julius II openly accused Alfonso of the crime during an acrimonious interview with

Alfonso's envoy, Carlo Ruini. Julius was a man of explosive temperament, deeply hostile to Alfonso at that time, but he was exceptionally well informed and only the Pope could have made such an accusation without fear of the consequences.

Wirtz argues that Alfonso had Ercole Strozzi killed out of jealousy because he himself was in love with Barbara, and that the timing of the crime, only thirteen days after their alleged marriage, is significant. But di Prosperi had reported on 16 September the previous year that Ercole had married Barbara Torelli, and Strozzi himself had announced his marriage in distinctly unromantic terms to Gonzaga in a letter of 23 September. Wirtz and indeed most historians seem to be unaware of this, which destroys their theory of the significance of the marriage in provoking Alfonso's homicidal jealousy. Jealousy there may have been on Alfonso's part but not of Barbara Torelli – rather, of Lucrezia. Alfonso had never liked Ercole Strozzi and had removed him from office as soon as he could. But his most cogent reason for disliking Strozzi was the part he played as go-between in the romance between Lucrezia and Gonzaga. It may even have been a warning signal to Francesco. Although Alfonso, reserved and secretive as he was, never gave any sign that he knew of the clandestine correspondence between his wife and his brother-in-law, it is inconceivable that Ippolito's intelligence system would not have picked up on it. Did his sister Isabella know or suspect something? It is entirely possible. Ferrara at night was as lawless as any other Italian city of the time, but it is not credible that such a violent murder could be committed by an ordinary criminal and the evidence of it, the body, dumped publicly in a main street in the city centre. Had it been any ordinary criminal, the Este would have been bound to pursue the case. They did not. Equally, they could have arranged for Strozzi simply to disappear. The violent nature of the incident and the alleged involvement of Masino del Forno point directly to Ippolito and Alfonso, who were not only constantly at odds with Francesco Gonzaga but also jealous for Este honour, touching as it did on the wife of Alfonso, mother of the Este heir, and the husband of Isabella.

Luzio absolves Alfonso of the murder, pointing the finger at the Bentivoglio, quoting from a letter which Barbara Torelli wrote to Gonzaga from Venice early the next year: 'Who took my husband from me, is causing his children to lose their inheritance and seeking to threaten my life and make me lose my dowry . . .' Yet in the next breath, Luzio claims that Alfonso was not only less bloodthirsty than had been rumoured but never left a crime unpunished, whatever the circumstances. In this case, however, he probably did. Luzio's conclusion was that the Bentivoglio killed Ercole to revenge themselves on Barbara for her intransigence over her dowry. Ercole Strozzi, supported by Lorenzo Strozzi, had taken Barbara's part in a dispute with her over her daughters' dowries but since Lorenzo later joined forces with Barbara's other son-in-law, Galeazzo Sforza, against her he can hardly have suspected the latter of involvement in Ercole's murder. And why should anyone have been willing to protect the Bentivoglio, stateless, under interdict and enemies of the Pope as they were? Although the brothers Guido and Lorenzo Strozzi had made common cause with Barbara to beg Francesco Gonzaga to pursue a vendetta against the killer or killers of Ercole, there is no evidence that they took it further. After five hundred years, the crime remains unsolved: as in the Borgia days, the killer was too important to be identified. And in Ferrara that pointed to the Este as either instigators of or complicit in the murder of Ercole Strozzi. It is always possible that Ippolito was the prime mover but, if he was, he could not have done so without Alfonso's agreement and Alfonso was in Ferrara when the crime took place.

The murder of Ercole Strozzi did not, however, deter Lucrezia from pursuing her passion for Gonzaga, although it certainly increased Gonzaga's reluctance to take risks. As we have seen, Lucrezia was reckless and determined in pursuing her objectives. As a Borgia, she enjoyed an element of danger: she also thought she could get away with it. She knew Alfonso was devoted to her and she had recently borne him his longed-for son. She thought, probably rightly, that she could manage him if she continued their harmonious relations at every level and conducted her private passion with discretion. In any case in Alfonso's absence she carried on a frequent official correspondence with Gonzaga on administrative matters. Somehow she induced Lorenzo Strozzi to step into his late brother's shoes as go-between. From Finale en route to Reggio on 30 June 1508, only a few weeks after Ercole's death, she wrote in her own hand a letter of recommendation to Gonzaga on behalf of Lorenzo who was to take it in person to Mantua: 'Since Count Lorenzo Strozzi is coming to you as no less devoted a servant of yours than was Messer Hercole his brother, I could not fail to write these few lines both to remind you of my goodwill towards you and to recommend the Count in every occurrence when he may turn to you, you will also hear from him personal matters of mine. I pray you to give him faith as if he were myself.' Strozzi's reward was to be the favour of Francesco and Lucrezia. In another letter in her own hand of 19 October she thanked Francesco for the favour he had shown Strozzi in some case which has given her the greatest pleasure 'for the love she bears the Count for his merit and virtues'.

This time no pseudonyms were used and the language was less passionate, so as not to arouse suspicion should it be intercepted. Strozzi signed the letters with his own name, but, reading between the lines, Lucrezia's continuing desire to see her recalcitrant lover is evident. She was at Reggio, accompanied by Strozzi, when he wrote to Gonzaga, attempting to lure Gonzaga to a rendezvous with her. The language was formal, the intention clear. The Most Illustrious Duchess, he said, wanted to let Gonzaga know that within eight or ten days she would have to leave for Ferrara because of the Duke's departure from there. But, because Her Ladyship wished to speak personally to him if possible, she urged him to come to Reggio because nothing in the world would give her more pleasure: 'I reminded her that Your Lordship was confined to bed: she said she would order many prayers to be said at Reggio and in Ferrara that Your Lordship would soon be free [from his illness] and come to her. Also that if it were permitted it would not have been difficult for her to go there and speak to you and visit you. She regrets his illness as much as if it were her own. More she never heard that Your Lordship was in bed, or she would have sent a message of condolence which she will do.' Lucrezia, he told Francesco, had been very ill of a bloody flux of which she has now recovered, but which prevented her from writing in her own hand to plead with him to come to Reggio by all means. 'I excused you on the grounds that you will not be able to come but Her ladyship commanded me that in any case I write to you and I have done what she ordered . . .' Lucrezia was so anxious for an answer, he said, that Francesco should either respond to his letter directly, where it would be delivered into her hands, or to Ferrara whence he would see that it 'flew to her'.[14]

Gonzaga does seem to have been genuinely ill, as he wrote in a graceful, affectionate letter dictated to his formidable secretary, Tolomeo Spagnoli, Isabella's *bête noire*, who was probably not unwilling to further his master's romance with her rival. Only the state he was in, Gonzaga wrote, could have prevented him from seeing the Lady Duchess, his most cordial sister, whose good wishes and prayers have had a restorative effect. He had heard of her illness with great displeasure, for 'such a fine body should be spared any infirmity'. He asked Strozzi to assure her that one of the principal reasons he wanted to be totally free of his malady was to see her again.[15]

Even one of Lucrezia's jesters, 'Martino de Amelia', entered into the game, writing from Reggio addressing Francesco as 'Illustrious Lord Marchese of Mantua, entirely the Duchess's' and describing how he had transformed himself into Gonzaga's image to console the Duchess and amuse the Duke and the Cardinal. Lucrezia, he said, had thought of visiting him but was now not going (possibly because of the arrival of Alfonso and Ippolito), signing himself 'Martin, your slave for the great love my Lady Duchess bears you'.[16] Lucrezia herself followed this up three days later with a private note to be sent to Francesco by a messenger carrying a letter from Alfonso, who would tell him of her date of departure from Reggio. Through October and November,

Lucrezia continued to send messages to Gonzaga via Strozzi, ostensibly asking him to further Strozzi's cause. At times she would scribble her own notes with a covering letter from Strozzi; sometimes Strozzi would be the bearer of messages from her 'which could not be written'. Gonzaga, however, remained in Mantua and Isabella visited Ferrara in November without him.

By this time relations between Francesco and Isabella were tense and contentious. For some years, more or less from the time that Lucrezia and Francesco had begun their relationship, the marriage had lacked affection. The letters between the couple evinced a 'restrained formality' and were mostly narrowly concerned with domestic matters.[17] On 1 October 1506 Francesco, in a letter to a friend who was about to marry, complained discouragingly that his own marriage seemed to have lasted twenty-five rather than seventeen years,[18] while, a few days after he wrote this, in a letter to him of 5 October Isabella complained pathetically that 'he had loved her little for some time past'. By now, on almost every subject, however petty, Lucrezia and Francesco, abetted by Lorenzo Strozzi, lined up against Isabella, who was supported by Alfonso and Ippolito. The first row developed from Isabella's visit to Ferrara when she persuaded her brothers that Lucrezia should take into her service a girl whom Francesco (probably from unworthy motives) wanted to remain in Mantua. At the behest of the three Este, Lucrezia was made to write to Mantua sending for the girl. She could not oppose Alfonso's wishes, however much she would have liked to please Francesco, as she wrote in an apologetic note, joking that the girl represented a pledge which would bring Francesco to Ferrara: 'Seriously my Lord, I could not have done more to serve you than I have done, but it has never been possible, for reasons which Count Lorenzo will write to you . . .'[19] Strozzi backed her up, saying that Alfonso and Ippolito had insisted she take the girl and made her send the horseman to Isabella for this purpose 'which on no account whatsoever Her Ladyship wished to do . . .' Indeed, in order to avoid having to write the letter, Lucrezia had had recourse to the convent of Corpus Domini for four days, but to no avail.

The second *casus belli* was the tempestuous widow Barbara Torelli, who had been in Venice and whom Isabella had taken under her wing. When Lorenzo Strozzi had asked her help to reconcile him with Galeazzo Sforza so that they could unite against Barbara over their wives' dowries, Isabella had rudely refused him. Now Torelli wished to return to Ferrara, her family home, to which Strozzi was strenuously opposed. Both he and Lucrezia believed that Isabella had supported the move and 'to such effect that she had persuaded the Duke and the Cardinal to protect and comfort her'. Gonzaga had apparently sided with Strozzi over this but the combined weight of the three Este had prevented Lucrezia from interfering. 'The Lady Duchess would do more for you than for anyone in the world,' Strozzi wrote, 'but in this case she has had to lay down her arms . . .'[20]

14. The Years of War, 1509–12

'The love, faith and trust she [Lucrezia] has in Your Lordship is of such an order that she has more hope in Your Lordship than in any other person in the world, and with all her heart she begs you not to abandon her in these times . . . [she] said to me: "Lorenzo, if it were not for the hope that I have in the Lord Marchese that in my every need he will aid and protect me, I would die of grief . . ."'

– Lorenzo Strozzi to Francesco Gonzaga, nominally leader of the papal forces against Ferrara, expressing Lucrezia's real feelings at a time of extreme danger and stress, 21 August 1510

Over the next three years Lucrezia was *de facto* ruler of Ferrara, as her city and state faced the threat of the Italian wars in general and the hostile ambitions of Pope Julius II in particular. With Alfonso almost continuously away fighting and with enemies on every side, she showed the administrative abilities and awareness of military affairs which her Borgia upbringing had taught her. She was also the head of a court and the mother of the heir with responsibility for his education and safety. As an added complication, for much of the time Alfonso and Francesco Gonzaga were fighting on opposing sides with Gonzaga heading the Pope's campaign against Ferrara; it took all Lucrezia's skills to keep him secretly on side.

On 10 December 1508 the treaty known as the League of Cambrai was signed. As with most such treaties, the public agreements were like the tip of the iceberg of proliferating understandings with numerous powers, including both Alfonso d'Este and Francesco Gonzaga. Ostensibly Cambrai was a treaty of peace between Louis XII of France and the Emperor, or 'Emperor

Elect', Maximilian, impoverished and impotent but still the feudal lord of many Italian cities. This agreement established Milan as a hereditary fief of the French King and was ostensibly directed towards a crusade against the Turks, often mooted but never executed. In reality it was directed against the overweening power of Venice on the Italian mainland. The power vacuum created by the crumbling of Cesare's dukedom of the Romagna had been filled by Venice, arrogant, opportunist and full of an unwarranted belief in its irreversible good fortune.

Haughty and greedy, the Venetians had offended everyone, bringing together an unprecedented coalition of major and minor powers against them. A second and secret treaty, to which the Pope and the King of Spain might be parties if they chose, was drawn up, binding the contracting powers to oblige Venice to restore all the cities of the Romagna to the Pope; the Apulian coast to the King of Spain; Roveredo, Verona, Padua, Vicenza, Treviso and Friuli to the emperor; Brescia, Bergamo, Crema, Cremona, Ghiara d'Adda and all the former fiefs of Milan to the King of France. The King of Hungary, should he join, was to get back all his former possessions in Dalmatia and Croatia, the Duke of Savoy to recover Cyprus while Ferrara and Mantua would be rewarded with all the lands taken from them by the Venetians. In essence it represented the dismemberment of the Venetian empire on the Italian mainland.

Alfonso had attempted to make an approach to Venice and been rebuffed, lashed by the tail of the Lion of St Mark for his temerity in scouting their dominions without permission. He had placated the Pope by acting against the attempt by the Bentivoglio to regain Bologna and he had renewed the family policy of close relations with France. On 20 April 1509 – to the disgust of Francesco Gonzaga – he was appointed Gonfalonier of the Church by the Pope, Venice was placed under interdict and the war began. On 14 May in the decisive battle of Agnadello the huge Venetian army of 50,000 mercenaries was defeated by French and papal troops. Although perhaps not fully realized in Venice at the time, it was the end of Venice's pretensions to power in Italy. Machiavelli condemned the Venetians for 'arrogance in prosperity and cowardice in adversity'. 'They imagined,' he wrote:

that they owed their prosperity to qualities which, in fact, they did not possess, and were so puffed up that they treated the King of France as a son, underrated the power of the Church, thought the whole of Italy too small a field for their ambition, and aimed at creating a world-wide empire like that of Rome. Then when fortune turned her back on them, and they were beaten by the French . . . they not only lost the greater part of their territory by the defection of their people, but, of their own accord, out of sheer cowardice and faint-heartedness, they gave back most of their conquests to the Pope and the King of Spain . . .[1]

War was the making of Alfonso: he showed courage, tenacity and political agility in the defence of his state, ably assisted by Ippolito, the warrior cardinal. Firstly, he removed the hated symbol of Venetian domination, the *visdomino*, a thorn in Ferrara's side since the last Venetian war. He politely withdrew his ambassador from Venice, upon which the Venetians confiscated his palace. More importantly for the economy of Ferrara, he recovered lands the Venetians had seized from Ferrara, including Este, from which his family had taken its name, and he restored the salt pans at Comacchio, abandoned since the Venetian prohibition of the making of salt there, and increased the tolls on goods passing through the Ferrarese from Bologna and the Romagna. The Venetians, enraged at his presumption, sent a fleet against him up the Po in December that year which Alfonso humiliatingly defeated. Alfonso's strength and defiance rested on his close alliance with Louis (not, however, the most dependable of allies), which Julius greatly resented. Increasingly the Pope's anger, xenophobia and aggression focused on the Duke of Ferrara.

The fortunes of war had not favoured Francesco Gonzaga and on 9 August 1509 the Venetians captured and imprisoned their former Captain General. While Lucrezia was distraught, the Este could not have cared less, particularly Isabella who felt free to give rein to her talent for government and political intrigue, untrammelled by the presence of her increasingly hostile husband and his clique. The Pope later alleged that Alfonso and Ippolito had schemed to keep him captive. According to Gonzaga's later testimony, only Lucrezia (whose letters to him of this period have all disappeared) wrote to him and was concerned about his fate while he was in his Venetian prison.

In the absence of their husbands, Lucrezia and Isabella exchanged war news. Little Ercole was very ill at the beginning of June and his doctor, Francesco Castello, was extremely concerned for him, while his anxious father sent twice daily for news. Lucrezia was pregnant again and indulging in another round of redecoration and reconstruction, this time of the set of rooms which had formerly been occupied by Isabella.

Throughout May, Lucrezia wrote frequently to Alfonso on military matters, sending him the latest news and asking his opinion on various matters. These were dangerous times of frequent troop movements; on one day alone she wrote to him three times, once to report that a force of some 1,500 troops was nearing Ferrara and had sent to ask her for free passage, allegedly to go and fight for the King of France; secondly, to report on the capture of Venetian infantry by the *podestà* of Porto, and the last asking his advice as to whether she should restore their arms to a body of troops to whom she had given free passage on the grounds that they disarmed. On May 31 she had letters from the *podestà* of Codigoro reporting on the presence of armed Venetian ships which they had followed for eight miles. They wanted artillery from Alfonso but Lucrezia advised that they should think only of their own defence and not begin skirmishes which could result in the Venetians reinforcing their fleet in greater numbers. Later that day, the news came to Ferrara of victory for Alfonso, who had recovered his former possession of the Polesine di Rovigo from Venice; Lucrezia wrote an enthusiastic letter of congratulations. The ambassadors of France and the Empire had arrived in Ferrara; she had arranged an honourable reception for them and had given them audience. Would Alfonso please let her know whether he would come to Ferrara to meet them or whether they should go to him because they were most anxious to talk to him. On 1 June she acknowledged Alfonso's letter saying the ambassadors should go to meet him at La Abbatia where he was about to besiege two towers; in wifely fashion she was sending 'a little tapestry and silver to entertain them'. On 4 June she had received news from the Governor of Ravenna, brother of Julius's legate at Bologna, complaining that the men of Codigoro had attacked his men and taken their goods. She had immediately written to order their restitution and had also tactfully smoothed things over in a letter to the Governor, assuring him of Alfonso's displeasure at such acts and that he intended to live on good terms with all his neighbours and especially the Pope's officers.

On 10 June, to the sound of gunfire and trumpets, Alfonso returned triumphant; mass was sung in the piazza, watched by the couple from their separate windows. Little Ercole had recovered and was seen by di Prosperi playing in his mother's room where Lucrezia was resting despite the turmoil in other parts of the apartment. That month a fire in the Palazzo del Corte destroyed the Sala dei Paladini and several other rooms with their curtains and hangings (*pavaglioni*). Alfonso was away again in July: the Venetians, intent on recovering the lands they had disgorged after Agnadello, retook Padua and then Este which, Lucrezia wrote to him, 'grieves me to my heart'. She had received appeals for help from the *podestà* of Lendinara and had sent telling him not to fear; she had also sent out reinforcements to various fortresses. She was by now accustomed to dealing with such matters and, she said, she would continue to do so until he returned to Ferrara 'which I hope can be soon: [meanwhile] in every occurrence I shall not for my part fail in every diligence and vigilance for the good and conservation of your affairs'.[2]

At the end of July, di Prosperi reported that Lucrezia had engaged a wet nurse and must be approaching the end of her term. He was premature: it was a difficult pregnancy, and early in August she was still heavily pregnant and felt pains. Angela Borgia arrived to keep her company. A few weeks later, on 18

August, desperate to get out of her apartments and possibly to pray for Gonzaga, news of whose capture by the Venetians she had received the previous day, she went to Corpus Domini in a carriage which almost precipitated the birth at the convent. She returned to Isabella's former rooms to await her delivery where, finally, on 25 August she gave birth to another son, named Ippolito in honour of his uncle, the cardinal; 'he is white and well-formed and resembles his father', di Prosperi reported.

That autumn Venice increased the pressure on Ferrara, and both the Este brothers were constantly in the field. At the end of November a Venetian force overwhelmed the Bastion of Lendinara; di Prosperi's dispatches took on a note of foreboding, almost a sense of siege. The Venetians were attempting to build a bridge over the Po and there was a skirmish when the Ferrarese tried to prevent them. 'I fear for our situation if the French and the Emperor do not divert the war from this direction,' he wrote, asking Isabella to persuade them to help her brothers. The fear in Ferrara was such that, on Alfonso's advice, Lucrezia had cancelled her intended journey to Modena to greet Elisabetta, now the widowed Duchess of Urbino, and her niece and daughter-in-law, Leonora Gonzaga, married to the present Duke of Urbino, Francesco Maria della Rovere, in case her departure would be misinterpreted as flight. 'The Duke's decision is most prudent,' approved di Prosperi, 'because of the terror I have seen here.' Ariosto was sent to Rome to ask for help and encountered such a furious welcome from Julius at Ostia that he fled, fearing to be thrown into the sea. At Ferrara, Lucrezia continued with her normal administration. On her orders the Guardaroba handed over a string of huge pearls which had belonged to the Duchess Eleonora and several fine pieces of her own jewellery to be pawned to raise money. Much of her silver had already gone the same way.[3]

The Venetians crossed the river by a bridge of boats, seized Comacchio and flooded through the Polesine di San Giorgio towards Ferrara. Ferrarese lives were lost, including that of the Este ally Count Lodovico Pico della Mirandola, decapitated by a

cannonball, a misfortune which greatly shocked the Italians, as
yet unused to artillery casualties. A large Venetian fleet lay in
readiness at Polesella and a message was sent by them to Ippolito
promising a good fight if he was willing, a challenge he accepted.
The Venetian ships floated high on the Po, swollen by recent
rains, presenting, Ippolito recognized, an easy target for the
Ferrarese artillery. At dawn on 22 December he made a surprise
attack, bombarding and sinking many of the ships; others were
captured and only two of the galleys escaped. The Venetians were
massacred by the Ferrarese as soon as they reached land and thirteen of their galleys taken back in triumph to Ferrara. On 27
December, Alfonso and Ippolito made a formal triumphal entry
into Ferrara on board the biggest of their prizes, armed and with
the standards of the Duke and of the Gonfalonier proudly raised,
the Venetian flags pointing downwards. Trumpets, small clarinets,
tabors, kettle drums played, and gunshots resounded on land and
water as they landed at San Paolo where Lucrezia waited to greet
them with fifty carriages of ladies. The procession with Alfonso,
wearing an armoured breastplate and a tunic of rich, curled
brocade, riding on a courser alongside Ippolito – for once in his
cardinal's robes – on a mule on his right hand, proceeded
triumphantly and noisily to the cathedral where the *Te Deum* was
sung and prayers offered to the Virgin and the two patron saints
of Ferrara, San Maurelio and San Giorgio. To complete the
triumph of the Este family, their holy ancestor, the blessed Beatrice
da Este, was heard over several days beating on the walls of her
tomb in Santo Antonio, presumably in celebration of the great
victory.

Unfortunately for the Este, the blessed Beatrice's knockings
only served to usher in the most dangerous year Alfonso and
Lucrezia would yet experience. Julius II had reverted to the policy
of Alexander VI and intended to re-establish the authority of the
papacy over the States of the Church, which included Ferrara.
With the cry of 'Out with the barbarians' he signalled his intention to expel the French from Italy which, considering that, as
cardinal, he had been among the first to invite them in, could

be considered a bit rich. He saw Venice as the only Italian power fit to provide a counterbalance against the French, and early in the new year of 1510 came to a secret peace with the Republic. He was furious with Alfonso for his friendship with France: as he told the Venetian envoy, 'It is God's will that the Duke of Ferrara should be punished and Italy freed from the hands of the French.'[4] The Cardinal d'Aragona warned Alfonso that an attack on Ferrara was to be the first stage of a campaign against the French by Julius in alliance with Venice and Ferdinand of Spain. 'The Pope wants to be lord and master of the world's game,' the Venetian envoy Domenico Trevisan warned the Signory on 1 April 1510.

In July 1510 Julius's campaign against Ferrara began. It was to be spearheaded in somewhat lackadaisical fashion by Gonzaga, released that month (thanks, it was rumoured, to the intervention of the Sultan with whom he traded in horses), and appointed by Julius Gonfalonier of the Church in place of Alfonso d'Este. Gonzaga's ten-year-old son Federico was sent to Rome to be kept by the Pope as hostage for his father's good behaviour. On 26 July, Lucrezia sent Bernardino di Prosperi to Francesco with an emotional letter in her own hand congratulating him on his 'most desired liberation' and thanking him for the message he had sent to her via Padre Francesco. It was also a plea for help: 'I pray the Lord God preserve Your Lordship for many years and that he will place his holy hand in these tribulations of ours and yours for which truly I have no less at heart than my own. And I pray Your Lordship with all my heart that in every matter which may help this state you will be pleased to do as I trust in you . . .'[5]

The war was to last until Julius's death in January 1513, only to be taken up again by his successor Leo X, the former Cardinal de'Medici. During these years Lucrezia, Alfonso and their family endured conditions of extreme danger, worse than any they had ever known. As the papal troops moved northwards through Ferrarese territory in the summer of 1510, on 9 August the Pope delivered the crushing blow of an interdict: Alfonso was excommunicated and deprived of the Duchy of Ferrara. Sanudo reported:

Today in consistory was read out the Bull depriving the Duke of Ferrara of all he has of the Holy Church, that is Ferrara, Comacchio and those things he has in Romagna, and Reggio which the house of Este was invested with by Pope Pius II; and similarly the Duke is excommunicated and anyone who gave him help or favour will be equally deprived. It is a most long Bull and tomorrow will be published in Bologna and printed. And there is a report that . . . France will abandon the Duke of Ferrara, and will not lend him any help, saying they do not wish to mix in the affairs of Ferrara, this being immediately in all things subject to the Holy See.[6]

On 19 August, the diarist noted the message from the Venetian envoy at Rome that Venice was to support the Pope in his enterprises against Ferrara and Genoa, and send a fleet to the Po with the announcement that anyone who wished to should go to damage the Duke of Ferrara.[7]

In this desperate situation, Lucrezia appealed to Francesco for help. On 12 August she sent Lorenzo Strozzi to him with private messages on her behalf. On 22 August she besought Francesco to order his officials to accept for safe keeping the herds and possessions at Hostia of her people of Mellara endangered by the taking of the Polesine di Rovigo by the Venetians and the recent interdict placed on Ferrara by the Pope. 'I would not know how nor would I be able to deny them any of their just petition, particularly of this kind in this case,' she wrote. 'I pray Your Lordship for love of me to signify to your officials that they should accept the livestock and possessions of my subjects for their security . . .'[8]

In mid August Sanudo reported that Alfonso had sent forty artillery pieces to Parma and that Lucrezia had asked Venice for a safe conduct for herself, her children and her possessions to go there, but that Venice did not want to grant it to her without licence from the Pope.[9] On 21 August there was panic in Ferrara;

Sanudo wrote that Lucrezia had her carriages ready to leave with her children for Milan but that the citizens rose up saying that if she left they would also flee the city, so she stayed. That very day, alone in charge at Ferrara since Alfonso was away in camp and Ippolito also, Lucrezia, despite Sanudo's report of panic, kept her head, informing Alfonso of all she was doing to help, including sending a spy to Venice to find out whether the Venetians were arming forces and, if so, of what kind. She also reminded him, among his many other preoccupations, 'of that affair of the Marchese [Gonzaga] about which you spoke to me before you left'. It can hardly be a coincidence that that same day she had Strozzi write a letter to Gonzaga conveying her feelings towards him: '. . . the love, faith and trust she has in Your Lordship is of such an order that she has more hope in Your Lordship than in any other person in the world, and with all her heart she begs you not to abandon her in these times, and to demonstrate effectively the fraternal love that Your Lordship bears her.' And as if that were not enough, Strozzi added a verbatim report of what she had told him: 'The Duchess said to me: "Lorenzo, if it were not for the hope that I have in the Lord Marchese that in my every need he will aid and protect me, I would die of grief . . ."'[10] There was a certain practicality behind these effusions: beyond the military and diplomatic capabilities of her husband and brother-in-law, maintaining her hold on Francesco's affections was the most effective form of insurance for Ferrara, which Gonzaga, as Julius's commander, was now pledged to attack. As we have seen, there was mutual dislike between the Este men and Gonzaga, a feeling which, as far as Francesco was concerned, now extended to his own wife. In view of the discussion about Francesco which Lucrezia says she had with Alfonso before he left, it seems likely that they agreed that she should act as a conduit between them – as to just how friendly, however, Alfonso was no doubt left in ignorance.

The twenty-first of August seems to have been a key day. Quite apart from the two letters she wrote to Alfonso and the one to Gonzaga, she wrote a third enclosing a letter containing important

news which she had received from one Abraham Thus, a Jewish
contact in Parma. The Este were known as protectors of the Jews.
During the fifteenth century the Jewish population of Ferrara had
developed rapidly: they were allowed autonomy as a community
and permitted to live wherever they wished in the city – although
in practice they mostly lived together in certain streets in an area
known as 'La Zuecca'. They were neither 'ghettoized' nor walled
off from the Christian inhabitants. Their activities were not confined
to money-lending: they were active as retailers, manufacturers and
tradesmen. They were exempt from the extra taxes demanded by
the papal legates but in 1505, confirming their privileges, Alfonso
had declared that they should share the – by now – heavy burden
of tax borne by the rest of the community. The Jewish population
had rapidly expanded after the expulsion of the Jews from Spain
and Portugal under Ferdinand and Isabella: on 20 November 1492
the fugitive Sephardim received their passports from Ercole and
on 1 February 1493 an agreement was made by which they shared
all the privileges of the established community: they were permitted to follow any trade, farm taxes, act as apothecaries and practise medicine among Christians. By the end of the century there
were some five thousand Jews in Ferrara and the community by
now included the sophisticated new arrivals with their international contacts in the silk and wool industries and in imports such
as pearls from India. The Spanish and Portuguese Jews in particular brought with them their superior artisan skills in gold and silver-
work and embroidery. Jews both professing and converted were
welcomed at court; as we have seen, one of Lucrezia's damsels, La
Violante, was Jewish, and Alfonso frequently played cards with a
Jewish friend. The Este protected the Jews against the Church and
secured their loyalty. Lucrezia herself wrote to Gonzaga on one
occasion to obtain justice for the heirs of 'the former Habraham
jew of Bresello' whose goods David the moneylender in Brescello
was threatening to sell: 'We have answered that we will inform
ourself of the details of this and what commission exists: and we
will not permit that any injustice be done to these heirs . . .'[11] In
return the Jewish community gave the Este their loyalty, particu-

larly when Ferrara was threatened by the Pope as Lucrezia's letter from Abraham Thus demonstrated.

On arrival at Parma, Thus wrote, 'At this hour I arrived here in Parma when I found that Modena was taken and it seemed to me that I could not send a letter by the Captain of Reggio, nor come myself which was my intention, but Messer Alfonso Ariosto finding himself here on the point of departure, it now seemed to me [best] to send a most satisfactory formal letter which I have obtained from the Gran Maestro [Jacques de Chabannes, seigneur de Lapalisse].' The Gran Maestro had told him personally that the affairs of the Bentivoglio were at present on hold pending a decision by the King of France which was expected imminently, and that he would do anything he could in the interest of the King of France and Lucrezia. However, he had not been able to provide troops for Modena for Signor Galeazzo (da Sanseverino, Master of the King's Horse) because he had to go towards Savoy to prevent the passage of the Pope's Swiss mercenaries. But he had also told Thus that if the Duke of Ferrara was in need of money he would see to it that the treasurer of the King of France would lend him it against pledges. He had heard the day before from Signor Galeazzo that the Duke had already sent to the Gran Maestro to this effect. 'This loss [of Modena] grieves me to my soul,' Thus wrote. 'However I pray Your Ladyship to bear this with your usual spirit because thus it will cause you less anxiety and thus God will provide: the Gran Maestro recognizes of what great moment is the State of Your Ladyship to the affairs of the King of France, and openly said to me that His Majesty would not fail [you] and that having heard of this case [of the need for money] he would make greater efforts to do that which was asked of him, recognizing [your] extreme need.'

He had spoken to Signor Galeazzo in Parma who would do everything he could for the service of the Duke and Duchess of Ferrara.

And speaking together of Your Ladyship's predicament we touched on the question of your Ladyship's sons, and to get them out of Ferrara should anything occur. I told him that perhaps Your Ladyship was minded when it was necessary to send them that they should go to him rather than any other living being. He answered that if Your Ladyship did this it would give him the greatest pleasure in the world. I thought to advise Your Ladyship of this in any case. I will not come to Your Ladyship as I had decided, for fear that these letters might fall into the hands of the enemy. And I will stay here three or four days to see what is happening. If Your Ladyship needs anything of me, know that I am most ready in every place, at any time, and in every [twist of] fortune. Signor Galeazzo is making every effort that Reggio should not be lost . . . he is waiting only on the answer of the Gran Maestro . . . He has pledged his treasure and friends to any need of Your Ladyship as soon as he is advised of it by you . . . M. de la Palisse is ill in Milan and recommends himself to Your Ladyship.[12]

In a letter of 22 August, Lucrezia wrote to Alfonso about Gonzaga again, concerned that the utmost pressure should be exerted on him to keep him from attacking the Este: 'Your Lordship writes that I must remind him about the affair of the Marchese [Gonzaga] which I spoke to you about. I tell you that it is to write to the Gran Maestro that he should write formally to the Marchese, even if it should come to pretexts and threats, that he should not attempt anything to damage Your Lordship nor molest you in any way.' She had received Alfonso's instructions about their son Ercole and was pleased with them, as the child was still a little indisposed. She meant to wait till he was cured and then choose twenty-five people to accompany him, headed, as Alfonso suggested, by a person of distinction at court. She would prefer M. Hercule da Camerino but he must choose as he thought most suitable. She retailed news of Count Guido Rangoni (whose family had intrigued with the papal legate to hand over Modena). 'It seems I should remind Your Lordship that it would be a good idea to remove the Capitano here of Castel Tealto as a precaution and if you do so give him some other position and I will provide someone to watch him closely.' Also she reminded him that he could send some infantry who had come from La Abbatia (where Rangoni now was) to Ferrara where they were doing nothing to Argenta.

By the next day, Ercole's state of health had deteriorated and Lucrezia thought he should not be subjected to the strain of travelling anywhere. She wanted Alfonso's opinion as to whether the young Ippolito should leave because it would be better that one of them were elsewhere before the ways were blocked. On the 24th she received good news from Alfonso, that help had arrived in the territories of Parma and Reggio. She had had his letter read out to the leading gentlemen of the city, which had greatly encouraged them, and had seen to it that the news was spread throughout the city. She acknowledged his information about enemy forces commanded by Gonzaga without comment. There was a report that some two hundred men had come from Bologna to attack the Torre del Fundo and burn the houses in San Martina, and that Masino del Forno had been ordered to put out spies. The next day Alfonso returned to Ferrara – 'because his eldest son is dying', Sanudo reported optimistically but incorrectly. Ercole made a complete recovery. It is worth noting that in not one of her letters written on the dates when Sanudo reported Lucrezia as being about to leave is there any mention of her planning to do so, only that her sons should escape while they still could, to avoid being taken hostage.

The Este were not about to be chased from their lands by the Pope as easily as the Baglioni from Perugia and the Bentivoglio from Bologna. Alfonso and Ippolito were strong and determined, expert in the arts of warfare and the use of artillery, while at Mantua Isabella, 'Machiavelli in skirts' as Luzio dubbed her, schemed and charmed to preserve her brothers' state. Unlike the Pope's previous victims, the Este family was popular in Ferrara, and when Ippolito called a meeting of the leading Ferrarese, they swore to defend the dynasty to the end. From the papal point of view, his Captain General Gonzaga was of dubious loyalty; he could hardly be expected wholeheartedly to push for the destruction of his brother-in-law's, or rather his sister-in-law's, state.

Julius II, who appears sincerely to have detested Alfonso, made every effort to stir up trouble between the brothers-in-law. He intimated that the Este had tried to keep Francesco as prisoner of the Venetians for as long as they could and that he had the evidence for it, showing 'villainous deeds' (*cose nephande*) relating to the process he had instituted against Masino del Forno who had fallen into his hands. The Pope had been delighted to hear of del Forno's capture by the Venetians, who handed him over in Bologna. Reacting very much as he had to the arrest of Cesare's Michelotto, Julius, Sanudo reported, 'wanted him because he is the confidant and minister of the betrayals and assassinations of the Cardinal [of] Ferrara'.[13] As the Archdeacon of Gabbioneta wrote to Gonzaga on 26 September 1510, the Pope wished to communicate to him things of capital importance but had expressly forbidden him under pain of excommunication to commit them to paper: 'then he said to me: I want to tell the Lord Marchese what those brothers-in-law of his wanted to do to him . . .'[14]

As a counterweight to Isabella, the Pope had cunningly instituted Francesco's scurrilous friend and procurer, Isabella's hated enemy, Lodovico 'Vigo' di Camposampiero, as his liaison officer with Gonzaga. He had presided over the attempted building of a bridge of boats across the Po at the frontier fortress of Sermide in Mantuan territory, and been frustrated by Alfonso's destruction of the bridge and confiscation of the boats which he took to Ferrara, to Francesco's rage. On 10 September, Lucrezia wrote, from her newly-founded convent of San Bernardino, an extraordinary, even piteous appeal to Isabella to intervene in yet another quarrel between Gonzaga and Alfonso, addressing her as 'My Most Illustrious Madam and as my Mother'

Your Excellency understands well enough in what great perils and difficulties is the State of your lord brothers, and particularly that which has come between the Lord Marchese and the Duke our consort, concerning those ships which were taken in Mantuan territory: and although it was not done to injure His Lordship, we have heard that His Excellency is very aggrieved by it. For this, with every instance and confidence I pray Your Excellency to be a good intermediary between Your Illustrious consort and mine, and that you hold as recommended to you the State of your lord brothers and together with them myself and my children . . .

She signed herself 'Your Most Beloved Daughter, Duchess of Ferrara'. Normally, she addressed Isabella as 'Illustrious lady my honoured sister-in law and sister' and signed herself 'Sister and sister-in-law, Lucretia, Duchess of Ferrara'.[15] That same month writing to thank Isabella for her present of twenty *cedri* and eighty *pomeranzi* (oranges) she found it necessary to add a postscript asking Isabella to intercede with Francesco to restrain some people who were intent on injuring the Duke's interests, and hoping that he would 'proceed wisely'.

Over the autumn and winter of 1510 the danger to Ferrara increased as the Pope himself came north to Bologna with the intention of gingering up his reluctant general, Gonzaga, who complained, as usual, of ill health as an excuse for inaction. In November he reported that he was being treated with mercury for his syphilis, an excuse with which the Pope, another sufferer, could sympathize. Caught between the support of the French (with whom he was in frequent contact) for Alfonso and the Pope's furious intent to take Ferrara, Gonzaga was indeed in an unenviable position. At Ferrara Alfonso, now backed by the French, was feverishly strengthening its fortifications – both men and women were reported to be working on a bastion in the lower part of the city which necessitated the demolition of several houses. Julius was 'beside himself because he believed he was soon going to have Ferrara,' Sanudo wrote. 'He threatens to sack Ferrara and lay it waste since it won't surrender and he would sooner see Ferrara ruined than it should fall into the hands of the French.'[16] Julius sent an envoy to Alfonso to demand the keys of the city. Alfonso, who was supervising the new fortifications in the Borgo di Sotto, took the envoy to see a gun called 'Devilchaser' (*Caza Diavoli*) and told him, 'These are the keys I would like to give the Pope.'

For Lucrezia and Alfonso the situation deteriorated through the winter: the papal troops, under Julius's nephew, Francesco Maria della Rovere, Duke of Urbino since Guidobaldo's death in 1508, had taken Modena. The Pope was ensconced in Bologna, although, fortunately for them, ill with a tertian fever and piles. In a bargain with Ferdinand of Spain in exchange for the Bull of Investiture for the Kingdom of Naples, however, he had negotiated for three hundred Spanish men-at-arms under the command of Fabrizio Colonna for the campaign against Ferrara. The French under Chaumont, who had advanced with the intention of reinstalling the Bentivoglio in Bologna, had retreated under the influence of indecision and bad weather. Sassuolo, Angela Borgia's town, fell in mid November, followed in mid December by Concordia, belonging to another Este ally, the Pico della Mirandola.

Worst of all was the news that the ferocious old pope had recovered his health and his energy. Despite the fierce cold and with snow on the ground he had himself carried on a litter to the siege of Mirandola, where Lodovico Pico's widow, Francesca, held out. As Francesco Guicciardini wrote, men marvelled that 'the supreme pontiff, the vicar of Christ on earth, old and ill . . . should have come in person to a war waged by him against Christians, encamped by an unimportant town where, subjecting himself like the captain of an army to fatigue and dangers, he retained nothing of the pope about him but the robes and the name'. Julius, convinced that he was being cheated by his commanders, including his nephew Francesco Maria della Rovere, who spent his time gaming with Fabrizio Colonna, roundly cursed his men in language so fruity that the Venetian envoy could not bring himself to repeat the exact words, even to his brother. On 19 January the Countess Francesca surrendered Mirandola to the Pope, but probably due to the deliberate dilatoriness of the papal commanders, nothing further was attempted against Ferrara for the moment. Ferrara by then was bristling with French troops, to such an extent that di Prosperi wrote that the Ferrarese were heartily sick of 'these French' and wished they would take themselves off somewhere else. Alfonso, however, was glad of their support and rode out with his artillery in late February to take La Bastia, an important fortification on the Po, where he obtained a significant victory. Alfonso was now regarded as a hero: di Prosperi proudly told Isabella how those present at La Bastia had said the victory was 'all his and that he was a man of such spirit and great prowess such as had never been seen the like'.

The Pope's explosions of rage against Ferrara – he told di Camposampiero: 'I want Ferrara and I will die like a dog rather than give up' – had alarmed Francesco, who feared for Lucrezia's safety. On 21 February he had written to the Archdeacon of Gabbioneta asking him to intercede with the Pope for the greatest clemency for Lucrezia, and for himself the assurance that she would be safe 'because the loving and faithful terms which only she used towards me in the time when I was in prison in Venice and so many connections that we had places an obligation on me now to show her my gratitude, and if the providence of His Holiness does not help us I do not know what will become of this poor woman who alone demonstrated such compassion for me'.[17]

Meanwhile, in Ferrara Lucrezia showed no signs of fear: although the normal carnival celebrations were suspended, she gave private parties for the French captains all through March. Led by the gallant Gaston de Foix, they greatly appreciated the oasis of gaiety and civilization which she created for them amid the devastation of war beyond the walls. The famous Chevalier Bayard, praising her linguistic gifts, left a record of the impression she made on him and his fellow Frenchmen: 'The good Duchess received the French before all the others with every mark of favour. She is a pearl in this world. She daily gave the most wonderful festivals and banquets in the Italian fashion. I venture to say that neither in her time nor for many years before this has there been such a glorious princess, for she is beautiful and good, gentle and amiable to everyone, and nothing is more certain than this, that, although her husband is a skilful and brave prince, the above-named lady, by her graciousness, has been of great service to him.'[18]

Lucrezia continued to play the gracious hostess to the French through the spring. Di Prosperi became more and more disapproving as he considered the times unsuited to dancing, given the devastation of the countryside. The chief goldsmith in Ferrara, he told Isabella, could not complete her order because he had too much to do for the Duchess. Lucrezia and Alfonso, however, knew only too well how important it was to keep the French happy and, if possible, in Ferrara. Among the constant excursions and alarums, however, things were not going well for the Pope. On 22 May news reached Ferrara that the Bentivoglio had returned to Bologna with the accord of the citizens; shortly afterwards the papal legate, Cardinal Alidosi, friend and protégé of Julius, was stabbed to death by Francesco Maria della Rovere. There were great celebrations at court: Alfonso gave a supper in the garden for the gentlemen of Ferrara while Lucrezia was visited and made much of by the nobility and ladies of the city. The Bolognese pulled down Michelangelo's bronze statue of Julius which had adorned the cathedral and donated it to Alfonso: he kept the head for his collection and melted down the body for a cannon which he named 'La Giulia'. The Ferrarese rejoiced in the streets and Lucrezia gave more parties in honour of de Foix and the French captains. Visiting her, di Prosperi found her 'very richly dressed and more magnificent than I have seen her for a long time'.

That same April, Francesco Gonzaga told Lorenzo Strozzi that he was eager that Lucrezia should come to Mantua as 'a relief from her present worries and travails and take some pleasure with him', assuring her that he was 'urgently hastening the completion of some new rooms in our palace of S. Sebastiano which we have established for her lodging'.[19]

In truth Lucrezia seems to have been worn out by all the festivities; on 16 June, di Prosperi reported that she had been ill and was convalescing. Four days later she decided to go to her convent of San Bernardino which she seems to have treated as if it were a health farm: 'she will stay there until she is purged and has taken the waters and dieted'. She would be there some time, he said. On the same day, Lucrezia wrote a note to Francesco in her own hand, her writing blotched and untidy: 'Finding myself weak from my sickness I will not write at length and also because truly it would be impossible to find words to express how yet again I feel myself obliged to Your Lordship for the favour he deigns to do me; with this letter I kiss your hand an infinity of times, leaving the rest to padre Fra Anselmo and the bearer of this, begging Your Lordship that if you know of anything in which I can serve you you will deign to command me.' Laura Bentivoglio Gonzaga, wife of Francesco's brother Giovanni, visited her there after she had purged herself and was about to take the waters. She found her on a bed dressed in light black silk with tight sleeves gathered at the wrist, a large turban-cap on her head covering her ears. They chatted about fashion, Lucrezia questioning Laura closely about the latest things in Mantua, asking her to send her some caps like the one she was wearing and wanting to copy her head ornament.[20] On 3 July, Lucrezia was still in San Bernardino: Alfonso visited her there but, because it was an enclosed convent, he was barred from entering and could only talk to her 'through the wheel'.

Lucrezia's health did not improve for all the treatments she subjected herself to in San Bernardino. The Queen of France had expressed a great desire to see her, having heard so much about her from the French captains, and there was a definite plan for her to leave for the French court. Bernardino di Prosperi reported on 5 July that the Queen had sent an envoy to invite Lucrezia with her eldest son to visit her at Grenoble. Ippolito was already at the French court and well received by the King and Queen who had, however, taken exception to the beards which he and his entourage had grown in fulfilment of a vow, and made them shave. On 20 July the journey was still on: Francesco had sent Lucrezia the gift of a mule and cob for which she thanked him in a handwritten note that day, adding the proviso that if she did not go, she would send them back to him. On the 29th in another emotional handwritten letter she told him that Alfonso had decided against her going 'because of this indisposition of mine'

and that she was sending the animals back to him via Count
Melina, who would give him personal messages from her.
Lucrezia's illness had proved difficult to shake off – on 12 August
she was back in San Bernardino '*incognita*', as di Prosperi described
it. It may have been that she had again been pregnant, since he
uses the verb *spazar*, which can be used to describe miscarriage
– Sister Laura had told him, he said, 'how she would "*spazar*"
that thing' if she continued.

Early in September Lucrezia departed for Reggio with a cavalcade of thirty horse, leaving her children behind in Ferrara. Later
she sent for them but Alfonso, possibly for fear of their being
captured, wanted them to remain in Ferrara, even though he
himself was spending most of the time in Ostellato. From Reggio,
Lucrezia continued to send Gonzaga affectionate messages. She
had hoped, she told him in November, to visit him on her way
back to Ferrara, but nothing came of it. Both she and Ippolito
were back in Ferrara by the end of November.

The war dragged on, prosecuted with unfailing energy by the
indomitable old pope who now put together another League,
this time with Ferdinand of Spain, Venice and the distant partici-
pation of Henry VIII, King of England, for the recovery of
Bologna and all other lands of the Church occupied by others
(i.e. Alfonso and the French). Spanish troops from Naples arrived
under Ramón Cardona. La Bastia was lost again and only the
presence of Alfonso with his troops and French lances in Ferrara
prevented the Spaniards from advancing on Ferrara. Alfonso came
and went with his troops and on 12 January brought the French
captains back for a festivity given by Lucrezia. Two days later he
was back before La Bastia which he succeeded in retaking and
in the process nearly lost his life, being struck on the forehead
by the ricochetting of a large piece of stone. Lucrezia's doctor,
Lodovico Bonaccioli, and another were sent to him and found
him in remarkably good spirits although he had bled from the
nose and mouth. He returned secretly to Ferrara in order not to
alarm the people and lodged in Lucrezia's rooms in the Castello
where a medical conference was being held. It was discovered

that no damage had been done to the bone beneath the wound, despite his having been struck with great force by the corner of a piece of masonry. Alfonso was lucky: in the bloody taking of the fortress 180 Spaniards and eighty Italians were killed, including three unfortunate Ferrarese prisoners. He was forced merely to wear a bandage round his head for several days and, in order not to embarrass their lord, obsequious courtiers followed suit.

The French returned to Ferrara from time to time throughout February and March for rest and recreation: this included jousting, duelling, feasting and then dancing in Lucrezia's rooms. For many of them it would be their last dance. On 11 April 1512, Easter Day, one of the bloodiest battles of the Italian wars took place outside the walls of Ravenna. It was a crushing defeat for the papal and Spanish forces in which Alfonso's artillery deployment was the determining factor. Ten thousand men were estimated to have been killed, among them the flower of the French army, notably the brilliant young Gaston de Foix, and Cesare's old companion-in-arms, Yves d'Alègre, and his twenty-eight-year-old son. Among the prisoners captured were Fabrizio Colonna and the papal legate, Cardinal de' Medici, the future Pope Leo X, whom Alfonso took back with him to Ferrara.

There he made a triumphal entry; the populace streamed out to greet him, on horseback and on foot, the children with bunches of flowers in their hands. The noise of tabors, bells and gunfire was such, di Prosperi exclaimed, that 'it seemed as if the city would fall down'. Riding into the piazza he dismounted at the cathedral to give thanks to St George, then rode to the Castello where Lucrezia was waiting for him on the Revelino. With him came the wounded and the dead, a piteous sight.[21] While the body of de Foix was borne back to France via Bologna, the wounded continued to arrive in the city over the following days. Among the prisoners was Fabrizio Colonna, under guard. It was reported from Ravenna, which had been given over to be sacked, that only Alfonso's prompt action in hanging a number of Gascons saved the women who had taken refuge in the churches, and the nuns in the convents, from rape.

In Ferrara the chief Italian prisoners were treated as guests: Fabrizio Colonna was permitted to go wherever he wished, accompanied only by el Modenese del Forno, captain of the light horse, and Messer Rainaldo Ariosto. The Cardinal de'Medici was taken hawking in the Barco. It was rumoured that he had been heard to say he thanked God for three things: first, for having done his duty and not taken flight like the Viceroy (Cardona) and the other Spaniards; second, for being alive; and third, for having fallen into the hands of the Duke of Ferrara, who had welcomed him and treated him not as a prisoner but like a father. Within less than two years, however, the future Leo X would forget his debt of gratitude to the Duke of Ferrara.

Lucrezia had continued to correspond with Francesco Gonzaga despite their being officially on opposing sides in this war. Strozzi seems to have faded from the picture as intermediary, to be replaced by Count Melina, with whom she had sent a hand-written note in January, 'to remind Your Lordship that you have in me a most obedient sister, desirous of your good and happiness as much as if it were her own health: may it please God to liberate us from these difficulties so that you can visit here presently as I desire beyond anything to see Your Lordship'.[22] A few weeks later she wrote again in her own hand via Count Melina, thanking Francesco for the letter he had written her despite his illness: 'May it please God to give you the grace to recover your health soon and be as well as I do desire.' Since Melina, now obviously in their confidence, was the bearer of her letter, she would say no more but leave it to him to deliver her messages. In March she asked him to help Angela Borgia by sending her letters on to the French ambassador at the imperial court and, if not, to recommend 'this business of Sassuolo' to the Cardinal-Bishop of Gurk (Matthaus Lang, the Emperor's favourite minister). She returned to the charge on behalf of her beloved Angela in May, asking him to forward letters from Cardinal Sanseverino to the Emperor and to Gurk, in favour of the 'business of Sassuolo', with one she herself had written to Casola, the Mantuan envoy at the imperial court: 'Because these letters are

important, I pray Your Excellency that you will for love of me
once more take up the task of seeing that they safely reach Casola
. . .' There were the usual requests for favours from him, for the
liberation of prisoners, for the cause of one of her singers, 'Nicolo
cantor', for the capture of certain prisoners requested by the
Capitano of Reggio, etc. For favours on Alfonso's side, di Prosperi
would address himself to Isabella 'for fear of causing trouble
between the signor Marchese and the Lord Duke . . .'

The battle of Ravenna saved Ferrara, but only for the time
being. It had been a pyrrhic victory for the French, who were
demoralized by the loss of some of their principal commanders,
notably the brilliant de Foix. They were forced to return to defend
their country against the King of Spain, who attacked through
Navarre, and the King of England in Guyenne. The time had
come for Alfonso, if he could, to make peace with the Pope and
save his state. But in Rome Julius II flew into a rage at the very
mention of Alfonso's name. He had been deeply offended since
he had heard of the fate of his statue in Bologna. Francesco
Gonzaga attempted to divert his attention from Ferrara by writing to di Camposampiero to persuade the Pope that he could
consider Ferrara as already his and his primary objective should
be to chase the French out of Italy.[23]

Under persuasion from the Gonzaga and their emissaries,
including the young hostage, their twelve-year-old son, Federico,
of whom Julius was extremely fond, the Pope agreed to send a
safe conduct, dated 11 June, for Alfonso to go to Rome and make
his submission. His safety was also guaranteed by his former prisoner, Fabrizio Colonna, who was to accompany him to Rome,
and by the Spanish ambassador. Julius was so delighted to hear
from Francesco Gonzaga that Alfonso would be coming to Rome
that he leapt out of bed shoeless and, wearing only his shirt,
capered triumphantly round his rooms, crying 'Julius' and 'the
Church' and singing out loud. Alfonso arrived in Rome on 4
July with a small company; Julius sent Federico Gonzaga out to
greet him and he entered the city supported by the principal
Roman aristocracy represented by Fabrizio Colonna and

Giangiordano Orsini. The Pope had offered him lodging in the Vatican, but the wary Alfonso preferred to stay in Cardinal d'Aragona's Palazzo San Clemente. On 9 July, Alfonso's formal absolution took place in the Vatican where the Pope had prepared what Isabella's friend and admirer, the humanist writer Mario Equicola, who accompanied him, described to Isabella as 'a sumptuous collation with all kinds of fruits . . . stunning confections [probably sugar statues], many various wines and fine music performed on viols'. In consistory, Alfonso kissed the Pope's foot and was embraced by him but mutual suspicion remained, fomented by Alfonso's enemies at court, Alberto Pio da Carpi, now imperial envoy, and Alfonso's treacherous cousin, Niccolò di Rinaldo d'Este (executed three years later at Ferrara for plotting against Alfonso), dripping poison in the Pope's ears. The Pope wanted Alfonso to release his brothers, particularly Ferrante who had recently smuggled a letter to him pleading for his help, and he wanted Ferrara. These conditions were completely unacceptable to Alfonso and, fearing a trap, he fled Rome on 19 July with Fabrizio Colonna, the pair forcing their way through the Porta San Giovanni and riding to Colonna's stronghold at Marino.

Lucrezia and Ippolito received letters, presumably containing the bad news, from Fabrizio Colonna on 21 July, although it was not generally divulged until early August. It would be three months before Alfonso, guarded by the Colonna, reached Ferrara after a tortuous journey northwards, dodging spies on the lookout for him. The Pope remained obsessed by Ferrara, and at a second meeting in Mantua of the 'Most Holy League' three decisions were taken – for the restoration of the Medici to Florence whence they had been expelled by the French; the restoration of Ludovico Sforza's son, Massimiliano, to Milan; and the conquest of Ferrara. While Francesco Gonzaga, pleading illness once again, withdrew from the discussions, Isabella played hostess, avid for information which might have a bearing on Ferrara and fruitlessly trying to divert the participants' attention elsewhere. The conference ended on 16 August and on the 17th she warned Ippolito that, although the participants could not agree as to who should be the first target for conquest, the much-feared Swiss mercenaries of the Pope were on the move towards Ferrara. Lucrezia, who had been ill for much of the summer, in the absence of Alfonso issued orders for the defence of the city. Artillery was taken out of the Castello and transferred to the bastions and ramparts. On 12 August she had received advice from Alfonso, as she wrote to Isabella, that at all costs the Este heir, Ercole, should be sent to safety to prevent his falling into the Pope's hands as a hostage for his father: 'I will be brief because the bearer of this letter will let you know in full what the decision of my lord and myself is concerning our son whom it is unnecessary to recommend to you. Only I beg you that in everything you can concerning this you will do as I have faith you will, for which I will be perpetually obliged to you . . .' To curry favour with the Marchioness, she congratulated Isabella on the 'fine court' she was holding for the meetings at Mantua.[24] On the same day she wrote an anguished letter to Francesco, passing on Alfonso's instructions by messenger and pleading with him not to fail Alfonso and herself and to help save Alfonso from the Pope. By the end of the month, she was writing to him of their 'extreme need' of men-at-arms. Even the Pope, having intercepted a similar letter from her, felt sorry for her and spoke 'very kindly and compassionately' of her.[25] Nonetheless, she had changed her mind about keeping Ercole with her. It was just as well.

15. Lucrezia Triumphant

'She shall ever grow in beauty, merit, fortune and good repute,
just like a tender plant in soft earth . . .'

– Ludovico Ariosto in praise of Lucrezia in
Orlando Furioso, Canto 13, line 69, 1516

That year of 1512 Alfonso and Lucrezia ordered three engraved silver votive plaques to thank the patron saint of Ferrara, San Maurelio, for the saving of the city after the battle of Ravenna. One of them is the only representation we have of Lucrezia with her son, the future Ercole II. It shows Lucrezia at the age of thirty-two, in profile, with her blonde hair bound with a jewelled diadem across her forehead, drawn back over her ears and held by a jewelled net, ending in a plait down her back. She is dressed in the height of contemporary fashion in a high-waisted dress, richly embroidered, with huge sleeves and a frilled *gorgiere* covering the top part of her breast. Draped over her right wrist is the latest fashion accessory, a small pelt of sable or ermine; with her left hand she holds little Ercole, aged five, presenting him to the saint who places his hand in blessing on the future Duke's bare head. She is attended by five extremely pretty women in dresses similar to her own but less richly patterned; three of them have the same bound-back hairstyles as Lucrezia, the other two have elaborately curled, shoulder-length hair; at least one of them is carrying a sable pelt. Another plaque shows Alfonso equipped for war, in armour kneeling before the saint, bearded and with wavy, shoulder-length hair, his helmet on the ground, and behind him his courser in rich harness, and two *staffieri*; one of them poses seductively in skin-tight doublet and hose, with an arm draped languidly over the horse's neck. The third depicts the prior of the Olivetan monastery of San Giorgio, Girolamo Bendedeo, guardian of the cult of San Maurelio, kneeling before the saint; in the background the towers and ramparts of Ferrara overlook the confluence of the Po di Volano and the Po di Primaro, where the citizens of Ferrara are going about their business on the river bank.[1]

It is particularly poignant to see Lucrezia as a mother at that time since, towards the end of August, while Alfonso was still at Marino on his way back from Rome, she received yet another personal blow: the death through illness at Bari of her eldest son, Rodrigo Bisceglie. He was twelve years old. She had not seen him since she had left Rome when he was two. Prostrate with grief, she fled to the convent of San Bernardino, remaining there the whole of September, unable to bring herself to write to anyone. When she did so, on 1 October, she wrote of 'finding myself completely overcome with tears and bitterness for the death of the Duke of Bisceglie, my most dear son . . .'

The tears were understandable, the bitterness too. Separation from Rodrigo had been an unwritten part of the deal which had taken her to Ferrara with the appearance of a virgin bride – '*pulcherrima virgo*', in the words of Ariosto. Reasons of state had decreed that she had not seen her eldest son since her departure from Rome to marry Alfonso.

There is evidence of some kind of agreement between the Este and the Borgias over Rodrigo in a document of 11 October 1505 in the Modena archives which describes not only Cardinal Cosenza as his guardian but Ippolito d'Este as one of his co-guardians.[2] He was brought up at the court of Isabella d'Aragona in Bari where she lived as Duchess in the city granted her by Ludovico il Moro. He was there in March 1505 when an entry in Lucrezia's wardrobe accounts mentions a doublet of damask and brocade which Lucrezia had had made and sent to Bari for him.[3] He appears to have shared a tutor named Baldassare Bonfiglio with Giovanni Borgia at Bari, but while Giovanni Borgia was allowed to come to Ferrara in 1506 and probably placed at the Pio estate at Carpi with Cesare's son, Girolamo, Rodrigo did not accompany him. That year, 1506, Lucrezia had apparently made plans to meet him with Duchess Isabella at the shrine of Loreto, but the meeting never took place. According to Gregorovius, both boys were in Bari in April 1508, sharing a tutor, Bartolommeo Grotto; Lucrezia had clothes made for them and paid for the tutor to buy a copy of Virgil for Giovanni.

Rodrigo Bisceglie had lived in some state at Bari: he received rents from his estates in Bisceglie and the Duchy of Corato. In February 1511, Duchess Isabella spent 100 ducats on a horse and harness for him.[4] An inventory of his goods taken after his death, presumably on Lucrezia's instructions, shows him finely equipped as befitted his rank as a young duke, albeit a minor one. There were quantities of rich clothes, belts and purses of gold, furnishings such as table carpets and carriage covers, trappings of velvet fringed with gold for coursers and mules, bed hangings and coverings and a commode – '*sedia a necessario*' – covered in red cloth with a copper vase, arms and armour including daggers in fine Spanish and German metalwork, and spurs and breastplates. His silver tableware included a fine salt gilded inside and out in the Spanish manner, silver gilt plates, dishes and ewers engraved with his arms.[5] His accounts were carefully preserved among Lucrezia's documents, and in the years following his death she succeeded in establishing herself as his heir although she was to discover that, as with so many noble families, the richness of the appanages belied the poverty of the income. On 9 October 1512 she wrote to Gonzaga asking him for a safe conduct for Jacopo de Tebaldi, the ducal chancellor, whom she was sending via Venice to Bari to deal with Duchess Isabella over Rodrigo's affairs: 'so that I should have those things which duly should come to me and because at present the journey there is not safe for any messenger of ours'. The recovery of Rodrigo's inheritance proved to be a protracted and tedious process and it was not until 1518 that it came to an end.

Di Prosperi reported to Isabella that Lucrezia was in such tribulation of spirit at the news of Rodrigo's death that there was no means of comforting her. Ippolito was on hand to console her on this occasion, as he had been on the deaths of Alexander and Cesare: as an ecclesiastic he was allowed inside the convent and, according to di Prosperi, spent many hours with her there. Alfonso was still making his tortuous way home, sending secret messages to Ippolito. When Isabella complained to Ippolito that he did not pass these messages on to her, the cardinal replied that he could not do so in case they were intercepted and Alfonso's whereabouts revealed to the Pope. Julius seized two of Alfonso's *staffieri* in the Marches and had them brought to Rome where he tortured them but they could tell him nothing. He kept up the pressure on the Gonzaga, sending a special representative to Mantua to promise Isabella great promotions for her children, including Ferrara for her son-in-law, Francesco Maria della Rovere, Duke of Urbino. He reminded Francesco that the Este had been the historical enemies of the Gonzaga, despite the present relationship, and Alfonso especially so, having always sought to do evil to the Marquis, to kill him and to mock him and hold him in little esteem, and that if he remained in Ferrara he would be the greatest enemy Gonzaga could have.[6] Against these intrigues, however, there was on the one hand, Isabella and Ippolito, standing shoulder to shoulder in the passionate defence of Ferrara, and on the other Francesco's devotion to Lucrezia.

Lucrezia and Francesco continued their correspondence through a new intermediary, Fra Anselmo. Gonzaga sent her *cedri* and truffles, she asked him for favours for her nuns. Gonzaga, for all his carnal sins, was, like Alexander, devout in his religious attachment to the Virgin Mary. On 2 November, Lucrezia wrote to him, asking that as he had been 'the most potent cause of comfort to my nuns and Mother Superior' to ensure that the Father Vicar General who had been in Mantua should enact what she had requested and create a new abbess before his return to Rome.

The lack of warmth between Lucrezia and Isabella continued, even over the death of Rodrigo Bisceglie. Isabella wrote to her crony, Sister Laura Boiarda, appointed by Lucrezia as abbess of the convent of San Bernardino, that she did not intend either to write in her own hand or send an envoy to condole with Lucrezia 'in case it renewed her grief', so she was entrusting Sister Laura to deal with it as she thought fit. Unsurprisingly, Lucrezia was offended at this breach of protocol, and complained to Fra Anselmo when he visited her on 7 October, saying that though his visit was a signal that Francesco still wished her well, 'nonetheless I feared that he had grown cold towards me . . . because it seemed to me that he had agreed with My Lady [Isabella] that none of them should be sent to visit me in this my sorrow of my son . . .' 'Believe me, My Lord, that this Lady is truly out of the ordinary,' the impressed friar reported to Francesco.[7] It was not until the end of the month that Isabella deigned to write an official letter of condolence which she entrusted to di Prosperi to deliver to San Bernardino. He, however, reported on 20 September that when he visited the convent that day Lucrezia had already left secretly, which he interpreted as a sign that Alfonso would soon be home. By the 9th, however, Lucrezia, dressed in mourning, had returned to San Bernardino and Alfonso did not arrive until the 14th.

Di Prosperi reported his triumphant arrival 'like Moses escaping from the Pharaoh', accompanied only by Masino del Forno and a few of his companions, having had a farewell supper with Fabrizio Colonna at Bondeno. He arrived 'in disguise and in a simple *burchiello*' (small boat) walked through the garden and entered the Castello: the entire populace crowded into the piazza to see him and the great bell of the fortress sounded. He went first to his *camerini* and then to Lucrezia's apartments to meet her in the 'second little room where they are used to dine in the winter'. There 'they embraced and caressed each other, remaining together for a little while and with their children, with happy countenances towards their gentlemen and everyone'.[8] Later, Alfonso went to talk to Ippolito and Federico Gonzaga da Bozzolo in his *camerini* for a long time, then to inspect the ramparts damaged by the recent floods. Afterwards he returned to spend a long time with Lucrezia in her rooms.

Alfonso was now a hero to the Ferrarese: 'Let [the Pope] do what he likes,' di Prosperi wrote to Isabella on 16 December 1512, 'because these people are more constant as time goes by and faithful to Your Illustrious House and to the Lord Duke your brother, and of this I am most certain . . .' Julius had succeeded in wresting from him all his lands apart from Argenta, Comacchio and Ferrara itself, but Alfonso was prepared to fight to the last, making a truce with the Venetians and signing up four thousand Italian and German troops. Francesco Gonzaga, however, now thought that Ferrara was finished and instructed his relation, Federico Gonzaga da Bozzolo, to abandon his efforts to help Alfonso or risk losing his state.

He also wanted Lucrezia safely at Mantua with him. On 22 December he wrote to the Archdeacon of Gabbioneta that he wanted favourable treatment for her: 'I want to be quite clear on one thing: if the Duchess of Ferrara, who has always in the past had great trust in me and towards whom as a woman I have great compassion and willingly would give her pleasure, if she would with confidence come here to our state without her husband and children, in what manner we are to behave to her without displeasing His Holiness . . .'9 Whether Lucrezia – let alone Alfonso – would have acquiesced in this plan we shall never know. She had not run away before when Ferrara had been in danger; it is more likely that Francesco's was the dream of a sick and lonely man. But the confidential correspondence continued: on 9 January 1513 she sent a private message by one of her gentlemen, Pietro Giorgio (?Lampugnano), with a covering note in her own hand. Francesco presumably sent private messages to her too, because on 4 February she wrote, again in her own hand, how glad she was to get good news of his convalescence from Messer Tolomeo (Spagnoli) and Lorenzo Strozzi who would have returned to him and would be able to tell him in person of her feelings towards him.10

Relations between Francesco and Isabella, however, had reached breaking point and they now led virtually separate lives, she in the ducal palace and he in his palace of San Sebastiano. According to Luzio they had not slept together since 1509 'for fear of the

pox'. Isabella had greatly enjoyed the independence and power
she had had while Francesco was imprisoned. While Francesco
was bound to the Pope by his military duties and, indeed, the
interests of his state, Isabella carried on diplomatic policy and
relations designed only to save her house of Este. Francesco had
his own clique hostile to her, which included his secretary,
Tolomeo Spagnoli, and, more distantly, the detested Vigo di
Camposampiero at Rome. Early in the new year of 1513, Isabella
left Mantua by mutual agreement 'for the sake of peace', as Luzio
put it, to spend carnival at Milan with her nephew, the recently
restored Duke Massimiliano Sforza, son of her sister Beatrice and
Ludovico il Moro. At Milan, she told Alfonso, she would be able
the better to use her influence with the Spanish Viceroy Ramón
Cardona, the imperial representative, the Cardinal-Bishop of
Gurk, and, of course, her nephew the Duke. On the eve of her
departure on 8 January, she wrote defiantly to Ippolito: 'the Pope
wants to have all the possessions of the house of Este in his power,
sooner may God ruin him and make him die as I hope it will
be . . .'

Isabella's wish was soon to be granted. On the night of 20–21
February 1513 Julius II died in the Vatican, just in time to save
Ferrara. He had made an agreement with the Emperor Maximilian
that the latter would not aid Alfonso d'Este, and, at the end of
January, Louis XII, Alfonso's principal protector, sent an envoy to
Rome to sue for peace. On 31 January, the Pope was reported
to be 'thinking of nothing else but the enterprise of Ferrara'
despite his illness. He was not too weak, however, to indulge in
one of his paroxysms of rage on hearing that certain cardinals
were giving a carnival banquet which he interpreted as an antici-
patory celebration of his death. Federico Gonzaga's tutor, Stazio
Gadio, reported him as being 'more terrible than ever' fulminat-
ing against 'that fleet of poltroons' and threatening that if they
took pleasure from his death 'he was not dead yet and he would
kill them all', particularly that 'beast', the Cardinal Agenensis,
promoter of the feast. It was to be his last rage: feeling himself
better he decided to indulge his passion for wine, tasting – or

rather drinking – no less than eight different varieties, with the result that that night he was overtaken by a fever from which he did not recover.

Patron of Michelangelo, Raphael and Bramante, Julius II had been a great pope in the temporal sense, the archetypal Renaissance pontiff along the lines of his hated predecessor, Alexander VI. The former Giuliano della Rovere had not been cut out for the spiritual life. As Guicciardini wrote, he would be considered a great pope by those who 'judge that it is more the office of the popes to increase with arms and the blood of Christians, the dominions of the Apostolic See than to labour, with the good example of their own lives and by correcting and caring for those fallen by the wayside, for the salvation of those souls, for which they boast that Christ appointed them his vicars on earth', adding that Julius would have been 'certainly worthy of great glory, if he had been a secular prince'.[11] Sanudo, writing from the Venetian point of view, did not see Julius as the patriot he is often made out to be. 'This pope,' he wrote, 'was the cause of Italy's ruin. Would to God he had died five years ago, for the good of Christianity, and of this republic and of poor Italy.' For all his xenophobic war cry 'Out with the barbarians! [i.e. foreigners]', he had done more than most to embroil the foreign powers in Italy in the ceaseless wars which were to bring about the ruin of Rome.

In Ferrara Lucrezia made no secret of her joy at the death of this 'Holofernes', as di Prosperi described him, the oldest and most virulent of her family's enemies who had destroyed Cesare and come near to destroying her too. While Alfonso discreetly celebrated at a dinner with his household, Lucrezia openly went about the town visiting a great number of churches to give thanks for their deliverance. For herself, her family and Ferrara it had been, as the Duke of Wellington said after the battle of Waterloo, 'a close-run thing'.

Julius II's successor was the cultivated, pleasure-loving, thirty-eight-year-old second son of Lorenzo the Magnificent, Cardinal Giovanni de'Medici, who took the name of Leo X. 'God has given us the papacy,' he told a friend. 'Let us enjoy it.' Alfonso and Lucrezia had high hopes of this new pope. But Leo, for all his pleasantness, was as avid for power and as ambitious for the advancement of his family as his father had been. He had never forgotten Lorenzo's instructions to him when he went to Rome for the first time as an extremely young cardinal, to make sure he preserved 'both the goat and the cabbages', i.e. to look after the interests of his family as well as those of the Church.

On 30 March, Lucrezia informed Francesco that Alfonso had left that morning with twelve companions for Rome in optimistic mood about his affairs, 'called by the Pope and encouraged by many Cardinals and other friends'. The next day Prospero Colonna arrived in Ferrara. He spent a long time with Lucrezia who had greeted him with the most beautiful of her gentlewomen, dining informally with Lucrezia and Angela, old acquaintances from the Roman days of Alexander's papacy, who persuaded him not to leave immediately as he had planned. Instead he went hunting with leopards and hawking in the Barco, and in the evening Antonio Costabili gave him a magnificent banquet – all the more remarkable, said di Prosperi, for it being a Friday – a meatless day under the Catholic calendar – and at such short notice.

Lucrezia sat at the head of the high table of a mixed company of select guests which included, of course, Angela Borgia. Di Prosperi considered the occasion so worthy of note that he had the menu and its ingredients copied out with the list of principal guests. Beginning with an amphora of rose water for the washing of hands, the table was set with milk bread, oat fritters and biscuits, marzipan and cakes made of pine-nut flour. The wines were Muscatel, Trebbiano, sweet new wine and other table wine. There were salads of chopped endive, lettuce, anchovies, capers and caper flowers and young cabbage. There were dishes of large prawns, sturgeon milk (? roe) mixed with sugar, cinnamon and rose water, presented as a first course. The boiled dishes were large pike, sturgeon, large ray, tuna and salted ray accompanied by juniper-flavoured soup and herb sauce. These were followed by fried pike, large tench, sturgeon, large trout and carp, accompanied by little freshwater fish, olives, oranges and lemons. Another course comprised small squid sliced, a spicy sauce, ravioli and zest of lemon. As if all this were not enough there was large pike in aspic, sturgeon and red mullet, and on the buffet three large ray, *tortelli alla lombarda*, and large eels in soup. Then came large eels roasted on the spit, huge herb omelets made with one hundred eggs each, pies, red caviar, an arrowroot tart and razorfish. There were oysters, scallops, sea truffles and winkles. For fruit there were pink apples, pears, cheese from Piacenza (*formato piacentino*), peeled almonds, sultanas, grapes and small plums, crisp, thin cakes and a punch made of brandy, sugar and cloves. Then after more rose water for washing their hands the guests were offered the confections of Maestro Vincenzo, sugared almonds in many colours, angelica sweets, pears and peaches preserved in *grappa*, *cedri*, preserved pine nuts and aniseed. At the beginning of dinner at the request of Lucrezia, the singers sang psalms in '*voce basse*' in place of reading, then lutes, viols and cornets were played while woodwind players greeted the entrance and departure of the guests.[12]

Isabella d'Este, now back in Mantua on the specific orders of her husband, was annoyed and jealous that Prospero Colonna had visited Ferrara without coming to visit her. She had sent to Lucrezia asking her to issue an invitation to him on her behalf but, Lucrezia wrote 'regretfully', 'had he still been here when your message arrived I would willingly have acted as your ambassador and used every diligence to obtain your object, but His Lordship had already departed for Correggio . . .' On 11 March, Gonzaga had written his wife a very angry letter, reminding her of her duty in insulting terms – 'she was of an age and discretion that she should not need reminding of it' and for public and private reasons 'she should return without further delay'. 'We are about to go to Gonzaga to greet Federico who should be already near here, for love of whom Your Ladyship will [no doubt] hasten, and beyond any other reason to put an end to all the gossip among the people here which we will not repeat, leaving it to Benedetto

Codelupo [Capilupo] who is most well informed of this . . . thus for whatever love you bear us we urge you to return immediately . . .'[13] The rumours to which Francesco was referring concerned a lampoon by Tebaldeo with scurrilous suggestions about Isabella and her old friend, Mario Equicola, author of the pro-women treatise *De mulieribus*, copies of which were pinned up on various walls in Mantua. Among other insults proffered by Francesco to Isabella in official letters written by his secretary and therefore public knowledge, had been the expression of his anger and bitterness at having 'a wife of the kind who always wants to have her own way and her own opinions', something which contemporaries would have considered the worst accusation a man could level at his wife. It is not surprising, therefore, to read that, according to Luzio, 'the cordiality of their old relations was never restored'.[14]

Lucrezia, however, remained on polite terms with Isabella, taking care to pass on to her – but not to Francesco – news of Alfonso in Rome, and forwarding to her Ippolito's more detailed accounts. Leo X had suspended the interdict on Alfonso for three months while his case was considered by five cardinals, and issued a brief addressing him as 'beloved son the noble Alfonso of Este, Duke of Ferrara' in order that he should attend the papal coronation on 12 April. Alfonso did so, very splendid in cloth of gold-curled brocade. Ominously, not a word had been said about possessions in the Romagna. Cento and La Pieve were to be discussed in the future and there was mention of the concession for salt at Comacchio and the restitution of Reggio. Lucrezia, however, remained groundlessly optimistic – 'we hope things will turn out excellently', she told Isabella. Where she had known very well what kind of man Julius II was, she, like most people, underestimated and misread Leo X. News came from Alfonso that the Pope had extended the suspension of the interdict for a further four months, promising to maintain him in his Duchy of Ferrara and to defend him against the hostile moves of any power against him. Alfonso dined with the Pope before leaving, 'most satisfied' with the soothing words he heard from Leo, delivered in the presence of his friend and protector, the Cardinal d'Aragona. It was agreed that further negotiations were to be carried on by Ippolito. Alfonso arrived home in Ferrara on 29 April 'well satisfied with His Holiness', Lucrezia reported to Isabella.

Indeed, briefly that spring things appeared to be going more smoothly for war-weary Ferrara and the beleaguered Este. Alfonso had retaken Cento and La Pieve on Julius's death, and with Venetian blessing recovered some of his former possessions in the Polesine. Alfonso and Lucrezia seem to have been very much partners in the affairs of Ferrara; in August, Sanudo reported that Giovanni Alberto della Pigna was in Venice to negotiate certain matters with the Council of Ten 'in the name of the Duke and Duchess of Ferrara'. But new hostile alignments were being drawn up with France and Venice on one side, the Pope, the Emperor, Spain and Henry VIII of England on the other. In May 1513 war broke out again; it was to last almost uninterrupted for the remainder of Lucrezia's life. The first sign of Leo's true intentions towards Ferrara came with his acquisition of Modena from the Emperor for 40,000 ducats; it was to be the base for a new state for his brother Giuliano de'Medici comprising Modena and Reggio, Parma and Piacenza, but principally Ferrara. As Guicciardini put it, 'Having purchased Modena, he bent his mind exclusively to acquire Ferrara, more with intrigues and threats than open force of arms; because this had become too difficult, Alfonso having seen the perils in which he stood, had attended to making the city impregnable . . . And his enemies were perhaps greater, although operating more secretly, than those of the time of Julius . . .' While Leo and his allies schemed against Ferrara, Alfonso aimed at the recovery of Modena and Reggio, showing himself as adept diplomatically as he was militarily.

In the dangers and difficulties of her life, Lucrezia had had increasing resort to religion for comfort. Convents had always been places of refuge for her from the strains of court life, first with the Borgias and then with the Este. At Ferrara she favoured the aristocratic convent of Corpus Domini of the order of the Poor Clares but her religious feeling ran deeper than merely

finding a peaceful retreat among sympathetic women. Perhaps as
a result of her experiences at her father's court and the tragedies
which had befallen her – particularly Cesare's death – she was
increasingly attracted by the radical reformist wing of the Church.
She kept the letters of the ascetic Dominican nun St Catherine
of Siena in her library but in practice she was a follower of the
Franciscan preacher San Bernardino of Siena, who had renewed
the ideals of St Francis of Assisi with his calls for charity and
social justice. She became a lay sister of the third Franciscan
order, and she had been among the founders of the Monte di
Pietà in Ferrara, designed specifically as a charitable foundation
for the poor. In 1510 she had founded her own convent of San
Bernardino in which she placed Cesare's illegitimate daughter,
Camilla Lucrezia. In 1516 she petitioned Leo X to institute a
stricter adherence to the rules of poverty; she received in return
a brief of permission written entirely in the fine hand of her
former lover, Pietro Bembo, now secretary to the Pope.[15] It was
she who chose the preachers for the Lenten sermons, among
them an Augustinian friar, Antonio Meli da Crema, with whom
she was particularly impressed. In April 1513 Fra Meli dedicated
to her the text of a book on the ascetic life entitled *Libro di vita
Contemplativa*, which at Lucrezia's express wish was written in
Italian so as to be more easily understood by lay people. In his
dedication Meli explicitly referred to Lucrezia as a woman who
'withdrawn from the vanity and show of the world, and fired by
the chaste divine love . . . engages herself in the instruction of
her damsels, not only those who have decided on [the path of]
virginity and religion but also those who propose to enter the
state of matrimony'.

The dedication was dated 10 April: three days before, di Prosperi
had reported that three of Lucrezia's damsels, including the daughter of Madonna Julia della Mirandola, had been accepted as nuns
of St Catherine of Siena. (In a letter of the same date to Francesco,
asking him to place Julia della Mirandola's son in the service of
Federico, Lucrezia refers to this girl as 'one of our dearest damsels'.)
Their formal reception into the convent of St Catherine was a

solemn public occasion attended by Lucrezia and a crowd of gentlemen, ladies and citizens, so that the church was overflowing. Dressed in white as brides of Christ, the three showed every sign of happiness and great contentment. 'May God make their hearts equally joyful,' di Prosperi commented glumly. Poor Madonna Julia, although not unhappy at her daughter's entering the convent, was reputed to be extremely worried that her son, who was presently in the service of the cardinal, might become a monk. It may be because of this that Lucrezia wrote the letter to Francesco at Madonna Julia's request, asking him to place her son Ercole with his son Federico.[16] While daughters were regarded as no loss and their dowries as nuns were very much smaller than they would have been as brides, sons were important for the support of the family and the continuance of the line, and becoming a monk would have been considered both eccentric and wasteful by aristocratic families.

Even over nuns there was a certain rivalry between Lucrezia and Isabella. A pre-emptive jealousy on Isabella's part prompted a mission by di Prosperi to visit Sister Laura Boiarda, whom Lucrezia had made abbess of San Bernardino, although, he admitted, nothing of interest was said, but that Sister Laura 'agrees that she holds Your Excellency as her principal Lady and Patroness . . .'

Di Prosperi ceased his correspondence with Isabella in June 1513, resuming it after a gap of six months with two letters of 18 and 24 December in which he reports his return home. The correspondence only resumes fully in January 1517, so there is a three-year gap in his invaluable daily reports of the Ferrarese court. Lucrezia continued to correspond with Francesco, sending him private messages and sweetmeats; but her correspondence with Isabella has a gap between April 1513, when Alfonso returned to Ferrara, and May 1516, during which period Isabella, avoiding Mantua as much as possible, was constantly on her travels. No correspondence survives between Alfonso and Lucrezia between the years 1510 and 1518. During this period Lucrezia gave birth to three more children, one of them a daughter, Leonora, named after Alfonso's mother, born on 4 July 1515, after yet another

difficult pregnancy and delivery, as she told Francesco Gonzaga:
'I have been very ill for ten days, very weak and afflicted
with complete loss of appetite and with other difficulties but it
has pleased God that this evening about the twenty-second hour
I was seized by a sudden pain unexpected and unthought of
because I thought I had not reached my term and gave birth. I
am so happy and the little girl to whom I have given birth is
well enough and it seems to me to have received from God one
of those pleasing graces which his divine Majesty is accustomed
to grant some meritorious person . . .'[17] The girl was to become
a nun at Corpus Domini.

   In April the previous year, Lucrezia had given birth to a third
son, another ill-fated Alexandro. Two years later from Belriguardo,
on 27 May 1516, she wrote to Francesco Gonzaga thanking him
for remembering her 'in this situation I find myself now' and for
sending her the '*tartufoli*' (truffles) which she particularly appreciated. The reason for her unhappiness became clear some weeks
later when, on 11 July 1516, she wrote to Gonzaga reporting her
son's death after a long illness:

The illustrious Don Alexandro, my last-born son, after having been ill
for a long time of an infirmity unfamiliar to our doctors and has always
been [afflicted] with ulcerations on his head and lately with a great
flux for which there was no remedy, and thus he was forced this past
night around the fourth hour to give up his blessed soul to God: which
has greatly afflicted me and has left me in the greatest grief which
could be expected, being a woman and a mother. It seemed to me my
duty to give you immediate notice so that you are aware of all that
befalls me, in adversity and prosperity: and I am sure that you will feel
because of it the sadness due to the love and consideration which I
bear you, and will feel compassion for the grief I feel which is immense:
it only remains to pray God to give me strength to bear with fortitude this most grave sorrow . . .'

That same year, however, there was consolation in the birth, on
1 November, of another son, this time a healthy baby, who was

named Francesco. It is a tempting, although unlikely, thought that she might have named him after Gonzaga.

Lucrezia had now borne Alfonso three healthy sons but her history of disastrous pregnancies, miscarriages still- and premature births and sickly, short-lived children could have been caused by Alfonso's syphilis. Unlike Francesco Gonzaga with Isabella, Alfonso maintained regular sexual relations with Lucrezia, resulting in repeated pregnancies which weakened her and eventually led to her death.

Lucrezia continued to keep in touch with her humanist circle, among them the poet Giangiorgio Trissino, with whom she had first become friendly in the summer of 1512 when he was in Ferrara.[18] She had consulted him later about the education of Ercole, writing on 18 September 1515 from Belriguardo to tell him that she had retailed their conversation to Alfonso who had been greatly pleased, and that they were both anxious that Ercole should begin his formal education as soon as possible. Could he possibly, she asked, without too much trouble to himself, find a tutor in grammar for the boy? She had not been able to write about this earlier because she had had no chance to speak to Alfonso, but she was also sending Ercole da Camerino to Ferrara to explain their ideas about it to him.[19] In November the recommended tutor, a Domine Niccolò Lazzarino, had still not arrived but, she told Trissino, who was apparently at the Emperor's court, enclosing the tutor's letter, he was hourly expected.[20] In March 1516, she wrote to Trissino saying that she and Alfonso were anxious to consult him personally as soon as he could get to Ferrara.[21]

Trissino, it would appear, had not been able to visit Ferrara, for Lucrezia wrote to him from Belriguardo on 1 June about how much they were hoping for his arrival to oversee Ercole's education: 'We advise you for your contentment that his preceptor until now could not be more satisfied with him, nor with greater hope of his gaining honours easily as we think you will have understood from his [the tutor's] letters.'[22] That month payments figured in the Este accounts for an Ovid and a Virgil purchased by the tutor 'Messer Nicol precepetore del Signore Don Hercule' for his pupil.[23] Two years later she was still in contact with Trissino and hoping to see him.

Meanwhile, Lucrezia had also been in touch with Aldus Manutius who had fled Venice for Ferrara after the defeat at Agnadello in 1509 and for the following four years had wandered the cities of northern Italy. Lucrezia was named executor in the will which he drew up in Ferrara in 1509, although not in a later version. At around that time, she also apparently offered support to establish the academy of intellectuals which had long been the printer's dream but which he never realized.[24] She encouraged Manutius to publish the edition of the poems of Tito and Ercole Strozzi, many dedicated to her, which eventually appeared in Venice in 1513. The book has a dedicatory preface by the printer to 'the Divine Lucretia Borgia, Duchess of Ferrara' in which he refers to their common desire to establish an academy at Ferrara. Three years later, Ludovico Ariosto's *Orlando Furioso*, on which he had been working since 1506, was first published in Ferrara, with frequent, laudatory references to Lucrezia: 'She shall ever grow in beauty, merit, fortune and good repute, just like a tender plant in soft earth . . .'[25] She appeared in the poem as a marble statue supported by their mutual friends, Antonio Tebaldeo and Ercole Strozzi.[26]

Lucrezia was nearing thirty-seven, considered old by Renaissance standards, when Francesco was born. In late December that year, rumours reached her of the death of Jofre and these were confirmed by the beginning of January. Lucrezia was now the last surviving of Vannozza's children: she had not seen Jofre since leaving Rome for Ferrara fifteen years earlier, and they do not appear to have corresponded; if they did, no letters have been preserved. After Cesare's fall, Jofre had retreated with the rest of the Borgia faction to Naples where Sancia became the mistress of Gonsalvo da Cordoba, Cesare's captor. By now thoroughly bored with Jofre, she had refused to have anything further to do with him. After her death, Jofre had subsequently married again, one Maria de Mila, who by her name was presumably a member of the family related to the Borgias. She bore him four children, and on his death his only son succeeded to the Principate of Squillace. Lucrezia received the news of her brother's death from his widow and son, Francesco, 'my nephew'. She wrote separately on 2 January to both the Gonzaga giving them the news. As might have been expected, her letter to Isabella was brief and couched in less emotional terms than the letter to Francesco. To the latter she wrote of the 'unexpected event which has greatly afflicted me and has caused me the sorrow which might be expected. I am sure Your Lordship,' she continued, 'for the relationship between us and the reverence I bear you, will have compassion for me and for love of me will feel regret . . .'[27] It is difficult to imagine that, apart from breaking one of the last links with her family past, Lucrezia really felt deeply bereaved by Jofre's death.

There had been other, more significant, deaths on the international front. On 1 January 1515 Louis XII died. Despite having contracted syphilis, the King had married, on 9 October 1513, Henry VIII's sister Mary; he was fifty-three and in failing health, she a beautiful girl of eighteen. His death was widely attributed to excessive indulgence in sex. Guicciardini accused him of 'greedily making use of the excellent beauty and youth of his new wife, a girl of eighteen, and, not considering his own years and weak constitution, was taken with a fever complicated by disorders due to a flux'. Francesco Vettori, Florentine ambassador to Rome, wrote gleefully that King Louis had brought out of England a '"filly" so young, so beautiful and so swift that she had ridden him right out of the world'.

Louis's heir, François d'Angoulême, a member of the cadet branch of the family, succeeded as Francis I. At the age of twenty and in contrast with the tired old man Louis had become, Francis had the aura of a Sun King about him, as Guicciardini wrote:

The new King's virtue, magnanimity, skill and generous spirit had aroused so much hope that it was universally admitted that for many years now no one had come to the throne with greater expectations.

For he united the highest grace with the flower of youth . . . outstanding physical beauty, the greatest liberality, deep humanity withal, and a thorough knowledge of things. Together with his title of King of France, he assumed the title of Duke of Milan, belonging to him not only because of the ancient claims of the Duke of Orleans but also as included within the investiture made by the Emperor according to the League of Cambrai; thus he had the same desire to recuperate it as his predecessor. He was goaded to this undertaking not only by his own inclination but also by the youth of the French nobility, the glory of Gaston de Foix, and the memory of so many victories which had been won by recent kings in Italy . . .'

Towards the end of June 1515, Francis set out for Italy determined to recover all the possessions which the French had lost there in the last years of Louis XII's reign. In July the Duke of Milan, Alfonso's nephew, the Pope, the King of Aragon and the Emperor signed a League for the defence of Italy. Venice was openly on the side of the French against the Emperor and so, more circumspectly, was Alfonso, although he prudently refused all attempts by both sides to make him declare himself. On 1 September, Sanudo reported that Alfonso's envoy had assured the Venetians that he was content to share fortunes with them and with the French:

He did not reveal any more and, to tell the truth, his excuse does not seem unreasonable. Not wishing to unite his forces with ours I should have thought that at least he should be willing to come here to meet us; but even this he has not wished to do and has made many excuses. I believe that in any case the aforesaid Lord Duke may not be a most cordial friend of Your Highness [the Doge of Venice]. All the same I believe that he will go to a good end with us and that he desires a prosperous success for the undertaking for his own particular interest because there is no doubt that if we lost he would also lose his state. We have had from His Excellency victuals and provisions and we have not failed to exchange with him good and cordial words.[28]

That month at Marignano the French defeated the fearsome Swiss army which had been defending Milan; Massimiliano Sforza was taken as hostage to France. Alfonso, it seemed, had backed the right side.

Lucrezia was once again left in charge at Ferrara during that autumn when Alfonso spent a good deal of time watching out for his interests in the French camp. Her principal role was to liaise with Venice, as Sanudo's reports of almost weekly letters from her to the Signory demonstrate. Alfonso was away until mid December, accompanied by his nephew Federico Gonzaga, now aged fifteen, providing her with news of the French and the Pope and of Spanish troop movements. Within a short time another old player was removed from the field: Ferdinand of Spain died on 23 January 1516 leaving his kingdom to his grandson, the Archduke Charles of Habsburg. Charles had inherited the dukedom of Burgundy from his father, while, as nephew to the Emperor Maximilian, there was a strong possibility he could also become his successor. As Ferdinand's heir he inherited the Aragonese claim to Naples, always a source of trouble for Italy. Alfonso continued to sit on his fence at Ferrara, keeping in touch with the French and the Venetians but refusing openly to take sides. When both the Emperor and the King of France demanded he send them men-at-arms, Alfonso promptly sent his troops out of the city so that he should not have to do so. In June the two Duchesses of Urbino, the widowed dowager Elisabetta and her niece Leonora, arrived as penniless refugees in Ferrara, having been driven out by the Pope in favour of his nephew, Lorenzo de'Medici. Meanwhile, Leo held on to Modena and Reggio (despite Alfonso having paid him back the 40,000 ducats he had paid the Emperor for them) and had by no means given up hope of laying hands on Ferrara. As the year 1518 opened, although ostensibly a year of peace in Italy it held out continuing problems for Alfonso, who continued to tread a careful line between France and the Pope.

16. The Last Year of Tranquillity

'Thus conditions were at peace in Italy and beyond the mountains'

– Francesco Guicciardini, writing of the year 1518

As Duchess of Ferrara, Lucrezia was required to be both splendid and domestic, playing a multitude of roles – Governor of the state, leader of a brilliant court, hostess, mother and wife. The suspension of military operations against Ferrara allowed her and Alfonso to enjoy life in the city and to continue to beautify their surroundings, a process necessarily interrupted by war.

Carnival of 1518 was exceptionally gay: at the instance of the Cardinal d'Aragona, Alfonso issued an edict permitting masking in the streets, although for fear of violence the maskers were only allowed to carry staves of a specified dimension and length. The usual spate of pre-Lenten marriages took place, among them that of one of Lucrezia's damsels, the daughter of Giovanni Valla to Ippolito da li Banchi. An unusual feature of the carnival festivities was tilting at the quintain by both young men and girls with lances of considerable size – 'including one Madonna of ours [i.e. Ferrarese] I leave to your imagination which one it was', di Prosperi primly commented. Even the young princes, Ercole and Ippolito, took part, 'with such dexterity that it was a pleasure to see them', he said. There was dancing in the Corte for three evenings running before the end of carnival.

But now, from 18 February, di Prosperi wrote, 'at court every one is keeping a Lenten way of life, even the little lords'. Alfonso had exempted them so that they could eat meat but they had pleaded with him to allow them to keep to the Lenten diet. Lucrezia was ill with a fever but she had kept Lent, as had Alfonso and the children.

The consumption of food throughout medieval and Renaissance Europe was governed by the dictates of the Church and regulated by a precise annual rhythm which predicated dietary regimes. According to the Church abstinence from eating meat and all animal products, including, to the distress of many, cheese, was the rule on Wednesday, Friday and Saturday as well as on the eve of important festivals and, of course, the forty days of Lent. Since for them fresh fish was always in relatively short supply and the prices high on days of '*magro*', the poor confined themselves to beans, chickpeas, fruit and vegetables while for the rich, as Antonio Costabili's banquet for Fabrizio Colonna showed, abstinence from meat was scarcely a hardship.

Due to the difficulty of keeping food fresh, the predominant taste in dishes of the day was of preservatives – salt or sugar. In Lucrezia's kitchen, the pig was the most useful animal, prepared in various ways and used in the making of salami, and sausages (*zambudelli*) and prosciutto. Salted ox tongues were also appreciated for their practicality. Sugar and spices from the East were important ingredients – among them pepper, cinnamon, nutmeg and tamarind, as were vegetables – radishes, carrots, garlic, onions, spring onions and leeks. Scented herbs were much in use – notably basil, sage, bay, marjoram, mint and rosemary. Sugar was the predominant luxury article in cooking, in meat and fish dishes as well as confectionery; it came via Venice from the Orient or via Genoa from Portuguese Atlantic sources, notably Madeira. Fruits in syrup of sugar and spices were particularly appreciated by Isabella d'Este who frequently requested them from Lucrezia's 'Vincentio spetiale'. They also raised capons, calves, peacocks and guinea fowl (*galline da India*), kid, ducks and swans, supplemented by game in season, and, given the lagoons, waterways and lakes of the Po area, they ate a great variety of fish, notably eels from Comacchio and *carpioni* provided by Isabella from Lake Garda. Then there were cheeses and pasta dishes.

Banquets were a ritual affair, often a movable feast held in different rooms at different seasons, with trestle tables covered with white cloths, napkins and choice decorations, the dressers or buffets (*credenze*) loaded with the family silver and gold plate, and crystal flasks. In the recent years of war, the Este plate – including Lucrezia's – had much of it disappeared in pawn or been melted down to provide finance for the defence of Ferrara, and the court had been reduced to eating off pottery made by Alfonso himself. Tapestries would be specially hung. Guests were offered perfumed water with which to wash their hands at the beginning of the meal and between courses – scented with rose petals, lemon, myrtle, musk; even the toothpicks were scented and the cloths changed after each course were often decorated with sweet-smelling herbs. Hot courses of at least eight dishes each from the kitchen alternated with cold courses served from the *credenza* and, at Lucrezia's court, the whole elaborate performance – the decoration of the table, *credenza* and room, the service and the organization of the musical accompaniment and *intermezzi* – was planned and choreographed by the most famous *scalco*, or steward, of the century, Cristoforo da Messisbugo, who entered the Este service in 1515. He came from an old Ferrarese family and his social status was high enough for him to have entertained Alfonso twice in his own house; his book, the *Banchetti*, published posthumously, was a bestseller. In entertainments, as in theatre and buildings, the Este court of the late fifteenth and first half of the sixteenth century set the standard for the other Italian courts.

Lucrezia's accounts books show the extent of her involvement in the running of her household. On 24 January 1516, for example,[1] her chancellor lists twenty-five heifers each known by name, among them 'Violet' and 'Rose'. A five-page bill details her commissions for shoes for herself and her household including Girolamo Borgia, Cesare's son. Another accounts book for 1507 details payments by 'Vincenzi banchero' (Vincenzi the banker) on Lucrezia's orders to a variety of recipients: to a Domenico Sforza for two flasks of Malvasia wine; to Ascanio da Vilaforo,

bookseller, for binding seven books for Lucrezia; salaries for her
staff including the faithful 'Sanzo spagnolo', Tullio, a member of
Giovanni Borgia's household, Bartolommeo Grotto, his tutor, and
Cola, another of his servants; a payment to her gentleman,
Sigismondo Nigrisolo, for the cost of a coffer he gave to Dalida
de'Puti, Lucrezia's singer; to a chairmaker, a table-decker (*aparec-
chiador*); Tromboncino and Porino, singers; il Cingano, 'the Gypsy',
a favourite of Alfonso's; to jewellers; a Spanish (probably Jewish)
embroiderer; a saddler; a 'Chatelina del forno', possibly a member
of the formidable family of Masino and El Modenese; and Tomaso
da Carpi, a painter.[2] The official annual accounts were consci-
entiously signed by Lucrezia herself. She was still signing them
in the last year of her life.

Alfonso had now resumed work on new rooms in the Corte
and his own particular *camerini* in the *via coperta*. In 1508, before
war had interrupted him, he had begun work on a 'studio of fine
marbles' designed for his collection of statues, ancient and modern,
and other antiquities and had already completed a small new
chapel constructed of fine marble and nutwood from Venice next
to the rooms. That same year he had taken delivery of a series
of marble reliefs from the sculptor Antonio Lombardo which he
had ordered two years previously for his 'Studio di Marmo'.
Twenty-eight of these are now in the Hermitage Museum in St
Petersburg, one of which is dated and inscribed 'In 1508 Alfonso,
third Duke of Ferrara, established this for his leisure and tranquillity', while another bears a quotation from Cicero expressive
of Alfonso's reserved character – 'Never less alone than when
alone'. Early in 1518 di Prosperi recorded Alfonso's building operations as proceeding 'at a furious pace'.[3] He was widening part
of the *via coperta* and building above it a sumptuous set of new
rooms. By early April they were working on the fabric and the
windows, so that now the family dined in the first *camera dorata*.
On the 17th, despite suffering from gallstones for which he was
purging himself and taking '*syropi*', Alfonso was reported as taking
great pains over the scaffolding of his rooms. The outside walls
of the *camerini* had been finished and the marble floors laid within

by the end of August.[4] On 4 October di Prosperi reported that Alfonso was overseeing daily the completion of the *camerini*, where the glass and wooden frames of the windows had already been installed though their surrounds had not been finished and it was doubted that Alfonso would be able to sleep there that winter. When Isabella saw it, he said, she would find it twice as pleasing as she had found it before: 'the more so that in that small piazza stalls have been set up as they used to be to sell goods as they did in the great piazza, to give a more pleasant aspect. Among other things you will see above all the exits to these *camerini* various heads and figures by antique and modern sculptors, and the studio most beautifully decorated and with its fine pavement . . .'

Work continued during Alfonso's absence at the French court that winter: 'There has been made a bridge or, as we say in our dialect, a *pezolo*, which crosses the way entering the *cortile* of the Corte; that is from the salon where the Duchess gives audience in the hot weather and connects with the apartments allotted to the daughters of Messer Hannibale [Bentivoglio] which were formerly occupied by Messer Niccolò da Correggio and before him used by Duke Borso. This bridge has been made for easier access to the Rooms of the Lady Duchess. And the beams above the Corridor of the Corte, that is the balcony of the Duke's Rooms which look over the vegetable market, are finished.'[5]

Alfonso was revealing an unsuspected passion and taste for decoration. His nephew, Isabella's son Federico, visiting Ferrara in June 1517, lodged in the first set of new rooms and was impressed, reporting that he had seen, probably in the Studio di Marmo, 'a most beautiful *camerino* all made of Carrara marble and panels with beautiful figures and foliation excellently worked and adorned with vases and statuettes modern and antique made of marble and metal . . .'[6] In Rome Raphael was looking out for ancient works of art for Alfonso, as Costabili reported to him. Alfonso employed the greatest contemporary artists. On 19 February 1518 Titian sent him designs for two balconies. All that year the decorations for the new rooms proceeded, including the installation of marble pavements, cornices, friezes, fireplaces, windows of glass and crystal glass, gilded ceilings and painted façades.

In February 1513 Mario Equicola wrote to Isabella that Alfonso 'cared only for commissioning pictures and seeing antiquities'. His major artistic project was the commissioning of a series of paintings by the great masters on classical subjects for his *camerino*. While in Rome for Leo X's coronation in 1513 he had tried without success to persuade Michelangelo to contribute, but the project actually began with Giovanni Bellini's *Feast of the Gods*, completed in 1514, and continued with three of Titian's greatest paintings, *The Worship of Venus, Bacchus and Ariadne* and *The Andrians*. He also commissioned a frieze and a canvas from Dosso Dossi for the same room.

All traces of Lucrezia's new decorations in the Castello and the Corte have vanished. Her earliest important commission was for a series of eight canvases in tempera on historical subjects, destined for the vaulted ceilings of her rooms in the Torre Marchesana in the Castello, originally ordered in 1506. As her interest in religion deepened so her taste in paintings changed. While her husband thought only of classical subjects, Lucrezia commissioned from Fra Bartolommeo a *Head of the Saviour* during his stay at court in early 1516.

Lucrezia's concern for the spiritual welfare of her citizens led her to back her confessor, Fra Thomaso, in a substantial move against the Dominican monks of Ferrara who had not been behaving themselves. In the presence of Alfonso, his gentlemen, the leading citizenry and the Vicar of the Order, they had been warned that if any one of them failed to conform to the observant life, he must leave the city within three days. The other monks and friars were alarmed that the same thing might happen to them. 'God make it that we see the other religious, priests and friars with the rest of Christendom come to a better reform,' di Prosperi wrote. She had, through the intercession of Isabella when she visited Ferrara in the autumn of 1517, obtained permission from Cardinal Gonzaga for Fra Thomaso to preach in the cathedral at Mantua that Lent.

Lucrezia Borgia

Relations between Lucrezia and Isabella had become more friendly than in the past, although there was always a certain spikiness between them. The balance of power had swung towards Lucrezia since the estrangement between Isabella and Francesco. Isabella was humiliatingly forced to have recourse to Lucrezia to obtain what she wanted from Francesco, over whom her enemy Tolomeo Spagnoli was increasingly in the ascendant. On one occasion she appealed to Lucrezia to obtain a pardon for a condemned man from Francesco. Lucrezia replied that although it had been much against her will to intervene to divert the course of justice, and she had not expected to get favours from Francesco as Isabella had seemed to think she would, nonetheless she would do anything in her power to help her and when she had read Isabella's commendation for the 'poor little man condemned to death' ('*quel poveretto condannato a morte*') she had written as best she could to Francesco, moved by the great pity the case had inspired in her. Moreover, she had even got 'the illustrious Lord Hercule' to write as well, while she had sent another letter in her own name to Messer Tolomeo. 'Your Ladyship may imagine what content I feel when also to me no favour is granted,' she continued.[7] She did in fact write to Gonzaga and to Tolomeo in favour of the '*poveretto*', one Gabriel Comascho, condemned to death for killing a constable. To Tolomeo she wrote asking him to bring the matter to Gonzaga's attention, and to Francesco himself she addressed a passionate plea for mercy. Comascho was a man 'of good family, and a person who has never been known to commit any other crime, and this killing was not deliberate but in a fight to which Comascho had been provoked'.[8] Isabella, meanwhile, appears to have haughtily complained, to which Lucrezia replied with some asperity: 'Your Excellency can be most certain that when you ask of me something which I cannot achieve, I am very sorry for it. And if I had had to write to the Illustrious Lord Marquis for my own purpose and need, I could not have written more warmly than I did for Gabriel Comascho to satisfy Your Excellency to whom I enclose the letters which I have received which are not as I would have wished . . .'[9]

On a more pleasant note, Lucrezia had thanked Isabella for a recipe for '*el Juleppo*' (?an infusion), which Isabella had sent her in the hope that it would do her good. Lucrezia had been unwell since Isabella left but she was sure that the '*Juleppo*' would help her 'principally because it comes from you who I know loves me like a sister: I will soon try it when the weather cools'. She did not know what was wrong with her but joked, 'it must be as '*Catherina che suona*', one of her musicians, sings 'because fortune wills it'.[10] References to Lucrezia's ill health become increasingly frequent in di Prosperi's reports over these years. On 4 March he wrote that Alfonso, who had been hawking in the Barco and was planning to hunt wolf, put off his plans because of Lucrezia's delicate state of health and forbade her from continuing her Lenten fasting and dieting.[11]

Five days later, however, she was seen in public again. On 14 March she dispatched an envoy, il Nasello, to Naples for what di Prosperi thought were negotiations regarding 'her brother, Don Giovanni', although it was more likely that it concerned the winding-up of Rodrigo Bisceglie's affairs. Giovanni Borgia, like Rodrigo Bisceglie, had been under the official tutelage of Cardinal Cosenza, who was joined in that office by Ippolito d'Este in November 1501, presumably in preparation for Lucrezia's marriage to Alfonso. Giovanni remained Spanish at heart: he liked to sign himself 'Don Juan de Borja' and his letter of condolence to Alfonso on Lucrezia's death was written not in Italian but in Castilian, in a looping, immature hand.[12] Giovanni Borgia was the one member of Lucrezia's extended family whom Alfonso found hard to stomach. While he liked Cesare's son Girolamo, and had him in his household after Alberto Pio left Carpi for Rome, Giovanni Borgia can best be described as a nuisance. It would appear that he was now back in Ferrara because in May one of his men killed a squire employed by the ducal sons. Enraged by such a 'cruel and arrogant case' touching on his own family, Alfonso was determined to arrest him and tortured other servants of Giovanni's suspected of having spirited the culprit away.[13] In June, di Prosperi reported that Lucrezia too was angry about the

case: 'Alberto di Petrato, a servant of the Lady Duchess was placed
in the Castello for having helped the escape of those of the household of Don Giovanni [Borgia] who murdered under the loggia
of the piazza a squire of the Lord's sons and it seems that Her
Excellency has been angry with him until now.' Lucrezia, however,
with her customary mercy, later released him. Giovanni Borgia
had gone to Rome before Alfonso arrived from Venice on 3 June,
'and it was conjectured that he had done so because he was no
longer well regarded by the Duke'.[14] He remained there until
early September when di Prosperi reported that he would be
given a pension by the King of France and would go to the
French court. He was to be a source of endless irritation to
Alfonso on his own visit there, and it is a measure of his deep
affection for Lucrezia that he did so much for the wretched youth.
The feckless creature had been nominated Duke of Camerino
by his father Alexander and among Lucrezia's papers are several
documents relating to the estate,[15] but on the fall of the Borgias
the Varano family, close connections of the Este, swiftly returned
there.

Not only was Lucrezia indulgent towards her worthless half-
brother, but she also looked out for the interests and education
of another half-brother, Rodrigo Borgia, her father's last child,
born in the final year of his pontificate. From two letters of the
faithful Borgia follower Juan Las Cases, written in May and
September 1518, it appears that this Rodrigo Borgia had gone
from Rome to Salerno in the Kingdom of Naples and that
Lucrezia had written somewhat peremptorily, demanding to know
how his studies were proceeding. Las Cases gave various excuses,
including illness, for failing to reply sooner and expressed a great
desire to go to Ferrara to see her 'to talk about old times'.[16] In
September, Las Cases wrote again assuring Lucrezia that the chaplain sent to tutor 'Dom Rodrigo' had been instructed as she
wished to get him to say his offices and to keep him 'in the love
and fear of God'.

Cesare's two illegitimate children, Girolamo and Camilla
Lucrezia, were under her eye in Ferrara, the former as a page

at court, the latter as a nun at San Bernardino. Both were now teenagers, having been born between 1501 and 1502 of mothers unknown, although in a document of 1509 legitimizing Camilla, Lucrezia stated that she was born of Cesare, married, and an unnamed married woman. Cesare's one legitimate child, his daughter by his wife, Charlotte d'Albret, Luisa or Louise, born in May 1500 and whom he had never seen, was just under seven years old when he died. She never visited Ferrara but wrote dutiful letters to her aunt Lucrezia.[17] She married, aged seventeen, an elderly and distinguished soldier and courtier, Louis de la Trémouïlle, in 1517. And Lucrezia, according to her accounts books, also kept in touch with Juan Gandia's widow and son.[18]

Early in May 1518 Alfonso went to Abano to take the waters for his health, leaving Lucrezia in sole charge (Ippolito having left the previous year with a huge retinue of hunting dogs, stallions and leopards to look after his interests in the bishopric of Eger in Hungary). 'The Lady Duchess has remained as Governor and is most expeditious in our affairs at present: it is true that sometimes she asks counsel of the Magistrates to assist her,' di Prosperi wrote on 16 May. 'And up till now they have tortured some persons arrested for going about without light at night, so everyone is on their guard . . .' This offence was apparently considered so grave that Alfonso had written to Lucrezia about it from Abano, demanding that they should be tortured because they were armed when arrested. Lucrezia responded, pleading not to be forced to torture them. Her letter gives an interesting insight not only into her own merciful character but into the class-based nature of Ferrarese justice. On 15 May she wrote to Alfonso giving her reasons for her actions:

More than one cause induced me not to torture [*dare la corda*] Giovanni Battista Bonleo, first because when he was arrested it was only just after the prescribed hour and he was wearing his day clothes and not things that would give rise to suspicion of any evil intent, but having only gone out and was returning home. And then I remembered the proclamation that the *corda* should not be given to any gentleman nor of the condition he is, I did not think I was wrong to have respect to his house and relations, but I have kept this decision between ourselves and released him on security of 200 ducats. And nor do I think I did wrong in releasing Verghezino because the *podestà* told me that Your Excellency had ordered him to have great respect for all the Cardinal's household, and the others were released at the instance of Sismondo Cistarello [probably Ippolito's untrustworthy wardrobe master, Sigismondo Cestarello] who gave a simple testimony that they were servants of the Cardinal ... but ... on investigation of this and suspecting it was not true, I ordered them to be re-arrested ...

In another letter of 19 May she attempted to calm Alfonso's anger against a son of Annibale Bentivoglio who had been accused of violence against the Ferrarese officers who were taking a Bolognese to prison and on the next day it was another case of mercy for a man arrested armed with a sword but without a light. This time it was 'Leonardo, a nephew of Giacomo di Lunardi, who has charge of il Boschetto who, when it was intended to proceed against him according to the proclamation, I was prayed by him that if I would not grant him any other grace ... he would willingly pay the 25 ducats than suffer the *tre tratti di corda*. I had him therefore held in prison until I could inform Your Excellency and have your opinion ...' Francesco Gonzaga was also bombarded with letters from Lucrezia in her role as administrator of justice, no less than three that month concerning the arrest of a criminal, Alfonso Rampino, 'my Ferrarese subject'.

On 24 May, Lucrezia addressed a housewifely letter to Alfonso requesting six guinea fowl eggs for hatching, reminding him that, when she had requested some of his fowl for a friend, he had told her that guinea fowl did not survive being moved and promised that he would give her eggs when the season came. At the end of the month while Alfonso was still away, this time having gone from Abano to Venice where he was most honourably received, the two Duchesses of Urbino, Elisabetta and Leonora, arrived on a formal visit. Lucrezia sent her sons out to meet them accompanied by the leading gentlemen and ladies of the court, while she herself waited to greet them, standing at the head of the marble staircase leading to the Corte. She accompanied them to their apartments above the loggia overlooking the piazza where Francesco Gonzaga used to stay and which were now normally occupied by her sons, who for the past month had been staying in the apartment in the great garden of the Castello.

She appears to have been ill again: Di Prosperi was guarded as to the nature of her illness: 'for a few days now she has not left her apartments because of an indisposition which I think you know of', he told Isabella on 30 May. Describing the Duchesses' visit to Alfonso, Lucrezia told him that she had put them in 'Your Lordship's rooms' and had given them not just one *camerino*, as he had ordered, but both *camerini* with the Stufa Grande, and had taken their own son Francesco to stay in her apartment, so that they could be more honourably lodged and she could have easy access to them. She had put Emilia Pia, Duchess Elisabetta's great friend, and the ladies in Don Ercole's rooms. Anxious to demonstrate to Alfonso the efforts she had made to make them comfortable and to present his possessions to the greatest advantage, she had heard that they wanted to see his '*boschetto*', the new villa – later known as the Belvedere – which Alfonso had begun to build five years earlier on a sandy island in the Po just outside Ferrara. She had had it furnished and arranged 'so that it will give them pleasure and they will praise it'. Yet, despite Lucrezia's efforts, di Prosperi told Isabella that the two Duchesses had 'taken little pleasure from their stay, principally because of the late hours which we are accustomed to eat'.

Lucrezia was unwell again in August and had not been seen since the 15th, which di Prosperi attributed to '*il solito male suo*' – her usual sickness – without giving details. She wrote to Alfonso about their sons: Ercole had gone that morning out of Ferrara, as he had ordered, but Ippolito stayed behind because he felt sick but did not appear to be in danger of serious illness. Perhaps because of concern for her and because she was not well enough to carry on government, Alfonso returned to Ferrara and plunged himself into administration: he divided his foreign secretariat between Opizo, or Obizzo, da Remi for Milan and France, and Bonaventura Pistofilo for Rome and Venice. In Lucrezia's place he himself gave audiences in the *Examine* – 'may God make it that he perseveres [in this] to the content and wellbeing of his subjects', commented di Prosperi which, with other subsequent remarks, implied that Alfonso was not much given to administration. A week later he was still energetically taking part, giving audiences before breakfast, and afterwards taking the *Examine* with the two secretaries, Hieronymo Magnanimo and the Counsellors of Justice. He was enjoying himself, di Prosperi said, particularly the audiences – 'as I remember did your Mother of most happy memory'. 'And, in truth, it is a most lordly thing and of the greatest contentment to his subjects . . . that no one can consider himself with too much influence with His Lordship but all are considered *almost equal* [my italics].' He took an interest in improving the defences of Ferrara, visiting every morning the quarter known as the Borgo di Sotto, where a fosse and ramparts were being created, the ramparts to be as high as or higher than the tallest palazzo in the city. Walls and towers were being built to house artillery. 'The pity of it is,' wrote di Prosperi, 'that almost all the houses in that Borgo are being levelled, including that beautiful monastery of S. Silvestro founded so long ago by San Maurelio, our patron saint.' When he returned to Comacchio, Lucrezia again took up the business of the *Examine* and gave audiences, which she did every day he was away.

Towards the end of November, Alfonso left for the French court to see if he could achieve some concrete action over Modena and Reggio. Leo had promised to hand over the two cities to Alfonso on payment of the 40,000 ducats which he [Leo] had paid the Emperor for them, plus 14,000 ducats he claimed to have spent on the administration of those cities. This had been formally agreed in a notarial document drawn up in Florence in February 1516, backed by Alfonso's two royal supporters, Francis I and Henry VIII, when Alfonso had promised to pay the money demanded by the Pope. Nothing, however, had resulted and Leo was now planning to marry his nephew, Lorenzo de'Medici, to a French princess and give him Ferrara. When summoned by Francis I to Paris to attend the entry of the English ambassadors in December following an Anglo-French rapprochement, Alfonso hastened to comply.

Before he left he called a meeting of the gentlemen and leading citizens and told them formally: 'I have called you here to tell you that the King of France's Majesty writes that I should go to him. That is all I have to say except that I commend to you my wife and children and my state [*le cose mie*]: and if anything untoward should happen that you should do for them what you would do for me.' For a man known to be taciturn, the words were few enough but all the more effective for that. His hearers remained 'moved and mute' for a while, then 'reminded him of the faith which the people had always shown him and that His Lordship should not doubt of it, to which he replied that this heartened him to leave and otherwise he would not have departed.'[19]

Lucrezia was left to govern in her own name, and to carry out the *Examine* and the audiences as usual. She frequently invited Alfonso's gentlemen to dine with her. Alfonso's concern for the safety of his family was shared by Lucrezia who wrote to Rome on the morning of his departure a letter to be communicated to the Pope in her name and that of Alfonso. It was intended to avert any suspicion Leo might have had concerning Alfonso's journey to France by underlining the fact that he had been summoned by the King of France, and to assure the Pope that, wherever he might be, Alfonso was most disposed to obey the Pope 'as his devoted and obedient son and servant'. She added her own profession of devotion to the Pope in whatever he wished and begged him, 'in the absence of the Duke to hold ourself, our children and state commended to him'.[20]

Shortly after Alfonso's departure for France, Lucrezia received news of her mother's death in Rome. 'My mother is still ill and her life must end soon,' she had written to Isabella. The term she used was '*la matre*' – the mother – not '*mia matre*' – my mother – unconsciously revealing the distance there had always been between herself and Vannozza. The news of her death did not reach Alfonso until he arrived in Paris: to his letter of condolence, Lucrezia replied in a handwritten letter referring to her mother's death in very curious terms: 'I thank Your lordship infinitely for the comfort you have given me in your most welcome letter . . . which has completely alleviated that small residue of chagrin which against my will I have sometimes felt for the death of my mother. That is enough, I do not want to hear any more of it . . .'[21]

The lack of grief is extraordinary when compared with the terms in which she spoke of the death even of Jofre. Lucrezia had not seen her mother since she had left Rome seventeen years before. While Cesare had been close to Vannozza, Lucrezia seems to have remained distant from her, devoted to her father and regarding Adriana de Mila as her mother. Few letters from Vannozza survive in the Este archives and those that do are businesslike rather than affectionate. The first, dated February 1515, asks for Lucrezia's and Alfonso's favour with the Duke of Milan against a Giovanni Paolo Pagnano in Milan who was claiming that she owed him 300 ducats. It is couched in the kind of complaining, almost hysterical, language that any daughter being asked a favour might find tiresome:

'This Pagnano,' Vannozza wrote,

thinks of nothing else but to give me some annoyance and trouble me as long as I live. Thus I pray Your Excellency that you should make every effort to ensure that I am once and for all freed of such persecution and to find some expedient so that I may no longer be in fear which certainly would be the cause of the total ruin of myself and the few means which I have. My need is that Your Excellency together with the Most Illustrious Lord Duke your consort should send a discreet and amiable servant to the Most Illustrious Duke of Milan with favourable letters from you, in which you pray the Most Illustrious Lord Duke to intervene with the said Paolo and induce him to perpetual silence and in the end order him that, given my good reasons, he must no longer molest me . . . He [Paolo] as a man lacking in respect has always wished to act against me, as if I were the most vile person in the world, thinking perhaps that I was abandoned and derelict of every help and favour, and that I would not find anyone to speak for me, but I thank almighty God . . . that neither He nor men of the world have abandoned me, and so again I pray and urge you with all the strength of my heart that Your Excellency will not fail me with your help and favour . . .

She signed herself 'La felice et infelice matre Vannozza Borgia' – 'The happy and unhappy mother, Vannozza Borgia.'[22]

Apart from politely wishing Lucrezia good health and that of her family, the letter contained nothing of a personal nature or expression of affection, which might be thought odd, considering that Lucrezia was some six months pregnant with her daughter Leonora and that her son Alexandro was perpetually ill.

Vannozza remained obsessed with the machinations of Pagnano, writing another complaining letter to Lucrezia about it. It seems that in Ippolito d'Este she found a more sympathetic ear, and indeed the tone of her letters to him is far more agreeable, even insinuating, as she returned to the charge against Pagnano. Between July and October 1515 she wrote him no fewer than five letters on the subject, the last thanking him with abject gratitude for his efforts: 'We have received a most welcome letter from Your Reverend Lordship,' she wrote on 14 September, 'for which we render you infinite thanks for the great love and charity you have borne us, particularly in this business of ours. No words could express our gratitude sufficiently so we pray to The Most High to keep you in that state which we most desire. Thus, I ask My Most Reverend and Illustrious Lord if possible that you could press this Pagnano in such a way that he will see the prudence of not disturbing me as he does. I swear to God that [I feel] shame rather than the loss that an usurious merchant should bring me to this . . .'[23]

Even the intervention of Ippolito, as Archbishop of Milan, had not produced an effect a month later. Ippolito fell ill and Vannozza was clearly panic-stricken, returning to the whining mode which she had used with Lucrezia. 'No words can express,' she wrote to him on 15 October,

the melancholy I feel at the sickness of Your Reverend Lordship and I have good reason to because I have no other hope in this world than Your Lordship and God knows that I do not rest day and night praying God that he should restore you to health and guard you from betrayals and traitors. And more, my Lord, I am most grieved that I am not in a position to come and be of service to you as I was to the late Duke and still more I am troubled by the persecution of Paolo Pagnano which would be enough if I was some woman or other that had no one and what grieves me more is that no regard is had for Your Lordship and for this My Lord I pray you that for the love you bear Jesus Christ you will not allow this man of nothing to tear me to pieces . . .

It was a question of 2,000 ducats owed over two or three years. If Ippolito could not settle it in her favour, she said, it would result in her dishonour and ruin.

The struggle against Pagnano was still going on in April 1517 when she again appealed to Ippolito for help. This time Pagnano, with the powerful help of Gian-Giacopo Trivulzio, Marshal of France and one of the most celebrated *condottieri* of his day, was trying to obtain sentence against her in a high court of law. She accused them of trying to have her and her emissary murdered. Signing herself 'La felice et infelice. Como matre' ('as mother'), the correspondence appears to have ended.

Money, as it would appear from the above, was a driving force in Vannozza's life. For all her complaints of ruin and destruction, she was a woman of considerable property. Apart from her handsome house in the Monti quarter, she owned other properties which she rented out: one large building contained three artisan's shops with rooms above. Two of the shops were inhabited by leather workers and their wives, who earned their living as laundresses, and one by a Florentine carpenter; above, two of the rooms were occupied by Margarita Mole and Lactantia, courtesans, the third by Madonna Montesina, 'a poor old Spanish woman'. In another building, rented out by Vannozza and also divided into three shops, one was occupied by a blacksmith, the two others by courtesans, one of them, Madonna Laura, a Spaniard, the other a cheap prostitute of the sort known as '*de la candeleta*' – by the candle in the window, a sign of their trade. In 1483, three years after Lucrezia's birth, she and her second husband, Giorgio della Croce, had rented the 'Leone', the first purpose-built inn in Rome and one of the most renowned, no doubt a profitable undertaking. She bought a second hostelry, the 'Vacca', near the Campo dei Fiori. She also appears to have raised money to finance her business undertakings: apart from borrowing from Paolo Pagnano, among the documents in the Archivio di Stato in Rome relating to her is a list of jewels, annotated 'List of the things which are in pawn'.[24]

In the latter years of her life, like other rich Roman matrons she bought peace for her soul and forgiveness for her sins with charitable donations. The fashionable church of Santa Maria del Popolo, much favoured by the Borgias, was a particular focus for her generosity. She endowed a chapel there in which Giorgio della Croce and their son Ottaviano were buried, as she was to be herself. She ordered marble ornaments for her chapel from the celebrated Andrea Bregno, including her arms, to be placed above the arch; she also donated a house on the Piazza Pizzo di Merlo, which may have been the one in which Lucrezia spent her early years, to this same church. In 1517 she donated the building which had been the Osteria della Vacca to the Ospedale di Santa Maria della Consolazione, a refuge for poor and sick women, with the condition that three masses should be said a year, one for her, one for Giorgio della Croce and one for Carlo Canale (the afterlife she envisaged for herself would certainly be crowded with men). To the same hospital she donated a silver bust of Cesare which disappeared, probably in the Sack of Rome in 1527.

Vannozza died on 26 November 1518, aged sixty years, four months and thirteen days. By the time of her death she had achieved wealth and respectability but she was still remembered principally for her association with Alexander VI and their children. Sanudo reported in a letter from Rome of 4 December 1518: 'The other day died Madama Vannozza who was the woman of Pope Alexander and mother of Duke Valentino and the Duchess of Ferrara.' News of her death was cried through Rome as befitted a celebrity of her stature, according to the letter: 'And that night I found myself in a place where I heard cry "*la parte*" in the Roman manner with these formal words, ". . . Know ye that Madonna Vannozza is dead, mother of the Duke of Gandia!"' As a member of Rome's most prestigious lay spiritual association, the Company of the Gonfalone, her funeral was well attended by the leading nobles and citizens. She was buried, Sanudo's correspondent continued, 'with pomp almost the equal of a cardinal . . . The chamberlains of the Pope attended which does not normally happen to anyone.' Her tombstone proudly recorded her relationship with Cesare, Juan – she even included Jofre – and Lucrezia, with their resounding titles. It was the only part of her tomb to survive and can still be seen today, removed to the porch of the little Basilica di San Marco, opposite the flamboyant Vittorio Emanuele Monument. Even the mass celebrated on the anniversary of her death (for which she had undoubtedly paid) was cancelled in the mid eighteenth century by the confraternity responsible, by then ashamed of the infamous Borgia connection.[25]

Alfonso and Lucrezia were a close partnership at this time, in their care for Ferrara and, above all, their children. His concern for her was obvious, as was his love. As Lucrezia had watched him mature over the difficult years of war, she had come to admire, respect and love him and she was proud of his achievements. When he reached Milan he took the trouble to write a letter in his own hand (which has since disappeared), a rare concession for a ruling prince. Lucrezia replied thanking him for the news of his arrival in Milan and 'what you have achieved there, and of your departure on your way [to France] . . .' She had clearly written to him on the day of his departure, the 24th, and she was reproving him for not having written to her sooner: 'Even if it arrived tardily it was timely enough to hear of your

wellbeing and that the tardiness was not your fault as I had thought
. . . God be praised for it and for mine and our children.' She
sent him all the latest news, enclosing a letter from Henry VIII
of England, thanking him for the lute which Alfonso had sent
him, and one from the Duchess of Milan asking for the stallions
to be sent as soon as possible. She also gave him the latest international news to keep him up to date: a friend had seen an autograph letter from Charles V, 'His Catholic Majesty', to the King
of France, reaffirming their friendship and asking for the King's
daughter, Charlotte, to be substituted for her sister, Louise, his
bride under the terms of the Treaty of Noyon, who had since
died.

Lucrezia had been kept informed since the outset of Alfonso's
journey by his companions, who included her favourite doctor,
Lodovico Bonaccioli, Alfonso Ariosto and Alfonso's secretary in
France, Bonaventura Pistofilo, who also wrote to his colleague in
Ferrara, Obizzo da Remi. En route on the day of Alfonso's departure Pistofilo wrote a hasty note to Obizzo saying that Alfonso
was in high spirits with his company and that Lucrezia should
be so too. From their correspondence it would appear that Alfonso,
although far less pious than his father, had inherited his interest
in saintly nuns and prophetesses. He commissioned Pistofilo to
find out whether there was anyone with a reputation for sanctity in the state of Monferrato where they had lodged with the
Marchioness and specifically to pass on to Lucrezia what Alfonso
himself had heard from her – that some months past, when the
Marquis was dying, she had brought in a holy woman from
Bologna who was reputed to have the gift of prophecy, 'but this
had brought them little fruit'.[26] At Turin, Alfonso received an
urgent message from the King to speed his journey to arrive
before the English envoys with their company of eight hundred
horse who were to be received with great pomp. Alfonso took
the post-horses provided, with a few companions – Sor Enea,
Messer Vincenzo, Alfonso Ariosto, il Cingano and il Mona, leaving the rest of his company to continue their normal journey.[27]

Lucrezia was delighted to hear of Alfonso's safe arrival in Paris

and replied thanking him effusively for the news; she was delighted
by his honourable reception by the King and Queen, by 'Madama'
('Madame Louise', the King's mother) and the leading nobles.
'Your letters have given me indescribable contentment, [the news]
has moved me to the heart,' she wrote, telling him she had passed
it on to her court to rejoice in. She was so pleased to hear that
his journey had proved useful and that she could reassure him
that everything in Ferrara was going well and peacefully in his
absence. She ended with family news. Their son Ippolito had a
rash and a slight temperature but nothing serious and neither one
nor the other troubled him. She suspected Francesco might be
about to go down with the same illness, 'however he eats well
and keeps fat and in these days I can hardly resist the urge to
bring him to Your Lordship at the accustomed hour'. Ercole was
well and continued to improve all the time. Their daughter was
well and fat: 'We all kiss your hand together . . .'[28]

She proudly kept Isabella informed of Alfonso's successes at
the French court, how he was welcomed and 'caressed' by the
King and Queen and 'Madama', and what an honourable place
he had been given at the formal reception of the papal legate.
She described his magnificent appearance in Notre Dame for the
swearing of the Anglo-French agreement: 'in a robe of cloth of
curled gold lined with ermine and in his bonnet, in place of a
medal, his beautiful great diamond which, by the reports of our
envoys, made a fine sight'.

Pistofilo and Bonaccioli wrote detailed reports of the magnificent entertainments – tournaments, jousts and banquets – with
which Francis was entertaining the English ambassadors: 'Yesterday
and today there were jousts in which the King took part dressed
in white with his company and M. St Paul [St Pol] led his company
dressed in black' in the great tournament on 22 December,
Pistofilo wrote. This spectacle was followed by dancing '*all'Italiana*'
to the sound of shawms in the presence of the King and the
English ambassadors until dinner was ready. 'There was so much
gold and silver displayed on the *credenze* that it would have satisfied the most avaricious soul,' the secretary reported. The scene

was lit by more than fifty torches in the hanging candelabra. The King sat in the middle of the table on a tribune beneath a baldachin in an armchair of gold brocade, with the English ambassadors alternating with the great ladies of the court on his right and left hand. Alfonso, Pistofilo noted proudly, was also among this most distinguished company. The meal was served 'in the royal manner' to the sound of trumpets, the dishes varied and copious. After dinner the tables were whisked away and there appeared twelve maskers dressed in black velvet who began to dance, then twelve others dressed in white velvet joined them, and then little by little many others, all most richly dressed and very elegant.

Giovanni Borgia had arrived safely, Alfonso wrote to Lucrezia from Paris on 26 December with a singular lack of enthusiasm. 'I have seen him and have set in train what is necessary for His Lordship for whom I will do all I can for love of Your Ladyship . . .' Lucrezia was always anxious about Giovanni Borgia's welfare: while Giovanni was on his way to Paris, she had written to Giovanni di Fino, their agent in Milan, informing him of Giovanni Borgia's arrival there. Many of Alfonso Ariosto's reports to Lucrezia concerned Giovanni, and his own and Alfonso's efforts to advance his cause at the French court. Ariosto told her that even before Borgia had arrived he (Ariosto) had spoken to the King, to de la Trémouïlle, Cesare's son-in-law, the Gran Scudero (Galeazzo da Sanseverino, *Grand Ecuyer* or Master of the King's Horse) and de Lapalisse about him but had not been able to speak to Madama because Alfonso was there much occupied with Her Highness. The King had answered Ariosto so kindly that he thought that His Majesty would not fail to do his best so that Lucrezia could have 'that courtesy that I told him you desired to have' (presumably to take Giovanni into royal service). Pistofilo reported on 20 December that Alfonso and company were well but that Alfonso had not yet presented Giovanni to the King.

Alfonso finally found an opportunity of presenting Giovanni to the King in the presence of M. de la Trémouïlle and the Gran Scudero, when he was 'seen and accepted', Bonaventura Pistofilo reported to Lucrezia on 23 December, but since the King was in such company he (Alfonso) could not present him with Lucrezia's letter of recommendation. Giovanni told Pistofilo that he wanted to send the letter to the Queen and Madama (instead of waiting to present it in person) whereupon Pistofilo reminded him that they could make him great and hold him dear. Borgia replied that he was ready to do any service but complained that they were too cold. 'For my part,' the harassed Pistofilo reported, 'I reminded this Don Giovanni of that which seemed to me to be of profit to him.' Eventually Giovanni succeeded in showing Lucrezia's letter to the King and Madama, 'by whom he is seen and welcomed very amiably when he attends them every day', but Pistofilo had to report that nothing had yet been decided about his service and Borgia was running short of money. By 21 January he was also running out of hope: 'The great promises made to Your Ladyship for the Lord Don Giovanni, seem to me to be very coldly executed, and I doubt that he will wish to stay here longer at his own expense. It pains me to have to write to Your Ladyship things that will be grievous, but . . . I feel I must because Your Ladyship should know everything.' Giovanni was to remain behind when the Ferrarese party left, with Alfonso's commendation to Madama and M. de Gramont (Gabriel, Cardinal-Bishop of Tarbes), but whether the tiresome and demanding young man ever received anything from them is not recorded. Lucrezia for her part thanked Alfonso warmly for all the care and favour he had shown Giovanni Borgia, 'that brother of mine'.

Alfonso's departure from Paris was delayed; the English ambassadors did not leave until 15 January but still he could not depart as Madama and the Gran Scudero were both ill and the King had left with his court for Saint-Germain to hunt stag. The Duke was therefore forced to wait until his return for a chance to talk about his affairs. He had written letters of thanks to the King and Cardinal (Thomas Wolsey) of England which the King had had read out in the English tongue, '*vulgar inglese*', to all the lords and gentlemen attending him. The King had said many 'amiable and honourable words about the Lord

Duke and Your Illustrious Ladyship, as I will demonstrate when I return to Ferrara,' Pistofilo reported. The papal legate had told him how much he wished to see Lucrezia if he could obtain licence from the Pope to pass by Ferrara. Meanwhile, Alfonso, with the leisure to go shopping, bought some civet cats which, Pistofilo wrote, 'have become very tame, so that His Excellency unleashes them and they allow themselves to be treated like dogs, they are young and beautiful, the male particularly so. Messer Poteghino has bought a little pony ['*ubinetto*'] for Ercole but it might be better for Francesco because it is very small.'

Alfonso finally left Paris on 24 January; on the eve of his departure he had dined privately with M. de Gramont and the Admiral (Guillaume Gouffier, seigneur de Bonnivet, admiral of France) together at his lodging. 'They told him the best things in the world', and when he left de Gramont presented him with the gift of a mule richly harnessed. For all the fine words, however, the mule seems to have been all that Alfonso actually received.

According to Pistofilo, the Duke was longing above everyone else to return to Ferrara. When Lucrezia heard the news she immediately wrote to Alfonso that 'any remnants of sorrow' for her mother's death in her heart had been effaced by her 'great joy and immense consolation at the news of your much desired swift return and the continuing good hope you give me of your affairs for which I thank the Lord God and await with high desire to hear from you personally of many other things which are too lengthy to write down . . .' Ippolito and Francesco were well, she told him, although Francesco had lost a little weight. 'I as usual listen to the readings of Galeazzo Boschetto with Ercole, who is very well.'

Alfonso arrived home on 20 February, having passed by Mantua. He went straight to see Lucrezia.

17. The End

'Having suffered greatly for more than two months because of
a difficult pregnancy; as it has pleased God on the 14th of this
month at dawn I had a daughter: and I hoped that having given
birth my illness also must be alleviated: but the contrary happened:
so that I must yield to nature: Our most clement Creator
has given me so many gifts, that I recognize the end of my life
and feel that within a few hours I shall be out of it . . .'

– Lucrezia to Pope Leo X, dictated on her deathbed, 22 June 1519

Alfonso celebrated his arrival home by proclaiming that carnival
should be celebrated with masking and tilting at the quintain.
He saw his sons – Ippolito had what may have been measles or
chicken pox (*varoli doppio*) and Ercole had a fever which was
thought to be the beginning of the same illness. Francesco,
however, was described by di Prosperi as in fine health 'and handsome and fresh as a rose, a very sweet little lord'. The elder boys
soon recovered and took part in the carnival masking and tilted
at the quintain but there were soon rumours that Lucrezia was
pregnant, and indeed, said di Prosperi, these days she had appeared
very troubled. Alfonso, therefore, had begun again to give audiences and to take the *Examine*: 'after which he retires with a few
people he likes'. He had issued new orders for his *camerini* that
no one should enter without permission except his pages and
men of his chamber.[1]

On 24 March, Francesco Gonzaga died of the syphilis which
had stalked him for years. Lucrezia had kept up her regular and
affectionate correspondence with him almost to the end. She had
written all through the previous winter and they had exchanged

international news, including the death of the Emperor Maximilian and speculation as to his succession. Francesco had sent her the latest news from Germany which he received from his agent there; she had written to him separately from Isabella of Alfonso's doings at the French court and of the Anglo-French negotiations. While expressing great affection for Francesco, she did not hesitate to tell him how much she was longing for Alfonso's arrival. And, beyond politics, there was religion, or rather superstition. On 24 January she had written to him in the most pious language congratulating him on the miraculous apparition of a dead nun in Mantua who had been seen to take the arm of a living nun, Sister Stephana: 'From this we must draw the conclusion that Our Lord God does not rest for the sins of our age to demonstrate his power, so that, moved by such a stupendous occurrence, we are disposed to have recourse to his mercy. And surely Your Lordship must rejoice that this should happen in your city, because where such cases occur, [people] are always turned to greater penitence, which alone can placate the wrath of God. And so I congratulate you . . .'

It is ironic that these two, one certainly committed to sins of the flesh, the other the daughter of the carnal Alexander and sister of the amoral Cesare, should have turned towards God in their later years. The reforming spirit expressed by Savonarola, the Ferrarese friar who had been the confidant of Duke Ercole and was executed at the stake in the reign of Alexander VI, had risen again under the stress of war and plague, for which the simple explanation was God's anger at 'the sins of our age'. Just over a year earlier, on 1 November 1517, Martin Luther had committed the act which let loose the Reformation when he nailed to the door of the church at Wittenberg the copy of his ninety-five theses against the buying, selling and offering of indulgences, which he saw as the flagrant ecclesiastical abuse of the time. No one yet foresaw the outcome of this act, least of all the current pope, Leo, who confined himself to ordering the head of Luther's monastic order, the Augustinian Eremites, to keep his monks quiet. Lucrezia herself saw nothing wrong in this ancient practice (nor did most of her contemporaries who eagerly abused the system: greedy Isabella d'Este was wont to seek indulgence or dispensation in order to eat cheese on meatless days).

Lucrezia's last surviving letter to Francesco, dated 19 March 1519, was loving with a note of valediction when she wrote thanking him for forwarding letters from Barcelona concerning 'Signor Hercule's' Spanish mission. The diligence he had shown in sending them expressly by the posts had once more shown her 'how you love me with [all] your heart, which although you have made this clear to me many times, still it pleases me on every occasion [whenever it happens] to realize it once again . . .'

After Francesco died, she sent a handwritten letter of condolence to Isabella to be taken to Mantua by messenger. She was too ill to go herself to offer her condolences, as Alfonso would – she was suffering another difficult pregnancy – yet her handwriting was still strong. It was hard to write an appropriate letter to the wife of a former lover, and she resorted to pious exhortation, begging Isabella to take this sorrow from the hand of God with her accustomed prudence, hoping that in his mercy some great good would come of it.[2] She also sent an official letter dated the same day, and wrote in her own hand to Francesco's son and successor, Federico, a rather more affectionate and personal letter than she had addressed to his mother, expressing her affection for him and wishing him 'every good and happiness' in his new estate.[3] One of the last letters she was to write would be to her delightful nephew, via a messenger, on 8 June 1519.

Lucrezia felt very unwell; the death of Francesco had unnerved her, as indeed had that of the Cardinal d'Aragona in January. On 26 April she wrote a curious letter to Alfonso, almost a premonition of her own death:

Talking the other day to a religious person, whose name I will tell Your Lordship when I see you, they said that everyone should be warned to take good care of themselves in these two months of which they hinted that they feared some danger. Although there is no other foundation than this which I have told you and you should give it no more faith than seems good to you, nonetheless I spoke of it to Hieronymo Ziliolo and since I could not write for finding myself somewhat stupefied in the head, I asked him to write to Messer Niccolò to advise you as you will now see, it seeming to me that the person of Your Lordship is of such importance that one could not fail to consider your security not to let you know of anything, however small.

Lucrezia was clearly anxious enough about this prognostication to take up her pen herself as soon as she felt well enough, so that there should be no misunderstanding or underestimation of the seriousness with which she herself regarded it.[4]

On 10 May, di Prosperi wrote of the 'love and concord' which demonstrably existed between Alfonso and Lucrezia, that she was pregnant and ill, praying that she would be cured of her infirmity 'to their contentment'. Their youngest son Francesco had almost died but was now well. On 15 June, the news was worse: 'The Duchess continues in her difficult pregnancy and not without great danger to herself so that she is very weak and cannot eat.' Bonaccioli counselled that it would be best if they induced or aborted the pregnancy so that she could regain her appetite and 'purge herself of the bad material that causes her illness'. But after she had produced 'a certain water which they say is a sign and preamble to imminent birth, they decided to go no further'. Alfonso showed great anxiety and spent a great deal of time at her side. 'God grant her a happy birth,' di Prosperi prayed, 'but people doubt it principally because of her weakness and because several women here have recently died of the same cause.'

He was unaware that, on 14 June, after an hour and a half's labour, Lucrezia had given birth to a baby girl so weak that she would not feed till the next day. Afraid that she might die unbaptized, Alfonso had her christened straightway, naming her Isabella Maria, with Eleonora della Mirandola, Count Alexandro Serafino and El Modenese del Forno as her godparents. Lucrezia had a little fever but it was hoped that she would soon be well. But by 20 June she was in a dangerous state and her doctors feared for her life, the more so since she had not been purged of the 'bad material' – believed to have been the accumulation of menstrual blood during pregnancy – and she was very weak. On the previous two nights she had had fits and the doctors prepared to bleed her. They cut off her hair. That morning blood flowed from her nose. Alfonso was frantic and the people of Ferrara anxious. Her life was despaired of and she was given just a few hours to live. She was incapable of speech and lost her sight. Alfonso remained by her side; suddenly she regained her senses and continued to improve until the thirteenth hour. 'If another paroxysm does not overtake her, the doctors give some hope of her convalescence,' di Prosperi wrote. 'God grant the Lord consolation because he is in such distress that more he could not be. And all this city will greatly grieve if she were to die.' That night and the following morning, the 22nd, she continued to improve and people began to think she might survive.

Lucrezia, however, was under no such illusion. As she was facing death, she dictated a letter to Leo X with her remaining strength:

Most Holy Father . . .
With every possible reverence of spirit I kiss the holy feet of Your Beatitude, and humbly recommend myself to the grace of Your Holiness: Having suffered greatly for more than two months because of a difficult pregnancy; as it has pleased God on the 14th of this month at dawn I had a daughter: and I hoped that having given birth my illness also must be alleviated: but the contrary happened: so that I must yield to nature: Our most clement Creator has given me so many gifts, that I recognize the end of my life and feel that within a few hours I shall be out of it, having however first received all the holy sacraments of the Church: And at this point, as a Christian although a sinner, it came to me to beseech your Beatitude that through your benignity you might deign to give from the spiritual Treasury some suffrage with your holy benediction to my soul: and thus devotedly I pray you: And to your grace I commend my lord Consort

and my children, all servants of your Beatitude. 'In Ferrara the 22nd day of June 1519 at the fourteenth hour.'
The humble servant of your Beatitude, Lucretia da este.[5]

Still Lucrezia did not die, but clung to life. Despite her piety, she felt in need of the highest benediction in the world to help her in the next. The Borgia past weighed heavily upon her; she had her young children and she did not want to leave them. In a postscript to his letter of the 22nd di Prosperi wrote, 'at this 23rd hour the Duchess still lives', but her burial had already been arranged. Even her death was not easy: on the morning of the 24th the doctors gave her up for dead, 'seeing the great fits and convulsions that came upon her'. They tried every way they could 'to open up the ways to purgation as they are wont to do in treating births', but whatever they tried failed, as did the continual orations and prayers of the convents of Ferrara. Alfonso never left her except to eat and rest a little. 'And thus the poor little woman is in her death throes without recognizing anyone or being able to speak . . .', di Prosperi wrote. '. . . May God have mercy on her soul and give comfort and good patience to the Lord when she does die, because truly his Excellency is grieving greatly. And yesterday in the procession he was as weak as if he had suffered a fever for some days. Wherefore it is now known truly the love that he bore her.'

Lucrezia died that night 'at the fifth hour', just over two months past her thirty-ninth birthday. Alfonso, 'in anguish of my soul', wrote two personal letters, to Federico Gonzaga, his nephew, and to an unnamed friend. To the first, he wrote, 'I cannot write without tears, so grave is it to find myself deprived of such a sweet, dear companion as she was to me, for her good ways and for the tender love there was between us. In so bitter a case I ask your consoling help but I know that you too will share my grief; and I would prefer someone to accompany my tears than to offer me consolation . . .'[6] To the second, he wrote how his 'most beloved consort, after an illness of several days with continual fever and *catarro* of the worst kind [which may have been tubercular], having received the sacraments of the Church with that devotion which

was in conformity with the rest of her life, has given up her spirit
to God: leaving me in the greatest imaginable anguish of soul
[for it is] the most unexpected and the greatest loss. I am writing to you about this grief that oppresses me so greatly and to
those who love me because . . . it seems that it may give me
some relief in my sorrow . . .'[7]

Postscript

Lucrezia was buried in the convent of Corpus Domini. Today she lies under a simple marble slab with Alfonso and two of their children, Alessandro and Isabella, her last born, who survived her by only two years, and Alfonso's mother, Eleonora d'Aragona. Beside them is the tomb of Lucrezia and Alfonso's eldest son, Duke Ercole II; in another lie his daughter, Lucrezia's granddaughter, also named Lucrezia, who died as a nun in the convent, and Eleonora d'Este, Lucrezia's only surviving daughter, who also became a nun in Corpus Domini.

In 1570 a devastating earthquake struck Ferrara, shattering much of the beauty of the city Lucrezia had known. Her grandson, Alfonso II, rebuilt the Castello but many churches and palaces still lay in ruins when he died, the last ruler of Lucrezia and Alfonso's legitimate line, in 1597. The following year, Cesare d'Este, Alfonso's illegitimate grandson by Laura Dianti, whom he took as mistress after Lucrezia's death, was expelled from the city by Pope Clement VIII who finally succeeded where Popes Julius and Leo had failed. Cesare d'Este retreated to Modena with what remained of the Este inheritance. The papal legate, Cardinal Aldobrandini, stripped Alfonso I's treasures, his Titians, from the *camerini*, and took them to Rome.

Ferrara, once one of the most glittering courts of Europe in the fifteenth and sixteenth centuries, sank into apathy under papal governance, becoming a shadow of its former self. There is still a romance about Ferrara. Boswell viewed it as 'the beautiful remains of a great city', while in 1846 Dickens wrote of the appeal of 'the long silent streets and the dismantled palaces where ivy waves in lieu of banners'. Gabriele d'Annunzio called it 'a city of silence'. The glory of the Este, however, has gone.

Archives

Cambridge University Library Archives, Acton Papers (CUL)

Acton MSS, Add. MSS 4757: correspondence of Gian Luca Pozzi in Rome with Ercole I d'Este concerning Lucrezia's marriage; correspondence of Gherardus Saraceni and Hector Berlinguer re the same and minutes by Ercole to the above

Add. MSS 4758: correspondence of Beltrando de'Costabili in Rome with Ercole

Add. MSS 4759: correspondence of Beltrando de'Costabili in Rome concerning illness and death of Alexander VI and fate of Cesare, and Julius II's reaction to attack on Giulio d'Este

Biblioteca Comunale Ariostea di Ferrara (BCAFe)

Lucrezia's accounts for 1507, Albo Estense Autografi, BCA, Classe I, 656

Papal brief to Lucrezia of 1516 concerning San Bernardino, MS coll. Antonelli, 272

Archivio di Stato di Mantova, Archivio Gonzaga (AG)

Correspondence Lucrezia Borgia to Francesco Gonzaga: Autografi 84, Busta 1, Busta 2, Busta 3, Busta 4, Serie E XXXi.2, Busta 1189

Correspondence Lucrezia Borgia to Isabella d'Este: Autografi 84, Busta 1, Busta 2, Busta 3, Busta 4, Serie E XXXi.2 Busta 1189

Isabella d'Este to Lucrezia Borgia, Copielettere, Busta 2993, 2994, liber 12, liber 15, liber 18

Isabella d'Este Family Correspondence: Copielettere to

Francesco Gonzaga, Ercole d'Este, Ferrante and Servitors with correspondence from the Este family, Busta 2993, liber 12, 13, 14

Isabella d'Este to Cesare Borgia, Busta 2993, liber 14

Ippolito d'Este to Isabella, Busta 1189; Alfonso d'Este to Isabella d'Este, E XXXI.2., Busta 1189, Alfonso d'Este to Francesco Gonzaga, E XXX 1.2., Busta 1189, Isabella d'Este to Alfonso d'Este, Busta 2994, liber 18; Ferrante d'Este to Francesco Gonzaga, Busta 1189; Giulio d'Este to Francesco Gonzaga, and to Isabella d'Este, Busta 1189

Bernardino di Prosperi to Isabella d'Este, 1502–19. More than seven hundred letters written from Ferrara covering the period of Lucrezia's life there: this is probably the most important and largely unexplored source providing not only an almost daily record of her life but a full chronicle of social and political events and people at court and in the city. Serie E XXX 1.3. Buste 1238–47

Archivio di Stato di Milano, Archivio Sforzesco (ASF)

Potenze Estere, Roma. Reg. Cartella 107; 109; 116; 123; 124; 126; 127; 128

Potenze Estere, Marca. Reg. Cartella 153

Potenze Estere, Mantova. Reg. Cartella 400

Archivio di Stato di Modena, Archivio Segreto Estense (ASE)

Correspondence Francesco Gonzaga to Lucrezia Borgia: Carteggio dei Principi Esteri, Busta 1181

Lucrezia Borgia correspondence with members of the Este family: Casa e Stato:

Lucrezia to Ercole I. Busta 141, Ercole I to Lucrezia, Camera Ducale, Minutario, Busta 5, Minute Ducali, Busta 69

Lucrezia to Alfonso I d'Este. Casa e Stato, Busta 141, Alfonso I
d'Este to Lucrezia. Casa e Stato, Carteggio dei Principi Estensi,
Busta 75
Lucrezia to Cardinal Ippolito d'Este. Casa e Stato, Busta 141
Lucrezia to Sigismondo d'Este, Casa e Stato, Busta 141
Lucrezia to Ferrante d'Este, Casa e Stato, Busta 141
Lucrezia to Giulio d'Este, Casa e Stato, Busta 141

Lucrezia Borgia General Correspondence, Casa e Stato, Busta 141,
Carteggio tra Principi Estensi
Letters by members of the Borgia family and others: Cancelleria
Ducale, Particolari, Busta 209, Fasc. 4 Borgia
Documents concerning Lucrezia Borgia anterior to her marriage
to Alfonso I, Casa e Stato, Busta 400
Documents concerning Lucrezia Borgia posterior to her marriage
to Alfonso I, Casa e Stato, Busta 400
Documents concerning the Borgia family: Casa e Stato, Busta 401,
other documents relating to Rodrigo d'Aragona, Duke of
Bisceglie. Casa e Stato, Busta 401, documents relating to the estate
of Rodrigo d'Aragona, Duke of Bisceglie, Busta 400
'Computo delle nozze della Ill. Madama Lucrezia 1501–1502' [Lists
of Jewels given by Ercole I to Lucrezia in 1502, and of her
company on her wedding journey to Ferrara] Camera Ducale,
Amministrazione dei Principi, n. 1128
Inventario di Guardaroba: 'Inventario 1502–3', Camera Ducale,
Amministrazione dei Principi – Lucrezia Borgia B1137
Lucrezia Borgia Household Accounts, ibid.: B1138 1506–8; B1131
1507–9; B1133 1506; B1132 1517–20, B1134 1514–19; B1136
1518–19

Bulls and papal briefs concerning Camerino: the creation of the
duchy and its Duke, Giovanni Borgia. Camera Ducale,
Amministrazione dei Principi, Busta 1127

Isabella d'Este to Alfonso I d'Este, Casa e Stato, Carteggio dei
Principi Estensi, Busta 133

Ercole I d'Este correspondence with his ambassador in France, Bartolommeo de'Cavalleri: Ambasciatori Esteri – Francia, 1500–1501, Busta 3

Ercole I d'Este correspondence with his ambassadors in Rome, Gian Luca Pozzi and Gherardo Saraceni, Ambasciatori Esteri – Roma, 1501–2, Busta 12

Ferrarese Ambassadors Manfredi and Cavalleri to Ercole I and Alfonso I concerning the marriage negotiations and posterior events including the death of Alexander VI and the fortunes of Cesare Borgia, 1503–4, 1506–7, Ambasciatori Esteri – Francia, Buste 3 and 4

Ercole I d'Este, Letterbook [*Minutario*] drafts of letters to various correspondents including the various ambassadors, Lucrezia, Cesare Borgia, Isabella d'Este and others, 1501–2, Cancelleria Ducale, Busta 5

Archivio Segreto Vaticano (ASV)

Borgia Family Letters: A.A. ARM I–XVIII, 5027; A.A. ARM I–XVIII, 5024

Source Notes

The Scene (pp. 1–3)

1. Guicciardini, *The History of Italy*, Book I, p. 4.

Chapter 1: The Pope's Daughter (pp. 11–24)

1. Gaspare da Verona, cited Gregorovius, *Lucretia Borgia*, p. 9.
2. Bonatto to Barbara of Brandenburg, 8 June 1460, in Luzio, *Isabella d'Este e i Borgia*, p. 471.
3. Pastor, *The History of the Popes from the Close of the Middle Ages*, vol. V, p. 388.
4. Ibid., p. 400.
5. Ross, *Lives of the Early Medici as told in their correspondence*.
6. Cesare's birth year is variously given as 1475 or 1476: I have adopted the date given by the most authoritative recent historian of the Borgias, Miquel Batllori, in *La Familia Borja*.
7. 18 March 1493, cited Luzio, *Isabella d'Este e i Borgia*, p. 477.
8. Batllori, *La Familia Borja*.
9. Cited in Bradford, *Cesare Borgia*, p. 23.
10. ASV, A.A. ARM I–XVIII, 5023, ff 61v–64r.

Chapter 2: Countess of Pesaro (pp. 25–49)

1. Guicciardini, *The History of Italy*, Book I, p. 10.
2. Ascanio to Ludovico, 3 February 1493, ASF, Potenze Estere, Roma, Reg. Cartella 107, ff 95–7.
3. Ibid.

4. Gianandrea Boccaccio, Bishop of Modena, 5 November 1492, in Gregorovius, *Lucretia Borgia*, p. 51.

5. Ercole to Alexander VI, 3 January 1493, in Gregorovius, p.55.

6. Ascanio Sforza to Ludovico Sforza, 3 February 1493, in ASF, Potenze Estere, Roma, Reg. Cartella 107, ff 95–7.

7. Sanchis y Sivera, Jose, *Algunos Documentos*, p. 52. Procida, or Proixita in Catalan spelling, married a Borgia connection, Caterina de Mila, in 1494.

8. Floramonte Brognolo, 10 June 1493, in Luzio, *Isabella d'Este e i Borgia*, p. 478.

9. Luzio, p. 120n.

10. Piergentile da Varano of Camerino, 18 June 1493, Luzio, p. 120.

11. Giovanni Lucido Cattanei, 6 August 1493, Luzio, p. 415.

12. Sanchis y Sivera, pp. 132–47.

13. 31 July 1493, see Batllori, *La Familia Borja*, p. 184.

14. Ibid.

15. ASV, A.A. ARM 5021, f 3rv, Viterbo, 31 [October 1493], this translation kindly provided by Milo Parmoor.

16. Sanchis y Sivera, pp. 54–5, this translation kindly provided by Milo Parmoor and Prof. Jaume Danti.

17. Cattaneo, 3 August 1493, Luzio, p. 415.

18. Ibid., 31 August 1493, Luzio, p. 416.

19. Ibid., 7 November 1493, Luzio, p. 418.

20. Gregorovius, p. 65.

21. Brognolo, 1 March 1494, Luzio, p. 482.

22. Ibid., 27 March 1494, Luzio, p. 483n.

23. G. Benedetto, 5 May 1494, Luzio, pp. 483–4.

24. Gregorovius, p. 72.

25. 4 April 1494, ASF, Potenze Estere, Roma, Cartella 109.

26. Sanchis y Sivera, pp. 78–9.

27. 18 May 1494, Sanchis y Sivera, p. 88.

28. Alexander VI to Gandia, 18 May 1494, Sanchis y Sivera, pp. 92–6.

29. Sanchis y Sivera, pp. 111–12.

30. Lucrezia to Alexander VI, Pesaro, 10 June 1494. ASV, A.A. ARM I–XVIII, 5027.

31. Giulia d'Aragona to Alexander VI, 10 June 1494. ASV, A.A. ARM I–XVIII, 5027.

32. Jacopo Dragoni to Cesare Borgia, 16 April 1494, ASV, A.A. ARM I–XVIII, 5027.

33. Lucrezia to Alexander VI, Pesaro, [?xxv] June 1494, ASV, A.A. ARM I–XVIII, 5027.

34. Caterina Gonzaga to Alexander VI, San Lorenzo, 8 July and 1 August 1494, ASV, A.A. ARM I–XVIII, 5027, ff rv and 14r.

35. Alexander VI to Giulia Farnese, n.d. [Rome, late June/early July 1494] ASV, A.A. ARM I–XVIII, 5027, f 32.

36. Alexander VI to Lucrezia, ASV, A.A. ARM I–XVIII, 5027, f 29.

37. Alexander VI to Lucrezia, 24 July 1494, from Florentine state archives, printed in Gregorovius, p. 74.

38. Lucrezia to Alexander VI, Pesaro, 27 July, 1494, ASV, A.A. ARM I–XVIII, 5027.

39. Virginio Orsini (drafted by Alexander VI) to Orsino Orsini, Monterotondo, 21 September 1494, ASV, A.A. ARM I–XVIII, 5027 f 42r.

40. Fra Theseo to Giulia Farnese, Bassanello, ASV, A.A. ARM I–XVIII, 5027, 28 October 1494.

41. Alexander VI draft minute to Giulia Farnese, 21 October 1494, ASV, A.A. ARM I–XVIII, 5027, f 28r.

42. Alexander VI draft minute to Adriana de Mila, ASV, A.A. ARM I–XVIII, 5027, 22 October 1494, f 28r.

43. Alexander VI draft minute to Cardinal Farnese, ASV, A.A. ARM I–XVIII, 5027, f 28r.

44. Giacomo Trotti to Ercole d'Este, 21 December 1494, in Gregorovius, p. 89.

Chapter 3: The Borgias Renascent (pp. 50–66)

1. Hollingsworth, *Patronage in Renaissance Italy: From 1400 to the Early Sixteenth Century*, pp. 273–4.

2. Giovanni Sforza to Francesco Gonzaga, Pesaro, 24 March 1495, in Luzio, *Isabella d'Este e i Borgia*, p. 487n.

3. Giovanni Sforza to Ludovico Sforza, ASF, Potenze Estere, Marca, Reg. Cartella 153.

4. Francesco Gonzaga to Ludovico Sforza, 4 March 1496, ASF, Potenze Estere, Mantova, Reg. Cartella 400.

5. Dolfo, *Lettere ai Gonzaga*, Letter XXIX, lines 393–5, p. 95.

6. Cardinal Ascanio Sforza to Ludovico Sforza, 7 April 1496, ASF, Potenze Estere, Roma, Reg. Cartella 116.

7. Ascanio to Ludovico, 16 April 1496; Giovanni Sforza to Ludovico, 17 April 1496; Stefano Taberna to Ludovico, 28 April 1496, ASF, Potenze Estere, Roma, Reg. Cartella 116.

8. Bradford, *Cesare Borgia*, p. 55.

9. Deposition by Anthoni Gurrea, 17 June 1494, ASV, A.A. ARM I–XVIII, 5024, f 126.

10. Bradford, p. 59.

11. Mallett, *The Borgias: The Rise and Fall of a Renaissance Dynasty*, p. 150.

12. Giovanni Sforza to Ludovico Sforza, Pesaro, 7 January 1497, ASF, Potenze Estere, Marca, Reg. Cartella 153.

13. G. C. Scalona to Francesco Gonzaga, 27 January 1497, Luzio, p. 493.

14. 10 April 1497, Ludovico Sforza draft letter to 'il Barone', ASF, Potenze Estere, Marca, Reg. Cartella 153.

15. Ludovico Sforza to Giovanni Sforza, 4 May 1497, ASF, Potenze Estere, Marca, Reg. Cartella 153.

16. Giovanni Sforza to Ludovico Sforza, 12 May 1497, ASF, Potenze Estere, Marca, Reg. Cartella 153.

17. Silvestro Calandra to Francesco Gonzaga, 6 June 1497, Luzio, p. 496.

18. Ferrarese envoy, in Pastor, *The History of the Popes from the Close of the Middle Ages*, vol. V, p. 505n.

19. 12 June 1497, Luzio, p. 497.

20. Sanudo, *I. Diarii*, vol. 1, pt. 1, col. 649.

21. Pastor, vol. V, pp. 520–21n.

22. Antonio Costabili to Ercole d'Este, 23 June 1497, ASE, Ambasciatori Esteri: Milano, Busta 13.

23. Cardinal Ascanio Sforza to Ludovico Sforza, August 1497, in Pastor, vol. V, p. 521n.

24. In Johannes Burchard, *Diarium sive Rerum Urbanum Commentarii*

(1483–1506), vol. 2, Alessandro Bracci to Florentine Signoria, 27 September 1497.

25. Document drawn up for Giovanni Sforza and Cardinal Ascanio Sforza in form of letter from the former to the latter, 20 November 1497, ASF, Potenze Estere, Marca, Reg. Cartella 153.

26. Draft divorce sentence, ASF, Potenze Estere, Marca, Reg. Cartella 153, following letter of 20 December 1497.

27. Thomasino Tormelli to Ludovico Sforza, 3 December 1497, ASF, Potenze Estere, Marca, Reg. Cartella 153.

28. Thomasino Tormelli to Ludovico Sforza, 21 December 1497, ASF, Potenze Estere, Marca, Reg. Cartella 153.

29. Ascanio Sforza to Ludovico Sforza, 23 December 1497, ASF, Potenze Estere, Roma, Reg. Cartella 153.

Chapter 4: The Tragic Duchess of Bisceglie (pp. 67–95)

1. Cristoforo Poggio to Francesco Gonzaga, 2 March 1498, in Luzio, *Isabella d'Este e i Borgia*, p. 503.

2. Saliceto to Ludovico Sforza, 29 July 1498, ASF, Potenze Estere, Roma, Reg. Cartella 126.

3. Cited in Burchard, *Diarium*, vol. 2, 29 July 1498.

4. Ibid., 14 September 1497.

5. Cardinal Ascanio Sforza to Ludovico Sforza, 2 May 1498, ASF, Potenze Estere, Roma, Reg. Cartella 126.

6. Cardinal Ascanio Sforza to Ludovico Sforza, 13 May 1498, ASF, Potenze Estere, Roma, Reg. Cartella 126.

7. The document was dated 31 August 1498 – ASF, Casa e Stato, Busta 400.

8. It was only on 10 June 1498 that Alexander finally issued a Bull cancelling her marriage contract with D. Gaspare da Procida, now described as Count of Almenara. ASF, Casa e Stato, Busta 400.

9. Laurencin, *Relaciónes de los Festines que se celebraron en el Vaticano con motivo de las Bodas de Lucrecia Borgia con Don Alonso de Aragon*.

10. Sanudo, *I Diarii*, vol. II, 23 October 1498.

11. 10 December 1498, ASF, Potenze Estere, Roma, Reg. Cartella 127.

12. The Prince of Asturias died of plague in October 1497.

13. Rome, 18 August 1499, transcript from document in archives of Spoleto, Gregorovius, *Lucretia Borgia*, pp. 117–18.

14. 18 August, 1499, Luzio, p. 431.

15. 16 August 1499, ibid.

16. Ascanio was not released until 3 January 1502 through the good offices of the Cardinal d'Amboise; he returned to Rome with him for the conclave which elected Pius III and died there of plague in May 1505.

17. See Malegonelle to Signoria of Florence, 4 April 1500, Burchard, vol. 3, p. 32n.

18. Sanudo, vol. III, col. 469, 3 July 1500.

19. Rome, 16 July 1500, Burchard.

20. Luzio, p. 519.

21. Sanudo, vol. III, col. 532, 19 July 1500.

22. Luzio, p. 521.

23. Cattaneo, 4 September 1500, in Luzio, p. 522.

24. Francesco Gonzaga to Giovanni Gonzaga, 1 October 1500, in Luzio, p. 524.

25. Copielettere d'Isabella d'Este, AG, Busta 2993, liber 14.

Chapter 5: Turning Point (pp. 96–110)

1. Lucrezia to Vincenzo Giordano, 31 October 1500, ASE, Casa e Stato, Busta 141.

2. Lucrezia to Vincenzo Giordano, 28 October 1500, ASE, Casa e Stato, Busta 141.

3. n.d. [October 1500], ff 89–90, 91 ASE, Casa e Stato, Busta 141.

4. 17 September, Luzio, *Isabella d'Este e i Borgia*, p. 522.

5. Bartolommeo de'Cavalleri to Ercole d'Este, 15 December 1500, ASE, Ambasciatori Esteri – Francia, Busta 3.

6. Ercole to Cavalleri, 14 February 1501, ASE, Ambasciatori Esteri – Francia, Busta 3.

7. Ercole to Cavalleri, 25 February 1501, 15 December 1500, ASE, Ambasciatori Esteri – Francia, Busta 3.
8. Cavalleri to Ercole, 18 March 1501, ASE, Ambasciatori Esteri – Francia, Busta 3.
9. Cardinal Ferrari to Ercole, 18 February 1501 and n.d., CUL, Acton MSS, Add. MSS 4757.
10. Cavalleri to Ercole, 26 May 1501, ASE, Ambasciatori Esteri – Francia, Busta 3.
11. Ercole to Cavalleri, 9 June 1501, ASE, Ambasciatori Esteri – Francia, Busta 3.
12. Ercole to Cavalleri, 14 June 1501, ASE, Ambasciatori Esteri – Francia, Busta 3.
13. Cavalleri to Ercole, Lyons, 22 June 1501, ASE, Ambasciatori Esteri – Francia, Busta 3.
14. Ercole to Cavalleri, 8 July 1501, ASE, Ambasciatori Esteri – Francia, Busta 3.
15. Cavalleri to Ercole, 10 July, Lyons, ASE, Ambasciatori Esteri – Francia, Busta 3.
16. Ercole to Cavalleri, 11 August 1501, ASE, Cancelleria ducale, minutario cronologica, Busta 5.
17. Cattaneo, 20 July 1501, Luzio, p. 532.
18. Cattaneo, 11 August 1501, Luzio, p. 533.
19. Ercole to Cesare Borgia, 6 August 1501, ASE, Cancelleria ducale, minutario cronologica, Busta 5.
20. Cardinal Ferrari to Ercole, 27 August 1501, CUL, Acton MSS, Add. MSS 4757.
21. Ercole to Cavalleri, 5 September 1501, ASE, Ambasciatori Esteri – Francia, Busta 3.
22. Ercole to Cavalleri, 30 October 1501, ASE, Ambasciatori Esteri – Francia, Busta 3.
23. Ercole to Lucrezia, 1 September 1501, ASE, Cancelleria ducale, minutario cronologica, Busta 5.
24. That summer he had also expropriated the lands of the other Roman baronial families, the Colonna, Savelli and Estouteville
25. Guicciardini, *The History of Italy*, Book I, p. 163.

Chapter 6: *Farewell to Rome (pp. 111–32)*

1. Burchard, *Diarium*, vol. 3, 17 September 1501.
2. 25 September 1501, CUL, Acton MSS, Add. MSS 4757, ff 64,
3. Ibid.
4. Berlinguer and Saraceni to Ercole, 27 September 1501, CUL, Acton MSS, Add. MSS 4757.
5. Lucrezia to Ercole, 28 September and 8 October 1501, ASE, Casa e Stato, Busta 141.
6. Ercole to Lucrezia, 14 October 1501, ASE, Cancelleria ducale, minutario cronologica, Busta 5.
7. Lucrezia to Ercole, 11 October 1501, Casa e Stato, Busta 141.
8. See Saraceni and Berlinguer to Ercole, 11 October 1501, CUL, Acton MSS, Add. MSS 4757.
9. Batllori, *La Familia Borja*, p. 4.
10. Letter of 4 March 1500, see Gardner, *Dukes and Poets in Ferrara*, p. 367n.
11. Cavalleri to Ercole, 26 August 1501, ASE, Ambasciatori Esteri – Francia, Busta 3.
12. Letter of 31 October 1501 in Gardner, p. 402n.
13. Lucrezia to Ercole, 28 October 1501, ASE, Casa e Stato, Busta 141.
14. Ercole to Lucrezia, 28 December 1501, ASE, Cancelleria ducale, Minute Ducali, Busta 69.
15. Rome, 8 October 1501, Saraceni and Berlinguer to Ercole, CUL, Acton MSS, Add. MSS 4757.
16. Rome, n.d., CUL, Acton MSS, Add. MSS 4757.
17. Cited in Gregorovius, *Lucretia Borgia*, p. 213.
18. See Beltrami, *La Guardaroba di Lucrezia Borgia*.
19. Burchard, vol. 3, 23 December 1501.
20. Luzio, *Isabella d'Este e i Borgia*, pp. 535–6.
21. Burchard, vol. 3, 23 December 1501.
22. Pozzi and Saraceni to Ercole, 30 December 1501, CUL, Acton MSS, Add. MSS 4757.
23. El Prete to Isabella 'relazione dello sposalizio della Borgia la sera

del 24 dicembre 1501' [transcript], AG, Autografi 84, Busta 4.

24. Pozzi to Ercole, 1 January 1502, ASE Ambasciatori Esteri – Roma, Busta 12.

25. Pozzi to Ercole, 6 January 1502, ASE Ambasciatori Esteri – Roma, Busta 12.

26. Beltrando Costabili to Ercole, 6 January 1502, CUL, Acton MSS, Add. MSS 4758.

Chapter 7: *The Road to Ferrara (pp. 133–55)*

1. Biblioteca Vaticana, manoscritto vaticano latino 3351, f 49, cited Sacerdote, *Cesare Borgia, la sua vita, la sua famiglia, e i suoi tempi*, p. 518.
2. Ercole to Ippolito, cited Gardner, *Dukes and Poets in Ferrara*, pp. 242–3.
3. Ercole to Ippolito, 19 August 1499, Gardner, p. 350.
4. Ercole to Ferrante, 8 April 1494, Gardner, p. 249.
5. Ercole to Ferrante, 27 February 1495, Gardner, p. 297.
6. Pozzi and Saraceni to Ercole, Foligno, 13 January 1502, ASE, Ambasciatori Esteri – Roma, Busta 12.
7. Ibid.
8. Ferrante d'Este to Isabella d'Este, Rimini, 22 January 1502, AG, Autografi 84, Busta 4.
9. Pozzi and Saraceni to Ippolito, Urbino, 18 January 1502, ASE, Ambasciatori Esteri – Roma, Busta 12.
10. Pozzi and Saraceni to Ercole, Urbino, 18 January 1502, ASE, Ambasciatori Esteri – Roma, Busta 12.
11. Pozzi and Saraceni to Ercole, Rimini, 22 January 1502, ASE, Ambasciatori Esteri – Roma, Busta 12.
12. Pozzi and Saraceni to Ercole, Cesena, 24 January 1502, ASE, Ambasciatori Esteri – Roma, Busta 12.
13. Pozzi and Saraceni to Ercole, Imola, 27 January 1502, ASE, Ambasciatori Esteri – Roma, Busta 12.
14. Marinello, *Gli Ornamenti delle Donne*, Venice, pp. 69–75.
15. Pozzi to Ercole, Bologna, 30 January 1502, ASE, Ambasciatori Esteri – Roma, Busta 12.
16. El Prete to Isabella d'Este, 19 January 1502, Luzio, p. 539.

17. Pozzi and Saraceni to Ercole, Bologna, 29 January 1502, ASE, Ambasciatori Esteri – Roma, Busta 12.
18. Pozzi and Saraceni to Ercole, Bentivoglio, 31 January 1502, ASE, Ambasciatori Esteri – Roma, Busta 12.
19. Costabili to Ercole, Rome, 17 January 1502, CUL, Acton MSS, Add. MSS 4758.
20. Costabili to Ercole, Rome, 20 January 1502, CUL, Acton MSS, Add. MSS 4758.
21. Isabella d'Este to Francesco Gonzaga, Ferrara, 1 February 1502, AG, Copielettere, Busta 2993, liber 12.
22. Tuohy, *Herculean Ferrara: Ercole d'Este (1471–1505) and the Invention of a Ducal Capital*, p. 14.
23. Ibid., p. 20.

Chapter 8: A New Life (pp. 156–83)

1. Zambotti, *Diario Ferrarese dall'anno 1476 sino al 1504*, p. 313.
2. Isabella d'Este to Francesco Gonzaga, Ferrara, 2 February 1502, AG, Copielettere, Busta 2993, liber 14.
3. 'Computo delle nozze della Ill.ma Madama Lucrezia 1501–1502', ASE, Camera Ducale, Amministrazione dei Principi, n1128.
4. Cited Luzio, *Isabella d'Este e i Borgia*, p. 541.
5. Costabili to Ercole, 1 April 1502, cited Gregorovius, *Lucretia Borgia*, p. 253n.
6. Isabella d'Este to Francesco Gonzaga, [?2] February 1502, AG, Copielettere, Busta 2993, liber 14.
7. Luzio, pp. 543–4.
8. Isabella d'Este to Francesco Gonzaga, 5 February 1502, AG, Copielettere, Busta 2993, liber 14.
9. Isabella d'Este to Francesco Gonzaga, 7 February 1502, AG, Copielettere, Busta 2993, liber 14.
10. 'Computo delle nozze della Ill.ma Madama Lucrezia 1501–1502', ASE, Camera Ducale, Amministrazione dei Principi, n1128.
11. Isabella d'Este to Francesco Gonzaga, 9 February 1502, AG, Copielettere, Busta 2993, liber 14.

12. Benedetto Capilupo to Francesco Gonzaga, February 9 1502, cited in Gardner, p. 422.

13. Isabella d'Este to Francesco Gonzaga, 11 February 1502, AG, Copielettere, Busta 2993, liber 14.

14. Bernardino di Prosperi to Isabella d'Este, Ferrara, 18 February 1502, AG, Serie E XXXI.3, Busta 1238.

15. Ercole to Alexander VI, 14 February 1502, see Gregorovius, doc. 38.

16. Di Prosperi to Isabella, 18 February 1502, AG, E XXXI.3, Busta 1238.

17. Di Prosperi to Isabella, 26 February 1502, AG, E XXXI.3, Busta 1238.

18. See Gundersheimer, *Art and Life at the Court of Ercole I d'Este: The 'De triumphis religionis' of Giovanni Sabadino degli Arienti.*

19. I am indebted to Dr Thomas Tuohy for this information.

20. Lucrezia's accounts for 1507, BCAFe, Albo Estense Autografi, BCA, Classe I, 656.

21. Zambotti, p. 338. The ladies who remained were 'Angela Borgia, Elisabetta senese [from Siena], Geronima Senese, Camilla Fiorentina [from Florence], Madona Juana Castigliana [from Castile], Black Catherina, two handmaids – Little Catherina and Eleonora, Madona Cecharella Puzeta from Naples with Cinzia and Margarita, her daughters'.

22. Zambotti, p. 337.

23. Di Prosperi to Isabella, Ferrara, 6 March 1502, AG, E XXXI.3, Busta 1238

24. Ibid.

25. Gundersheimer, p. 21.

26. Lucrezia to Sigismondo d'Este, Belfiore, 26 June 1502, ASE, Casa e Stato, Busta 141.

27. Isabella d'Este to Lucrezia, Isabella to Geronima Borgia, Mantua, 18 February 1502, AG, Copielettere, Busta 2993, liber 12.

28. Gundersheimer, pp. 22–4.

29. Di Prosperi to Isabella, 27 June 1502, AG, E XXXI.3, Busta 1238.

30. Letter of 27 June 1502, in Luzio and Renier, *Mantova e Urbino*, p. 125.

31. Report of delegation 26 June 1502, in Bradford, p. 179.

32. Lucrezia to Ercole, 13 July 1502, ASE, Casa e Stato, Busta 141.

33. Di Prosperi to Isabella, 16 July 1502, AG, E XXXI.3, Busta 1238.

34. Di Prosperi to Isabella, 24 July 1502, AG, E XXXI.3, Busta 1238.

35. Di Prosperi to Isabella, 28 July 1502, AG, E XXXI.3, Busta 1238.

36. Costabili to Ercole, 13 July 1502, CUL, Acton MSS, Add. MSS 4758, f 169.

37. Di Prosperi to Isabella, 8 September 1502, AG, E XXXI.3, Busta 1238.

38. Costabili to Ercole, 8 September 1502, CUL, Acton MSS, Add. MSS 4758, f 172.

39. Saraceni to Ercole, 8 September 1502, CUL, Acton MSS, Add. MSS 4758, f 147.

40. Di Prosperi to Isabella, 6 October 1502, AG, E XXXI.3, Busta 1238.

41. Matarazzo, in Bradford, p. 182.

42. Isabella d'Este to Francesco Gonzaga, 23 July 1502, in Bradford, p. 185.

43. Bradford, p. 197.

44. Gregorovius, pp. 284–5.

45. Di Prosperi to Isabella, 10 January 1503, AG, E XXXI.3, Busta 1239.

Chapter 9: The Heavens Conspire (pp. 184–207)

1. Cited in Luzio, *Isabella d'Este e i Borgia*, p. 697.

2. Di Prosperi to Isabella, 16 January 1503, AG, E XXXI.3, Busta 1239.

3. Isabella d'Este to Lucrezia, 4 February 1502, AG, Copielettere, Busta 2993, liber 12.

4. Luzio, p. 699. There is no other evidence for this.

5. Lucrezia's wardrobe inventory: Inventario di Guardaroba, 'Inventario 1502–3', ASE, Camera Ducale, Amministrazione dei Principi, Lucrezia Borgia B1137.

6. See Shankland, *The Prettiest Love Letters in the World: Letters Between Lucrezia Borgia and Pietro Bembo 1503–1519*, p. 21.

7. Pietro Bembo to Carlo Bembo, 15 January 1503, in Shankland.

8. Wirtz, *Ercole Strozzi, Poeta Ferrarese (1473–1508)*, in *Atti della Deputazione Ferrarese di Storia Patria*, vol. 16, pt. II, p. 52.

9. 3 June 1503, Shankland, Letter I.

10. Both letters of 8 June 1503, Shankland, Letters II and III.

11. 19 June 1503, Shankland, Letter IV.

12. Shankland, op. cit., Letters V and VI.

13. Late June 1503, Shankland, Letter VII.

14. Cited in Bradford, *Cesare Borgia*, p. 213.

15. Costabili to Ercole, 5 July 1503, CUL, Acton MSS, Add. MSS 4759.

16. Clough, 'Niccolò Machiavelli, Cesare Borgia and the Francesco Troche Episode', in *Medievalia et Humanistica*, Fasc. 17.

17. 14 July 1503, Shankland, Letter IX.

18. 18 July 1503, Shankland, Letter X.

19. 24 July 1503, Shankland, Letter XII.

20. 12 August 1503, Shankland, Letter XIII.

21. Costabili to Ercole, 14 August 1503, CUL, Acton MSS, Add. MSS 4759.

22. 22 August 1503, Shankland, Letter XIV.

23. Ercole to Seregni, Belriguardo, 24 August 1503, cited in Gregorovius, *Lucretia Borgia*, pp. 287–8.

24. Cavalleri to Ercole, 8 September 1503, ASE, Ambasciatori Esteri – Francia, Busta 3.

25. Di Prosperi to Isabella, 26 August 1503, AG, E XXXI.3, Busta 1239.

26. Francesco Gonzaga to Isabella, 22 September 1503, cited in Gregorovius, pp. 288–9.

27. Sanudo, *I Diarii*, vol. V, col. 111.

28. Lucrezia to Ercole, Medelana, 3 October [1503], misplaced by archivist under Lucrezia's correspondence with Alfonso d'Este, ASE, Casa e Stato, Busta 141.

29. Ercole to Lucrezia, Codigoro, 4 October 1503, mistranscribed by Gregorovius according to Gardner, *Dukes and Poets in Ferrara*, see pp. 436–7.

30. Document of 3 May 1503 in ASE, Casa e Stato, Busta 400. Documenti riguardanti Lucrezia Borgia posteriormente al matrimonio con Alfonso I.

31. 5 October 1503, Shankland, Letter XV.
32. 18 October 1503, Shankland, Letter XVI.
33. 25 October 1503 (Noniano) and 2 November 1503 (Ferrara), Shankland, Letters XVII and XVIII.
34. 5 January 1504, Shankland, Letter XIX.

Chapter 10: The Dark Marquis (pp. 208–28)

1. See Bradford, *Cesare Borgia*, p. 252.
2. Sanudo, *I Diarii*, vol. V, col. 210.
3. 23 September 1505, Shankland, *The Prettiest Love Letters in the World: Letters Between Lucrezia Borgia and Pietro Bembo 1503–1519*, Letter XXXI.
4. Zambotti, *Diario Ferrarese dall'anno 1476 sino al 1504*, 2 January 1504.
5. Copy letter in ASE, Cancelleria Ducale, Particolari, Busta 209, Fasc. 4 Borgia.
6. Mirafuentes had been in touch with Lucrezia as Cesare's trusted representative via her chamberlain, Sancho, since late June. See Mirafuentes to Lucrezia, Forlì, [?29] June 1504, ASE, Cancelleria Ducale, Particolari, Busta 209, Fasc. 4 Borgia.
7. Printed in Gardner, *Dukes and Poets in Ferrara*, pp. 444–5.
8. Costabili to Ercole, 4 August 1504, Gardner, p. 450n2.
9. Gardner, p. 449.
10. 25 July 1504, Shankland, Letter XXVI.
11. 10 February 1505, Shankland, Letter XXX.
12. Luzio, *Isabella d'Este di Fronte a Giulio II*, p. 14n3.
13. Dolfo, *Lettere ai Gonzaga*, Letter IX.
14. Ibid., Letter XXVII.
15. Ibid., Letter VII.
16. See undated letter [post 1509] by Isabella d'Este to Alfonso d'Este in ASE, Casa e Stato, Carteggio dei Principi Estensi, Busta 133.
17. Lucrezia to Francesco Gonzaga, 11 April (marked by archivist '1502'), mistakenly filed with Lucrezia's correspondence with Isabella, AG, Autografi 84, Busta 1.
18. Loc. cit. supra.

19. Cited Luzio, *Isabella d'Este e i Borgia*, p. 705.
20. Lucrezia to Ercole, 21 May 1502, ASE, Casa e Stato, Busta 141.
21. Lucrezia to Francesco Gonzaga, 28 May 1504, AG, Autografi 84, Busta 1.
22. Francesco to Lucrezia, cited Luzio, p. 706n.
23. Lucrezia to Francesco, Ferrara, 13 May 1504, AG, Autografi 84, Busta 1.
24. Lucrezia to Francesco, Ferrara, 18 July 1504, AG, Autografi 84, Busta 1.
25. Alfonso d'Este to Isabella, Ferrara, 3 October 1504, AG, E XXXI.2, Busta 1189.
26. Amendola, *The Mystery of the Duchess of Amalfi*, pp. 174–6.
27. Sanudo, vol. VI, col. 30.
28. Zambotti, cited Gardner, p. 451.
29. Gardner, loc. cit. supra.
30. Luzio, pp. 705–6.
31. Giustinian, *Dispacci*, vol. 3.

Chapter 11: Duchess of Ferrara (pp. 229–49)

1. Di Prosperi to Isabella, 1 March 1505, AG, E XXXI.3, Busta 1240.
2. Gardner, *Dukes and Poets in Ferrara*, p. 496.
3. Lockwood, *Music in Renaissance Ferrara 1400–1500*, p. 201.
4. Luzio, *Isabella d'Este e i Borgia*, p. 710n.
5. Lucrezia to Alfonso d'Este, Modena, 1 July 1505, ASE, Casa e Stato, Busta 141.
6. Jacques de Chabannes (1470–1525), seigneur de Lapalisse, 'Grand Maitre' (in Italian 'Gran Maestro') until 1515 when he was created Marshal of France.
7. Lucrezia to Francesco Gonzaga, Reggio, 18 August 1505, AG, Autografi 84, Busta 1.
8. Lucrezia to Ippolito d'Este, Reggio, 19 and 26 August 1505, ASE, Casa e Stato, Busta 141.
9. Lucrezia to Alfonso, Reggio, 10 October 1505, ASE, Casa e Stato, Busta 141.

10. 30 September 1505, Shankland, *The Prettiest Love Letters in the World: Letters Between Lucrezia Borgia and Pietro Bembo 1503–1519*, Letter XXXII.

11. 29 November 1505, Shankland, Letter XXXIII.

12. Lucrezia to Francesco, Reggio, 24 October 1505, AG, Autografi 84, Busta 1.

13. Luzio, p. 711.

14. Lucrezia to Alfonso, Borgoforte, 29 October 1505, ASE, Casa e Stato, Busta 141.

15. Belriguardo, 3 November 1505, in a secretarial hand, Casa e Stato, Busta 141.

16. Isabella d'Este to Alfonso d'Este, 23 September 1505, AG, Copielettere, Busta 2994, liber 18.

17. Ferrante d'Este to Francesco Gonzaga, Reggio, 24 September 1505, AG, Busta 1189.

18. Alfonso d'Este to Isabella and Francesco Gonzaga, 5 and 6 November 1505, both in AG, Busta 1189.

19. Costabili to Ippolito d'Este, 14 November 1505, CUL, Acton MSS, Add. MSS 4759.

20. Bacchelli, *La Congiura di Don Giulio d'Este*, vol. 2, p. 85.

21. James, *The Letters of Giovanni Sabadino degli Arienti (1481–1510)*, p. 231, n1.

22. Di Prosperi to Isabella, 24 December 1505, AG, E XXXI.3, Busta 1240.

Chapter 12: The Congiura (pp. 250–67)

1. Di Prosperi to Isabella, 21 March 1506, AG, E XXXI.3, Busta 1241.

2. Bacchelli, *La Congiura di Don Giulio d'Este*, vol. II, p. 179.

3. Ibid., p. 227.

4. Ibid., p. 229.

5. Lucrezia to Francesco, 28 December 1506, AG, Autografi 84, Busta 2.

6. Bradford, *Cesare Borgia*, p. 283.

Chapter 13: 'Horrors and Tears' (pp. 268–89)

1. Sanudo, *I Diarii*, vol. VII, col. 56.
2. Gardner, *Dukes and Poets in Ferrara*, p. 512n.
3. Lucrezia to Ippolito, 1 May 1507, ASE, Casa e Stato, Busta 141.
4. Luzio, *Isabella d'Este e i Borgia*, pp. 725–6.
5. Letter of 27 August 1507, Luzio, p. 716.
6. Lucrezia to Francesco, Ferrara, 9 September 1507, AG, Autografi 84, Busta 2.
7. Di Prosperi gives a description of the comedy in a letter to Isabella of 8 March 1508, AG, E XXXI.3, Busta 1242.
8. Luzio, p. 717.
9. Ibid., p. 719n.
10. Letter of 3 April 1508, Luzio, p. 720.
11. Capilupo to Gonzaga, 11 April 1508, Luzio, p. 722.
12. Letter of 25 April 1508, Luzio, p. 724.
13. Letter of 30 August 1508, Luzio p. 154.
14. Reggio, 21 August 1508, Luzio, p. 731.
15. Mantua, 25 August 1508, Luzio, p. 732.
16. Letter of 26 August 1508, Luzio, p. 732.
17. James, *The Letters of Giovanni Sabadino degli Arienti (1481–1510)*, p. 65.
18. Ibid., p. 62.
19. Lucrezia to Francesco, 30 December 1508, AG, Autografi 84, Busta 2.
20. Letter of 1 January 1509, Luzio, p. 731.

Chapter 14: The Years of War, 1509–12 (pp. 290–315)

1. See Pastor, *The History of the Popes from the Close of the Middle Ages*, vol. VI, p. 314.
2. Lucrezia to Alfonso, 18 July 1509, plus undated drafts, ASE, Casa e Stato, Busta 141.

3. Di Prosperi to Isabella, 17 December 1509, AG, E XXXI.3, Busta 1242.

4. Shaw, *Julius II: The Warrior Pope*, p. 259.

5. Lucrezia to Francesco, Ferrara, 26 July 1510, AG, Autografi 84, Busta 2.

6. Sanudo, *I Diarii*, vol. XI, col. 114.

7. Ibid., col. 129.

8. Lucrezia to Francesco, 22 August 1510, AG, Autografi 84, Busta 2.

9. Sanudo, vol. XI, col. 153.

10. Luzio, *Isabella d'Este di Fronte a Giulio II*, pp. 8–9.

11. Lucrezia to Francesco, 14 October 1505, AG, Autografi 84, Busta 1.

12. Abraham Thus to Lucrezia, n.d. [?August 1510], filed with Lucrezia's letters to Alfonso, ASE, Casa e Stato, Busta 141.

13. Sanudo, vol. XI, col. 466, 25 September 1510.

14. Luzio, p. 9 and n2.

15. Lucrezia to Isabella, 10 September 1510, AG, Autografi 84, Busta 2.

16. Sanudo, vol. XI, col. 279.

17. Luzio, p. 47.

18. Gregorovius, *Lucretia Borgia*, p. 332 and n.

19. Luzio, p. 59n.

20. Ibid., p. 78n.

21. Di Prosperi to Isabella, 15 April 1512, AG, E XXXI.3, Busta 1244.

22. Lucrezia to Francesco, Ferrara, 27 January 1512, AG, Autografi 84, Busta 3.

23. Francesco to Vigo di Camposampiero, 17 June 1512, Luzio, p. 130n.

24. Lucrezia to Isabella, 12 August 1512, AG, Autografi 84, Busta 3.

25. Luzio, p. 172.

Chapter 15: Lucrezia Triumphant (pp. 316–35)

1. The plaques were executed by Giannantonio da Foligno, leading member of a family of goldsmiths and engravers, originally from Foligno but for many years settled in Ferrara, where Giannantonio carried out commissions for the nobility and particularly for Lucrezia. His work features in her Inventory of jewels of 1516–19.

2. ASE, Casa e Stato, Busta 401.

3. Gregorovius, *Lucretia Borgia*, p. 335.

4. 21 February 1511, 'Ordini d'Isabella d'Aragona, Duchessa di Milano', ASE, Casa e Stato, Busta 401.

5. ASE, Casa e Stato, Busta 401.

6. Luzio, *Isabella d'Este di Fronte a Giulio II*, p. 169.

7. Ibid., p. 173n.

8. Di Prosperi to Isabella, 15 October 1512, AG, E XXXI.3, Busta 1244.

9. Luzio, p. 184n.

10. Lucrezia to Francesco, 4 February 1513, AG, Autografi 84, Busta 3.

11. Shaw, *Julius II: The Warrior Pope*, pp. 314–15.

12. Di Prosperi to Isabella, 2 April 1513, enclosing information on the banquet of 1 April 1513, AG, E XXXI.3, Busta 1245.

13. Luzio, p. 213.

14. Ibid., p. 214.

15. BCAFe, MS, coll. Antonelli, 272.

16. Lucrezia to Francesco, 7 April 1513, AG, Autografi 84, Busta 3.

17. Lucrezia to Francesco, 4 July 1515, AG, Autografi 84, Busta 3.

18. See letter by Ippolita Sforza Bentivoglio to Trissino mentioning Lucrezia's esteem for him, 1 June 1512, in Morsolin, *Giangiorgio Trissino. Monografia d'un gentiluomo letterato nel secolo XVI*, p. 387.

19. Morsolin, Lucrezia to Trissino, Belriguardo, 18 September 1515, doc. XXX, p. 397.

20. Morsolin, Lucrezia to Trissino, Ferrara, 22 November 1515, pp. 397–8.

21. Morsolin, Lucrezia to Trissino, 26 March 1516, loc. cit. supra.

22. Morsolin, Lucrezia to Trissino, 1 June 1516, p. 404.

23. Laureati, *Da Borgia a Este: due vite in quarant'anni*, p. 55.

24. See Lowry, *The World of Aldus Manutius: Business and Scholarship in Renaissance Venice*, p. 203.

25. Canto 13.69.

26. Canto 42.83.

27. Lucrezia to Francesco, 2 January 1517, AG, Autografi 84, Busta 3.

28. Sanudo, *I Diarii*, vol. XXI, cols 18–19.

Chapter 16: The Last Year of Tranquillity (pp. 336–59)

1. Lucrezia Borgia Household Accounts, ASE, Camera Ducale, Amministrazione dei Principi, 'Libro di entrate e uscite', 1514–19, B1134.

2. BCAFe, Classe I, 656, Albo Estense Autografi.

3. Di Prosperi to Isabella, 18 February 1518, AG, E XXXI.3, Busta 1246.

4. Di Prosperi to Isabella, 30 August 1518, AG, E XXXI.3, Busta 1246.

5. Di Prosperi to Isabella, 26 December 1518, AG, E XXXI.3, Busta 1246.

6. Hope, 'The "Camerini d'Alabastro" of Alfonso d'Este', in *The Burlington Magazine*, vol. CXIII, no. 824, November 1971, p. 649.

7. Lucrezia to Isabella, 19 August 1518, AG, Autografi 84, Busta 4.

8. Lucrezia to Francesco, letters of 20, 21 and 23 August 1518, AG, Autografi 84, Busta 4.

9. Lucrezia to Isabella, Ferrara, 26 August 1518, AG, Autografi 84, Busta 4.

10. Lucrezia to Isabella, Ferrara, 17 October 1517, AG, Autografi 84, Busta 3.

11. Di Prosperi to Isabella, 4 March 1518, AG, E XXXI.3, Busta 1246.

12. Giovanni Borgia to Alfonso, 8 July [1519], ASE, Cancelleria Ducale, Particolari, Busta 209, Fasc. 4 Borgia.

13. Di Prosperi to Isabella, 1 May 1518, AG, E XXXI.3, Busta 1246.

14. Di Prosperi to Isabella, 16 June 1518.

15. ASE, Camera Ducale, Amministrazione dei Principi, Busta 1127.

16. Juan Las Cases to Lucrezia, 12 May 1518, ASE, Cancelleria Ducale, Particolari, Busta 209, Fasc. 4 Borgia.

17. Louise de Valentinois (Luisa Borgia) to Lucrezia, Lyon, 16 March [?1514] ASE, Principi Esteri.

18. ASE, Camera Ducale, Amministrazione dei Principi, B1134.

19. Di Prosperi, 26 November 1518, AG, E XXXI.3, Busta 1246.

20. Draft letter by Lucrezia to an unnamed cardinal, 24 November 1518, ASE, Casa e Stato, Busta 141.

21. Lucrezia to Alfonso, n.d. [?1519], marked by archivist as 2 January, ASE, Casa e Stato, Busta 141.

22. Vannozza to Lucrezia, February 1515, ASE, Cancelleria Ducale, Particolari, Busta 209, Fasc. 4 Borgia.

23. Vannozza to Ippolito, 14 September 1515, ASE, Cancelleria Ducale, Particolari, Busta 209, Fasc. 4 Borgia.

24. See Sacerdote, *Cesare Borgia, la sua vita, la sua famiglia, e i suoi tempi*, p. 843.

25. Ibid., p. 848.

26. Bonaventura Pistofilo to Lucrezia, 24 November 1518, ASE, Cancelleria Ducale, Particolari, Busta 6.

27. Pistofilo to Lucrezia, Lyons, 4 December 1518, ASE, Cancelleria Ducale, Particolari, Busta 6.

28. Lucrezia to Alfonso, Ferrara, 23 December 1518, ASE, Casa e Stato, Busta 141.

Chapter 17: The End (pp. 360–66)

1. Di Prosperi to Isabella, 17 March 1519, AG, E XXXI.3, Busta 1247.

2. Lucrezia to Isabella, 31 March 1519, AG, Autografi 84, Busta 4.

3. Lucrezia to Federico Gonzaga, AG, 31 March 1519, Autografi 84, Busta 4.

4. Lucrezia to Alfonso, apparently unpublished, 26 April [1519], ASE, Casa e Stato, Busta 141.

5. Lucrezia to Leo X, ASE, Carteggio tra Principi Estense, Busta 141, f 42.

6. Alfonso to Federico Gonzaga, AG, Autografi 84, Busta 4.

7. Alfonso to unnamed friend, ASE, Casa e Stato, Busta 400.

Bibliography

Ady, C. M., *The Bentivoglio of Bologna*, Oxford, 1937

Amendola, Barbara Banks, *The Mystery of the Duchess of Malfi*, Stroud, 2002

Ariosto, Ludovico, *Orlando Furioso*, trans. Guido Waldman, Oxford, 1974

Bacchelli, Riccardo, *La Congiura di Don Giulio d'Este*, 2 vols, Milan, 1931

Batllori, Miquel, *La Familia Borja*, Obra Completa vol. IV, Biblioteca D'Estudis I Investigacions, Tres I Quatre, Barcelona, 1994

—, ed., *De Valencia a Roma, Cartes Triades dels Borja*, Barcelona, 1998

Bellonci, Maria, *Lucrezia Borgia, la sua vita e i suoi tempi*, 6th edn, revised and augmented, Verona, 1942

Beltrami, Luca, *La Guardaroba di Lucrezia Borgia*, [Milan], 1903

Bernardi, Andrea, ed. G. Mazzatinti, *Cronache forlivesi*, Bologna, 1895

Birbari, Elizabeth, *Dress in Italian Painting 1460–1500*, London, 1975

Borella, Marco, ed., *Este a Ferrara, Il Castello per la città* (exhibition catalogue), Milan, 2004

Bradford, Sarah, *Cesare Borgia*, London, 1976

Burchard, Johannes, *Diarium*, ed. L. Thuasne, 3 vols, Paris, 1883–5

—, *Liber notarum*, ed. E. Celani, Rerum Italicarum Scriptores, xxxii, 2, Città di Castello, 1907 ff

—, *At the Court of the Borgia*, selections from the *Diarium*, ed. and trans. G. Parker, London, 1963

Burckhardt, Jacob, *The Civilisation of the Renaissance in Italy*, trans. S. G. C. Middlemore, London, 1989

Calendar of State Papers Henry VIII 1509–14, ed. J. S. Brewer, vol. I, 1862

Castelli, Patrizia, 'Cronache dei loro tempi . . . le "allegrezze degli Sforza di Pesaro 1445–1512"', in *Historica Pisaurensia*, vol. II, Pesaro, 1989

Castiglione, Baldassare, *The Book of the Courtier*, trans. George Bull, London, 1976

Cartwright, Julia (Mrs Ady), *Isabella d'Este, Marchioness of Mantua, 1474–1539. A Study of the Renaissance*, 2 vols, London, 1903

—, *Beatrice d'Este, Duchess of Milan, 1475–1497*, London, 1920

Chiappini, Luciano, *Gli Estensi*, Varese, 1967

Clough, Cecil H., 'Niccolò Machiavelli, Cesare Borgia and the Francesco Troche Episode', in *Medievalia et Humanistica*, Fasc. 17, 1966

—, 'Niccolò Machiavelli's Political Assumptions and Objectives', in *Bulletin of the John Rylands Library*, vol. 53, no. 1, Manchester, 1970

—, ed., *Cultural Aspects of the Italian Renaissance: Essays in Honour of Paul Oscar Kristeller*, 1976

Dean, Trevor, *Land and Power in Late Medieval Ferrara. The Rule of the Este, 1350–1450*, Cambridge, 1988

—, and K. J. P. Lowe, eds, *Marriage in Italy, 1300–1650*, Cambridge, 1998

Dizionario biografico degli Italiani, Rome, Istituto della Enciclopedia Italiana, vol. 1, 1960 et seq.

Dolfo, Floriano, ed. Marzia Minutelli, *Lettere ai Gonzaga*, Edizioni di Storia e Letteratura, Rome, 2002

Ehrle, F., and Stevenson, H., *Les fresques du Pinturicchio dans les salles Borgia au Vatican*, Rome, 1898

Eiche, Sabine, 'Towards a Study of the "Famiglia" of the Sforza Court at Pesaro', in *Renaissance and Reformation*, n.s. 9, 1985, pp. 79–103

—, 'Architetture Sforzesche', in *Pesaro tra Medioevo e Rinascimento*, Venice, 1989, pp. 269–303

—, 'La corte di Pesaro dalle case malatestiane alla residenza roveresca', in *La corte di Pesaro: Storia di una residenza signorile*, ed. M. R. Valazzi, Modena, n.d., pp. 13–55

Farinelli Toselli, Alessandra, ed., *Lucrezia Borgia a Ferrara*, Ferrara, 2002

Fioravanti Baraldi, Anna Maria, *Lucrezia Borgia 'la bellà, la virtù, la fama onesta'*, Ferrara, 2002

Gardner, Edmund G., *Dukes and Poets in Ferrara: A Study in the Poetry, Religion and Politics of the Fifteenth and Early Sixteenth Centuries*, London, 1904

Giustinian, Antonio, *Dispacci*, ed. Pasquale Villari, 3 vols, Florence, 1876

Goodgal, Dana, 'The Camerino of Alfonso I d'Este', in *Art History*, vol. 1, no. 2., June 1978, pp. 162–90

Grafton, Anthony, *Cardano's Cosmos: The Worlds and Works of a Renaissance Astrologer*, Cambridge, Mass., 1999

Gregorovius, F., *Lucretia Borgia*, trans. J. L. Garner, London, 1903

Guerzoni, Guido, *Le Corti Estensi e la Devoluzione di Ferrara del 1598*, Modena, 2000

Guicciardini, Francesco, *The History of Italy*, trans. and ed. with notes and an introduction by Sidney Alexander, New York and London, 1969

Gundersheimer, Werner L., ed., *Art and Life at the Court of Ercole I d'Este: The 'De triumphis religionis' of Giovanni Sabadino degli Arienti*, Geneva, 1972

—, *Ferrara, The Style of a Renaissance Despotism*, Princeton, NJ, 1973

Hollingsworth, Mary, *Patronage in Renaissance Italy: From 1400 to the Early Sixteenth Century*, London, 1994

—, *The Cardinal's Hat: Money, Ambition and Housekeeping in a Renaissance Court*, London, 2004

Hope, Charles, 'The "Camerini d'Alabastro of Alfonso I d'Este"', in *The Burlington Magazine*, vol. CXIII, no. 824, November 1971, pp. 641–50, and no. 825, December 1971, pp. 712–21

—, 'Alfonso d'Este's Camerino' (exhibition catalogue), 2003

James, Carolyn, *The Letters of Giovanni Sabadino degli Arienti (1481–1510)*, Florence, 2002

Jardine, Lisa, *Worldly Goods*, London, 1996

Johnson, Paul, *The Renaissance*, London, 2000

Knecht, R. J. *Francis I*, Cambridge, 1982

Laureati, Laura, *Da Borgia a Este: due vite in quarant'anni*, in *Lucrezia Borgia*, exhibition catalogue, Ferrara, 2002

Laurencin, Marques de, *Relaciónes de los Festines que se celebraron en el Vaticano can motivo de las Bodas de Lucrecia Borgia con Don Alonso de Aragon*, Madrid, 1916

Lockwood, Lewis, *Music in Renaissance Ferrara 1400–1500*, Oxford, 1984

Lowry, Martin, *The World of Aldus Manutius: Business and Scholarship in Renaissance Venice*, Oxford, 1979

Luzio, Alessandro, *Isabella d'Este di Fronte a Giulio II negli ultimi tre anni del suo pontificato*, Milan, 1912

—, *Isabella d'Este e i Borgia, con nuovi documenti*, Milan, 1916

—, and Renier, R., *Mantova e Urbino, Isabella d'Este ed Elisabetta Gonzaga nelle Relazioni Famigliari e nelle Vicende Politiche*, Turin, 1893

Machiavelli, Niccolò, *The Prince*, trans. G. Bull, London, 1961

—, *Legazioni e Commissarie*, ed. S. Bertelli, 3 vols, Milan, 1964

—, *Niccolò Machiavelli, The Chief Works and others*, selected and trans. A. Gilbert, North Carolina, 1965

Malacarne, Giancarlo, *Sulla Mensa del Principe, Alimentazione e banchetti alla Corte dei Gonzaga*, Modena, 2000

Mallett, Michael, *The Borgias: The Rise and Fall of a Renaissance Dynasty*, London, 1969

—, *Mercenaries and their Masters, Warfare in Renaissance Italy*, London, 1974

Marinello, Giovanni, *Gli Ornamenti delle Donne*, Venice, 1574

Martines, Lauro, ed., *Violence and Civil Disorder in Italian Cities, 1200–1500*, 1972

Martufi, Roberta, Presentazione di Ippolito Pizzetti, *Diletto e Maraviglia, Le ville del colle San Bartolo di Pesaro*, Pesaro, (?) 1986

Masson, Georgina, *Courtesans of the Italian Renaissance*, London, 1975

Messisbugo, Cristoforo da, *Banchetti, Composizioni de Vivande e apparecchi*, a cura F. Bandini, Venice, 1960

Monson, Craig A., ed., *The Crannied Wall: Women, Religion, and the Arts in Early Modern Europe*, Ann Arbor, Mich., 1992

Morsolin, Bernardo, *Giangiorgio Trissino. Monografia d'un gentiluomo letterato nel secolo XVI*, 2nd edn, Florence, 1894

Partner, P., *The Lands of St Peter: The Papal State in the Middle Ages and the Early Renaissance*, London, 1972

Pastor, Ludwig, *The History of the Popes from the Close of the Middle Ages*, ed. F. I. Antrobus, vols V–VI, London, 1898

Pistofilo, Bonaventura, *Vita di Alfonso I d'Este*, in Atti e memorie della Reale Deputazione di Storia Patria per le provincie modenesi, series I, vol. III, 1865

Queirazza, Giuliano Gasca, S. J., *Gli Scritti Autografi di Alessandro VI nell 'Archivium Arcis'*, Turin, 1959

Roscoe, William, *The Life and Pontificate of Leo the Tenth*, 4 vols, London, 1827

Ross, Janet, *Lives of the Early Medici as told in their correspondence*, London, 1910

Rubinstein, Nicolai, *Lucrezia Borgia*, 1971

Sacerdote, Gustavo, *Cesare Borgia, la sua vita, la sua famiglia, e i suoi tempi*, Milan, 1950

Sanchis y Sivera, Jose, *Algunos Documentos y Cartas privadas que pertencieron al segundo Duque de Gandia don Juan de Borja*, Valencia, 1919

Sanudo, Marin, *I Diarii*, vols 1–27, Venice, 1879–90

Saxl, F., *The Appartamento Borgia*, Lectures, vols I and III, London, 1957

Shankland, Hugh, trans., *The Prettiest Love Letters in the World: Letters Between Lucrezia Borgia and Pietro Bembo 1503–1519*, London, 1987

Shaw, Christine, *Julius II: The Warrior Pope*, Oxford, 1993

Sikorski, Darius, *Brandani e il segreto dell'Età dell'Oro: verso una ricostruzione della cronologia e decodificazione dei significati nel Palazzo di Pesaro*, in 'Pesaro nell'età dei Della Rovere', III.2, Venice, 2001, pp. 247–306

Strong, Roy, *Feast: A History of Grand Eating*, London, 2002

Thornton, Peter, *The Italian Renaissance Interior 1400–1600*, London, 1991

Tuohy, Thomas, *Herculean Ferrara: Ercole d'Este (1471–1505) and the Invention of a Ducal Capital*, Cambridge, 1996

Vancini, Gianna, ed., *Lucrezia Borgia nell'opera di cronisti, letterati e poeti suoi contemporanei alla corte di Ferrara*, Ferrara, 2002

Wind, Edgar, *Pagan Mysteries in the Renaissance*, London, 1958

Wirtz, Prof. Maria, *Ercole Strozzi, Poeta Ferrarese (1473–1508)*, in Atti della Deputazione Ferrarese di Storia Patria, vol. 16, pt II, Ferrara, 1906

Zambotti, Bernardino, *Diario Ferrarese dall'anno 1476 sino al 1504*, ed. G. Pardi, Rerum Italicarum Scriptores, t. 24, pt. vii, Bologna, 1934–7

Zerbinato, *Croniche di Ferrara*, Ferrara, 1989

Index

SARAH BRADFORD

GEORGE VI

In the first major biography of the King to be published in thirty years, Sarah Bradford draws on new archive material, hitherto unknown or suppressed, and privileged interviews with members of the royal circle to present an acclaimed portrait of a man not born to be king, but who stepped out of his brother's shadow to lead his country through war, austerity and social change, laying the foundations for the reign of his daughter, Elizabeth II.

'Triumphantly successful' *Sunday Times*

'Vivid, thorough and enjoyable' *Independent*

'Engrossing' *Financial Times*

'Sarah Bradford looks set to inherit Lady Longford's mantle as Royal biographer supreme' *Mail on Sunday*